Hazard Mitigation in Emergency Management

Hazard Mitigation in Emergency Management

Tanveer Islam

Jeffrey Ryan

AMSTERDAM • BOSTON • HEIDELBERG • LONDON
NEW YORK • OXFORD • PARIS • SAN DIEGO
SAN FRANCISCO • SINGAPORE • SYDNEY • TOKYO

Butterworth-Heinemann is an imprint of Elsevier

Acquiring Editor: Sara Scott
Editorial Project Manager: Hilary Carr
Project Manager: Punithavathy Govindaradjane
Designer: Mark Rogers

Butterworth-Heinemann is an imprint of Elsevier
The Boulevard, Langford Lane, Kidlington, Oxford OX5 1GB, UK
225 Wyman Street, Waltham, MA 02451, USA

ISBN: 978-0-12-420134-7

British Library Cataloguing-in-Publication Data
A catalogue record for this book is available from the British Library

Library of Congress Cataloging-in-Publication Data
A catalog record for this book is available from the Library of Congress

For Information on all Butterworth-Heinemann publications
visit our website at http://store.elsevier.com/

Working together
to grow libraries in
developing countries

www.elsevier.com • www.bookaid.org

Contents

THEMATIC SECTION 2 ASSESSING RISK—KNOW THY ENEMY!

THEMATIC SECTION 3 MITIGATION STRATEGIES, TOOLS, AND TECHNIQUES—WHAT CAN BE DONE?

Foreword

Hazards, natural such as an earthquake, a hurricane, or a tornado, and man-made such as terrorist attack or oil spill, occur all the time. Our societal goal is to prevent a hazard from becoming a disaster. Hazards such as a tornado striking an open prairie do not cause a disaster. I have been involved in tornado research for the past four decades including tornado chasing activity (I managed to photograph a couple of them but there were no cell phones or videos in the 1970s when I chased tornadoes in West Texas). Fortunately, the tornadoes I found were in open areas and did not cause any disaster.

A natural hazard, such as an earthquake occurring in a populated area or a hurricane striking a city along the coast, has the potential to causing a disaster. A hazard becomes a disaster when it affects a large, populated area and causes injuries and fatalities to people and damage to structures. With proper planning and making communities resilient disasters can be avoided. This book is a compendium of strategies to prevent a hazard from becoming a disaster. The authors have developed a comprehensive book on hazard mitigation. The book is an outstanding compilation of material on natural and man-made hazards, government regulations, hazard mitigation tools, and several notable best practices of hazard mitigation. It deals with all hazards (natural and man-made), all stakeholders (emergency managers, students of emergency management), and covers all phases (mitigation, preparedness, response, and recovery). Comprehensive emergency management is discussed as a holistic approach that recognizes various aspects of a disaster.

The twelve chapter volume covers virtually all subjects related to disaster mitigation. The contents in chapters range from description of hazards to best practices for mitigation. Chapters in the book deal with local, state, and national regulations, descriptions of natural and man-made hazards, considerations of vulnerability, and risk assessment and mitigation strategies. This book will be very useful to emergency managers as well as to students and practitioners who aspire to be involved in emergency planning and hazard mitigation.

The book defines the duties of the emergency managers as focusing on the larger picture and during the greatest time of need act as a clearing house for resources and a focal point for communication and collaboration. This definition of duty is important because the emergency managers should not get tied-up focusing only on a specific task to respond to a disaster, but should organize the overall response in the short term as well as in the long term. They have to be in tune with a bigger picture from preparedness to recovery and bringing the community to normalcy as soon as possible after an event.

Regulations and roles of the local, state, and federal governments in hazard mitigation are discussed in Chapters 2 and 3. A chronological listing of major mitigation policy initiatives in the United States is presented in the introductory chapter which provides history of government involvement in hazard mitigation. Chapter 2 gives the major regulations developed by the federal government while Chapter 3 deals with implementations of the regulations. Chapter 3 also provides the description of disaster risk reduction strategy by the United Nations.

Natural hazards are divided into atmospheric (hurricane, tornado, etc.), hydrologic (flood, etc.), geologic (earthquake, landslide, etc.), and other hazards such as tsunami and wildfire. Man-made hazards come from hazardous materials, chemical and biological agents, nuclear threat, cyber terrorism, high yield explosives, and others. Chapters 5 and 6 give examples of these hazards to put scale of mitigation in proper perspective.

The authors weave together vulnerability and risk assessment with mitigation strategies and tools for mitigation that are currently available. These vulnerability, risk, and mitigation strategies are of immense use to city planners, city managers, city council members, and emergency planners. Each community can plan emergency management for various hazards that each one might face.

The last chapter on best practices in mitigation is unique. It contains specific examples of past disasters, natural and man-made, which have taught us the lessons to be learned. Beyond the lessons, what actions in mitigation are taken for each case are presented. This chapter describes a number of mitigation best practices implemented in the United States and in other countries. At the international level, many countries have implemented exemplary projects, such as the safe island program in Maldives (sea level rise hazard), climate change adaptation project in Canada, and seismic upgrading of public schools in the Philippines. A collection of links for hazard-related database and hazard mitigation plans of the states, countries, and regional levels are also provided. The compilation of various sources of hazard mitigation information and tools make this book an excellent resource for all stakeholders interested in hazard mitigation.

Some of the distinctive and useful items throughout the volume are "Critical Thinking" boxes, illustrations and tables in each chapter, and references with resource URLs for websites at the end of each chapter. The "Critical Thinking" boxes are an excellent resource for raising some important questions. In addition, several chapters have discussion questions that would be useful when the book is used in classroom as a text. These items are properly interspersed throughout the book with readers and users in mind. This is a special advantage of this book.

Dr. Islam, senior author of the book, has been involved in studying about hazards and disaster mitigation strategies since his graduate studies at Texas Tech University. I was on his graduate committee while he conducted dissertation research related to cyclone disasters in Bangladesh. From my personal experience of documenting damages caused by hurricanes and tornadoes (for this work I am elected to the National Academy of Engineering), I can attest that this is an excellent reference book for emergency managers and hazard mitigation professionals and as a textbook for students pursuing emergency management studies.

Kishor C. Mehta, Ph.D.
Program Director
Hazard Mitigation and Structural Engineering (HMSE)
Civil, Mechanical and Manufacturing Innovation(CMMI)
National Science Foundation; and
P.W. Horn Professor of Civil Engineering
Texas Tech University

Acknowledgments

The authors wish to thank their spouses and family members for being patient and giving them the necessary time and support to finish this project. In addition, the authors thank Jacksonville State University (JSU) doctoral student Melissa Pinke for researching many of the mitigation strategies discussed in Chapters 9 and 10. Finally, thanks to all students and practitioners of emergency management and business continuity, who continually serve their communities and organizations with passion and great distinction. Their efforts, invisible to most that they serve, save lives, protect property, and preserve the environment.

Thematic Section

1

Mitigation Framework

PREFACE AND INTRODUCTION

Civilizations have been affected by natural disasters for millennia. As humanity has progressed through the Industrial Revolution, world wars, and the Information Age, the threats to people, property, and the environment have become more complex and serious. Furthermore, governments have grown more complex and serving. Just as death and taxes are certain and unavoidable, disasters (both natural and manmade) will occur. Emergency management is now comprehensive and holistic. It includes concepts and programs that address the myriad of hazards we face pre- and post-disaster. Post-disaster, we must respond to and recover from their effects. Pre-disaster, we can prepare ourselves for the most likely hazards. We may also mitigate some of those hazards to lessen their impact or prevent them altogether. To most people outside the emergency management profession, these concepts and programs are transparent.

This textbook introduces readers to hazard mitigation. Included is a thorough review of the hazard mitigation framework, involving private and governmental agencies and the rules and regulations governing mitigation, the risk assessment process, and mitigation strategies, tools, and techniques that are currently available to prevent or lessen the impact of natural and manmade hazards.

Until now, there was no textbook that holistically addressed mitigation for both natural and manmade hazards or that examined this subject using the all-hazards approach. This book can be used as a text-book for classes or as a reference for emergency management and business continuity professionals in the government, military, and private sectors.

GOALS AND LEARNING OBJECTIVES

The primary goal of this book is to give readers an understanding of mitigation and the mitigation planning process. Readers will learn the full spectrum of hazards posed to society and how to create hazard mitigation plans to combat these hazards. Case studies of mitigation projects and mitigation plans are presented that illustrate the development of a hazard mitigation plan and the mitigation planning process. This text discusses government programs, private-sector initiatives, and regulations that encompass hazard mitigation. Users of this book will get the opportunity to develop skills in using mitigation tools such as HAZUS-MH.

Specific learning objectives for this textbook are outlined as follows:

- Recognize the relationships of hazards and their potential behaviors that may ultimately lead to a disaster
- Understand how local, state, and federal emergency management agencies (EMAs) can mitigate the effect of a potential threat
- Acquire a general knowledge of and be able to discuss the laws and regulations that support the regulatory environment for the practice of emergency management and hazard mitigation in the United States and other countries
- Understand the hazard mitigation planning process and be able to evaluate the effectiveness of proposed hazard mitigation measures
- Build on knowledge of the use of risk assessment in hazard mitigation
- Expand the ability to use and apply a sound methodology to quantify the benefit-cost analysis of proposed hazard mitigation measures
- Develop a mitigation strategy
- Identify the knowledge and skills to maintain a mitigation plan
- Understand dependency relationships in hazard mitigation

ORGANIZATION

The book is organized into three thematic sections. Part 1 provides a conceptual understanding of mitigation as a phase of emergency management and the mitigation planning process. It also focuses on explaining the hazard mitigation framework, the rules and regulations related to hazard mitigation, and the players involved in this framework including federal, state, local governments, and the private sector. Part 2 outlines and details the process of risk assessment for both natural and manmade hazards. This section also gives a thorough overview of all possible hazards that a community might face and how to assess these risks. Part 3 covers in detail the mitigation strategies for natural and manmade hazards. This will include structural and nonstructural mitigation measures, as well as strategies to combat terrorism/bioterrorism, technological hazards, and chemical, biological, radiological, nuclear, and explosives (CBRNE). Mitigation tools, such as geographic information systems (GIS), Hazards United States (HAZUS), and their applications are shown with tutorials. Finally, case studies are presented that illustrate the best practices of mitigation planning process in the United States and around the world. A compendium of mitigation resources and links are also included.

Introduction

OBJECTIVES

The study of this chapter will enable you to:

1. Understand the emergency management cycle and how mitigation fits into it
2. Understand the meaning and importance of an all-hazards approach to the profession of emergency management
3. Understand the meaning of hazards and disasters
4. Discuss the history and evolution of hazard mitigation
5. Discuss the hazard mitigation planning process and the structure of a functional hazard mitigation plan
6. Discuss the benefits of mitigation planning

Essential Terminology: All hazards, all-hazards approach, comprehensive emergency management, hazard, disaster, mitigation, preparedness, resilience, response, recovery, risk, vulnerability, hazard mitigation plan, mitigation planning process.

Nature, as we know her, is no saint.

Ralph Waldo Emerson

EMERGENCY MANAGEMENT CYCLE AND MITIGATION

Emergency management practitioners, scholars, and students require a complete understanding of *hazard mitigation*. Before diving straight into mitigation strategies and practices, we need to discuss some very basic terms and lay a good foundation of knowledge about comprehensive emergency management and how it relates to the emergency management practitioner. Next, we will delve into where mitigation fits into the emergency management life cycle and how it came to be included as one of the four phases.

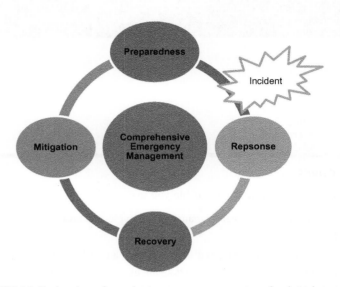

■ **FIGURE 1.1** The four phases of comprehensive emergency management are often depicted as a cycle. Ideally, community officials seek to mitigate and prevent hazards. They spend most of their time preparing for those hazards. Inevitably, an incident occurs. These officials respond to save lives, stabilize the incident, and preserve property and the environment. Finally, they embark on long- and short-term recovery operations. During recovery is a great time to implement a hazard mitigation plan with the aim to restore the community in such a way that hazards are more efficiently mitigated or prevented.

Comprehensive emergency management is a holistic approach to the emergency management profession that recognizes that all phases of a disaster, incident, or catastrophic event need to be addressed. The four phases of emergency management are mitigation, preparedness, response, and recovery. The emergency management cycle is a continuous cycle in which the completion of each phase leads into the beginning of the next phase. Refer to Figure 1.1 for the four phases of the comprehensive emergency management life cycle.

Emergency management professionals play a crucial role in all phases of disasters, even though they may not be primarily responsible for performing the myriad needed functions. For example, emergency managers would not actually work at a shelter. Instead, they would coordinate with the location operator, volunteer organizations, regional public health officials, their state's emergency management agency (EMA), local law enforcement, and others to ensure that the shelter was established and safe, and all needs were being met. Emergency managers maintain a focus on the larger picture, and during the greatest times of need, they act as a clearing house for resources and a focal point for communication and collaboration.

Comprehensive emergency management also encompasses an ***all-hazards approach***. Emergency managers should complete a hazard vulnerability analysis (HVA) to determine all the hazards that their community is vulnerable to and prioritize the hazards based upon likelihood of the event and the resulting outcome. This will give the emergency manager and his or her partners a baseline for preparation and mitigation measures. "The hazard/vulnerability analysis should address three major components of vulnerability: hazard exposure, physical vulnerability, and social vulnerability." (Waugh & Tierney, 2007) Each community will be unique in the vulnerabilities they face, based on these three factors.

Another aspect of comprehensive emergency management is the inclusion of all partners (i.e., stakeholders) in the decision-making and planning process. Emergency management partners include government officials, first-responder organizations, community leaders, organizations that serve functional needs populations, and businesses. Including these partners ensures that the needs of the whole community are addressed and the resources to meet those needs are identified before a disaster strikes. Another benefit that comes from the inclusion of all stakeholders is that it enables emergency managers to identify unmet needs (gap analysis) so that contingency plans can be made to address those needs. Inclusiveness also garners buy-in for plans and disaster relief strategies, which increases collaboration and cooperation during an incident.

Comprehensive emergency management seeks to build resilient communities. Resilient communities are formed by an active participation in preparedness activities and with the utilization of mitigation techniques. All phases and activities should be planned for and executed in a way that promotes social equity, defined as the fair management and distribution of public programs, policies, and services. The preservation of resources for future generations, intergenerational equity, should be a primary goal.

Preparedness

Often thought of as the beginning of the cycle, the preparedness phase of emergency management (refer to Figure 1.2) protects lives and property. It consists of planning, development of procedures, and gathering of resources. Plans, procedures, and resources allow communities to be ready for any disaster that may strike. The preparedness phase eases the response phase by having all response aspects in place and ready to be activated timely. Through planning, the preparedness also helps guide the recovery phase.

Preparedness is planning for activities that will take place immediately before, during, and immediately after a disaster occurs (Schwab, Eschelbach, & Brower, 2007). Preparedness includes activities such as training emergency personnel, response procedures, and evacuation

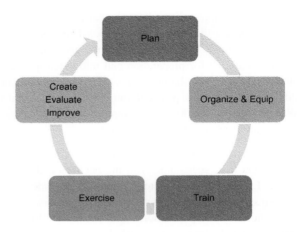

■ **FIGURE 1.2** The preparedness phase can be viewed as its own cycle. It begins with the creation of a comprehensive, functional response plan that involves all community stakeholders. The plan specifies what it takes to organize and equip the community for all hazards. Community organizations should come together to train and exercise the plan. After action, reviews from exercises and training sessions should be used to evaluate and improve the plan.

planning. These activities are planned as short-term solutions to restore critical functions and public safety. Networking, information dissemination, and community outreach are integral parts of emergency management. Federal-level planning is conducted according to the National Incident Management System (NIMS), which defines disaster response capabilities in six areas: command and management, preparedness, resource management, communication and information, supporting technologies, and ongoing management (Perry & Lindell, 2007). NIMS is a national framework, with adaptable qualities to suite any community.

Local emergency managers should develop and maintain a cohesive, all-inclusive emergency operations plan (EOP). The start of the EOP planning process considers the hazard, its effects, and any possible ramifications, and identifies the threat. Once these are identified, the success of a plan will depend heavily on the support of community members, officials, and media. Planning should also involve community stakeholders from each of the three groups: social, economic, and governmental. Planning for disasters is particularly difficult because the time available to reach the public's focus is limited, usually occurring soon after a disaster. The basic EOP should define and include the emergency planning authority, the aim and scope, the statement of purpose, the situation and assumptions, the overall concept of operations, documentation of agreements, provisions for response training, and procedures for administering the EOP (Waugh & Tierney, 2007). Additional documents may be added to the basic plan as annexes resulting from a community preparedness analysis. Hazard-specific and functional annexes may be added as a result of information gathered during hazard exposure, physical vulnerability, and social vulnerability assessments.

In order to know the hazard exposures, populated hazardous areas should be identified, such as communities near nuclear plants, fault lines, floodplains, and coastal areas. The community's history of disasters can help determine the probability that a hazard will turn into a disaster. Disaster impacts can be categorized into six groups: speed of onset, availability of perceptual cues, intensity of impact, scope of impact, duration of impact, and probability of impact. There are three aspects of physical vulnerabilities: humans, agriculture, and structures (Lindell, Prater, & Perry, 2007). The most susceptible people are the very young, the very old, the physically or mentally disabled, and those with a weakened immune system. *Agricultural vulnerability* refers to the consequences of disaster impact for any agricultural product and is defined in terms of transportation or distribution. The more diverse the community's agriculture, the more difficult it is to determine its vulnerability. Structural vulnerability arises when building are constructed by using designs and materials that are incapable of resisting stresses imposed by disaster agents. Local damage assessments from previous disasters provide insight. Plans must address a series of stages of housing recovery as provisions for temporary shelters are usually established in the EOP. The burden of providing shelter is not always taken on by the local government; partnership organizations can provide this service, such as the American Red Cross. *Social vulnerabilities* are a person's or group's ability to anticipate, prepare for, cope with, resist, and recover from disasters. The demographic makeup and distribution of the community can assist in assessing social vulnerability.

Performing strategic, operational, and resource analysis can reveal the weaknesses and strengths of the EOP, and opportunities to refine it. The success of emergency management directly relates to the success of collaboration. A strategic analysis includes continual evaluation of the following: HVA, community content, community perceptions, goals for risk communication, mitigation planning, and recovery planning. The review is followed by two other tasks in the continuing hazard phase: operational analysis and resource analysis (Lindell et al., 2007).

The operational analysis can use supporting information gathered in the strategic analysis. Evaluating and reviewing management and communication with the public is the focus of this review. The following areas are examined in an operational analysis: Local EMAs, the jurisdictional EOP, training and exercise needs, processes for protective measures, hazard adjustment incentives, sanctions and innovations, risk communications, and communications interoperability.

There are elements of the strategic analysis that provide input to the operational analysis. For example, the information gathered for mitigation and recovery planning would directly relate hazard adjustment incentives, sanctions, and innovations. This in turn would relate to the community content analyzed in the strategic analysis, with the knowledge that the community content would render a clearer picture for developing effective practices in raising public awareness and communications. A strategic analysis supports the ability to get messages to vulnerable populations (Lindell et al., 2007).

States and local jurisdictions devote significant time, energy, and resources toward developing disaster response plans and emergency management capabilities. Training is conducted to validate and incorporate the plans into accepted procedures operationally. Actions taken by states and local jurisdictions related to disaster preparedness are often motivated by federal funding.

There are three types of exercises. The tabletop exercise is the least complex exercise type and is often used to acquaint participants with plans or changes in plans. This is a verbal exercise where a scenario is read and the participants explain their actions and responsibilities within the scenario. Functional exercises test one or more functions in an emergency plan in a field setting designed to realistically approximate disaster conditions. Functional exercises can vary depending upon the objective. However, there are some constants, such as timing and realism. The full-scale exercise is a culmination of all planning efforts conducted in a realistic setting. The objective is to practice response scenarios before a disaster occurs. Each type of exercise is important and has its place. For example, it would be difficult to have a productive full-scale EOP without a solid understanding of it, that which could be gained through a tabletop exercise. Exercises at all levels provide simulated experiences.

Preparedness activities are created with a successful response in mind linking the two phases and necessitating linkage through continuity planning. Continuity of operations (COOP) is preparation of service provisions during and after a disaster. Specifically, the delivery of essential services during and after a disaster differs from continuity of government (COG). COG is concerned with the survival of the government. State and local governments sometimes combine COOP and COG; they are both plans of integration. Despite the combining of mass amounts of information, the plan should not be massively large. Lengthy plans become unusable during an emergency (Lindell et al., 2007). The COOP is cross-referenced with business continuity plans and linked to the jurisdictional mitigation plan. The key words are cross-referenced and linked; a necessary connection required when a disaster surpasses the ability of one community to continue operations on its own. Thus, where one emergency manager is handling a disaster response, the need to connect with other emergency managers and the like through the hierarchy must be easily understood and smooth. Transitioning into the recovery phase, COOP should form a bridge (Lindell et al., 2007). COOP is effective only if it is integrated with the jurisdictional EOP.

Response

The response phase is exactly what it sounds like—the response to a disaster. It begins when the disaster begins or early notifications are given (refer to Figure 1.3). For example, when the National Weather Service initiates a tornado warning, the response phase has started. Response includes activation of resources and assets in order to lessen the impact of the disaster and return the community to normal or a new normal as soon as possible. The goals of response are to protect the

■ **FIGURE 1.3** The response phase begins with the onset of an incident or disaster. It is comprised of immediate and ongoing activities, tasks, programs, and systems to manage the effects of an incident that threatens life, property, operations, or the environment. The first priority is lifesaving, followed by stabilization of the scene. Other priorities include protection of property and protection of the environment. *Image courtesy of the FEMA Photo Library.*

population, limit damage from initial impact of the disaster, and reduce the effects of any secondary impacts. Secondary impacts are caused by the initial disaster and include elements such as power outages, loss of water systems, and sewer systems.

The response phase occurs at the onset of an incident (emergency, disaster, or catastrophic event) (refer to Figure 1.3). It marks the execution of the EOP, either in part of in total. During the response phase, the coordination of activities is conducted through an emergency operations center (EOC). *Coordination* can be defined as a series of actions that assesses agent- and response-generated demands, gathers demand-relevant resources, and deploys those resources efficiently and effectively. Disaster operations are dynamic; a highly changing state must be monitored. Essentially, in order to fulfill the coordination of responsibilities, the changes in the responsibilities need monitoring. The EOC is also a point-of-information dissemination to incident commands. All information regarding the response filters through the EOC. Heightened information access at the EOC lessens the sharing of incorrect, incomplete, or ambiguous information; it is the most effective structure for public information dissemination (Lindell et al., 2007).

The EOC is activated under the stress of time-sensitive situations. Disasters require flexibility within operating procedures. Improvising must take place without violating policy. The EOC should have a designated space for such visitors and a public information officer to distribute information. During a disaster, the entire concept of an operation may need to endure a metamorphosis to manage the increased demand for service, combined with the lack of immediately available resources. The operational mode may need to transition from serving individuals to serving the masses. It is designed to increase or decrease functions, depending upon the incident in which it is activated. Once it is activated, the emergency management coordinator decides which services and functions are needed, thus tailoring the EOC to the event (Lindell et al., 2007). The EOC command is divided into four sections that perform the functions: administration, planning, logistics, and operations.

Overcoming some of the challenges in responding to a disaster involves knowing the roles of other responding agencies and trusting their abilities to perform their duties. Wherever a disaster occurs, the local government organizations are the first to respond and react to address the needs of its people. Mutual aid from surrounding areas and the state government may be requested or offered. Given the magnitude of the event, assistance from the federal government can be requested.

The assistance that the federal government can bring to bear during a catastrophic event will likely improve the situation. In a catastrophe, local government and perhaps states will not have the resources needed to respond adequately. The National Response Framework (NRF) and Emergency Support Function (ESF) annexes provide a sound plan for coordinating federal resources into the response effort. However, having a state and federal response greatly increases the complexity of the event. The meshing of local roles and responsibilities has the potential to overlap and bear inconsistencies if they are not standardized. Disastrous events are fraught with unknowns. Disorder occurs when agencies responding to a disaster are unable to put the event into a known context and cannot agree on a course of action. The length of the impact phase is contingent upon the type of disaster. Immediately following the impact phase, the emergency phase consists of life-sustaining activities such as search and rescue. The separation of the response phase into recovery can be ambiguous; all facets of a community cannot recover simultaneously.

Recovery

The recovery phase begins as lifesaving efforts come to a close in the response phase. The first priority in this phase is to restore community infrastructure as quickly as possible. This infrastructure refers to water systems, sewer systems, and electrical systems. The long-term goal of recovery is to return the community to normal, or at least a new, accepted definition of normal.

Recovery is the collective effort of all other phases, and as such, it is extremely difficult to define (refer to Figure 1.4). It can be viewed as a social process requiring the involvement of many partnerships necessary to guide a multifaceted course of action (Waugh & Tierney, 2007). Recovery can be categorized as short-term or long-term activities. Short-term activities include the regaining of basic support services, including search and rescue and donations management. Long-term recovery is weighed into the social processes of recovery, though not by itself.

It is difficult to determine recovery needs prior to impact because of the unique circumstances that each disaster brings. While emergency management is knowledge based and forward thinking, it is not an exact science. Provisions can be planned prior to impact which address all community dimensions based on an event magnitude scale of small-scale event, normal disaster, and catastrophic event. The dimensions of a community are social and psychological needs, housing, economic sector, environment, and infrastructure and lifelines. It is important to identify

■ **FIGURE 1.4** The recovery phase includes efforts to restore infrastructure and the social and economic life of a community to normal. In the short term, recovery may mean bringing necessary lifeline systems up to an acceptable standard while providing for basic human needs and ensuring that the societal needs of individuals and the community are met. Once a level of stability is achieved, the jurisdiction can begin recovery efforts for the long term, restoring economic activity and rebuilding community facilities and family housing with attention to long-term mitigation. *Image courtesy of the FEMA Photo Library.*

and establish priorities to reduce confusion and duplication of effort. Furthermore, the recovery process requires activating partnerships ideally established through preparedness activities. Presently, relief operations include the establishment of multi-agency resource centers (MARCs). A MARC provides an inclusive, one-stop hub for recovery assistance. Though not recommended, these activities sometimes occur after impact. Recovery provides a window of opportunity to garner stakeholder support and public attention and apply for federal funding; a chance to rebuild safer and resilient communities through mitigation measures is provided.

Mitigation

Mitigation is any activity or action taken that reduces or eliminates hazard risks to citizens and property. Whenever possible, a primary objective of a good mitigation program is to prevent disasters from occurring. Mitigation is an ongoing phase in which communities continually pursue mitigation efforts through thoughtful planning and effective leadership. When natural disasters are prevented or human behavior is changed, the impact of natural disasters are greatly reduced. While most natural disasters are nearly impossible to prevent, changing human behavior can prevent loss of life, as well as loss of property. Mitigation activities include planning, strategizing, and implementation of action items before an incident occurs.

Mitigation activities are planned for long-term hazard resistance and reduction. An *all-hazards approach* to mitigation planning involves consideration of all hazards with the potential of causing harm. The end product of this approach is a hazard mitigation plan, a document that presents policies and strategies that will reduce vulnerability to hazards when those policies and strategies are put into action. Mitigation includes activities such as land use controls, critical facility mapping, and preserving the natural environment. Such activities require a varied breadth of organizations to research, plan, and execute.

The law establishing provisions is the Disaster Mitigation Act (DMA) of 2000; Federal Emergency Management Agency (FEMA) is the administering agency. Federal appropriations can also be distributed on a cost-share basis (Schwab et al., 2007). Usually, the federal government carries the majority of the cost. However, the allocation of grant funds is contingent upon the adoption of hazard mitigation plans. Enforced responsibilities through federal guidelines and incentives, such as funding for mitigation projects, are executed at the local level.

Community development and growth do not occur in isolation. Intervals of activity and inactivity occur; however, thorough planning will be guided by a vision. Temporal qualities necessitate the inclusion of mitigation techniques into city planning. Since mitigation is most effective planned in conjunction with development, it too must be guided by a vision. A hazard mitigation plan can be developed as a stand-alone document, a local land use or comprehensive addendum, or as an integrated component of the local emergency operations plan. Therefore, a flexible element to hazard mitigation planning exists. The chosen plan should guide development decisions so that vulnerability to hazards is reduced. There are four basic phases that aid in determining the most appropriate context. Collaborating with affected parties is crucial, and rallying the community and stakeholders can provide useful guidance. The inclusion of individuals increases perspectives. Input from various perspectives increases the chance of success, and errors unnoticed by emergency management personnel can be recognized by others. Ideally, collaboration will increase community satisfaction. The hazard and community exposure assessment, as well as measurable goal setting, verifies if a multijurisdictional approach is needed. Finally, the selected plan must be implemented and evaluated. Development is dynamic; the hazard mitigation plan should reflect this characteristic through periodic revisions. Mitigation is an ongoing effort to lessen the impact through predisaster activities. It can take place years, months, or even decades before a disaster. Success is measured by what does *not* occur (that is, avoidance and prevention are key). This causes mitigation to be put off until after a disaster.

There are two approaches to mitigation: structural and nonstructural, which can be placed into six broad categories. Structural engineering projects consist of engineering and technology used to armor against forces of nature, such as a dam. These projects tend to be very expensive and can fail. Local authorities may seek cheaper prevention alternatives. Property acquisition and land-use plans are cost-effective prevention mitigation approaches. However, they may also limit the use of land for public services. Property protection practices seek to increase the resilience of existing structures through elevation, floodproofing, windproofing, and seismic retrofitting. Preserving nature and healthy ecosystems are an often-overlooked but effective mitigation technique. Often, nature has already provided mitigation measures for disasters, such as wetlands that are able to absorb large amounts of water. Public awareness and understanding that face the community are essential for effective hazard management activities. Education and information dissemination are important functions of local governments to protect health and safety in the community. Emergency services protect people and property during and immediately after a disaster or hazard event.

Many mitigation efforts are federally funded and carried out at the local level. Thus, certain local powers are prescribed to mitigate in the form of zoning ordinances, subdivision regulations, building codes, and flood damage prevention ordinances. Zoning regulates how property within the jurisdiction may be used by dividing the community into districts. Zoning maps define the location of the various districts. Overlay zones apply conditions to development in addition to, or in place of, the standard zoning ordinance for a certain area. This is effective for high-hazard areas. Bonus and incentive zoning is the practice of allowing developers to exceed the limits of current regulations, such as building height and floor area, in return for certain dispensations. Subdivision ordinances govern development land for sale. Developers may be required to pay for impacts on the community, such as fees to help pay for the demands of new construction will place on local facilities and services. Subdivision regulations prohibit the use of land subject to flooding, wildfire, or erosion. Building codes enforce standards and requirements for structural integrity, design, and construction materials used in commercial and residential structures. Local governments can reject the proposal or require revisions before granting approval.

Local governments can use eminent domain to condemn property for certain community needs, such as schools and roads. However, eminent domain is rarely used for this purpose. Usually, land is purchased from a willing seller through the acquisition program. Ideally, the acquisition will result in removal of the property from the private market to be returned to a natural hazard impact absorbing area.

The requisition of funds, the adopting of a hazard mitigation plan, and local land use decisions are primarily responsibilities of the state and local governments. However, state and local governments do not own all the land. Federally owned areas, such as wildlife and forest, by nature limit the residential population and therefore decrease the hazard risk. Military bases increase the residential population of the area, as military members, base employees, and their respective families will move nearby.

Sizeable mitigation activities fall under the federal government. Specifically, the U.S. Army Corps of Engineers carries out flood control and navigation structure projects: levees, dams, seawalls, and beach nourishment. This is a significant conflict as the U.S. Army Corps of Engineers can only carry out the intended use, set forth by Congress, of the appropriated funds. There is no independent authority to set construction priorities and little ability to consider the broader effects of the projects that Congress assigns (Schwab et al., 2007).

CRITICAL THINKING

Often, an expensive mitigation project is initiated during long-term recovery operations. Why? If returning the community to normalcy is the goal of recovery, how does an expensive mitigation project make disaster victims feel like things are returning to normal?

Mitigation should lead to sustainable communities. Sustainable development can be defined as development that meets the current needs without compromising the ability of future generations to meet their own needs. It requires viewing everything in a networked context, thus complicating the prediction process of disaster relief. Truly sustainable communities are hazard-resilient and consider disaster prevention, along with issues of environmental stewardship, quality of life, economic vitality, and a fair legacy for future generations.

Unsustainable land uses lead to vulnerability. Unchecked patterns of growth emphasize sprawling development place intense pressure on the natural environment. The economy to withstand disasters is best accomplished by placing people and property in hazard-safe locations and by integrating mitigation building techniques into the construction process. A disaster can fast-forward a declining economy, and it can also provide an opportunity for a community to make positive changes and focus new energy on revitalizing areas of blight or neglect.

Mitigation encourages long-term reduction of hazard vulnerability. Preparedness saves lives and property and facilitates response operations through predisaster plans and training. Research indicates that the majority of households in vulnerable communities are not adequately prepared for environmental disasters. Efforts must be seen across all sides of the community to achieve community resiliency. It is a shared responsibility among the local government, the stakeholders, the public, and the surrounding areas.

UNDERSTANDING HAZARDS AND DISASTERS

Although the terms *hazard* and *disaster* are often used interchangeably, they have different meanings. According to FEMA, "Hazard means an event or physical condition that has the potential to cause fatalities, injuries, property damage, infrastructure damage, agricultural loss, damage to the environment, interruption of business, or other types of harm or loss" (FEMA, 1997). Chapters 5 and 6 of this book describe in great detail natural and manmade hazards that a community might face. On the other hand, a disaster is a singular event that results in widespread losses to people, infrastructure, or the environment caused by any natural or manmade hazards (Cutter, 2001). A disaster is different from a routine emergency in the sense that routine emergencies can be managed by local resources or with assistance from others in the area by using normal operating techniques, with very little displacement (Altay & Green, 2006). Examples of routine emergencies include a fire, a vehicle accident, or other events that typically can take place in an area and be prepared for ahead of time. An event becomes a disaster when the local resources are stressed to the point where the normal operating techniques are no longer adequate and government assistance is required to respond to the situation (Altay & Green, 2006). The Robert T. Stafford Disaster Relief and Emergency Assistance Act (FEMA, 2013) defines a major disaster as follows.

Table 1.1 provides a list of the top 10 deadliest disasters since 1900 caused by different hazards.

HISTORY AND EVOLUTION OF HAZARD MITIGATION

This section of the chapter describes the history of modern emergency management in the United States, highlighting major mitigation policies and framework. A chronological list of major mitigation policy initiatives is provided in Table 1.2.

> Any natural catastrophe (including any hurricane, tornado, storm, high water, wind-driven water, tidal wave, tsunami, earthquake, volcanic eruption, landslide, mudslide, snowstorm, or drought), or, regardless of cause, any fire, flood, or explosion, in any part of the United States, which in the determination of the President causes damage of sufficient severity and magnitude to warrant major disaster assistance under this Act to supplement the efforts and available resources of States, local governments, and disaster relief organizations in alleviating the damage, loss, hardship, or suffering caused thereby.

Table 1.1 Deadliest Disasters Since 1900

Rank	Disaster	Deaths (approx.)
1	1931 central China floods	2,500,000–3,700,000
2	1976 Tangshan earthquake, China	250,000–779,000
3	1938 Huang He River flood, China	500,000–700,000
4	1970 Bhola cyclone, East Pakistan (now Bangladesh)	500,000
5	2010 Haiti earthquake	316,000
6	1920 Haiyuan earthquake	235,502
7	2004 Indian Ocean tsunami and earthquake	230,210
8	1975 Typhoon Nina–Banqiao dam failure, China	210,000
9	2008 Cyclone Nargis, Myanmar	146,000
10	1935 Yangtze River flood, China	145,000

Source: Chicago Tribune (n.d.).

Table 1.2 A Chronological Listing of Major Mitigation Policy Initiatives in the United States

Year	Mitigation Policy Initiative	Significance
1803	Congressional Act of 1803	To provide financial assistance to Portsmouth, NH, a town devastated by fire
1849 and 1850	The Swamp Land Acts	Reclamation of wetlands in Mississippi Valley
1917	Flood Control Act of 1917	First flood control law
1928	Flood Control Act of 1928	To expand federal flood control funding
1936	Flood Control Act of 1936	Helped develop many reservoir, levee, and channelization projects
1950	Disaster Relief Act of 1950	First nationwide framework for disaster response and relief
1968	National Flood Insurance Act	Creation of the National Flood Insurance Program (NFIP)
1974	Disaster Relief Act of 1974	Mitigation requirements introduced to receive financial aid
1977	Earthquake Hazards Reduction Act	Provide finding for earthquake research, education, and training
1979	Executive Order 12127	Creation of FEMA
1988	Robert T. Stafford Disaster Relief and Emergency Assistance Act of 1988	Federal assistance for state and local governments; established the Hazard Mitigation Grant Program (HMGP)
1993	Mitigation Directorate was created within FEMA	Mitigation has become the cornerstone of emergency management
2000	Disaster Mitigation Act of 2000	New requirements were set for state, local, and tribal governments to implement mitigation planning projects
2002	Homeland Security Act of 2002	DHS was created; terrorism became the major focus
2011 and 2012	FEMA introduced the "Whole Community Approach" and Threat Hazards Identification and Risk Assessment (THIRA)	Creation of resilient communities becomes a focus

Prior to the 1930s, the U.S. government was not heavily involved in disaster relief. The first example of federal government involvement was an 1803 congressional act passed to provide financial assistance to Portsmouth, a town in New Hampshire that was devastated by fire (Haddow, Bullock, & Coppola, 2008). The Swamp Land Acts of 1849 and 1850 were the first significant federal flood control laws, and they helped in the reclamation of millions of acres of wetlands in the lower Mississippi Valley (Arnold, 1988). The Mississippi River Commission was formed in 1879 in response to a series of floods especially due to a major Mississippi River flood in 1874. However, the Flood Control Act of 1917 was the first flood control law passed by the House Committee on Flood Control. Another significant flood on the Mississippi River in 1927 became the initiative for the Flood Control Act of 1928, which enhanced federal flood control funding and created awareness for the problem. Until the 1930s, the responsibility of the federal government and Congress was mainly confined to passing a bill to provide assistance to the victims after a specific disaster.

The Flood Control Act of 1936 was also an important milestone in flood mitigation, as it led to the development of hundreds of reservoir, dam, levee, dike, and channelization projects. The Flood Control Act of 1936 gave increased authority to the U.S. Army Corps of Engineers and other federal agencies to design and build flood control projects. Before this act was passed, there was no nationwide flood control program by the federal government despite the long history of severe flooding in the country. According to Arnold (1988), the main reasons for this were.

First, the national government's modest financial resources seemed to preclude federal financing of expensive flood control measures during the 19th century. Second, there were formidable engineering and economic obstacles to flood control by methods other than levees, such as reservoirs. Third, the relatively modest growth of cities along the nation's rivers kept flood damage fairly low until the end of the 19th or the beginning of the 20th century. Finally, many political leaders believed that federal aid for flood control was unconstitutional.

Prior to the 1950s, although the federal government did provide occasional assistance to victims after specific disaster events, there was no ongoing framework for federal disaster assistance to state and local governments. The American Red Cross, a largely volunteer organization, was the primary relief agency operating under federal charter. With the passage of the Disaster Relief Act of 1950, the first nationwide framework for disaster response and relief came into existence (Godschalk, Beatley, Berke, Brower & Kaiser 1999). This era is also known for the Cold War and the rise of civil defense. Communities were encouraged to build shelters to protect themselves from nuclear attack from the then–Soviet Union. The Federal Civil Defense Administration (FCDA) was established to provide federal support for civil defense activities. Almost every community participated in civil defense programs, and each community had a civil defense director to oversee such programs. In reality, these officers were the first recognized face of emergency management in the United States (Haddow et al., 2008).

The most significant event during the 1960s was the creation of the National Flood Insurance Program (NFIP), with the passage of National Flood Insurance Act of 1968. A series of major disasters occurred during the 1960s, including Hurricane Betsy in 1965. Hurricane Betsy was a category 4 hurricane that killed and injured hundreds of people and caused about $1.42 billion (in 1965 U.S. dollars) in damage along the Gulf Coast. The financial losses from Hurricane Betsy led to the creation of the NFIP to provide insurance as a protection against future floods and to reduce government assistance after disasters.

Meanwhile, subsequent versions of the Disaster Relief Act of 1950 (which authorized assistance for individual victims, as well as state and local governments) were introduced in 1953, then in 1970, and then again in 1974. The Disaster Relief Act of 1974 is highly significant, as Congress mandated specific prerequisites for financial aid for the first time. Section 406 of the Disaster Relief Act of 1974 requires that all recipient jurisdictions will take steps to evaluate and mitigate natural hazards. Later, more requirements were stipulated with the passage of the Robert T. Stafford Disaster Relief and Emergency Assistance Act of 1988, and finally, the Disaster Mitigation Act of 2000.

Also, in 1977, the National Earthquake Hazards Reduction Program (NEHRP) was created by the Earthquake Hazards Reduction Act of 1977. The purpose of this program is to provide funding for research, understating and mapping of seismic hazards, and education and technical assistance. Through the leadership of the U.S. Geological Survey (USGS), substantial research has been done in understanding and the mapping of seismic hazards.

Perhaps the most significant milestone of emergency management in the United States was the creation of FEMA. Prior to the existence of FEMA, there were a number of federal agencies working on some aspect of risk and disasters, and it was frustrating for states and local government officials to get immediate assistance in the aftermath of a disaster. A group of state civil defense directors, led by Lacy Suiter of Tennessee and Eric Jones of Illinois, launched an effort through the National Governor's Association to consolidate federal emergency management functions under one lead agency (Haddow et al., 2008). Through their efforts, FEMA was created in 1979 by the consolidation of the following five agencies: the Defense Civil Preparedness Agency, from the Pentagon; the Federal Insurance Administrator, from the Department of Housing and Urban Development (HUD); the Federal Disaster Assistance Administration, from HUD; the Federal Preparedness Agency, from the

First, Federal authorities to anticipate, prepare for, and respond to major civil emergencies should be supervised by one official responsible to the President and given attention by other officials at the highest levels. Second, an effective civil defense system requires the most efficient use of all available resources. Third, whenever possible, emergency responsibilities should be extensions of federal agencies. Fourth, federal hazard mitigation activities should be closely linked with emergency preparedness and response functions.

General Services Administration (GSA); and the National Fire Prevention and Control Administration, from the Department of Commerce.

On June 19, 1978, President Jimmy Carter transmitted to Congress Reorganization Plan Number 3 (3 CFR 1978, 5 U.S. Code 903), which proposed the establishment of a new federal agency, FEMA. The new agency consolidated the aforementioned agencies, and its director would report directly to the president. Reorganization Plan Number 3 stated several fundamental organization principles.

The Three Mile Island Nuclear Power Plant accident in Pennsylvania on March 28, 1979, added impetus to the creation of FEMA. This incident was the worst disaster in U.S. nuclear power plant history, and the way in which the federal government responded to this event was heavily criticized by national media and the public. After congressional review and concurrence, FEMA was officially established on March 31, 1979, by Executive Order 12127. The establishment of FEMA following this event was a much-needed measure by the Carter Administration and well received in general.

The next notable event in U.S. mitigation history was the creation of the Robert T. Stafford Disaster Relief and Emergency Assistance Act of 1988, commonly known as the Stafford Act. It is an amended version of the Disaster Relief Act of 1974. The Stafford Act is an important milestone, as it created the provision for disaster preparedness and for federal assistance for states and local governments through FEMA following a presidential disaster declaration. The act also established the Hazard Mitigation Grant Program (HMGP) to provide grants to states and local governments to implement long-term hazard mitigation measures after a major disaster declaration. Moreover, the act requires states to develop and adopt hazard mitigation plans (HMPs) as a condition for receiving disaster assistance. The Stafford Act was amended in 2000 by the passage of the Disaster Mitigation Act of 2000 (DMA 2000) and again in 2006 with the Pets Evacuation and Transportation Standards Act.

In 1993, President Bill Clinton appointed James Lee Witt as the director of FEMA, and he brought a new style of leadership to the agency. Mitigation suddenly received priority and unprecedented support from the government. The Mitigation Directorate was created within FEMA on November 28, 1993. The new era of emergency management began and mitigation became a cornerstone of FEMA and emergency management. For the first time in the history of federal disaster assistance, mitigation—sustained action taken to reduce or eliminate long-term risk to people and their property from hazards and their effects—has become the cornerstone of emergency management (FEMA 1995, p. vii).

As mentioned previously, the Stafford Act was amended in 2000 with the passage of DMA 2000, with a new set of requirements that emphasize the need for state, local, and tribal governments to implement mitigation planning projects. The requirement for a state HMP is continued as a condition of disaster assistance, with added incentives for increased coordination and integration of mitigation activities at the state level. DMA 2000 also established a new requirement for local mitigation plans and authorized up to 7 percent of HMGP funds available to a state for development of state, local, and Indian tribal mitigation plans (FEMA, 2000).

Terrorism and homeland security became the major focus after the Al Qaeda terrorist attacks on September 11, 2001. President George W. Bush signed the Homeland Security Act of 2002 (HS Act; Public Law 107–296) on November 25, 2002, which created the Department of Homeland Security (DHS) to protect the United States within, at, and outside its borders in the civilian sphere. A total of 22 existing federal agencies, including FEMA, were incorporated into the new department. Under this new structure, FEMA would focus exclusively on response and recovery (Haddow et al., 2008). The Homeland Security Presidential Directive 5 (HSPD5) requires that all federal, state, and local agencies be compliant with the National Incident Management System (NIMS) and operate under the Incident Command System (ICS) to manage emergencies. These administrative requirements must now be met before state and local governmental agencies receive federal funding.

CRITICAL THINKING

In your opinion, which mitigation policy initiative is the most significant in the history of hazard mitigation? Defend your answer.

One sad chapter in FEMA's history came in 2005, when the agency failed to respond adequately after Hurricane Katrina hit the Gulf Coast. Although Katrina was a category 3 hurricane at landfall, it became the costliest hurricane in U.S. history, with an estimated $108 billion in damages and more than 1800 fatalities. The Hurricane Katrina debacle raised many concerns about FEMA's capabilities, which prompted the government to conduct a thorough review to find out what went wrong and what would be needed to remedy those problems. A report called "The Federal Response to Hurricane Katrina: Lessons Learned" was released in February 2006, with 125 recommendations and 11 critical actions. In the wake of Hurricane Katrina, strides have been made toward the creation of "resilient communities" (Comfort, Boin, & Demchak, 2010). FEMA introduced the "Whole Community Approach" in December 2011 and the Threat Hazards Identification and Risk Assessment (THIRA) in April 2012, to incorporate the community into the process of emergency management in order to enhance community resilience.

THE HAZARD MITIGATION PLANNING PROCESS AND THE HAZARD MITIGATION PLAN

Hazard mitigation planning is the process of determining how to reduce or eliminate the loss of life and property damage resulting from natural and human-caused hazards (FEMA 386-1, "Getting Started: Building Support for Mitigation Planning"). State, Indian tribal, and local governments are required by DMA 2000 to develop a HMP as a condition for receiving certain types of disaster assistance from FEMA. There are four basic phases in the mitigation planning process, as shown in Figure 1.5.

■ **FIGURE 1.5** Hazard mitigation planning is a four-step process. First, you must organize your resources. Then, you need to assess risks. From there, you can develop a plan to mitigate hazards. Finally, implement your plan and monitor progress. All of this would lead to a constant process of updating the plan with progress made and addressing new risks. *Image courtesy of FEMA.*

Organize Resources

The first phase of the mitigation planning process involves organizing resources such as identifying and assembling the necessary technical information, funding, staff, and political and public support. The efforts for organizing resources can be done in three steps (Figure 1.6):

> *Step 1:* The first step toward organizing resources involves measuring the level and source of community support for planning and working

■ **FIGURE 1.6** Organizing resources involves three steps. First, you need to assess the community support for developing a hazard mitigation plan. Then you establish a planning team with subject matter experts. Also, you must obtain public input during the mitigation planning process. *Image courtesy of FEMA.*

on areas where gaps have been identified. It is also important in this step to determine the scope of the mitigation plan and clearly define the planning area. Mitigation plans can be developed for a single jurisdiction, such as a city, or for multiple jurisdictions developed by various entities, including villages, towns, cities, counties, special districts, regional planning commissions, and tribal governments. In terms of a multijurisdictional plan, each entity that falls within the planning area is responsible for participating in and adopting the mitigation plan.

Step 2: Whether there is an established planning team or you are in the process of forming one, it is essential that you assess the expertise and capabilities of all team members that may contribute to the hazard mitigation plan. The assessment will enable you to determine if more subject matter experts should be recruited for the planning team.

Step 3: It is important to obtain public input during the hazard mitigation planning process. Therefore, the planning team should develop a detailed schedule to obtain public input at certain key stages in the mitigation planning process, which are:

- At the beginning of the planning process, to inform the public about your planning efforts and for them to learn about resources that are important to the community
- At the conclusion of the risk assessment cycle, to report on your findings
- When developing goals and discussing alternative mitigation actions for mitigation strategy
- During the implementation stage, to inform the public of your progress.

Frequently used methods to obtain public input include public meetings, questionnaires, and visual definition surveys (FEMA 386-1, "Getting Started: Building Support for Mitigation Planning").

Risk Assessment

The next planning step is to analyze the hazards facing the community by conducting a risk assessment (see Figure 1.7). *Risk assessment* is the process of measuring the potential loss of life, personal injury, economic injury, and property damage resulting from hazard events. This is done by assessing the vulnerability of people, buildings, and infrastructure to specific hazards. This step is essential because it evaluates the degree to which injuries and damages may occur and provides the foundation for the rest of the mitigation planning process (FEMA 386-2, "Understanding Your Risks: Identifying Hazards and Estimating Losses").

According to FEMA, there are four primary steps (Figure 1.7) associated with conducting risk assessment:

Step 1: Identification of hazards affecting the community
Step 2: Profiling of hazards to determine hazard-prone areas and magnitude of each hazard

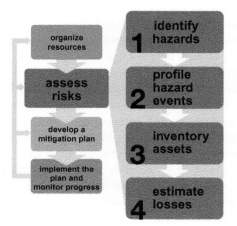

■ **FIGURE 1.7** Risk assessment is a four-step process. The first step is to identify hazards that may affect your community. The next step involves developing hazard event profiles. Then you inventory assets and assess vulnerability. Finally, you estimate potential losses from hazards. *Image courtesy of FEMA.*

Step 3: Inventory of assets vulnerable to those hazards, assess vulnerability of these assets, and establish priorities by determining which assets are most valuable to the community
Step 4: Estimating potential losses

Chapters 5 and 6 of this book provide detailed descriptions of a number of natural and man-made hazards that are useful in the hazard identification process. Chapter 7 discusses the methodology of conducting hazard vulnerability assessment and impact analysis, which includes all the steps of the risk assessment process.

In addition to these four primary steps, risk assessment should include information about repetitive loss structures and how these might best be addressed in the mitigation strategy portion of the plan. FEMA, through the Federal Insurance Administration (FIA), defines a repetitive loss structure as a structure for which there has been more than one flood insurance claim of at least $1000 within any 10-year period since 1978. Also, a general description of land uses within the jurisdiction and an analysis of development trends should be provided so that mitigation options can be considered in future land use decisions.

Developing the Mitigation Plan

Once the risk assessment phase has been completed, the findings are used to write mitigation strategies for the community to reduce potential losses. This is also a four-step process (Figure 1.8):

Step 1: The first step is to formulate goals and objectives in concert with loss estimation identified in the risk assessment. Public participation is essential in this step to obtain information while developing goals and objectives.
Step 2: Next is to identify and analyze a range of mitigation actions that needs to be prioritized. According to FEMA, mitigation plans only require a review of benefits and costs to prioritize actions, although a community may wish to complete a benefit-cost analysis (BCA) for its own purposes. Normally, a BCA is required only when a community applies for a grant to implement the action (FEMA 386-3, "Developing the Mitigation Plan: Identifying Mitigation Actions and Implementation Strategies").
Step 3: Once mitigation actions are identified and prioritized, the planning team must prepare an implementation strategy identifying

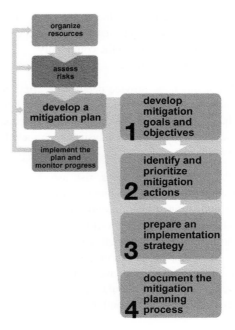

■ **FIGURE 1.8** Steps for developing the plan include developing mitigation goals and objectives, identifying and prioritizing mitigation actions, preparing an implementation strategy, and finally, documenting the mitigation planning process. *Image courtesy of FEMA.*

the responsible agency or organization, funding source, and time frame for completing each project.

Step 4: Documenting the mitigation planning process helps to organize all relevant information into a coherent, practical plan to meet the DMA 2000 criteria.

FEMA HOW-TO SERIES DOCUMENTS FOR HAZARD MITIGATION PLAN

FEMA published a number of mitigation planning documents in their "How-To Series." The following documents provide step-by-step guidelines how to develop a hazard mitigation plan (HMP):

- FEMA 386-1, "Getting Started: Building Support for Mitigation Planning"
- FEMA 386-2, "Understanding Your Risks: Identifying Hazards and Estimating Losses"
- FEMA 386-3, "Developing the Mitigation Plan: Identifying Mitigation Actions and Implementation Strategies"
- FEMA 386-4, "Bringing the Plan to Life: Implementing the Hazard Mitigation Plan"

Implement the Plan and Monitor the Progress

A number of considerations (see Figure 1.9) or steps are associated with this phase described in detail in the FEMA 386-4, "Bringing the Plan to Life: Implementing the Hazard Mitigation Plan." These include:

■ *Sensitivity of information:* The planning team should be cautious about incorporating and releasing sensitive information in the mitigation plan. For instance, disclosing the specific location of archeological sites or details about certain cultural practices and traditions could be detrimental and result in the destruction of the very resources that the planning team is striving to protect. In addition, providing details about the vulnerability of soft targets may be detrimental to national security efforts.

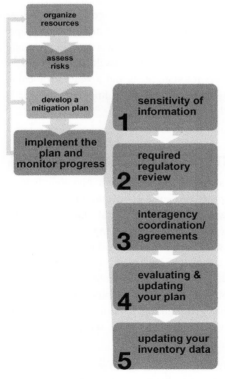

■ **FIGURE 1.9** Considerations for implementing the plan and monitor progress. The Planning Team should be in compliance with all rules and regulations during the implementation phase and carefully monitor the progress. *Image courtesy of FEMA.*

- *Required regulatory review:* It is essential that the planning team is in compliance with the rules and regulations during the implementation phase.
- *Interagency coordination/agreements:* During implementation, the planning team will want to continue to coordinate closely with all its partners with whom it has been working throughout the planning process. These include local or regional planning entities, local building officials, and others who have helped the planning team develop the plan.
- *Evaluating and updating plan:* It is also important to assess the mitigation plan and update changes to jurisdictional boundaries, land uses, and new development. If lands have been added or removed from the planning area, this can affect the risk assessment.
- *Updating inventory data:* A strategy for revising and updating inventory data can be developed based on the evaluation results. Although updating the plan should occur at least every 10 years, certain circumstances, such as a surge in population growth or a serious disaster event, may warrant more frequent updates of inventory information. It may be worthwhile to update the inventory when the hazard mitigation plan itself must be updated: a maximum of every 3 years for state plans and 5 years for local plans (FEMA 386-4, "Bringing the Plan to Life: Implementing the Hazard Mitigation Plan").

THE BENEFITS OF MITIGATION PLANNING

In addition to saving lives, mitigation planning helps save money by reducing the impacts and costs of natural and manmade hazards. A study by the Multihazard Mitigation Council finds that each dollar spent on mitigation saves a community an average of $4 (FEMA, n.d.). Disasters are expensive, with many costs associated with them. First, there are direct financial costs from damage and destruction that need to be handled immediately. These include debris removal, rebuilding homes, repairing infrastructure, and reestablishing commerce and industry. Without appropriate mitigation measures in place, more damages may occur, which incur more costs from the governments (hence, paid by taxpayers).

Besides direct financial costs, a community may suffer from long-term economic losses from a disaster as local businesses and industries may close permanently or suspend operations for an extended period (Schwab et al., 2007). An example of such occurrences comes from the 2010

■ **FIGURE 1.10** The Deepwater Horizon oil spill began on April 20, 2010 in the Gulf of Mexico due to the explosion and sinking of the Deepwater Horizon oil rig operated by British Petroleum (BP). An estimated total of 4.9 million barrels of oil was discharged for 87 days until the well was capped on July 15, 2010. *Image courtesy of NOAA.*

Deepwater Horizon oil spill disaster in the Gulf of Mexico (Figure 1.10), which caused the fishing industry in the state of Louisiana to shut down for a long period of time, with an estimated cost of about $2.5 billion in losses (Walsh, 2010).

Also, there are environmental impacts associated with hazard events. The Deepwater Horizon oil spill is considered to be the worst environmental disaster in the United States; it released about 4.9 million barrels of crude oil into the Gulf of Mexico, which caused a great deal of damage to marine life and species, and surrounding beaches.

Mitigation planning helps communities become more sustainable and disaster resilient by taking appropriate mitigation measures based on risk assessment. Also, it allows focusing on implementing mitigation projects in areas at risk of hazards by setting priorities.

■ CONCLUSION

Comprehensive emergency management is approaching emergency management from a broad and inclusive perspective. All hazards, all partners, and all phases of emergency management are addressed. Adopting this mind-set in emergency management programs will lead to more resilient and sustainable organizations and communities, which will be better prepared to recover from disaster.

The impacts of disasters on residents and their communities can be mitigated through effective local emergency planning, which includes organized efforts at the community and household levels. Presently, local emergency planning should include communicating risk and providing information about planning and preparedness measures. Even so, the majority of households in vulnerable communities are not adequately prepared for environmental disasters. Ideally, the best future predictors are facts, knowledge of people's behavior, and the hazard in question. In theory, disaster awareness and training programs should motivate individuals to take action. Efforts must be seen across all sides of the community to achieve community resiliency. It is a shared responsibility among the local government, the stakeholders, the public, and the individual.

The four phases of emergency management can be viewed as a continuous life cycle. Beginning with the preparedness phase, emergency managers focus their efforts on making their communities ready for the most serious hazards facing them. The overall goal of preparedness is to be ready to respond and recover from these hazards should they affect the community. A primary objective of preparedness would be to predict risk and then address it through the creation of functional plans, the acquisition of resources, and the coordination of an effective response. The response phase begins at the onset of an incident (emergency, disaster, or catastrophe). The primary goal of response activities is to save lives. Following this, first responders and community officials will seek to stabilize the incident, save property and environment. Actions during the response phase should be in keeping with the concepts and principles prescribed in the NIMS. This would include a unity of effort and a scalable, flexible and tiered response. Typical activities include search and rescue, triage, treatment and transport of victims, and establishment of an EOC.

Response activities will lead to the recovery phase, which can be further broken down into short- and long- term recovery efforts. The overall goal of recovery is to return the community to a state of normalcy. Short-term recovery operations will seek to restore essential functions in a community by clearing roads, removing debris, restoring utilities, and providing temporary shelter to disaster victims. This could endure for a period ranging from a few weeks to a few months. Long-term recovery efforts, which could be going on for months to years, will seek to rebuild damaged structures and may include the provision of temporary housing for disaster victims. Rebuilding a community can be quite extensive and expensive. If we have to build something again, why not rebuild it better? This is what makes the recovery phase a good time for mitigation monies to help communities with costly structural mitigation projects like flood water control measures and storm shelters. The mitigation phase seeks to reduce or prevent the impact of hazards. Mitigation strategies can be structural and nonstructural. A good hazard mitigation plan considers all important hazards facing a community so that exposure to risk is minimized, thus reducing or preventing damage. Implementation of mitigation strategies can save lives and protect property. Progressive and knowledgeable emergency managers will utilize a combination of structural and nonstructural methods to achieve their mitigation goal. A combination of federal, state and local funds will have to be applied to make costly structural mitigation projects become a reality. Having shovel-ready projects to hand may be the key to success. The goals, objectives, and typical activities for each phase of the emergency management life cycle have been summarized in Table 1.3. It outlines the four phases of the emergency management life cycle, the goals and objectives of each and some typical activities that might be taking place in each phase.

Hazards and disasters are not the same; *hazard* is the potential, and *disaster* is the actual event. A disaster is different from a routine emergency because routine emergencies can be managed by local resources or with very little displacement, while during a disaster, local resources are stressed, the normal operating techniques are no longer adequate, and government assistance is required.

Table 1.3 The Four Phases of the Emergency Management Life Cycle, the Goals and Objectives of Each and Some Typical Activities that might be Taking Place in Each Phase

Phase	Overall Goal	Objectives	Typical Activities
Mitigation	Reduce or prevent the impact of hazards	■ Reduce public exposure to risk ■ Reduce or prevent damage to property ■ Reduce adverse environmental and financial impacts of hazards	■ Levee construction ■ Implement land use restrictions
Preparedness	To be ready to respond to and recover from hazards	To predict risk and address it through: ■ Creation of functional plans ■ Acquisition of resources ■ Coordination for an effective response	■ Development of an Emergency Operations Plan ■ Exercises, training and drills
Response	To save lives, protecting property and the environment.	■ To stabilize the incident ■ Tiered response ■ Scalable, flexible and adaptable ■ Unity of effort	■ Search and Rescue ■ Triage and transport of victims ■ Establish an EOC
Recovery	Return community to a state of normalcy	To restore essential functions in a community affected by disaster by: ■ Rebuilding damaged structures ■ Clearing roads and removing debris ■ Restoring utilities	■ Provide temporary shelter and housing ■ Restore power, water and other utilities

Mitigation has a long and interesting history in the United States, with many turning points. As described in this chapter, the disaster assistance and mitigation framework has evolved slowly and still continues to evolve. However, since the 1990s, mitigation has become the cornerstone of emergency management. The Disaster Mitigation Act of 2000 requires state, Indian tribal, and local governments to develop HMPs as a condition for receiving certain types of disaster assistance from FEMA. This chapter presents an outline of the structure of a functional hazard mitigation plan. Section 1 of this book describes the mitigation framework, including the associated rules and regulations and the role of governments and the private sector. Components of the risk assessment process for both natural and manmade hazards are described in section 2. Finally, section 3 highlights current mitigation strategies, tools, techniques, and best practices in the United States and around the world.

DISCUSSION QUESTIONS

1. Discuss the four phases of comprehensive emergency management. State the goals and objectives of each. Give some examples of activities in your workplace for each of the four phases.
2. What is the meaning and importance of an all-hazards approach to the profession of emergency management?
3. How does mitigation fit into the emergency management cycle? Consider this from a planning and implementation point of view.
4. What is the difference between a hazard and a disaster?
5. Discuss the history and evolution of hazard mitigation.
6. Discuss the hazard mitigation planning process and the structure of a functional HMP.
7. Discuss the benefits of mitigation planning.

WEBSITES

Federal Emergency Management Agency (FEMA). Plan, Prepare, and Mitigate. http://www.fema.gov/plan-prepare-mitigate

Federal Emergency Management Agency (FEMA). Emergency Management Institute. http://training.fema.gov/EMIWeb/edu/

Federal Emergency Management Agency (FEMA). National Incident Management System. http://www.fema.gov/national-incident-management-system

REFERENCES

Altay, N., & Green, W. G., III (2006). Interfaces with other disciplines OR/MS research in disaster operations management. *European Journal of Operational Research*, *175*, 475–493.

Arnold, J. L. (1988). *The evolution of the 1936 flood control act*. Fort Belvoir, VA: Office of History, U. S. Army Corps of Engineers.

Chicago Tribune (n.d.). 25 Deadliest disasters. Retrieved from <http://www.chicagotribune.com/sns-viral-natural-disaster-deaths-photogallery.html>. Accessed October 1, 2014.

Comfort, L., Boin, A., & Demchak, C. (Eds.), (2010). *Designing resilience* Pittsburgh, PA: University of Pittsburgh Press.

Cutter, S. (2001). *The changing nature of risks and hazards* (Chapter 1). *American Hazardscapes: The regionalization of hazards and disasters*. Washington, DC: Joseph Henry Press.

Godschalk, D. R., Beatley, T., Berke, P. R., Brower, D. J., & Kaiser, E. J. (1999). *Natural hazard mitigation: Recasting disaster policy and planning*. Washington, DC: Island Press.

Haddow, G., Bullock, J., & Coppola, D. (2008). *Introduction to emergency management* (3rd ed.). Burlington, MA: Elsevier Butterworth-Heinemann.

Lindell, M. K., Prater, C. S., & Perry, R. W. (2007). *Introduction to emergency management*. Hoboken, NJ: John Wiley & Sons.

Perry, R., & Lindell, M. (2007). *Emergency planning*. Hoboken, NJ: John Wiley & Sons.

Schwab, A. J., Eschelbach, K., & Brower, D. J. (2007). *Hazard mitigation and preparedness*. Hoboken, NJ: John Wiley & Sons.

U.S. Federal Emergency Management Agency (FEMA) (1995). *Mitigation: Cornerstone for Building Safer Communities*. Washington, DC: FEMA.

U.S. Federal Emergency Management Agency (FEMA) (1997). *Multihazard identification and assessment*. Washington, DC: FEMA.

U.S. Federal Emergency Management Agency (FEMA) (2000). *Disaster mitigation act of 2000*. Washington, DC: FEMA.

U.S. Federal Emergency Management Agency (FEMA) (2013). *The Robert T. Stafford disaster relief and emergency assistance act*. Washington, DC: FEMA.

U.S. Federal Emergency Management Agency (FEMA). (n.d.). What is mitigation? Retrieved from <http://www.fema.gov/what-mitigation>.

Walsh, B. (2010). With oil spill (and blame) spreading, Obama will visit Gulf, Time, May 1, 2010. Retrieved from <http://content.time.com/time/health/article/0,8599,1986323,00.html>.

Waugh, W. L., & Tierney, K. (Eds.), (2007). *Emergency management: Principles and practice for local government* Washington, DC: International City/County Management Association; ICMA Press.

Chapter 2

Mitigation Rules and Regulations

OBJECTIVES

The study of this chapter will enable you to:

1. Discuss the genesis and salient features of the Stafford Act

2. Discuss the importance of the Disaster Mitigation Act

3. Discuss the requirements and procedures for state, local, and tribal mitigation plans in federal regulations

4. Understand and explain other important rules and regulations that affect hazard mitigation planning activities

5. Discuss examples of rules and regulations from other countries that have had an impact on mitigation planning and programs

Essential Terminology: Disaster legislation, Disaster Mitigation Act of 2000, Disaster Relief Act, Disaster Relief and Emergency Assistance Act of 1988 (Stafford Act), Code of Federal Regulations (CFR), Coastal Barrier Resources Act (CBRA), Coastal Zone Management Act (CZMA), Clean Water Act (CWA), National Environmental Policy Act (NEPA), National Flood Insurance Act, Disaster Countermeasures Basic Act (Japan), Civil Contingencies Act (CCA) (UK), Civil Defence Emergency Management (CDEM) Act (New Zealand), Disaster Management Act of 2005 (India).

Principles and rules are intended to provide a thinking man with a frame of reference.
  General Carl von Clausewitz (1780−1831), Prussian military theorist

DISASTER LEGISLATION 101

In the United States prior to 1950, Congress provided funding for disaster relief and recovery efforts on a case-by-case basis. That meant that each time there was a major disaster in the United States, the legislative branch of government would have to convene, draft, propose, and pass into law a bill that would provide funds for the relief effort. This cumbersome and time-consuming process was put to rest by the *Federal Disaster Relief Program (FDRP)*. The FDRP, established in September 1950, authorized the government to provide disaster response assistance for state and local governments. However, a far greater and more costly task in the wake of a major disaster is long-term recovery, which is needed to reestablish a community. The FDRP did not cover such efforts. Therefore, in 1966, Congress passed the *Disaster Relief Act*, which augmented the FDRP to allow federal assistance in recovery (Baca, 2008).

In the mid-1970s, U.S. governors discussed their concerns about the fractal nature of disaster relief operations spread about over numerous federal agencies. In addition, they expressed a need for a new federal agency that would be responsible for comprehensive emergency management, which would include preparedness, mitigation, response, and recovery. The National Governors Association (NGA) met in August 1978 and produced a report requesting this action, which was sent to President Jimmy Carter. President Carter agreed with the NGA, and the Federal Emergency Management Agency (FEMA) was created under Executive Order 12148 on March 31, 1979. As such, FEMA became responsible for disaster-related "functions from the Departments of Defense (civil defense) and Housing and Urban Development (federal disaster assistance), [the] General Services Administration (federal preparedness), and the Office of Science and Technology Policy (earthquake hazards reduction)." President Carter also transferred to FEMA disaster-related legal authority inherent in the presidency or within other federal agencies. In addition, Executive Orders 12127 and 12148 consolidated authority for manmade and natural disaster preparation, mitigation, response, and recovery within a single federal agency (Baca, 2008).

History of the Stafford Act

Robert Theodore Stafford (1913–2006) was a Republican U.S. senator from Vermont (Figure 2.1). Before becoming a senator in 1971, he served twice as an army officer during World War II and the Korean War. He was elected to serve as attorney general and lieutenant governor for the state of Vermont before being elected governor in 1958. Senator Stafford is well known for sponsoring and proposing legislation in support of educational and environmental issues. Indeed, Stafford loans have helped millions of Americans attend institutes of higher learning. Senator Stafford is also known for sponsoring the Clean Air Act (CAA), which was voted into law in 1963. However, what he is probably best known for is the *Stafford Act* (whose full

- Robert T. Stafford (1913–2006)
- Advocate for educational programs
  and the environment
- Proponent for reform of comprehensive
  legislation to provide better support for local
  and state governments in the wake of disaster

■ **FIGURE 2.1** Senator Robert T. Stafford (R-VT) served six terms in Congress. He is best known for sponsoring the Disaster Relief and Emergency Assistance Act of 1988; U.S. Code, Title 42, Chapter 68, entitled *Disaster Relief* (the Stafford Act). *Image courtesy of the Biographical Directory of the United States Congress.*

name is the Disaster Relief and Emergency Assistance Act of 1988), a key piece of legislation passed in 1988. The Stafford Act, still the major legislation under which FEMA operates, provides a framework for continued disaster relief (Baca, 2008).

When a disaster strikes, response and relief efforts begin locally. Emergency workers will be tasked and local resources depleted. By definition, a disaster will overwhelm a community and its internal resources to the point where assistance will be needed. The municipality may request assistance using mutual aid agreements. Requests for support will be sent to the state emergency management agency (EMA) if mutual aid by itself is insufficient. The state EMA may request assistance from neighboring states as well. If the mayor of the affected community believes that federal assistance will be needed, he or she will make a formal request to the governor, who will assess the situation and determine what action to take. Normally, the governor will review the damage assessment and send a team to survey the damage. The governor then declares a state of emergency and request a Presidential Disaster Declaration under the Stafford Act. The FEMA administrator reviews the damage assessment and request and then makes a recommendation to the secretary of the Department of Homeland Security (DHS). The president will make the final decision. In this politically charged, media-saturated, high-visibility world we live in, most true disasters get a Presidential Disaster Declaration in very short order. In fact, state and federal assets can be seen "leaning forward," especially if the disaster has a predictable quality to it (e.g., hurricane).

The Stafford Act, which was signed into law in 1988, is probably the most important piece of federal legislation to emergency management professionals. Yet, it is also probably the one that is least read and studied by the same group (B. Long, personal communication, 2013). To truly appreciate this seminal document and what it achieved, one would have to look back at how disaster response, relief, and recovery were funded and accomplished at the national level prior to its inception.

The Stafford Act gives the federal government the authority to assist states during a state of emergency. FEMA coordinates these financial, logistical, and technical resources. Funds have already been appropriated by Congress. After the state has activated its emergency response plan and help is requested, FEMA determines whether to issue the declaration. The president may make one of two declarations, a major presidential disaster or an emergency. An emergency may be granted even if the federal government has not been contacted. If the president determines that the incident can cause consequences for the nation and lives need to be saved quickly, he can declare an emergency. Normally, this is short-term (in days) and requires a 10% match by the state. This is also appropriate if the disaster occurs on federal property. A major disaster declaration may be granted only if requested by the state. It is a long-term resource that requires up to a 25% match in funding by the state. Congress has the authority to provide additional funds if needed.

The Stafford Act also provides a temporary waiver of certain Medicare and Medicaid requirements. It provides several types of assistance. The first is reimbursement to states that provide mutual aid. The second is financial and resource support for pandemic influenza. Funds may not be duplicated. Individual assistance is granted in the forms of housing, grants, and low-cost loans. Businesses may be eligible as well. For major disasters only (not emergency declarations), mitigation assistance in the immediate area may be funded. This may be the perfect opportunity to prepare a community for upcoming disasters and decrease the risk that such events will cause devastation. The thought behind this is: If you have to rebuild something, why not rebuild it so that it is better able to withstand the disaster that destroyed it? Costs for temporary and long-term workers, such as those that remove debris and rebuild structures, can be reimbursed. The Stafford Act is instrumental in providing aid to those areas that are unable to respond to disasters independently, helping the community recover.

CRITICAL THINKING

Concerns expressed by policymakers and experts suggest that current Stafford Act declarations are inadequate to respond to, and recover from, highly destructive events. There are arguments for and against amending the act to add a catastrophic declaration amendment.

If such an amendment were approved, catastrophic declarations could be invoked for high-profile, large-scale incidents that threaten the lives of many people, cause tremendous damage, and pose significant challenges to timely recovery efforts. In your opinion, is the current version of the Stafford Act insufficient for large-scale events like Hurricane Katrina and Superstorm Sandy?

DISASTER MITIGATION ACT (2000)

The Disaster Mitigation Act of 2000 (DMA 2000) was signed into law in October 2000. It was used to override some of the mitigation requirements previously established in the Stafford Act. The DMA 2000 allows local governments to obtain funding from the Hazard Mitigation Grant Program (HMGP) when mitigation planning is conducted before a disaster occurs. To obtain funding, jurisdictions must prove that mitigation activities being conducted are based on the planning activities and identified risks.

DMA 2000 changed the environment of mitigation activities by taking the mitigation planning requirements to the local level and working to ensure that all levels of government are included in the planning process. Prior to the DMA, only state jurisdictions were required to have mitigation plans. For jurisdictions to receive grant funding and disaster funding, there must be an approved mitigation plan in place prior to a disaster occurring. These requirements encourage jurisdictions to conduct mitigation activities through funding opportunities incentives.

Some provisions include:

- *Plan requirements:* Any jurisdiction wanting reimbursements for disasters must have a preestablished mitigation plan approved before the disaster occurs. That being said, jurisdictions are allowed to submit multijurisdictional plans when the submitting jurisdiction has participated in the development of the plan.
- *Planning process:* The public must be given the opportunity to provide input into the plan. In addition to the public being allowed to participate, neighboring jurisdictions must be given the opportunity to take part in the planning process.
- *Plan content:* The plan must include documentation of the planning process, a risk assessment, and a mitigation strategy. The final element of plan content is that there must be documentation related to the formal adoption of the plan.
- *Plan review/updates:* Plan reviews are required to be conducted at least every three years. In addition, jurisdictions must be able to prove that they have made progress toward identified mitigation activities.

One study that proves that there is a return on investment associated with hazard mitigation and hazard mitigation grants is a benefit-cost analysis of FEMA Hazard Mitigation Grants (Rose et al., 2007). This research project revealed that the most cost-effective mitigation activity is flood mitigation (Figure 2.2). In addition to flood mitigation being most effective, the study showed that the most grant funding mitigation activity is flood mitigation, followed by wind and tornado mitigation activities.

■ **FIGURE 2.2** At the Douglas County Disaster Recovery Center, FEMA mitigation specialist Loida Pagan provides information to a flood-affected resident. Severe storms and flooding damaged many homes here, and mitigation assistance can help repair the community so that it is not only rebuilt, but more damage resistant. *Image and description courtesy of FEMA. Picture by George Armstrong.*

CRITICAL THINKING

While the emergency management community enjoys a much greater understanding of mitigation possibilities and pitfalls, translating ideas to actions remains one of the greatest challenges. How has DMA 2000 changed the environment for mitigation practice? What are the key provisions of this act? What is the distinction between structural and nonstructural approaches to mitigation, and why is it important to employ both? What evidence could you give to a community planner that expensive mitigation projects are cost effective?

REQUIREMENTS AND PROCEDURES FOR STATE, LOCAL, AND TRIBAL MITIGATION PLANS

State, local, and Indian tribal governments are required to develop a hazard mitigation plan as a condition for receiving certain types of non-emergency disaster assistance, including funding for mitigation projects from the federal government. The Robert T. Stafford Disaster Relief and Emergency Assistance Act (Public Law 93-288), as amended by DMA 2000, provides the legal basis for developing these plans, which were described earlier in this chapter. The requirements and procedures for state, local, and tribal mitigation plans are explained in detail in the Code of Federal Regulations (CFR) at Title 44, Chapter 1, Part 201[1].

Requirements and Procedures for State Mitigation Plans

In terms of standard state mitigation plans, the requirements and procedures stated in the CFR are as follows:

- States are required to have an approved standard state mitigation plan following the criteria established in Section 201.4 of the CFR. Section 203 of the Stafford Act authorizes mitigation planning grants provided through the Predisaster Mitigation (PDM) program. According to the CFR, "[t]he mitigation plan is the demonstration of the State's commitment to reduce risks from natural hazards and serves as a guide for State decision makers as they commit resources to reducing the effects of natural hazards."
- The mitigation planning process is essential to developing and maintaining a good state mitigation plan and should include coordination with other state agencies, appropriate federal agencies, interested groups, and be integrated to the extent possible with other ongoing state planning efforts, as well as other FEMA mitigation programs and initiatives.
- Some provisions in Section 201.4 regarding the content of a state mitigation plan include:
  - ❑ The plan should include a description of the planning process; e.g., how it was prepared, the agencies involved in the process, and other details.
  - ❑ In a "Risk Assessments" section, it must provide a statewide overview of natural hazards and risks that should allow the state to compare potential losses and to prioritize mitigation measures and jurisdictions for receiving technical and financial assistance.
  - ❑ The plan should provide a blueprint of mitigation strategy for the state for reducing the losses identified in the risk assessment. This section must include a description of state goals and objectives to mitigate and reduce potential losses; a discussion of the state's predisaster and postdisaster hazard management policies, programs, and capabilities to mitigate the hazards in the area; a discussion of state funding capabilities for hazard mitigation projects; and a general description and analysis of the effectiveness of local mitigation policies, programs, and capabilities. Also, the plan must

---

[1] U.S. Code, Title 44, Chapter 1, Part 201 is entitled "Mitigation Planning."

feature an identification, evaluation, and prioritization of cost-effective, environmentally sound, and technically feasible mitigation actions and activities and an explanation of how each activity contributes to the overall mitigation strategy. The plan should also identify current and potential sources of federal, state, local, or private funding to implement mitigation activities.

❑ The state mitigation plan should also include a section on the coordination of local mitigation planning that incorporates a description of the state process to provide assistance to the development of local mitigation plans, a time frame by which the local plans will be reviewed, coordinated, and linked to the state mitigation plan, and criteria for prioritizing local jurisdictions to receive assistance from the state.

❑ The plan should include a maintenance process describing the method and schedule for monitoring, evaluating, and updating the plan. Also, the plan must be formally adopted by the state prior to submittal for final review and approval.

❑ The plan must be reviewed and revised to reflect changes in development, progress in statewide mitigation efforts, and changes in priorities and resubmitted for approval to the appropriate regional administrator every five years.

Enhanced State Mitigation Plans
States can also develop enhanced mitigation plans. A state that has an approved enhanced mitigation plan is eligible to receive increased mitigation funds after a Presidential Disaster Declaration. According to CFR, the funding level is 20% of the total estimated eligible Stafford Act disaster assistance under HMGP. In order to be eligible for this increased HMGP funding, the plan must be approved by FEMA five years or earlier than the disaster declaration. Along with all elements of the standard state mitigation plan, an enhanced state mitigation plan must demonstrate that the state has developed a comprehensive mitigation program, effectively uses available mitigation funding, and is capable of managing the increased funding. As of June 30, 2014, only 10 states have FEMA-approved enhanced state mitigation plans: California, Florida, Georgia, Iowa, Missouri, Nevada, North Carolina, Ohio, Washington, and Wisconsin (FEMA, n.d.a).

Requirements and Procedures for Local Mitigation Plans

Local mitigation plans usually serve as the basis for a state to provide technical assistance and prioritize project funding. According to CFR

Title 44, Chapter 1, §201.6, "[t]he local mitigation plan is the representation of the jurisdiction's commitment to reduce risks from natural hazards, serving as a guide for decision makers as they commit resources to reducing the effects of natural hazards."

In terms of local mitigation plans, the requirements and procedures stated in the CFR are as follows:

1. A local government must have a mitigation plan approved in order to receive HMGP project grants. A local government must have an approved mitigation plan to apply for any mitigation project grants.
2. To be eligible for Flood Mitigation Assistance (FMA) project grants, plans only need to address the requirements related to flood hazards and must be clearly identified as being flood mitigation plans. These plans will not meet the eligibility criteria for other mitigation grant programs unless flooding is the only natural hazard that the jurisdiction faces.
3. For small and impoverished communities, regional administrators may grant an exception to the plan requirement. In these cases, a plan will be completed within 12 months of the award of the project grant.
4. Multijurisdictional plans may be accepted so long as each jurisdiction has participated in the process. Statewide plans will not be accepted as multijurisdictional plans.

The public should be involved in the planning process for the development of an effective plan. The planning process shall include all of the following:

1. An opportunity for the public to comment on the plan during the drafting stage and prior to plan approval
2. An opportunity for neighboring communities, local and regional agencies involved in hazard mitigation activities, as well as businesses, academia, and other private and nonprofit interests to be involved in the planning process
3. Review and incorporation of existing plans, studies, reports, and technical information

The plan content is similar to the state mitigation plan. Some provisions in Section 201.6 regarding the content of a local mitigation plan include:

- Documentation of the planning process (e.g., how it was prepared, the agencies involved in the process, and how the public was involved)
- In the "Risk Assessments" section, sufficient information should be provided to enable the jurisdiction to identify and prioritize

appropriate mitigation actions to reduce losses from identified hazards. This section should include:

(a) A description of the type, location, and extent of all natural hazards that can affect the jurisdiction.

(b) A description of the jurisdiction's vulnerability to the hazards, including an overall summary of each hazard and its impact on the community. The plan should describe vulnerability in terms of:
- The types and numbers of existing and future buildings, infrastructure, and critical facilities located in the identified hazard areas;
- An estimate of the potential dollar losses to vulnerable structures
- A general description of land uses and development trends within the community so that mitigation options can be considered in future land use decisions.

(c) For multijurisdictional plans, the risk assessment section must assess each jurisdiction's risks facing the entire planning area.

The mitigation strategy must provide the jurisdiction's blueprint for reducing the potential losses identified in the risk assessment. This section shall include:

- A description of mitigation goals and objectives to reduce potential losses from the identified hazards.
- A section that identifies and analyzes a comprehensive range of specific mitigation actions and projects being considered to reduce the effects of each hazard, with particular emphasis on new and existing buildings and infrastructure.
- A mitigation action plan describing how the actions will be prioritized, implemented, and administered by the local jurisdiction.

The "Plan Maintenance Process" section should include:

- The method and schedule of monitoring, evaluating, and updating the mitigation plan within a five-year cycle
- A process by which local governments incorporate the requirements of the mitigation plan into other planning mechanisms such as comprehensive or capital improvement plans, when appropriate
- Discussion on how the community will continue public participation in the plan maintenance process

The plan review should meet the following criteria:

- Plans must be submitted to the state hazard mitigation officer (SHMO) for initial review and coordination. The state will then send the plan to the appropriate FEMA regional office for formal review and approval. Where the state point of contact for the FMA program is different from the SHMO, the SHMO will be responsible for coordinating the local plan reviews between the FMA point of contact and FEMA.

- The regional review will be completed within 45 days after receipt from the state.
- A local jurisdiction must review and revise its plan to reflect changes in development, progress in local mitigation efforts, and changes in priorities, and resubmit it for approval within five years in order to continue to be eligible for mitigation project grant funding. Status of local government mitigation planning is graphically represented in Figure 2.3.

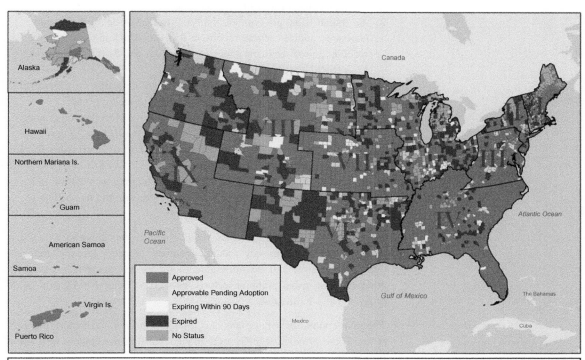

■ **FIGURE 2.3** Local mitigation plan status in the United States by state (as of June 30, 2014). *Image courtesy of FEMA.*

Requirements and Procedures for Tribal Mitigation Plans

Similar to state and local mitigation plans, the requirements and procedures of the Indian tribal mitigation plan are described in CFR, Title 44, Chapter 1, §201.7. According to the CFR, "[t]he Indian Tribal Mitigation Plan is the representation of the Indian tribal government's commitment to reduce risks from natural hazards, serving as a guide for decision makers as they commit resources to reducing the effects of natural hazards."

Here are the requirements and procedures of the tribal mitigation plans established in Section 201.7:

1. Indian tribal governments applying to FEMA as a grantee must have an approved tribal mitigation plan meeting the requirements of Section 201.7 as a condition of receiving nonemergency Stafford Act assistance and FEMA mitigation grants.
2. An Indian tribal government applying to FEMA as a grantee may choose to address severe repetitive loss properties in their plan to receive the reduced cost share for the FMA and Severe Repetitive Loss (SRL) programs.
3. Indian tribal governments applying through the state as a subgrantee must have an approved tribal mitigation plan meeting the requirements of this section in order to receive HMGP project grants and may require a tribal mitigation plan for the RFCP. Also, a tribe must have an approved tribal mitigation plan in order to apply for all FEMA mitigation grant programs.
4. Multijurisdictional plans may be accepted as long as each the Indian tribal government has participated in the process and has officially adopted the plan.

The mitigation planning process should include coordination with other tribal agencies, appropriate federal agencies, adjacent jurisdictions, and interested groups, and be integrated to the fullest possible extent with other ongoing tribal planning efforts, as well as other FEMA mitigation programs and initiatives.

The plan content of tribal plans is similar to the state and local mitigation plans. Some provisions in Section 201.7 regarding the content of a tribal mitigation plan include:

- Documentation of the planning process; e.g., how it was prepared, the agencies involved in the process, and how the public was involved.
- In the "Risk Assessments" section, sufficient information should be provided to enable the Indian tribal government to identify and

prioritize appropriate mitigation actions to reduce losses from identified hazards. The components of this section are similar to the local mitigation plan.

■ The sections concerning mitigation strategy, plan maintenance, and review and updates in tribal plans are the same as in local mitigation plans. According to the CFR, a plan must be formally adopted by the governing body of the Indian tribal government prior to submittal to FEMA for final review and approval. Plans must be submitted to the appropriate FEMA regional office for formal review and approval. Indian tribal governments who would like the option of being a subgrantee under the state must also submit their plan to the SHMO for review and coordination.

OTHER IMPORTANT RULES AND REGULATIONS AFFECTING HAZARD MITIGATION

The following rules and regulations are not directly related to emergency management, but they can result in reducing hazard vulnerability as a by-product of their main objectives. The programs and activities derived from these acts affect hazard mitigation indirectly, and we can refer to these as *indirect mitigation programs.*

Coastal Barrier Resources Act (CBRA)

Federal programs such as the National Flood Insurance Program (NFIP) provide financial incentives that encourage building in areas that are prone to repeated natural hazards, such as flooding, hurricanes, and coastal erosion. Previously, coastal areas, especially barrier islands, were under increased risk due to such federal activities (Figure 2.4). The *Coastal Barrier Resources Act (CBRA)* of 1982, also called Public Law 97–348, is an innovative federal law that made federal expenditure and financial assistance ineligible for relatively undeveloped coastal barriers along the Atlantic and Gulf coasts. The U.S. Congress passed CBRA in 1982 and established the John H. Chafee Coastal Barrier Resources System (CBRS), which consists of 584 units comprised of nearly 1.3 million acres of land and associated aquatic habitats. The act made these areas ineligible for most new federal expenditures and financial assistance (U.S. Fish and Wildlife Service, n.d.a).

In 1990, the Coastal Barrier Improvement Act (CBIA) reauthorized the CBRA and expanded the CBRS to include undeveloped coastal barriers along the Florida Keys and Great Lakes, in Puerto Rico, and in the U.S. Virgin Islands. An additional 271 units of coastal barriers, called

■ **FIGURE 2.4** An unnamed Louisiana coastal barrier island. *Image courtesy of NOAA.*

otherwise protected areas (OPAs) and comprising 1.9 million acres of land and associated aquatic habitats, were added as a new category for conservation purposes to the CBRS (U.S. Fish and Wildlife Service, n.d.a).

Although CBRA prevents federal funds being spent on these islands in the CBRS system, it does not restrict activities of the private sector or the local or state governments to facilitate coastal development (Schwab et al., 2007). As a result, large infrastructure projects such as bridges and causeways are built by many states and local communities to connect these barrier islands to mainland, which encourages private developers to build multistory condominiums, beach houses, and other infrastructure on these islands. However, studies have shown that areas that are not eligible for federal funding and value-added programs are developed much more slowly than other areas, if at all (Schwab et al., 2007; Salveson & Godschalk, n.d.).

Coastal Zone Management Act (CZMA)

The *Coastal Zone Management Act (CZMA)* was passed in 1972 by Congress to encourage coastal states to develop and implement coastal zone management plans (U.S. Fish and Wildlife Service, n.d.b). Congress recognized the importance of coastal zones to the entire nation and wanted to meet the challenges of continued growth in coastal zones. Therefore, the act establishes a national policy to "preserve, protect, develop, and where possible, to restore or enhance the resources of the nation's coastal zone." The CZMA is administered by the Office of Ocean and Coastal Resource Management (OCRM) at the National Oceanic and Atmospheric Administration (NOAA) and applicable to states along the Atlantic and Pacific oceans, the Gulf Coast, and the Great Lakes (NOAA, n.d.a).

Although participation is voluntary, the CZMA has been a great success. All 35 coastal and Great Lakes states and territories (with the exception of Alaska) participate in the national Coastal Zone Management Program (CZMP) established under this act. The CZMA gives states a great deal of authority to get involved in hazard mitigation planning through the CZMP. Some of the key mitigation measures of this program include:

- Shoreline management and retreat; e.g., setback regulations, shoreline development, and stabilization
- Posthazard reconstruction management; e.g., regulating repair and reconstruction after a coastal hazard
- Managing development in hazardous areas
- Protecting wetlands and natural resources
- Addressing sea level rise
- Encouraging or requiring local governments to incorporate hazard mitigation in their comprehensive plans
- Developing special area management plans for coastal areas prone to hazards (Schwab et al., 2007)

The CZMA also established the National Estuarine Research Reserve System (NERRS), a network of 28 protected areas established by partnerships between the NOAA and coastal states (Figure 2.5). The reserves represent different biogeographic regions that are protected for long-term research, water-quality monitoring, education, and coastal stewardship (NOAA, n.d.b). Each reserve is managed by a state agency or university with input from local stakeholders. NOAA provides funding, guidance, and technical assistance to manage these reserves.

Clean Water Act (CWA)

The *Clean Water Act (CWA)*, passed in 1972 as the Federal Water Pollution Control Act, is the primary federal law in the U.S. governing water pollution, and it also helps reduces the impacts of hazards in communities. The objective of the CWA is to restore and maintain the chemical, physical, and biological integrity of the waters of the United States by reducing and removing pollutants discharged into them (EPA, n.d.). The CWA pollution control programs include both point sources (i.e., pollution discharged from a specific source, such as a pipe) and nonpoint sources (e.g., urban or agricultural runoff).

■ FIGURE 2.5 Location of the 28 protected reserves in the United States. *Image courtesy of NOAA.*

Section 404

Section 404 of the CWA contains provisions to prohibit the discharge of dredged or fill materials into waters unless a permit issued by the U.S. Army Corps of Engineers (USACE). In addition to the permit, Section 404 requires that the impacts from dredge and fill activities should be mitigated through restoration or through the creation of new wetlands (Schwab et al., 2007). Such provisions of protecting wetlands are important, especially for flood mitigation as wetlands (Figure 2.6) can absorb floodwaters and also act as a storage that can supply water during dry periods.

Although Section 404 of the CWA is very useful for protecting wetlands and flood mitigation, there are some limitations of this program. According to Schwab et al. (2007), these limitations include:

- The 404 permit is required only for discharging dredged and fill materials. There is no requirement or restriction for other ways of damaging or destroying the wetlands, and many wetlands are disappearing without any discharge taking place.

■ **FIGURE 2.6** A Great Blue Heron catches a fish in a Wetlands estuary. *Image courtesy of NOAA.*

- The definition of wetland is not clearly defined in Section 404. For instance, USACE does not have the authority to issue permits for isolated wetlands, as they are not adjacent to a navigable waterway.
- There have been criticisms regarding the issuance of permits that they are not rigorously enforced and almost readily granted without considering the wetland mitigation and restoration requirements.

National Environmental Policy Act (NEPA)

The *National Environmental Policy Act (NEPA)* was passed in 1969 in response to public concerns about the degradation of the quality of the human environment (i.e., physical, biological, social, and cultural) in the United States and to consider the environmental impacts of major federal projects. NEPA establishes a national policy for the protection and maintenance of the environment by providing a process which all federal agencies must follow. The act has also established the President's Council on Environmental Quality (CEQ), which creates regulations for implementing NEPA. The CEQ requires each federal agency, including FEMA, to write their own NEPA compliance regulations to fit their particular programs. FEMA's regulations at 44 CFR Part 10, DHS's Management Directive 5100.1, and the Council on Environmental Quality regulations at 40 CFR Part 1500–1508 implement the NEPA requirements for FEMA (FEMA, n.d.b).

There are three levels of analysis that a federal agency may undertake to comply with the law: categorical exclusion (CE), environmental assessment (EA) and Finding of No Significant Impact (FONSI), and environmental impact statement (EIS). They are described in the next sections.

Categorical Exclusion (CE)

According to 40 CFR, "categorical exclusion" means "a category of actions which do not individually or cumulatively have a significant effect on the human environment and which have been found to have no such effect in procedures adopted by a federal agency in implementation of these regulations" (Sec. 1507.3), and for which, therefore, "neither an environmental assessment nor an environmental impact statement is required..." (Sec. 1508.4).

Environmental Assessment (EA) and Finding of No Significant Impact (FONSI)

Environmental assessments (EAs) are used to determine if significant environmental impacts would occur as a result of a proposed action or a project funded by a federal agency. EAs are concise public documents that include evidence and analysis regarding the significance of environmental impacts of the proposed action, a listing of alternatives, and a listing of agencies and persons consulted. An EA concludes with one of two decision documents—either a Finding of No Significant Impact (FONSI) or Notice of Intent to Prepare an Environmental Impact Statement (EIS). A FONSI is part of the EA and presents the reasons why an action will not have a significant effect on the human environment.

Environmental Impact Statement (EIS)

An environmental impact statement (EIS) is a critical examination of any potential impacts from the proposed project and proposed alternatives. The EIS process starts with a Notice of Intent to Prepare an EIS and concludes with a Record of Decision (ROD), a document that explains the reasons for selecting a certain action. The EIS is available to the public for information and comment. An EIS must include:

- A description of the proposed action, including the need for it and its benefits
- A description of the environmental setting and areas to be affected
- An analysis of all environmental impacts related to the action
- An analysis of reasonable alternatives to the action
- Identification of ways to reduce or avoid adverse environmental impacts

■ **FIGURE 2.7** Flooding in the Lower Ninth Ward of New Orleans after Hurricane Betsy. *Image courtesy of NOAA.*

National Flood Insurance Act

Frequent flooding along the Mississippi River and widespread flood damages from Hurricane Betsy in 1965 (Figure 2.7) prompted Congress to pass the *National Flood Insurance Act* in 1968. Prior to this act, private insurance companies were reluctant to cover flood damages. The act created the Federal Insurance Administration (which at that time was in the Department of Housing and Urban Development) and made flood insurance available for the first time through the NFIP (FEMA n.d.c). Along with the National Flood Insurance Act of 1968, the NFIP program is also administered by the Flood Disaster Protection Act of 1973 (FDPA). The FDPA requires the purchase of flood insurance mandatory for all properties located in the Special Flood Hazard Areas. Details of the NFIP program are discussed in Chapter 3.

The *National Flood Insurance Reform Act of 1994* (Reform Act) comprehensively revised the federal flood insurance statutes. "The purpose of the Reform Act is to increase compliance with flood insurance requirements and participation in the NFIP in order to provide additional income to the National Flood Insurance Fund and to decrease the financial burden of flooding on the federal government, taxpayers, and flood victims."[2] The Reform Act also applied flood insurance requirements directly to the loans purchased by agencies that provide government insurance or guarantees, such as the Small Business Administration, Federal Housing Administration (FHA), and the Veterans Administration (FDIC, n.d.).

On July 6, 2012, President Barack Obama signed into law the ***Biggert-Waters Flood Insurance Reform Act of 2012*** (BW-12), which reauthorized the NFIP and made a number of reforms aimed at making the program more financially and structurally sound. One of the objectives of this legislation was to increase the rates to reflect true flood risk, as well as make the program more financially stable. However, on March 21, 2014, President Obama signed the Homeowner Flood Insurance Affordability Act of 2014 into law, which repealed and modified certain BW-12 provisions and lowered the rate increases on some policies, prevented some future rate increases, and implemented a surcharge on all policyholders. It also repealed certain rate increases that have already gone into effect and provided refunds to those policyholders (National Association of Insurance Commissioners, n.d.).

RULES AND REGULATIONS IN OTHER COUNTRIES
Japan

In Japan, the Disaster Countermeasures Basic Act of 1961 (Act No. 223) provides the institutional framework for disaster prevention and management. The act was passed in 1961 in response to repeated typhoons and earthquakes that occurred during the 1940s and 1950s (World Bank, n.d.). The act established the Central Disaster Management Council (CDMC) as the national coordinating body for disaster management that formulates the overall policy for disaster risk management. It also establishes guidelines for the organization, functioning, powers, and responsibilities of central and local disaster management councils. The CDMC is chaired by the prime minister, and its members come from line ministries; semipublic organizations such as NHK, the national public broadcasting organization; the Nippon Telegraph and Telephone Corporation, commonly known as NTT; the Japanese Red Cross; the Bank of Japan; and representatives from academia (Figure 2.8). The act was revised following the occurrence of the Hanshin Awaji Earthquake in 1995, resulting a new version that passed in June 1997.

The CDMC prepares the Basic Disaster Management Plan in accordance with the Disaster Countermeasures Basic Act, which is the master plan and

---

[2]H.R. Conf. Rep. No. 652, 103d Cong. 2d Sess. 195 (1994) (Conference Report).

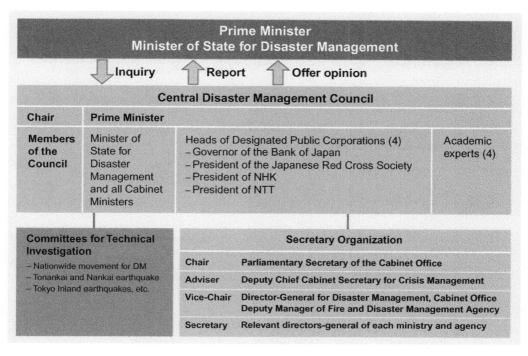

■ FIGURE 2.8 Structure of the CDMC. *Image courtesy of the World Bank.*

the basis for disaster risk management activities in Japan. The plan clarifies the duties of the central government, public corporations, and local governments in implementing measures. The plan also describes the sequence of disaster countermeasures such as preparation, emergency response, recovery, and reconstruction for various types of disasters (World Bank, n.d.).

The municipal government plays a fundamental role in disaster management according to the Disaster Countermeasure Basic Act and is responsible for establishing a local disaster management plan, emergency operations such as warning systems, issuing evacuation recommendations and orders, and flood fighting and relief activities (Figure 2.9). In cases where a municipality is so widely and heavily devastated that it cannot carry out many of its primary roles, the prefectural government shall issue evacuation recommendations and orders instead of the municipality.

United Kingdom

Similar to the United States, the evolution of emergency management in the United Kingdom (UK) took its first steps with the passage of the

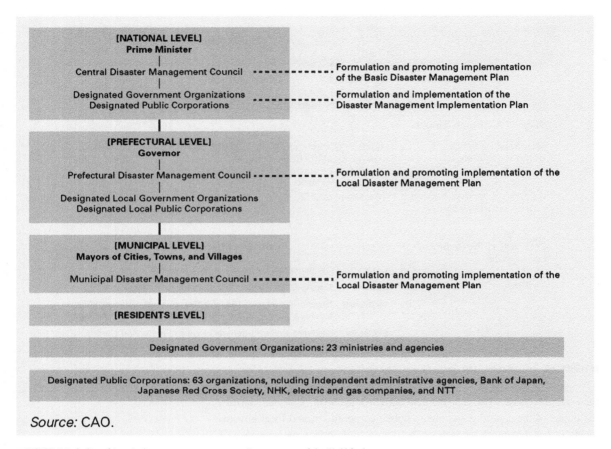

Source: CAO.

■ **FIGURE 2.9** Outline of Japan's disaster management system. *Image courtesy of the World Bank.*

Civil Defense Act of 1948 during the Cold War due to the growing risk of nuclear attack (Kapucu, n.d.). The central government did not put any mandatory requirements for local government agencies and organizations in requesting regional and national resources to manage emergencies. In 1986, the Civil Defense in Peacetime Act was passed, which recognized a central and local government approach to disaster relief. Following numerous reviews of the emergency management system, the *Civil Contingencies Secretariat (CCS)* was started in July 2001 under the Ministry of the Interior. The CCS established a central focus and framework for responding and preparing for emergencies at the national, regional, and local level (O'Brien & Read, 2005). The purpose of CCS is to improve the resilience of central government and the UK to handle emergencies and disasters. Later, the *Civil Contingencies Act (CCA)*

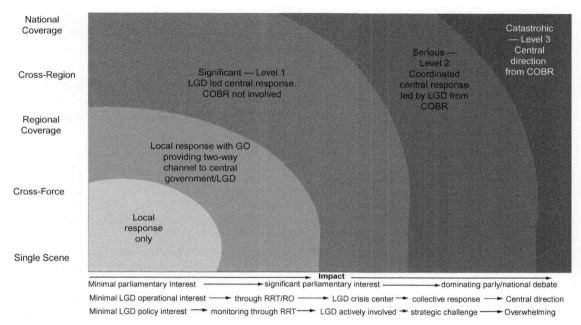

■ **FIGURE 2.10** Central government engagement model in the UK. *LGD*, Lead Government Department; *GO*, Government Office; *RRT*, Regional Resilience Team; *RO*, Regional Office; *COBR*, Cabinet Office Briefing Room. *Image courtesy of the Government of UK.*

of 2004 introduced a single framework for civil protection in UK and brought new changes, such as replacing and updating former Civil Defense and Emergency Power legislation (Kapucu, n.d.).

Although central government plays a significant role, the structure of emergency management in UK is decentralized. Most emergencies or incidents, such as road accidents, small impact floods, and other events, are mainly handled by local agencies and first responders. Central government can engage in emergencies only based on three different levels of significance; i.e., Level 1 as significant emergency, Level 2 as serious emergency and Level 3 as catastrophic emergency (Cabinet Office, 2010).

Figure 2.10 depicts the process of involvement of central government agencies based on the level of significance of disasters. It depicts the Cabinet Office Briefing Room (COBR, or COBRA), is a dedicated crisis management facility of the UK government, which is activated in the incidents or events of national significance. A Level 1 emergency, such as a riot or a severe natural disaster, does not necessarily require activation of the COBR rather the support of central government is provided through Lead Government Departments (LGDs). Any disaster with Level 2 impact, such as a major terrorist attack or outbreak of disease, requires support and coordination of government and other departments and is coordinated from COBR by the LGD. Finally, a Level 3 catastrophic emergency, such as a nuclear attack or a terrorist attack with the scale and size of 9/11, requires immediate involvement of central government and is led by COBR/Civil Contingencies Committee (CCC). The Cabinet Office is responsible for overall disaster management and LGD.

Australia

Although Australia was not directly threatened from World War II, it established a nationwide air-raid protection program in 1938, later known as *civil defense* during the Cold War (Peters & McEntire, n.d.). These programs were run by the states, and they developed their own volunteer civil defense or air-raid precaution organizations. By constitution, states were responsible for the protection and preservation of civilian life and property; and there was no national policy in place. The air-raid protection programs were disbanded by 1954, but as trained and organized community "public safety assets," the volunteer civil defense units were increasingly called on to respond to natural disasters by states.

However, the Black Tuesday fires of Tasmania in February 1967 were the seminal point for the development of structured national emergency management sector in Australia. The disaster initiated a call for the establishment of a national disaster fund and a national disaster organization in the federal parliament by the newly appointed deputy leader of the Federal Labor Party, Lance Bernard (Peters & McEntire n.d.). In February 1974, the Natural Disasters Organization (NDO) was established within the Department of Defence. The NDO served Australia for a number of decades after its creation. In January 1993, the NDO was replaced by an agency named Emergency Management Australia (EMA). EMA is the agency currently responsible for planning and coordinating the commonwealth's physical assistance to the states and territories under the Commonwealth Government Disaster Response Plan (COMDISPLAN).

According to the Commonwealth of Australia (2009):

> *The purpose of the Australian Emergency Management Arrangement... is to provide the Australia public with a high level overview of how Australia addresses the risks and impacts of hazards through a collaborative approach to the prevention of, preparedness for, response to and recovery from emergency.*

EMA is guided by four policy pillars (EMA, 1998):

- All hazards approach
- Comprehensive approach (including all disaster phases)
- All agencies (or integrated) approach
- Prepared community approach

Ironically, Australia does not have any national law to direct and legally mandate the activities of the EMA (Peters & McEntire, n.d.). Instead, EMA is guided by a realization at all levels of government that the impact of some emergencies could be particularly severe or widespread and exceed the capability of a single state or territory (Commonwealth of Australia, 2009). During the mid-eighties, the Australian Interservice Incident Management System (AIIMS) was developed which is similar to the National Incident Management System (NIMS) in the United States (Australasian Fire Authority Council, 2004). The objective of AIIMS is to organize resources from diverse agencies and jurisdictions to respond successfully to large-scale national or regional emergency or disaster (Perry, 2003; Annelli, 2006).

Since state and territory governments have responsibility by constitution for emergency management within their jurisdiction, they have the laws, funding mechanisms and organizational arrangements in place to deal with disasters (Commonwealth of Australia, 2009). For instance, the Queensland government passed the Disaster Management Act 2003 and its main objectives are (i) to help communities mitigate the potential adverse effects of an event, prepare for managing the effects of an event, and effectively respond to, and recover from, a disaster or an emergency situation; (ii) to provide for effective disaster management for the state; (iii) to establish a framework for the management of the State Emergency Service and emergency service units to ensure the effective performance of their functions (Queensland Parliamentary Counsel, 2014). In Australia, when a state or territory declares a disaster, it must mobilize its resources to respond and manage the event alone unlike in the United States. However, if requested, the Australian government via EMA will provide and coordinate physical assistance to the state or territory in event of a major natural, technological or civil defense emergency (Peters & McEntire, n.d.).

New Zealand

In New Zealand, the Ministry of Civil Defence and Emergency Management (MCDEM) is the central government agency responsible for emergency management. It was established in July 1999 within the Department of Internal Affairs. In 2002, the *Civil Defence Emergency Management (CDEM)* Act was passed (replacing the Civil Defence Act

The *Civil Defence Emergency Management Act 2002* (CDEM) is the key law of the New Zealand CDEM framework. However, other legislation, regulations, and policies that contribute to hazard risk reduction and emergency management in New Zealand include "the Biosecurity Act of 1993 (legal basis for excluding, eradicating and managing pests and unwanted organisms); Building Act of 2004 (controls new construction and alteration, demolition and maintenance of existing buildings) and the building code; the Epidemic Preparedness Act of 2006 (providing statutory powers around the prevention and response to outbreak of epidemics); the Health Act of 1956 (covering all aspects of health including emergency powers); Local Government Act of 2002 (provides for democratic and effective local government that recognizes the diversity of New Zealand communities); Policing Act of 2008 (states the functions and provides for the governance and administration of the New Zealand Police); and the Resource Management Act of 1991 (promoting the sustainable management of natural and physical resources)" (Webb and McEntire, n.d.).

of 1983), which provided more significant statutory powers and duties to the MCDEM. Through the CDEM Act, the central government has established a comprehensive, risk-based approach to the management of all hazards, with a primary goal being to support communities to be resilient and self-reliant. The act establishes structures at the local, regional, and national level to support the management of hazardous disasters at the local level (Department of Internal Affairs, 2005).

The CDEM Act of 2002 requires the establishment of CDEM groups, which are a consortium of local authorities working in partnership with emergency services, lifeline utilities, local businesses, community groups and others to deliver CDEM at the local level. Each group is required to prepare a CDEM Group Plan consistent with the National CDEM Strategy. The CDEM Act of 2002 and the National CDEM Strategy including other national strategies and legislation such as the Resource Management Act (RMA), the National CDEM Plan, the Guide to the National CDEM Plan, and CDEM Group plans including government agency (e.g., Ministry of Agriculture and Forestry (MAF)) and non-govt agency (e.g., Society for the Prevention of Cruelty to Animals (SPCA)) operational plans, all form part of the New Zealand CDEM framework, as illustrated in Figure 2.11 (Webb and McEntire, n.d.). The main strength of the New Zealand CDEM framework is that although this is a national framework, most implementation is

■ **FIGURE 2.11** The New Zealand CDEM framework. *Image courtesy of the New Zealand government.*

developed to the local government. The activities of the CDEM are focused on the '4Rs' approach—reduction, readiness, response, and recovery—which is similar to the four phases of emergency management.

India

On December 26, 2005, the first anniversary of the devastating Indian Ocean tsunami of 2004, the parliament of India passed the ***Disaster Management Act 2005***. The act provides a legal and institutional framework for "the effective management of disasters and for matters connected therewith or incidental thereto." It provides the legal framework to establish the National Disaster Management Authority (NDMA), State Disaster Management Authority (SDMA) and District Disaster Management Authorities (DDMAs) at the National, state and District levels. The act also establishes the National Institute of Disaster Management (NIDM) to undertake training and capacity building, and to provide assistance to state governments and state training institutions. In addition, the act provides guidelines for the creation of the National Disaster Response Fund, National Mitigation Fund, and establishment of funds by State Government and Ministries and Departments for emergency procurement (India Disaster Knowledge Network, n.d.).

In 2009, the government approved the National Policy on Disaster Management, which aimed to minimize the losses to lives, livelihoods, and property caused by natural or manmade disasters developing a holistic, proactive, integrated, multidisaster-oriented and technology-driven strategy. The themes associated with the policy include community-based disaster management, capacity development in all spheres, consolidation of past initiatives and best practices, and cooperation with agencies at national and international levels with multisectoral synergy.

■ CONCLUSION

The Stafford Act is the principal authority governing federal emergency and disaster response in the United States. The act authorizes the president to issue three categories of declaration: major disasters, emergencies, and fire assistance declarations in response to incidents that overwhelm the resources of state and local governments. Once a declaration is issued, a wide range of federal disaster assistance becomes available to eligible individuals and households, public entities, and certain nonprofit organizations.

Disaster assistance authorized by the Stafford Act is appropriated by Congress and provided through the Disaster Relief Fund. Emergency declarations supplement and promote coordination of local and state efforts, such as evacuations and protection of public assets. They may also be declared prior to the impact of an incident to protect property, public health, and safety and to reduce or avert the threat of a major disaster or catastrophe. Major disaster declarations are issued after an incident and constitute broader authority to help states and localities, as well as families and individuals, recover from the damage caused by the event. Fire assistance declarations provide grants to state and localities to manage fires that threaten to cause major disasters.

The Disaster Mitigation Act (DMA) of 2000, which amended the Stafford Act, made federal requirements for local governments to develop hazard mitigation plans. Prior to this act, there was not a defined structure for mitigation development and planning on the local level, nor was there any set of standards for anyone to follow. This act assisted the large and small communities to not only become aware of their challenges, but forced them to see what they were not expecting and plan for it. Another key point of the DMA is that it encourages cooperation between the state and local governments and also sometimes state to state.

State, local, and Indian tribal governments are required to develop a hazard mitigation plan as a condition for receiving certain types of non-emergency disaster assistance, including funding for mitigation projects from the federal government. The requirements and procedures for state, local, and tribal mitigation plans are described in this chapter in detail, as explained in the CFR at Title 44, Chapter 1, Part 201.

Also, there are many rules and regulations that do not focus on hazard mitigation but can result in reducing hazard vulnerability as a by-product of their main objectives. These include the CBRA, CZMA, CWA, NEPA, National Flood Insurance Act, etc. The programs and activities derived from these acts can be referred to as *indirect mitigation programs.*

In Japan, the Disaster Countermeasures Basic Act of 1961 (revised in 1997) provides the institutional framework for disaster prevention and management. The act has established the CDMC as the national coordinating body for disaster management that formulates the overall policy for disaster risk management. The CDMC prepares the Basic Disaster Management Plan in accordance with the Disaster Countermeasures Basic Act, which is the master plan and the basis for disaster risk management activities in Japan.

In the United Kingdom, the Civil Contingencies Secretariat is the lead emergency management organization, which functions under the Minister of the Interior and provides the framework for responding and preparing for emergencies at the national, regional, and local levels. The CCA is the primary regulation that establishes a single framework for civil protection in the UK. Although the central government plays a significant role, the structure of emergency management in the UK is decentralized. The central government can engage in emergencies only based on different levels of significance.

Australia does not have any national law to direct and legally mandate the activities of the EMA. Instead, it is guided by a realization at all levels of government that the impact of some emergencies could be particularly severe or widespread and exceed the capability of a single state or territory. Since state and territory governments have a responsibility by constitution for emergency management within their jurisdiction, they have the laws, funding mechanisms, and organizational arrangements in place to deal with disasters such as Disaster Management Act 2003 by Queensland.

The Civil Defence Emergency Management Act of 2002 is the key law of the New Zealand CDEM framework. The MCDEM under the Department of Internal Affairs is the central government agency responsible for emergency management. Other legislation, regulations, and policies that contribute to hazard risk reduction and emergency management in New Zealand include the Biosecurity Act of 1993, Building Act of 2004, Epidemic Preparedness Act of 2006, Health Act of 1956, Local Government Act of 2002, Policing Act of 2008, and the Resource Management Act of 1991.

In India, the Disaster Management Act of 2005 provides a legal and institutional framework for the effective management of disasters and establishes the National Disaster Management Authority, State Disaster Management Authority, and District Disaster Management Authorities at the national, state, and district levels.

DISCUSSION QUESTIONS

1. Discuss the timeline and creation of important legislation that affects how your national authority or government agency provides disaster relief and recovery support for areas devastated by a disaster.
2. Determine how often the Stafford Act has been utilized in your state over the past five years, and for which events.
3. What are the most salient features of the Stafford Act?
4. In your opinion, how might the Stafford Act be amended to better serve the needs of the United States? Are there recent examples of where this act has failed?
5. Discuss the requirements and procedures for state, local, and tribal mitigation plans in the CFR?
6. Describe the CBRA and CBRS.

7. Describe the significance of the CZMA. What is NERRS?
8. Discuss briefly about the CWA and how it helps in flood mitigation.
9. Discuss the three levels of analysis that a federal agency may undertake to comply with NEPA.
10. Discuss the role of the National Flood Insurance Act in reducing federal cost.
11. Discuss briefly the following topics:
    a. Japan's Disaster Countermeasures Basic Act and the role of the CDMC
    b. The UK's CCS and CCA
    c. EMA
    d. New Zealand's CDEM Act and the CDEM framework
    e. The Disaster Management Act 2005 in India

WEBSITES

Robert T. Stafford Act. http://www.fema.gov/robert-t-stafford-disaster-relief-and-emergency-assistance-act-public-law-93-288-amended

Stafford Act (as amended). https://www.mwcog.org/security/security/otherplans/stafford.pdf

Short biography of Robert T. Stafford. http://bioguide.congress.gov/scripts/biodisplay.pl?index=S000776-publisher=Biographical

Disaster Mitigation Act (2000). http://www.fema.gov/media-library/assets/documents/4596

International Disaster Law. http://www.ifrc.org/en/what-we-do/disaster-law/

Code of Federal Regulations for Mitigation Planning. http://www.ecfr.gov/cgi-bin/text-idx?c=ecfr&sid=e63c0b17b2c76390184c081f4e63611d&rgn=div5&view=text&node=44:1.0.1.4.53&idno=44

FEMA Fact Sheet on the Coastal Barrier Resources Act. http://www.fema.gov/media-library/assets/documents/17075

National Coastal Zone Management Program. http://coast.noaa.gov/czm/

Clean Water Act. http://www2.epa.gov/laws-regulations/summary-clean-water-act

National Environmental Policy Act. http://www.epa.gov/compliance/nepa/

National Flood Insurance Act. http://www.fca.gov/Download/1968&1973FloodActs.pdf

Biggert-Waters Flood Insurance Reform Act of 2012. www.fema.gov/media-library/assets/documents/31873; https://www.fema.gov/media-library/assets/documents/31946

Disaster Countermeasures Basic Act (Japan). http://www.ifrc.org/docs/IDRL/Japan_DMAct_1961.pdf

Civil Contingencies Act (UK). http://www.legislation.gov.uk/ukpga/2004/36/contents

New Zealand Civil Defence Emergency Management Act. http://www.legislation.govt.nz/act/public/2002/0033/latest/DLM149789.html

Disaster Management Act 2005 (India). http://atingl.nic.in/Downloads/THE%20DISASTER%20MANAGEMENT%20ACT%202005.pdf

REFERENCES

Annelli, J. F. (2006). The National Incident Management System: A multi-agency approach to emergency response in the United States of America. *Revue Scientifique et Technique—Office International Epizooties, 25*(1), 223–231.

Australian Fire Authority Council (2004). *The Australian Inter-service Incident Management System: A management system for any emergency.* East Melbourne, Victoria, Australia: AFAC Limited.

Baca, A.M. (2008). History of disaster legislation. Federal Emergency Management Agency. On Call. *Disaster Reserve Workforce News.* September. Washington, DC.

Cabinet Office. (2010). *Central Government Arrangements for Responding to an Emergency.* Retrieved from <https://www.gov.uk/government/uploads/system/uploads/attachment_data/file/60816/conops-2010-overview.pdf>.

Commonwealth of Australia. (2009). Australian emergency management arrangements. Attorney-General's Department. Retrieved from <http://www.em.gov.au/documents/Australian%20Emergency%20Management%20Arrangements.pdf>.

Department of Internal Affairs. (2005). Briefing for incoming minister, Civil Defence. Retrieved from <https://www.dia.govt.nz/Pubforms.nsf/URL/CDEMBIMOctober2005.pdf/$file/CDEMBIMOctober2005.pdf>. Accessed July 24, 2014.

Emergency Management Australia (EMA). (1998). *Australian Emergency Management Glossary Manual 03.* Retrieved from <https://www.em.gov.au/Documents/Manual03-AEMGlossary.PDF>.

Federal Deposit Insurance Corporation (FDIC). (n.d.). Flood disaster protection. Retrieved from <https://www.fdic.gov/regulations/compliance/manual/pdf/V-6.1.pdf>.

Federal Emergency Management Agency (FEMA). (n.d.a). Multi-hazard mitigation plan status. Retrieved from <http://www.fema.gov/multi-hazard-mitigation-plan-status>. Accessed July 28, 2014.

Federal Emergency Management Agency (FEMA). (n.d.b). National Environmental Policy Act. Retrieved from <http://www.fema.gov/environmental-planning-and-historic-preservation-program/national-environmental-policy-act>. Accessed July 28, 2014.

Federal Emergency Management Agency (FEMA). (n.d.c). National Flood Insurance Act of 1968 and Flood Disaster Protection Act of 1973. Retrieved from <http://www.fema.gov/media-library/assets/documents/7277>. Accessed July 30, 2014.

India Disaster Knowledge Network. (n.d.). Institutions. Retrieved from <http://www.saarc-sadkn.org/countries/india/institution.aspx>. Accessed September 6, 2014.

Kapucu, N. (n.d.) Emergency and crisis management in the United Kingdom: Disasters experienced, lessons learned, and recommendations for the future. Comparative Emergency Management Book. FEMA Emergency Management Institute, Emmitsburg, Maryland.

National Association of Insurance Commissioners. (n.d.). National Flood Insurance Program (NFIP). Retrieved from <http://www.naic.org/cipr_topics/topic_nfip.htm>. Accessed July 3, 2014.

National Oceanic and Atmospheric Administration (NOAA). (n.d.a). Coastal Zone Management Act. Retrieved from <http://coast.noaa.gov/czm/act/>. Accessed July 5, 2014.

National Oceanic and Atmospheric Administration (NOAA). (n.d.b). National Estuarine Research Reserve System. Retrieved from <http://www.nerrs.noaa.gov/>. Accessed July 9, 2014.

O'Brien, G., & Read, P. (2005). Future UK emergency management: New wine, old skin? *Disaster Prevention and Management*, *14*(3), 353–361.

Perry, R. (2003). Incident management system in disaster management. *Disaster Prevention and Management*, *12*(5), 405–412.

Peters E., & McEntire, D. (n.d.). Emergency management in Australia: An innovative, progressive and committed sector. Comparative Emergency Management Book. FEMA Emergency Management Institute, Emmitsburg, Maryland.

Queensland Parliamentary Counsel. (2014). Disaster Management Act 2003. Retrieved from <https://www.legislation.qld.gov.au/LEGISLTN/CURRENT/D/DisastManA03.pdf>. Accessed July 5, 2014.

Rose, A., Porter, K., Dash, N., Bouabid, J., Huyck, C., Whitehead, J., et al. (2007). Benefit-Cost Analysis of FEMA Hazard Mitigation Grants. *Natural Hazards Review*, *8*(4), 97–111. Available from http://dx.doi.org/10.1061/(ASCE)1527-6988 (2007)8:4(97).

Salveson, D., & Godschalk, D. (n.d.) Development on coastal barriers: Does the Coastal Barrier Resources Act make a difference? *Report to the Coastal Alliance*. Washington, DC: Coastal Alliance.

Schwab, A. J., Eschelbach, K., & Brower, D. J. (2007). Hazard mitigation and preparedness. Hoboken, NJ: John Wiley and Sons.

U.S. Environmental Protection Agency (EPA). (n.d.). Wetlands compensatory mitigation. Retrieved from <http://water.epa.gov/lawsregs/guidance/wetlands/upload/2003_05_30_wetlands_CMitigation.pdf>. Accessed August 5, 2014.

U.S. Fish and Wildlife Service. (n.d.a). Coastal Barrier Resources Act. Retrieved from <http://www.fws.gov/cbra/Act/index.html>. Accessed August 6, 2014.

U.S. Fish and Wildlife Service. (n.d.b). Coastal Zone Management Act. Retrieved from <https://www.fws.gov/laws/lawsdigest/COASZON.HTML>. Accessed August 6, 2014.

Webb, C., & McEntire, D. (n.d.). Emergency management in New Zealand: Potential disasters and opportunities for resilience. Comparative Emergency Management Book. FEMA Emergency Management Institute, Emmitsburg, Maryland.

World Bank. (n.d.). Disaster Management Plans, Knowledge Note 2-2. Retrieved from <http://wbi.worldbank.org/wbi/Data/wbi/wbicms/files/drupal-acquia/wbi/drm_kn2-2.pdf>. Accessed September 15, 2014.

The Role of Governments in Hazard Mitigation

OBJECTIVES

The study of this chapter will enable you to:

1. Understand and discuss FEMA's Hazard Mitigation Assistance Program

2. Understand the role of federal appropriations

3. Understand and discuss other federal mitigation programs

4. Understand the role of regulatory power in state and local government mitigation activities and local government structure

5. Understand the concept of disaster risk reduction and its implementation

6. Discuss other notable mitigation efforts on the international front

Essential Terminology: Hazard mitigation assistance (HMA), base flood, repetitive loss properties, severe repetitive loss properties, 100-year floodplain, Special Flood Hazard Area (SFHA), home rule, Dillon's Rule, disaster risk reduction (DRR), International Strategy for Disaster Reduction (ISDR), Hyogo Framework for Action (HFA)

Government's first duty is to protect the people, not run their lives.
President Ronald Reagan

INTRODUCTION

One of the primary responsibilities for any government is to protect the lives and property of its citizens. Governments play a significant role in hazard mitigation, as they create mitigation rules and regulations and execute mitigation programs. Chapter 2 discussed the legal framework of mitigation within which government agencies operate. Usually, government agencies implement large-scale mitigation projects such as dams and levees, regulate land use and development, and assist communities with funding for hazard mitigation activities (Mileti, 1999). Also, organizations such as the United Nations (UN) play an important role assisting governments worldwide, especially in developing countries in mitigation and disaster risk reduction (DRR) activities. This chapter will provide an extensive overview of various federal mitigation programs in the United States and the role of state and local governments in implementing hazard mitigation activities, and will also explore notable mitigation efforts on the international front, including the DRR strategy by the UN Office for Disaster Risk Reduction.

FEDERAL MITIGATION PROGRAMS IN THE UNITED STATES

The Mitigation Directorate of the Federal Emergency Management Agency (FEMA), officially known as the **Federal Insurance and Mitigation Administration (FIMA)**, is responsible for most of the federal mitigation programs in the United States. The Mitigation Directorate was established on November 29, 1993, as mitigation became the cornerstone of emergency management under the leadership of former FEMA director James Lee Witt. FIMA has stakeholders in federal, state, local, and tribal governments, as well as in the private sector, which include partners such as professional associations and nongovernmental groups involved in public policy and administration, insurance, higher education, building sciences, and urban planning (FEMA, n.d.a). The Mitigation Directorate is comprised of three divisions: Risk Reduction, Risk Analysis, and Risk Insurance.

The main authorized programs run by the Mitigation Directorate are the hazard mitigation assistance (HMA) programs. These include the Hazard Mitigation Grant Program (HMGP), Predisaster Mitigation (PDM), and the Flood Mitigation Assistance (FMA) program, Severe Repetitive Loss (SRL), Community Rating System (CRS), National Earthquake Hazards Reduction Program (NEHRP) and the National Flood Insurance Program (NFIP).

Hazard Mitigation Assistance Program

The HMA grant programs by FEMA are designed to provide funding to protect life and property to mitigate disasters. Currently, there are three HMA programs, described in the next sections.

HMGP

The HMGP was established by the Robert T. Stafford Disaster Relief and Emergency Assistance Act (the Stafford Act). Section 404 of this act authorizes the program to provide grants to states and local governments to implement long-term hazard mitigation measures after a major disaster declaration made by the president. Since 1988, Section 404 has been amended four times to (1) increase the share of federal assistance and authorize property acquisition grants, (2) stimulate state mitigation planning, (3) reduce the maximum amount of federal aid, and (4) establish a sliding scale for the awards (Bea, 2010).

The purpose of the HMGP is to reduce the loss of life and property due to natural disasters and to enable mitigation measures to be implemented during the immediate recovery from a disaster. States that have an approved hazard mitigation plan (HMP) in effect at the time of the Presidential Disaster Declaration may receive additional HMGP funding. Indian tribes or other tribal organizations and private nonprofit organizations are also eligible for HMGP grants as primary or subapplicants. Individual homeowners and businesses may not apply directly to the program; however, an eligible applicant or subapplicant may apply on their behalf (FEMA, n.d.b).

HMGP is the largest source of federal funding for state and local mitigation activities that derives from the Disaster Relief Fund (DRF) rather than from line item appropriations. The amount of funding is based on a percentage of the total disaster assistance package as calculated by damage loss estimates. Therefore, the larger the disaster, the more mitigation funds are made available (Schwab et al., 2007). However, the Post-Katrina Emergency Management Reform Act of 2006 adjusted the percentage amounts for HMGP awards by establishing a scale that authorizes a higher percentage (15% of the total Stafford Act assistance in a state) for major disasters in which no more than $2 billion is provided, 10% for assistance that ranges from above $2 billion to $10 billion, and 7.5% for major disasters that involve Stafford Act assistance of more than $10 billion to $35.3 billion. The current statutory provisions do not address what percentage would be used to determine hazard mitigation funding for disasters that exceed $35.3 billion. It would appear that special legislation would need to be enacted to provide mitigation funding for any disaster in excess of that amount (Bea, 2010).

Although HMGP funds are allocated following a major disaster declaration, the funds generally may be used for any eligible hazard mitigation activity, even if it is not related to the catastrophe that led to the declaration. These include construction activities, such as dams to protect from hazards, retrofitting of facilities, elevating structures in flood-prone areas, enforcement of building code, and public awareness campaigns.

DRF and the Role of Federal Appropriations

The Disaster Relief Fund (DRF) is the primary source of funding for federal assistance. The Congress appropriates money to the DRF to ensure that money is available to help disaster-stricken communities. The DRF is funded annually and is a "no-year" account, meaning that any unused funds from the previous fiscal year are carried over to the next fiscal year. Also, when the balance of the DRF becomes low, Congress provides additional funding through both annual and supplemental appropriations to replenish the account (Bea, 2010).

Most federal grants and other forms of aid are distributed on a cost-share basis, meaning that the recipient has to share a portion of the costs. The current amount of federal assistance for mitigation projects can be as much as 75% of each project's cost (FEMA, n.d.c). However, the local matching can be in-kind support such as labor, land, facilities, and other resources. Federal grant application, therefore, is a cumbersome process because of this cost-sharing policy, and small local emergency management agencies (EMAs) often find it difficult to fulfill the requirements with their limited staff and resources.

The role of federal appropriations in emergency management is often as a "carrot-and-stick approach" to policy development and implementation. While states remain largely independent of federal direction, the federal government can influence emergency management policy through incentives (the carrot) or penalties (the stick). Federal appropriations are typically awarded to the states, which in turn allocate the resources to local communities. Appropriations generally have strings attached, meaning the federal government requires recipients of such funds to have certain policies and procedures in place before they can qualify for the funds. For example, states that do not adopt an HMP jeopardize federal disaster relief funding. Those entities that go beyond the minimum requirements—adopting an enhanced HMP may receive larger percentages of federal funding for mitigation projects. This ensures that the state and local governments are taking responsibility for their communities, not relying solely on the federal government to provide aid.

PDM Grant Program

The PDM program was established by Section 203 of the Disaster Mitigation Act (DMA, 2000). The objective of this program is to reduce losses and suffering "resulting from natural disasters" and provide a source of funding to ensure "the continued functionality of critical services and facilities after a natural disaster (Sec. 101, P.L. 106-390; DMA, 2000). Unlike the HMGP grant, the PDM program does not require a disaster declaration to provide mitigation funding to state and local governments. Prior to PDM, FEMA initiated a program called **Project Impact** during the Bill Clinton administration to stimulate predisaster mitigation efforts. With the passage of DMA 2000, Section 203 authorizes FEMA to expand federal predisaster mitigation assistance in order to reduce federal disaster relief costs, save lives, and protect property (Bea, 2010).

The PDM program provides technical and financial assistance to state and local governments for hazard mitigation planning and projects on an annual basis. The PDM projects must be cost-effective and designed to reduce injuries, loss of life, and damage and destruction of property, including damage to critical services and facilities (Sec. 101, P.L. 106-390; DMA, 2000). According to FEMA (2002), the PDM program "emphasizes the importance of strong state and local planning processes and comprehensive program management at the state level." Figure 3.1 shows how to apply for FEMA's hazard mitigation assistance including the PDM program.

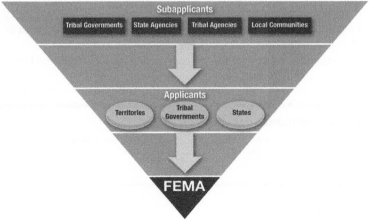

■ **FIGURE 3.1** An HMA application submission flowchart. On the top is a chart of an upside pyramid with three levels. The first level is the subapplicant level, which includes tribal governments, state agencies, tribal agencies, and local communities. The second level is the applicant level, applicable for territories, tribal government and states. *Image courtesy of FEMA.*

Project Impact
FEMA started the Project Impact program in 1997 to encourage public-private partnerships to create disaster-resistant communities. The program provided financial and technical assistance to communities to mitigate and minimize hazard vulnerability. Project Impact communities were designated in all 50 states, the U.S. Virgin Islands, and Puerto Rico (Schwab et al., 2007). The project grew from seven pilots to over 250 communities, and partners include private, nongovernmental, media, volunteer organizations, universities, and professional organizations, along with federal, state, tribal and local governments (Anderson & Pierce, 2013). FEMA provided $1 million in seed money to each community for mitigation projects and disaster reduction actions (Godschalk, Beatley, Berke, Brower & Kaiser 1999). Although Project Impact was highly successful in some communities, it was discontinued as a national program in 2001 after the DMA was passed in 2000.

FMA Program

The FMA program was established by the National Flood Insurance Act of 1968 and was later amended as part of the National Flood Insurance Reform Act of 1994. It provides funds for projects to reduce or eliminate risk of flood damage to buildings that are insured under the NFIP (discussed in the next section) on an annual basis (FEMA, n.d.d).

There are three types of FMA grants available to applicants:

- Planning grants, to prepare flood mitigation plans
- Project grants, to implement measures to reduce flood losses, such as elevation, acquisition, or relocation of NFIP-insured structures
- Management cost grants, for the grantee to help administer the FMA program and activities

CRITICAL THINKING
Why is it that the role of federal appropriations is often referred to as a "carrot-and-stick approach" to policy development and implementation? *Quid pro quo!*

NFIP

NFIP was established by the National Flood Insurance Act of 1968 to reduce the growing cost of federal disaster assistance from widespread flooding and to provide people a means to financially protect themselves through insurance. The program offers flood insurance to homeowners, renters, and business owners if the community participates in it. Communities that participate in NFIP are required to adopt and enforce a floodplain management ordinance that meets minimum requirements, and flood insurance is available to them as a financial protection against flood losses. Communities that do not enforce these ordinances can be placed on probation or suspended from the program and will not be eligible for flood insurance under the NFIP.

The NFIP is administered by FEMA, which identifies flood hazard areas throughout the United States and its territories by producing Flood Hazard Boundary Maps (FHBMs), Flood Insurance Rate Maps (FIRMs), and Flood Boundary and Floodway Maps (FBFMs). Several areas of flood hazards are commonly identified on these maps. One of these areas is the Special Flood Hazard Area (SFHA), a high-risk area defined as any land that would be inundated by a flood having a 1 percent chance of occurring in any given year (also referred to as the **base flood**) (FEMA, n.d.d).

Community participation in the NFIP is voluntary, although some states require NFIP participation as part of their floodplain management program. However, Congress passed the Flood Disaster Protection Act in 1973, which created the mandatory purchase requirement for all federally backed home mortgages, including mortgages issued by lending institutions that are federally regulated or insured (Wetmore, 2013; Schwab et al., 2007).

Besides the FMA grants, two other grant programs were established and funded by the NFIP. The Severe Repetitive Loss (SRL) program provides funding for severe repetitive loss properties, and the Repetitive Flood Claims (RFC) program is intended for certain repetitive loss properties where there is no local government sponsor. **Repetitive Loss Properties (RLPs)** are defined as buildings with two or more NFIP claim payments of over $1000 each within a 10-year period since 1978. Such properties represent only 1–2% of the total NFIP-insured properties, but the program pays out an average of more than $200 million annually for RLPs, which account for 25–30% of the total claim payments (Schwab et al., 2007). In 2004, the Flood Insurance Reform Act created a new category of RLPs known as **Severe Repetitive Loss Properties (SRLP)**. Buildings that have four or more NFIP claim payments of over $5000 each, or the cumulative amount exceeds $20,000, or if at least two claims cumulatively exceed the building's value, such properties would be considered as SRL properties (FEMA, n.d.d; Wetmore, 2013).

Flood Mapping and Flood Insurance Study (FIS)

Most of the known floodplains in the United States have been mapped by FEMA, which administers the NFIP. When a flood study is completed for the NFIP, the information and maps are assembled into a flood insurance study (FIS). An FIS is a compilation and presentation of flood risk data for specific watercourses, lakes, and coastal flood hazard areas within a community. It includes causes of flooding.

The FIS report and associated maps delineate SFHAs, designate flood risk zones, and establish base flood elevations (BFEs), based on the flood that has a 1% chance of occurring annually (namely, the 100-year flood). The study may have three components:

■ The FIS—Flood Insurance Study text
■ The FIRM—Flood Insurance Rate Map
■ A separate Flood Boundary and Floodway Map (FBFM) that was issued as a component of the FIS for each community studied prior to 1986 (FEMA, 2001)

The **100-year flood** designation (Figure 3.2) applies to any area that has a 1% chance, on average, of flooding in any given year. However, a

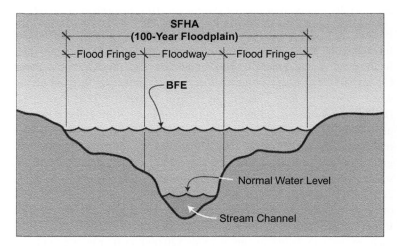

■ **FIGURE 3.2** An SFHA identified in the FIRM, which is an area that has a 1% chance of being flooded in any given year, also known as the 100-year floodplain. The elevation of the water surface resulting from a 100-year flood or base flood is known as the BFE (FEMA, 2001). *Image courtesy of FEMA.*

100-year flood could occur two years in a row or once every 10 years. The 100-year flood is also referred to as the *base flood*, and it is the standard that has been adopted for the NFIP. This is a national standard that represents a compromise between minor floods and the greatest flood likely to occur in a given area and provides a useful benchmark. **Base flood elevation (BFE)**, as shown on the FIRM, is the elevation of the water surface resulting from a flood that has a 1% chance of occurring in any given year.

A floodway is a stream channel and that portion of the adjacent floodplain that must remain open to permit passage of the base flood without raising the water surface elevation by more than one foot. A **Special Flood Hazard Area (SFHA)** is the shaded area on a FIRM that identifies an area that has a 1% chance of being flooded in any given year (100-year floodplain).

FIRMs show different floodplains with different zone designations as indicated in Table 3.1.

CRS

The CRS was initiated as a voluntary program in 1990 under the NFIP for recognizing and encouraging communities that exceed the minimum requirements of the NFIP. Any community in full compliance with the minimum NFIP floodplain management requirements may apply to join the CRS. As of March 2014, nearly 3.8 million policyholders in 1296 communities participate in the CRS by implementing local mitigation, floodplain management, and outreach activities that exceed the minimum NFIP requirements (FEMA, 2014). Although CRS communities represent only 5% of the over 22,000 communities participating in the NFIP, more than 67% of all flood insurance policies are written in CRS communities.

CRS Classification

The CRS uses a class rating system (refer to Table 3.2) to determine flood insurance premium reductions for residents. Communities usually enter the program at a CRS class 9 or class 8 rating, which entitles residents in SFHAs to a 5% discount on their flood insurance premiums for a class 9, or a 10% discount for class 8. As a community engages in additional mitigation activities, it becomes eligible for increased premium discounts and promote to upper classes.

Table 3.1 Flood Zones used by FEMA on the FIRMs to Categorize Different Floodplain Areas

Zone A		The 100-year or base floodplain. There are six types of A zones:
	A	The base floodplain mapped by approximate methods, i.e., BFEs are not determined. This is often called an unnumbered A zone or an approximate A zone.
	A1-30	These are known as numbered A zones (e.g., A7 or A14). This is the base floodplain where the FIRM shows a BFE (old format).
	AE	The base floodplain where base flood elevations are provided. AE zones are now used on new format FIRMs instead of A1-A30 zones.
	AO	The base floodplain with sheet flow, ponding, or shallow flooding. Base flood depths (feet above ground) are provided.
	AH	Shallow flooding base floodplain. BFEs are provided.
	A99	Area to be protected from base flood by levees or Federal flood protection systems under construction. BFEs are not determined.
	AR	The base floodplain that results from the de-certification of a previously accredited flood protection system that is in the process of being restored to provide a 100-year or greater level of flood protection.
Zone V and VE	**V**	The coastal area subject to a velocity hazard (wave action) where BFEs are not determined on the **FIRM.**
	VE	The coastal area subject to a velocity hazard (wave action) where BFEs are provided on the FIRM.
Zone B and Zone X (shaded)		Area of moderate flood hazard, usually the area between the limits of the 100-year and 500-year floods. B zones are also used to designate base floodplains of lesser hazards, such as areas protected by levees from the 100-year flood, or shallow flooding areas with average depths of less than one foot or drainage areas less than 1 square mile.
Zone C and Zone X (unshaded)		Area of minimal flood hazard, usually depicted on FIRMs as exceeding the 500-year flood level. Zone C may have ponding and local drainage problems that do not warrant a detailed study or designation as base floodplain. Zone X is the area determined to be outside the 500-year flood.
Zone D		Area of undetermined but possible flood hazards.

Source: Mitigation Planning How-To Guide #2 by FEMA.

The CRS classes for local communities are based on 18 creditable activities, organized into four categories (Schwab et al., 2007):

- Public Information. This series includes elevation certificates, map information, outreach projects, hazard disclosure, flood protection information, and flood protection assistance.
- Mapping and Regulations. This series includes additional flood data, open space preservation, higher regulatory standards, flood data maintenance, and stormwater management.
- Flood Damage Reduction. This series includes floodplain management plans, acquisition and relocation, flood protection (retrofitting), and drainage system maintenance.
- Flood Preparedness. This series credits flood warning programs, levee safety, and dam safety.

Table 3.2 Credit Points Earned, Classification Awarded and Premium Reductions Given for Communities in the NFIP CRS

CRS Class	Credit Points (cT)	Premium Reduction	
		In SFHA	Outside SFHA
1	4,500+	45%	10%
2	4,000–4,499	40%	10%
3	3,500–3,999	35%	10%
4	3,000–3,499	30%	10%
5	2,500–2,999	25%	10%
6	2,000–2,499	20%	10%
7	1,500–1,999	15%	5%
8	1,000–1,499	10%	5%
9	500–999	5%	5%
10	0–499	0	0

Source: CRS Coordinator's Manual *by FEMA.*
SFHA: Zones A, AE, A1–A30, V, V1–V30, AO, and AH.
Outside the SFHA: Zones X, B, C, A99, AR, and D.
Preferred Risk Policies are not eligible for CRS premium discounts because they already have premiums lower than other policies. Preferred Risk Policies are available only in B, C, and X Zones for properties that are shown to have a minimal risk of flood damage.
Some minus-rated policies may not be eligible for CRS premium discounts.
Premium discounts are subject to change.

Are Federal Programs and Disaster Assistance Creating a Moral Hazard?
In economics, the term **moral hazard** is defined as "any situation in which one person makes the decision about how much risk to take, while someone else bears the cost if things go badly" (Krugman, 2009). Prior to the implementation of the NFIP, private companies were reluctant to cover damages incurred from floods. As a result, fewer people used to live in the flood-prone and coastal areas. With the passage of the National Flood Insurance Act of 1968, flood insurance becomes available through the NFIP, which provides protection for people living in the floodplains. However, critics say that federal disaster aid and payment for insured losses in many ways negate the original intent of the NFIP and cost federal taxpayers billions of dollars (National Taxpayers Union, 2009). Due to the implementation of federal programs such as NFIP and federal disaster assistance, common sense or basic survival instincts are overlooked when development decisions are made in hazardous areas. In addition, more tax dollars are used in federal disaster assistance as more people choose to live in harm's way and these increasing costs are also paid by the tax payers who live in safer areas.
All of these factors create a moral hazard, which reduces the incentives to take responsibility for avoiding hazards (Schwab et al., 2007).

NHP

The National Hurricane Program (NHP) is a multiagency partnership among several federal agencies, including FEMA, National Oceanic and Atmospheric Administration (NOAA) and its National Weather Service (NWS), U.S. Department of Transportation (USDOT) and U.S. Army Corps of Engineers (USACE). Established in 1985, the program helps protect communities and residents from hurricane hazards through various projects and activities such as developing hurricane evacuation plans, assessment of storm surge and wind impacts (Figure 3.3), and hazard and

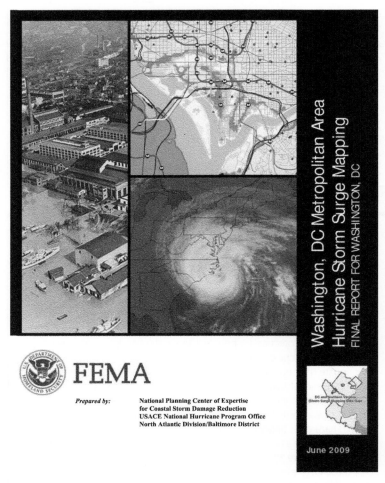

■ **FIGURE 3.3** The cover page of the *Final Report for Hurricane Storm Surge Mapping for Washington, DC Metro Area*, prepared by the NHP. *Image courtesy of FEMA.*

vulnerability analyses. Especially, the NHP program conducts Hurricane Evacuation Studies (HES) that guide the decision-making process in hurricane-prone areas to protect citizens (FEMA, n.d.e). The HES studies help state and local communities to establish evacuation plans, identifying appropriate shelters, determining probable effects of a hurricane, and predicting public responses.

The program gives priority to mitigation, which saves lives and property from hurricane damage through prevention and proper insurance. Some of the hurricane mitigation measures of this program include:

- Assessing building performance after significant hurricanes and coastal storms
- Developing designs for hazard-resistant construction in new buildings
- Developing designs and retrofitting techniques for existing buildings
- Recommending improvements in state and local regulatory programs

Although the NHP is highly effective for hurricane mitigation and preparedness, it is severely underfunded (Schwab et al., 2007). Annually, it receives $5.86 million from the government, which consists of $2.91 million for FEMA program activities and $2.95 million for the Emergency Management Performance Grant program. These funds are directed into general state funds for hurricane preparedness and mitigation activities (FEMA, n.d.e).

NEHRP

The National Earthquake Hazards Reduction Program (NEHRP) was established by the Congress when it passed the Earthquake Hazards Reduction Act of 1977, Public Law (PL) 95–124. The goal of NEHRP is "to reduce the risks of life and property from future earthquakes in the United States through the establishment and maintenance of an effective earthquake hazards reduction program." The program involves four primary federal agencies: FEMA, National Institute of Standards and Technology (NIST), U.S. Geological Survey (USGS), and the National Science Foundation (NSF). Refer to Figure 3.4 for a breakdown of agencies that make up the NEHRP.

The NEHRP projects include research, development, and implementation activities. The objective of the NEHRP research is to advance our understanding of why and how earthquakes occur and its impacts on the natural and built environments. The research projects are funded mainly through the NSF in the earth sciences, social sciences, and engineering. The research results are used to develop earthquake risk-reduction measures that are put into practice through the program's implementation

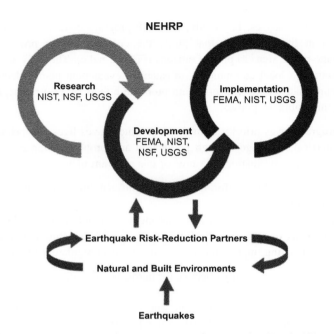

■ FIGURE 3.4 NEHRP agencies and their activities in terms of research (NIST, NSF, and USGS), development (FEMA, NIST, NSF, and USGS), and implementation (FEMA, NIST, and USGS). NEHRP collaborates with earthquake risk-reduction partners to understand why and how earthquakes occur and affect both natural and constructed environments (FEMA, n.d.f). *Image courtesy of FEMA.*

efforts. NIST's applied earthquake engineering research is integrated with the development of performance-based tools, guidelines, and standards for its Earthquake Risk Mitigation Research and Development program. Also, USGS develops innovative technologies, systems, and products related to earthquakes. These products are useful to a variety of audiences, including emergency responders, infrastructure managers, scientists, the news media, and the public. The implementation activities are conducted primarily by FEMA through publication and dissemination. FEMA also sponsors Hazards United States (HAZUS) training for loss estimation by an earthquake that helps states and localities with preparedness and response planning and to assess the need for specific risk-reduction strategies (FEMA, n.d.f).

Structural Mitigation Projects by USACE

Along with administering the 404 wetlands program of the Clean Water Act (CWA) and issuing permits for dredging and fill activities in wetlands, the USACE involves in the design and construction of many structural mitigation projects in coastal and watershed areas, especially for flood control and shoreline and riverbank protection. Although a large number of USACE-constructed flood protection projects are owned by sponsoring jurisdictions or agricultural districts, the agency continues to maintain and operate about 400 dams and reservoirs across the United States (Schwab et al., 2007).

Some of the USACE projects, such as flood protection for New Orleans, have been characterized as being "pork barrel" since faulty design and substandard construction caused failure of levees and flooding in New Orleans as was witnessed to devastating effect during Hurricane Katrina (Grunwald, 2007). Critics also argue that in reality, coastal erosion— and flood control—related projects by USACE only reduce vulnerability for the short term, but increase vulnerability in the long term by encouraging development in these areas. However, these land use decisions are made by state and local authorities; the federal government plays no role in the decision-making process regarding land use and managing their shores and floodplains (Schwab et al., 2007).

ROLE OF STATE AND LOCAL GOVERNMENTS IN HAZARD MITIGATION

State and local governments play an important role in carrying out emergency management functions, including mitigation plans and projects. As mentioned in the previous chapter, the DMA 2000 requires all states to prepare HMPs, and states can receive additional funding for implementing mitigation projects if they have an approved enhanced mitigation plan. All 50 states, U.S. territories, and the District of Columbia have offices and agencies of emergency management, which serve as the primary organization for coordinating emergency management activities at the state level. Many federal programs, such the Coastal Zone Management Program (CZMP), are run in partnership with the states. Each state and U.S. territory has a state hazard mitigation officer (SHMO), who is the primary contact between federal government and the state (Schwab et al., 2007). In addition to implementing mitigation programs and projects in partnership with the federal government, state governments have engaged in mitigation measures that involve the private sector and local stakeholders as partners. These include mitigation programs related to property management, building construction, and personal response to risk (Edwards & Goodrich, 2013).

State legislation is also an important factor in implementing mitigation at the state and local levels. The state laws govern land-use regulations, building codes, insurance, and real estate and environmental regulations in each state. It authorizes and creates agencies to oversee the implementation of these regulations. State also dictates the regulatory power that a local government can exercise. In 1868, Judge John F. Dillon invented what became known as **Dillon's Rule** as a result of his distrust of the local government due to extreme corruption (Coester, 2004). According to Dillon's Rule, a local government may only engage in activities specifically authorized by the state government. Consequently, Dillon's Rule became the basis of U.S. municipal law, as 31 states apply it to all municipalities (National League of Cities, n.d.). These include Arizona, Arkansas, Connecticut, Delaware, Georgia, Hawaii, Idaho, Kentucky, Maine, Maryland, Michigan, Minnesota, Mississippi, Missouri, Nebraska, Nevada, New Hampshire, New York, North Carolina, North Dakota, Oklahoma, Pennsylvania, Rhode Island, South Dakota, Texas, Vermont, Virginia, West Virginia, Washington, Wisconsin, and Wyoming.

Due to the inflexibility of Dillon's Rule, many states began to adopt home rule provisions in the early 1900s that conferred greater authority to their local governments. **Home rule** is a delegation of power from the state to its subunits of governments (including counties, municipalities, towns or townships or villages). It creates local autonomy and limits the degree of state interference in local affairs. Currently, 10 States employ home rule: Alaska, Iowa, Massachusetts, Montana, New Jersey, New Mexico, Ohio, Oregon, South Carolina, and Utah. Also, some states employ Dillon's Rule for only certain municipalities: Alabama, California, Colorado, Illinois, Indiana, Louisiana, and Tennessee.

CRITICAL THINKING

What are the implications of adopting Dillon's Rule or home rule for a state in terms of hazard mitigation?

Since all disasters are considered to be local, the powers available to local government are crucial for all phases of emergency management, including mitigation. Land use regulation is one of the effective means of mitigation used throughout the United States. Using the regulatory power granted by the state, local governments can control the growth and development within its jurisdictions, ensure public safety, and protect the natural environment. Such regulatory powers include zoning ordinances, subdivision regulations, acquisition, easement, purchase and transfer of development rights, eminent domain, and building codes. Chapter 9 describes in detail about these tools for land use control and management.

Also, comprehensive plans, which are sometimes referred to as *land use plans*, serve as the basis for regulation of property uses. As the term *comprehensive* suggests, this is an all-inclusive approach to addressing the issue of a community's future growth. A comprehensive plan is the formal document produced through this process that establishes guidelines for the future growth of a community. The plan also provides guidelines on mitigation measures such as zoning, subdivision ordinances, and capital improvement programs. Prior to DMA 2000, when states were not required to develop a HMP, some states had legislation that required the inclusion of hazard mitigation elements into local comprehensive plans. These elements could be land use or building codes to limit development in hazardous areas or the inclusion of postdisaster elements in those plans. For example, California, Florida, South Carolina, and North Carolina required local governments to include provisions for natural hazard mitigation in their comprehensive plans (Brody, Godschalk & Burby 2003).

Local Government Structure

It is important to know the structure of the local government in the United States and its political machinery that is essential to implement mitigation strategies. The Code of Federal Regulations (44 CFR Part 201) defines local government as any county, municipality, city, town, township, public authority, school district, special district, intrastate district, council of governments (regardless of whether the council of governments is incorporated as a nonprofit corporation under State law), regional or interstate government entity, or agency or instrumentality of a local government; any Indian tribe or authorized tribal organization, or Alaska Native village or organization; and any rural community, unincorporated town or village, or other public entity.

There are five basic types of local government in the United States, which are described in the next sections.

Counties

A total of 48 of the 50 states in the United States are divided into counties. The counties of Connecticut and Rhode Island are geographical regions, and they do not have any functioning government. In Alaska and Louisiana, these county-type government units are called *boroughs* and *parishes*, respectively. Counties are administrative units of states and perform state-mandated duties. They also have policy-setting and decision-making responsibilities. Basic functions of counties include property assessment, record keeping (land, statistics), revenue collection, law enforcement, jails, election, judicial function, road maintenance, and emergency services. Counties may also deliver additional services, such as health care, social services, utility services, pollution control, mass transit, and industrial and economic development.

Municipalities

Municipalities are formed by the state through a charter or other means to provide general government for a defined area with certain characteristics, such as urbanized and high population density. Municipalities are referred to as *cities*, *towns*, *hamlets*, *villages*, or *boroughs* throughout the United States. They are authorized to make decisions for communities and to implement policies and programs. Generally, municipalities have greater decision-making authority and discretion than do counties (Schwab et al., 2007).

The three main types of municipal government are:

- Mayor council: This type of municipal government is mostly found in older, larger, or very small cities. Mayor-council municipal government is popular in the Mid-Atlantic and Midwest. Depending on the strength of the mayor, there are two varieties in this type-
  a. Strong mayor council: In this form mayor is elected by the voters and holds significant administrative and budgetary authority and has veto power over the council.
  b. Weak mayor council: In this form power and authority are fragmented. The council holds significant administrative and budgetary authority. The council elects the mayor.
- City commission: In this form, voters elect an individual commissioner. Each commissioner is responsible for a specific department and tends to be its advocate. Commissioners generally make policy. One commissioner serves as mayor, who presides over commission meetings. The commission has both executive and legislative functions.
- Council city manager: This form is found in cities with populations over 10,000. The council appoints a professional city manager. The city manager in turn appoints and removes department heads, oversees delivery of services, prepares the budget, and makes policy recommendation to the city council (Schwab et al., 2007). The manager is quite powerful in many communities and can play an activist role in local affairs, such as promoting mitigation measures to all local government departments.

Towns and Townships

Towns and townships are general-purpose units of local government. In some states, such as all the New England states, New Jersey, Pennsylvania, Michigan, New York, and Wisconsin, towns and townships have broad powers and function like other general purpose units of government. In some other states, such as Illinois, Indiana, Kansas, Minnesota, Missouri, Nebraska, North Dakota, Ohio, and South Dakota, towns and townships have more limited authority. The functions of this type of local entities include road maintenance and law enforcement.

Councils of Governments (COGs)

Councils of governments (COGs) are voluntary associations of local governments. Such associations are also called *regional councils*. COGs are formed when services can be provided more efficiently on a regional basis or when they are needed to deal with a problem that crosses the boundary of individual local government. They provide services in cooperation with the members of the associations, including programs for senior citizens, environmental planning, land use planning, economic development, operating specialized transit system, and other services. Local government units that are in lack of resources can benefit by forming COGs.

Special Districts

Special districts are single-purpose units of local governments concerned with one specific service. Special districts are created to perform specific functions or to address specific issues in the community, such as school administration, fire protection, sewage and water management, drainage and flood control, redevelopment and disaster recovery, and many more. The services of special districts can be extended beyond the borders of general-purpose local governments such as counties and municipalities. Special districts can be created to tackle regional problems that encompass multiple counties. For example, a flood control district can be created to deal with flooding of a river that runs through several counties.

CRITICAL THINKING

If you were the emergency manager in a mid-sized municipality, what would be some of the advantages of having a council-manager type of local government for pushing a hazard mitigation agenda through the local policy-making process?

NOTABLE MITIGATION EFFORTS ON THE INTERNATIONAL FRONT

DRR and the International Strategy

Disaster risk reduction (DRR) is "the concept and practice of reducing disaster risks through systematic efforts to analyze and reduce the causal factors of disasters" (UNISDR, n.d.). The scope of DRR is much broader than conventional humanitarian response and relief activities, as it aims to save lives through disaster reduction strategies. Examples of DRR strategies include reducing exposure to hazards, lessening vulnerability of people and properties, and improving preparedness and early warning systems (UNISDR, 2004).

The UN Office for Disaster Risk Reduction, also known as the UN International Strategy for Disaster Reduction (UNISDR), is the focal point of the UN system for coordinating DRR around the world. UNISDR was established in December 1999 as a successor of the International Decade for Natural Disaster Reduction (1990–1999), which was launched by the UN General Assembly in 1989. According to the UN, the **International Strategy for Disaster Reduction (ISDR)** reflects a major shift from the traditional emphasis on disaster response to disaster reduction, and in effect seeks to promote a "culture of prevention" (UNISDR, n.d.).

The UNISDR is the secretariat mandated by the UN General Assembly to implement the strategy worldwide through governments of the UN member countries. These governments have committed to take action for DRR and have adopted a guideline to reduce vulnerabilities, which is known as the **Hyogo Framework for Action (HFA).** The first 10-year plan came out during the World Conference for Disaster Reduction held in Kobe, Hyogo, Japan in 2005 (hence the name for the framework). It brings together governments, international agencies, disaster experts, and many others into a common platform to reduce disaster losses substantially by 2015 by building the resilient nations and communities.

The ISDR system that implements HFA (Figure 3.5) has many levels of action that include global, regional, national, and thematic platforms (Matsuoka & Shaw, 2011). The global platform is the main forum that assesses HFA implementation progress at all levels and creates awareness about the DRR. Regional platforms are focused on specific regions and comprised of representatives of governments, national platforms, regional intergovernmental organizations, and different UN offices. National platforms provide leadership nationally on DRR and are comprised of governments, nongovernmental organizations (NGOs), academic institutions,

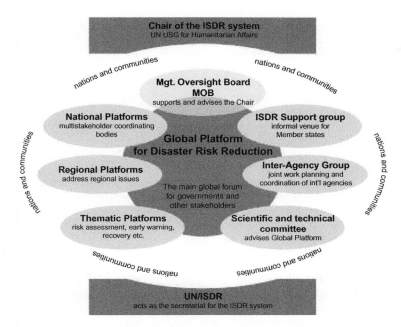

■ FIGURE 3.5 The ISDR System that implements the Hyogo Framework for Action (HFA). The Global Platform for DRR is the main forum, which assesses the progress of implementation at regional, national and thematic levels. *Image courtesy of UNISDR.*

professional associations, private sector, media, etc. Thematic platforms are focused on specific topic or thematic area and comprised of specialized partnerships and networks. These mainly include technical and scientific bodies that have expertise on issues related with global, regional, or national concerns.

HFA

The HFA outlines five priorities for action and offers guiding principles and practical means for achieving disaster resilience. These are:

Priority Action 1: Ensure that DRR is a national and a local priority with a strong institutional basis for implementation.

Countries that develop policy, legislative, and institutional frameworks for DRR and that are able to develop and track progress through specific and measurable indicators have greater capacity to manage risks and to achieve widespread consensus for, engagement in, and compliance with DRR measures across all sectors of society.

Priority Action 2: Identify, assess, and monitor disaster risks and enhance early warning.

The starting point for reducing disaster risk and for promoting a culture of disaster resilience lies in the knowledge of the hazards and the physical, social, economic, and environmental vulnerabilities to disasters that most societies face, and of the ways in which hazards and vulnerabilities are changing in the short and long term, followed by actions taken on the basis of that knowledge.

Priority Action 3: Use knowledge, innovation, and education to build a culture of safety and resilience at all levels.

Disasters can be substantially reduced if people are well informed and motivated toward a culture of disaster prevention and resilience, which in turn requires the collection, compilation, and dissemination of relevant knowledge and information on hazards, vulnerabilities, and capacities.

Priority Action 4: Reduce the underlying risk factors.

Disaster risks related to changing social, economic, and environmental conditions and land use, and the impact of hazards associated with geological events, weather, water, climate variability, and climate change are addressed in sector development planning and programs, as well as in postdisaster situations.

Priority Action 5: Strengthen disaster preparedness for effective response at all levels.

At times of disaster, impacts and losses can be substantially reduced if authorities, individuals, and communities in hazard-prone areas are well prepared and ready to act and are equipped with the knowledge and capacities for effective disaster management.

Source: UNISDR (n.d.).

Challenges in DRR Strategy

Although governments worldwide have committed to DRR, some governments are more successful than others at implementing it. Disaster losses in developing countries amounted to $862 billion since the inception of DRR in 1990 until 2010 (Kellet & Caravani, 2013). Financing DRR initiatives is one of the main factors in this development. Research shows that funding for DRR is not distributed uniformly among member countries by the UNISDR. There is a high concentration of funding in a relatively small number of middle-income countries. From 1990 to 2010, the top 10 recipients received a total of nearly $8 billion, and the remaining 144 just $5.6 billion combined (Kellet & Caravani, 2013). Many high-risk countries have received negligible levels of funding for DRR compared with emergency response. For instance, Niger, Eritrea, Zimbabwe,

Kenya, and Malawi are highly drought-affected countries, but their combined DRR financing for the 1990—2010 period was only $116.5 million, which was the same as Honduras.

Although there has been progress implementing HFA at the national level, participation from local and city governments in DRR activities has been unsatisfactory (Matsuoka & Shaw, 2011). Since all disasters are local, it is important to integrate local governments and stakeholders into the implementation process. In order to address this issue, the ISDR Asia Regional Task Force on Urban Risk Reduction (RTF-URR), which is one of the regional thematic platforms of the ISDR system, developed a guideline for local governments called *A Guide for Implementing the Hyogo Framework for Action by Local Stakeholders* (Matsuoka & Shaw, 2011).

In March 2015, a new framework for disaster risk reduction was adopted for 2015—2030 at the UN World Conference on Disaster Risk Reduction in Sendai, Japan. The Sendai Framework outlines seven global targets to be achieved over the next 15 years, which include:

a. Substantially reduce global disaster mortality;
b. Substantially reduce the number of affected people globally from disasters;
c. Reducing economic losses from disasters in relation to global GDP;
d. Substantial reduction in disaster damage to critical infrastructure and disruption of basic services including health and education facilities;
e. Increasing the number of countries adopting national and local disaster risk reduction strategies;
f. Enhanced international cooperation to implement the Sendai Framework by 2030; and
g. Increasing the access to multi-hazard early warning systems and disaster risk information and assessments (UN General Assembly, 2015).

Based on the experience of the Hyogo Framework, the Sendai Framework set the following four priority areas to address the challenges and shortcomings of DRR implementation:

1. Understanding disaster risk.
2. Strengthening disaster risk governance to manage disaster risk.
3. Investing in disaster risk reduction for resilience.
4. Enhancing disaster preparedness for effective response, and to "Build Back Better" in recovery, rehabilitation and reconstruction (UN General Assembly, 2015).

Earthquake and Tsunami Warning System in Japan

Japan is highly vulnerable to earthquakes and associated tsunamis. In 2011, for instance, the country was hit by a 9.0 magnitude earthquake, which then triggered a 23-foot tsunami; the disaster killed 15,887 people. However, the damage and loss of life was likely limited due to Japan's innovative earthquake and tsunami warning system (Knight, 2011). The system was developed by the Japan Meteorological Agency (JMA), which is a government agency of the Ministry of Land, Infrastructure, Transport, and Tourism.

The system was first triggered during the 2011 earthquake; it automatically issued public alerts through television channels and cell phones when the first wave was detected, providing time for people to prepare for the powerful shocks to come. The system also caused many industrial facilities and transportation services to shut down automatically (Knight, 2011). It also detected tsunamis resulted from the earthquake in coordination with the Pacific Tsunami Warning Center (PTWC) in Hawaii and sent warnings to possible affected regions.

According to the JMA website, "The Earthquake Early Warning system provides advance announcement of the estimated seismic intensity and expected arrival time of principal motion when an earthquake occurs. These estimations are based on prompt analysis of the quake's focus and magnitude using waveform data obtained from seismographs near the epicenter (Figure 3.6). The Earthquake Early Warning system is aimed at mitigating earthquake-related damage by allowing countermeasures such as promptly slowing down trains, controlling elevators to avoid danger, and enabling people to quickly protect themselves in various environments such as factories, offices, houses and near cliffs" (JMA, n.d.).

For the tsunami warning system, JMA estimates the possibility of tsunami generation from seismic observation data. If a damaging tsunami is expected in coastal regions, JMA issues a tsunami warning/advisory for each region within around 2–3 min of the quake (Figure 3.7). If tsunamis are generated by seismic events that may affect other countries, JMA coordinates with the PTWC and issues warnings for long-propagating tsunamis (JMA, n.d.).

Flood Control in the Netherlands—The Delta Works

There is a saying that "God created the world, but the Dutch made the Netherlands." Located in western Europe, the Netherlands is highly susceptible to flooding from the North Sea, as much of the land is below sea level. But the Dutch have been successful not only at protecting the Delta, but also at reclaiming a large portion of their land from the sea.

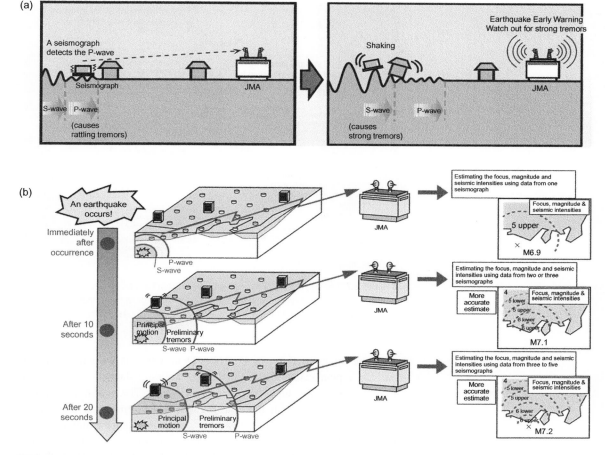

■ **FIGURE 3.6** Japan's Earthquake Alert System. When an earthquake occurs, a seismograph detects the P-wave, and the JMA immediately provides the announcement of the estimated seismic intensity and expected arrival time of principal motion. More accurate estimates are provided within 10 and 20s. *Image courtesy of the JMA (http://www.jma.go.jp/jma/en/Activities/earthquake.html).*

The Delta Works in the Netherlands, which is a series of construction projects in the southwest of the Netherlands to protect a large area of land around the Rhine-Meuse-Scheldt delta from the sea, is a prime example of flood control and mitigation. The Department of Public Works (known as Rijkswaterstaat, which is now the Ministry of Infrastructure and Environment) conducted a study in 1937 and decided to close all the river mouths in this area to shorten the Dutch coastline, thus reducing the number of dikes that had to be raised (Deltawerken, n.d.).

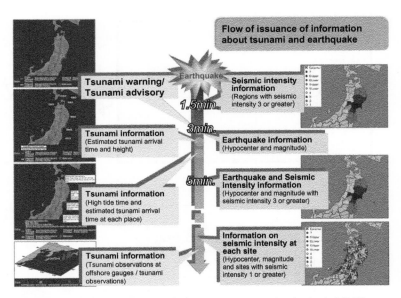

■ FIGURE 3.7 Time sequence for issuance of information on tsunamis and earthquakes by JMA. When an earthquake occurs, JMA estimates the possibility of tsunami generation from seismic observation data and issues a tsunami warning/advisory for each region within 2—3 min. of the quake. *Image courtesy of the JMA.*

After the infamous flood of 1953, the Delta Commission was formed to execute a plan called the Deltaplan by building dams, sluices, dykes, levees, and storm surge barriers (Figure 3.8). The original plan was completed in 1997 with the construction of a storm surge barrier, the Maeslantkering (Figure 3.9), which is one of the largest moving structures on Earth. However, the Delta Works were finished in 2010 with the official opening of the last strengthened and raised retaining wall near the city of Harlingen, Netherlands. Along with the Zuiderzee Works in the North Sea, the Delta Works have been declared as one of the Seven Wonders of the Modern World by the American Society of Civil Engineers (ASCE).

Advantages of the Delta Works

Besides shortening the total length of the dikes by 700 km, the Delta Works have many other advantages, including the following:

- It improves the freshwater supply for agriculture as the border between freshwater and saltwater is moved farther west and less fresh water is required to balance the freshwater-saltwater division.

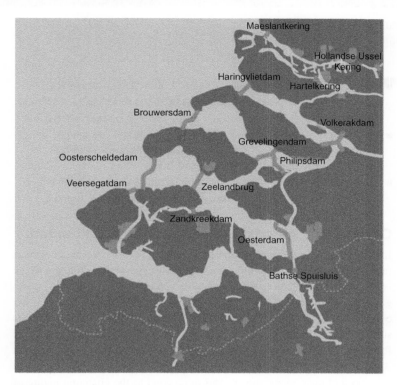

■ **FIGURE 3.8** Map of the Delta Works in Zeeland, the Netherlands. *Image courtesy of Deltawerken.*

■ **FIGURE 3.9** The Maeslantkering, a storm surge barrier located at Hoek van Holland. The barrier is important in protecting South Holland against flooding from the North Sea. The barrier helps protect an important area where millions of people live and work. *Image courtesy of the Rijkswaterstaat, Netherland's Department of Public Works.*

- It improves the complete water balance of the Delta area as the streams in this area are able to be manipulated more easily. Different types of sluices allow fresh water in, or polluted or excess water out.
- It encourages traffic between the many islands and peninsulas. Large parts of the province of Zeeland had literally been isolated for centuries. The building of the Zeeland Bridge helps increase mobility.
- It influences new developments in the areas of nature and recreation and supports the inland waterways shipping (Deltawerken, n.d.).

Climate Change Adaptation in the United Kingdom

Implications from climate change are widely reported in an enormous (and growing) body of credible research that suggests that climate change is a reality. The International Panel on Climate Change (IPCC) categorizes climate change impacts into two groups: fast or "extreme weather events," such as hurricanes and flash floods; and "slow onset" events such as sea level rise (IPCC, 2012). The United Kingdom (UK) is at the forefront of climate change adaptation and mitigation. The National Adaptation Programme (NAP) was initiated by the UK government to develop a climate-ready society and to respond to the changing nature of climate risks. The objectives of the NAP cover four main areas (HM Government, 2013):

- Increasing awareness
- Increasing resilience to current extremes
- Taking timely action for long-lead time measures
- Addressing major evidence gaps

Policies and projects have been developed related to built environment, infrastructure, healthy and resilient communities, agriculture and forestry, natural environment, business, and local government, with a number of focus areas. Proactive adaptation planning stimulates enterprise in a global market for adaptation goods and services. In 2010−2011, these goods and services were worth £2.1 billion, with over 21,000 employees in the UK. Also, the Climate Change Programme was launched in November 2000 by the British government in response to its commitment agreed at the 1992 UN Conference on Environment and Development. The aim of the program is to cut significantly all greenhouse gas emissions, including carbon dioxide, that contribute to global warming.

■ CONCLUSION

This chapter began with descriptions of various federal mitigation programs in the United States, including the HMA, NFIP, NHP, NEHRP, and structural mitigation projects by USACE. There are currently three HMA programs (HMGP, PDM, and FMA), through which FEMA provides funding to communities to mitigate disasters. This chapter described all three HMA grant programs, including the role of federal appropriations to award mitigation grants. NFIP offers flood insurance to homeowners, renters, and business owners, thus helps reduce the growing cost of federal disaster assistance from widespread flooding.

The chapter also discussed major components of the NFIP, including flood mapping, flood insurance study, and the CRS. The NHP is a multiagency partnership among several federal agencies that helps protect communities and residents from hurricane hazards through various mitigation projects. NEHRP is another multiagency federal program that is committed to reducing future earthquake risks by means of innovative research, development, and implementation. The USACE is involved in the design and construction of many structural mitigation projects in coastal and watershed areas, especially for flood control and shoreline and riverbank protection. The chapter also described the role of state and local governments in hazard mitigation exercising regulatory powers and explains the local government structure, and concluded with the description of DRR strategies by the United Nations and other notable mitigation efforts initiated by governments in different countries, including Japan, the Netherlands, and the UK.

DISCUSSION QUESTIONS

1. Discuss the three types of HMA grant programs by FEMA.
2. Discuss briefly the NFIP and define the following terms:
   a. RLPs
   b. Severe Repetitive Loss Properties
   c. 100-year floodplain
   d. BFE
   e. Flood zones and SFHAs
   f. CRS
3. Discuss the NHP and the NEHRP.
4. Discuss the role of regulatory powers in state and local government mitigation functions.
5. Discuss the local government structure in the United States.
6. Define DRR. Describe the importance of the HFA in DRR. What are the challenges in DRR strategy?
7. Discuss the following international mitigation efforts:
   a. The Earthquake and Tsunami Warning System in Japan
   b. The Delta Works in the Netherlands
   c. Climate change adaptation strategies in the United Kingdom

WEBSITES

FEMA HMGP

https://www.fema.gov/hazard-mitigation-grant-program

National Flood Insurance Program CRS

https://www.fema.gov/national-flood-insurance-program-community-rating-system

UN Office for Disaster Risk Reduction

http://www.unisdr.org/

The Netherlands Ministry of Infrastructure and the Environment

http://www.rijkswaterstaat.nl/en/

United Kingdom NAP for Climate Change

https://www.gov.uk/government/uploads/system/uploads/attachment_data/file/209866/
  pb13942-nap-20130701.pdf

REFERENCES

Anderson, R., & Pierce, I. (2013). Public-private partnerships in mitigation initiatives. In A. Jerolleman, & J. J. Kiefer (Eds.), *Natural hazard mitigation*. Boca Raton, FL: CRC Press.

Bea, K. (2010). Federal Stafford Act disaster assistance: Presidential Declarations, eligible activities, and funding. Congressional Research Service (CRS) Report. Prepared for Members and Committees of Congress. Retrieved from <http://biotech.law.lsu.edu/blaw/crs/RL33053_20100316.pdfl>. Accessed October 3, 2014.

Brody, S. D., Godschalk, D. R., & Burby, R. J. (2003). Mandating citizen participation in plan making: Six strategic planning choices. *Journal of the American Planning Association*, 69(3), 245–264.

Coester, A. (2004). Dillon's rule or not? Retrieved from <http://www.celdf.org/downloads/Home%20Rule%20State%20or%20Dillons%20Rule%20State.pdf>. Accessed October 4, 2014.

Deltawerken. (n.d). The Delta Works. Retrieved from <http://www.deltawerken.com/Deltaworks/23.html>. Accessed October 4, 2014.

Edwards, F. L., & Goodrich, D. C. (2013). State initiatives. In A. Jerolleman, & J. J. Kiefer (Eds.), *Natural hazard mitigation*. Boca Raton, FL: CRC Press.

Federal Emergency Management Agency (FEMA). (2001). Mitigation planning how-to guide #2: Understanding your risks: Identifying hazards and estimating losses (FEMA 386-2).

Federal Emergency Management Agency (FEMA). (2002). 44CFR parts 201 and 206—Hazard mitigation planning and Hazard Mitigation Grants Program: Interim final rule.

Federal Emergency Management Agency (FEMA). (2014). Community rating system fact sheet. Retrieved from < http://www.fema.gov/media-library-data/1395661546460-d6859e8d080fba06b34a6f1a4d0abdba/NFIP_CRS_March+2014+508.pdf >. Accessed October 19, 2014.

Federal Emergency Management Agency (FEMA). (n.d.a). Federal Insurance and Mitigation Administration. Retrieved from <https://www.fema.gov/what-mitigation/federal-insurance-mitigation-administration>. Accessed October 8, 2014.

Federal Emergency Management Agency (FEMA). (n.d.b). Hazard Mitigation Grant Program. Retrieved from <https://www.fema.gov/hazard-mitigation-grant-program>. Accessed October 8, 2014.

Federal Emergency Management Agency (FEMA). (n.d.c). Hazard mitigation—Emergency Management Institute training course. Emmitsburg, MD.

Federal Emergency Management Agency (FEMA). (n.d.d). National Flood Insurance Program. Retrieved from <https://www.fema.gov/national-flood-insurance-program>. Accessed October 8, 2014.

Federal Emergency Management Agency (FEMA). (n.d.e). National Hurricane Program. Retrieved from <https://www.fema.gov/region-iii-mitigation-division/national-hurricane-program>. Accessed October 8, 2014.

Federal Emergency Management Agency (FEMA). (n.d.f). National Earthquake Hazards Reduction Program. Retrieved from <https://www.fema.gov/national-earthquake-hazards-reduction-program>. Accessed October 8, 2014.

Godschalk, D. R., Beatley, T., Berke, P. R., Brower, D. J., & Kaiser, E. J. (1999). *Natural hazard mitigation: Recasting disaster policy and planning*. Washington, DC: Island Press.

Grunwald, M. (2007). The Threatening Storm. Hurricane Katrina—Two years later, Katrina Anniversary Special Issue. *Time*. Retrieved from <http://content.time.com/time/specials/2007/article/0,28804,1646611_1646683_1648904,00.html>. Accessed October 9, 2014.

HM Government. (2013). The National Adaptation Programme: Making the country resilient to a changing climate. Retrieved from <https://www.gov.uk/government/uploads/system/uploads/attachment_data/file/209866/pb13942-nap-20130701.pdf>. Accessed October 9, 2014.

Japan Meteorological Agency (JMA). (n.d.). Monitoring of earthquakes, tsunamis and volcanic activity. Retrieved from <http://www.jma.go.jp/jma/en/Activities/earthquake.html>. Accessed October 10, 2014.

Kellett, J., & Caravani, A. (2013). Financial disaster risk reduction: A 20-year story of international aid. Retrieved from <http://www.odi.org/sites/odi.org.uk/files/odi-assets/publications-opinion-files/8574.pdf>. Accessed October 10, 2014.

Knight, W. (2011). How Japan's earthquake and tsunami warning systems work, technology review. Retrieved from <http://www.technologyreview.com/view/423279/how-japans-earthquake-and-tsunami-warning-systems-work/>. Accessed October 10, 2014.

Krugman, P. (2009). *The return of depression economics and the crisis of 2008*. New York, NY: W. W. Norton & Company.

Matsuoka, Y., & Shaw, R. (2011). Linking resilience planning to Hyogo Framework for Action in cities. In R. Shaw, & A. Sharma (Eds.), *Climate and disaster resilience in cities. Community, environment, and disaster risk management* (Vol 6, pp. 129–147). Bingley, UK: Emerald Group.

Mileti, D. S. (1999). *Disasters by design: A reassessment of natural hazards in the United States*. Washington, DC: Joseph Henry Press.

National League of Cities. (n.d.). Local government authority. Retrieved from <http://www.nlc.org/build-skills-and-networks/resources/cities-101/city-powers/local-government-authority>. Accessed October 10, 2014.

National Taxpayers Union. (2009). NTU testifies on the National Flood Insurance Program. Retrieved from <http://www.ntu.org/governmentbytes/detail/ntu-testifie-sonthe-national-flood-insurance-program>. Accessed October 10, 2014.

Schwab, A. J., Eschelbach, K., & Brower, D. J. (2007). *Hazard mitigation and preparedness*. Hoboken, NJ: John Wiley & Sons.

UN General Assembly. (2015). Sendai framework for disaster risk reduction 2015−2030, Third United Nations World conference on disaster risk reduction, Sendai, Japan, 14−18 March 2015. Agenda item 11. Adoption of the final outcomes of the Conference. Retrieved from < http://www.wcdrr.org/uploads/Sendai_Framework_for_Disaster_Risk_Reduction_2015-2030.pdf >. Accessed May 18, 2015.

UN International Strategy for Disaster Reduction (2004). *Living with risk: A global review of disaster reduction initiatives*. Geneva: UN International Strategy for Disaster Reduction.

UN International Strategy for Disaster Reduction. (n.d.). What is disaster risk reduction? Retrieved from <http://www.unisdr.org/who-we-are/what-is-drr>. Accessed October 7, 2014.

Wetmore, F. (2013). The National Flood Insurance Program and the Community Rating System. In A. Jerolleman, & J. J. Kiefer (Eds.), *Natural hazard mitigation*. Boca Raton, FL: CRC Press.

Chapter 4

Mitigation in the Private Sector

OBJECTIVES

The study of this chapter will enable you to:

1. Understand the role of the private sector in hazard mitigation
2. Discuss public-private partnerships (PPPs) and their importance to mitigation
3. Understand the concept of sustainability and its relevance to hazard mitigation
4. Understand and discuss the concept of community resilience
5. Discuss the sustainable livelihood approach and the Pentagon model
6. Discuss the "whole community" approach
7. Understand and discuss business continuity planning, including business impact analysis (BIA) and IT disaster recovery plans (IT DRPs)

Essential Terminology: Private sector, public-private partnership (PPP), critical infrastructure, sustainable development, resilience, sustainable livelihood, Pentagon model, human capital, social capital, natural capital, physical capital, financial capital, whole community approach, business continuity, business impact analysis (BIA), information technology disaster recovery plan (IT DRP)

Building sustainable cities—and a sustainable future—will need open dialogue among all branches of national, regional, and local government. And it will need the engagement of all stakeholders—including the private sector and civil society, and especially the poor and marginalized.

Ban Ki-moon, UN Secretary-General

INTRODUCTION

The role of the private sector in hazard mitigation is critical and manifold. Private-sector consultants and firms are often involved in local mitigation activities, and they work in state and federal mitigation projects as contractors. For instance, the Disaster Mitigation Act of 2000 (DMA 2000) requires all local governments to have a written hazard mitigation plan in place in order to receive federal funding after a disaster, but many communities do not have enough resources or expertise to develop and update a hazard mitigation plan on their own. So, they turn to private-sector consultants to accomplish the tasks. According to Schwab (2010), at least 50% of local hazard mitigation plans in California involve the use of consultants. Another way that the private sector is involved in hazard mitigation with the government is through public-private partnerships (PPPs). In order to protect community assets, infrastructure, and the economy from natural and manmade disasters or terrorist attacks, public safety agencies are establishing partnerships with private-sector organizations for building sustainable and hazard resilient communities (FEMA, n.d.d). The Ready Campaign and Citizen Corps of the Federal Emergency Management Agency (FEMA) is an example of a PPP. In 2011, FEMA introduced the "whole community" approach to promote PPPs and help building community resilience. Also, economic losses from disasters are staggering, and since private entities own most of the nation's infrastructure and businesses, protection of critical infrastructure and business continuity are vital for the U.S. economy. This chapter will discuss several important relevant concepts, such as PPPs, sustainability, community resilience, the sustainable livelihood approach, the whole community approach, and business continuity planning to help broaden our understanding of the role that the private sector plays in community hazard mitigation.

WHAT IS THE PRIVATE SECTOR?

The **private sector** is usually defined as organizations and entities that are not part of any governmental structure (FEMA, n.d.g). It includes a broad spectrum of entities ranging from nonprofit organizations (e.g., faith-based and volunteer groups), for-profit organizations, commerce, and industries. The Code of Federal Regulations (CFR) allows private-sector entities to be involved in hazard mitigation activities and in the mitigation planning process. According to the CFR (44 CFR 201).

The private sector drives a large percentage of a country's economy; therefore, it is often hit the hardest during a natural or manmade disaster. In order to reduce damages from disasters, it is important that the private sector works together in collaboration with the government. In 12 December 2013, as FEMA administrator Craig Fugate, said in a

The planning process shall include an opportunity for neighboring communities, local and regional agencies involved in hazard mitigation activities, and agencies that have the authority to regulate development, as well as businesses, academia, and other private and non-profit interests to be involved in the planning process.

speech at a gathering of U.S. private-sector leaders, "There is no way government can solve the challenges of a disaster with a government-centric approach. It takes the whole team" (FEMA, n.d.i).

PPPs

Public-private partnerships (PPPs) are collaborative relationships built on the needs, capabilities, and communication channels of public- and private-sector partners (FEMA, n.d.d). In a PPP, partners bring their own unique sets of capabilities that can be employed to meet certain needs, and they should communicate their needs, as well as capabilities to all members of the partnership. Anderson and Pearce (2013) describe PPPs as "collaborative, cooperative groups with the aim of proactively addressing community issues, such as pre-disaster mitigation, as no one sector can accomplish this on its own."

Partnerships can take different forms, depending upon their objectives and purposes. Some partnerships are formal based on legal agreements and may address issues such as contracting, acquisition, and cobranding. Others are less formal, even in the form of a listserv or a communication channel (FEMA, n.d.d). In order to be effective and successful, partnerships should be publicly accessible, dedicated, resourced, engaged, and sustainable (PADRES). PPPs can be designed to fulfill the PADRES requirements and yet can have different structures, goals, and functions (FEMA, n.d.d).

In emergency management, PPPs can provide significant value by conducting a variety of functions, including:

- Community outreach and awareness projects
- Participating in mitigation planning and projects
- Participating in emergency operation centers
- Conducting joint training activities
- Ensuring the efficient and effective use of available resources during an emergency
- Developing and enhancing plans for integration of nongovernmental entities in preparedness, mitigation, response, and recovery

Partnerships with the private sector are also highly encouraged in the National Response Framework (NRF), the National Incident Management System (NIMS), and the National Infrastructure Protection Plan (NIPP) documents. One of the five principles of the NRF is "engaged partnerships" meant specifically for private-sector leaders. Private sector outreach falls under Emergency Support Function (ESF) #15—External

Affairs, which is an annex to the NRF. The NIMS provides a proactive approach explaining the roles to guide agencies and the private sector to work together during emergencies.

Critical infrastructure is largely owned and operated by the private sector. According to the NIPP, **critical infrastructure** represents "systems and assets, whether physical or virtual, so vital to the United States that the incapacity or destruction of such systems and assets would have a debilitating impact on security, national economic security, national public health or safety, or any combination of those matters." The NIPP is a national-level plan that provides the road map for safer, more secure, and more resilient communities. The plan defines overall roles and responsibilities for public and private partners and outlines a comprehensive approach for managing the threats that face critical infrastructure. The private-sector entities can participate in information-sharing mechanisms, join in community planning activities, and use the NIPP Risk Management Framework as a model for evaluating threats to their operations.

A broad PPP known as the Sector Partnership Model provides a basis for national-level coordination. This framework is comprehensive because it involves virtually every sector of the national economy and connects to all levels of government. This partnership balances the needs and interests of an incredibly diverse group of partners who share a common interest—to protect the nation's infrastructure and make it more resilient to attacks, natural hazards, or other kinds of emergencies (Figure 4.1). The partnership approach includes a hotline that connects private-sector and government partners across all the sectors (DHS, 2013).

The UN developed a global partnership between UN International Strategy for Disaster Reduction (UNISDR) and members of the private sector to mobilize actions to reduce the risk of disasters (UNISDR, n.d.). It is known as Disaster Risk Reduction Private-Sector Partnerships (DRR-PSP). The DRR-PSP has five essential objectives:

- Promote and develop PPPs for disaster risk reduction (DRR) to analyze the root causes of continued nonresilient activity.
- Use private-sector expertise and strengths to advance DRR and mitigation activities, including enhanced resilience and effective response.
- Foster a collaborative exchange and dissemination of data, sharing information on assessment, monitoring, prediction, forecasting, and early warning purposes and actions between the public and private sectors.

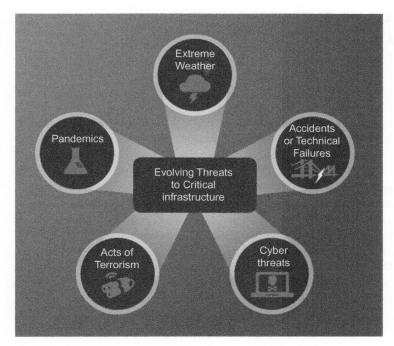

■ **FIGURE 4.1** Evolving threats to critical infrastructure. *Image courtesy of the U.S. Department of Homeland Security.*

- Support national and local risk assessments and socioeconomic cost-benefit analyses and capacity building, and demonstrate opportunities where resilience building and DRR are a sound economic strategy, with attractive returns and competitive advantages.
- Support the development and strengthening of national and local laws, regulations, policies, and programs that enhance DRR and improve resilience (UNISDR, n.d.).

CRITICAL THINKING

A local electric utility company covers several counties in northeast Alabama and partners with local county emergency management agencies. The partners conduct joint exercises and trainings to test communication channels and ensure that appropriate information is shared during a disaster. While the public sector and the company communicate regularly, there are no formal leaders, bylaws, or rules that govern the partnership. What kind of partnership best explains its purpose?

EXAMPLES OF PPPs
Citizen Corps

Citizen Corps was started in 2002 as a PPP initiative to strengthen community safety by bringing government and community leaders together in all-hazards emergency planning, preparedness, mitigation, response, and recovery. The program is administered by FEMA but implemented locally by communities across the United States. FEMA coordinates the effort of helping communities to establish local Citizen Corps Councils and their programs. Council members include emergency managers, first responders, volunteer organizations, faith-based organizations, schools, hospitals, businesses, neighborhoods, and individual citizens. Citizen Corps activities include collaborative community planning and capacity building, integration of community resources, outreach and localized preparedness education and training, emergency communications to all population segments, drills and exercises, and volunteer programs (FEMA, n.d.c). FEMA, the U.S. Department of Justice, and the U.S. Department of Health and Human Services jointly administer five programs through the Citizen Corps, which include Community Emergency Response Teams (CERTs), Fire Corps, Neighborhood Watch, Medical Reserve Corps, and Volunteers in Police Program (VIPS).

ChicagoFIRST

ChicagoFIRST Coalition for Homeland Security is a nonprofit association of private firms in the Chicago metropolitan area (Chicagoland) that collaborates with one another and with government agencies at all levels to promote the resilience of its members and the Chicago business community.

On the recognition that emergencies, natural disasters, and terrorist events have their greatest effects in the region in which they occur, this PPP was originally formed in 2003 to develop solutions to common problems through working groups, roundtables, workshops, and exercises (ChicagoFIRST, n.d.). ChicagoFIRST has the following resources and capabilities: (i) a seat in the Emergency Operations Center; (ii) resources to help prepare for, respond to, and recover from disasters; (iii) web resources; and (iv) participation in the local fusion center; and critical public sector relationships (FEMA, n.d.j).

Although ChicagoFIRST can pursue grants for specific projects, it relies entirely on funding itself through dues from its members. This partnership has dedicated staff in order to engage the public sector and to achieve the goals of the organization.

Ready Campaign

Started in 2003, the Ready Campaign is a national public service advertising (PSA) campaign program designed to educate and empower Americans to prepare for and respond to emergencies, including natural and manmade disasters. The goal of the program is to get the public involved and ultimately to increase the level of basic preparedness across the nation. In 2004, DHS and FEMA launched Ready Business, an extension of the Ready Campaign that focuses on business preparedness. The Ready Campaign conducts recruitment annually for National Preparedness Month, which establishes contacts with over 3000 businesses, state and local governments, and community-based organizations. The Ready Campaign participates in joint training and exercises with the public and private sectors. The program uses the following methods of communication—e-mail alerts, in-person meetings, conferences and other events, teleconferences, websites, media outreach, and public service announcements (Ready Campaign, n.d.).

SUSTAINABILITY AND COMMUNITY RESILIENCE

As previously mentioned, public safety agencies are establishing PPPs with private-sector organizations for the purpose of building sustainable and hazard resilient communities. Therefore, it is important to know the concepts of sustainability and community resilience. Hazard literature frequently refers to both of these concepts "as the guiding principles behind effective hazard planning" (Tobin, 1999). In theory, sustainable and hazard-resilient communities are able to diminish the effects of certain disasters and recover more quickly.

The Concept of Sustainability

In 1987, the World Commission on Environment and Development (also known as the Brundtland Commission) defines **sustainable development** as "development that meets the needs of the present without compromising the ability of future generations to meet their own needs." The sustainable development framework considers economic, social, and environment factors. This concept, referred to as the "sustainability triad" (Figure 4.2), aims to develop and provide the tools necessary to overcome a community's vulnerability in the face of disaster (Oviatt & Brett, 2010). Essentially, sustainability means that decisions made by the present generation will not reduce the options of future generations, but rather will pass on to them a natural, economic, and social environment that will provide a high quality of life.

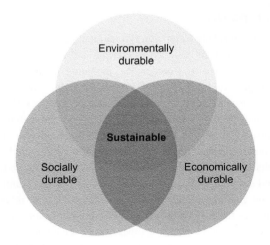

■ **FIGURE 4.2** The sustainability triad is often known as the three E's—economy, environment, and equity—essential factors for making a community sustainable. *Image courtesy of the National Park Service.*

Economic vitality is essential to sustainability. When recovering economically from a disaster, a community would like to retain existing businesses, promote continued or new economic development, and ensure that businesses are reconstructed safer, smarter, and stronger than before (FEMA, n.d.f). Hazard mitigation strategies can help communities keep local businesses and economic infrastructure out of hazard-prone areas or protect them from the impacts of disasters, promoting a more sustainable economy. Preserving the integrity of natural and physical systems is the most important environmental indicator of sustainability. Hazard mitigation plays a vital role in limiting environmental degradation and helps the preservation of natural systems such as wetlands, floodplains, and dunes. Mitigation strategies such as restricting development in active fault or landslide zones will increase a community's resilience to natural hazards by preventing potentially disastrous situations. In terms of social aspects, disasters can have social consequences such as loss of security, severe stress, and anxiety that can affect a community's sustainability. Hazard mitigation can prevent such social impacts by protecting communities from disasters and helping make communities sustainable.

According to Schneider (2006), there are six basic principles that should be adhered to in order to mitigate hazard and contribute to a sustainable community. These six principles are:

- Human activities in the community should maintain and, if possible, enhance environmental quality.
- The quality of life that community members want must be defined and planned for, not only for themselves but for future generations.

- Local resilience to and responsibility for disasters must be fostered. This suggests that communities must take responsibility for their involvement in comprehensive emergency management, mitigating hazards, understanding environmental resources, and implementing the steps to reduce damage and withstand disaster.
- Sustainable communities are tied to vital local economies. This implies that mitigation planning should take into account the need to use local resources instead of building a dependence on regional or state resources whenever possible.
- Local and regional resources and ecosystems should be preserved for future generations.
- Community members should be involved in mitigation planning activities, and a consensus building approach should be used.

Mileti (1999) describes sustainable hazard mitigation, which is similar to these six principles and highlights the need to preserve resources for future generations and understand the variability of the natural environment. An assessment on the volcanic disaster at Montserrat (in 1995), an island in the Caribbean, shows that these principles do contribute to sustainable hazard mitigation and that it is important to make sure that future generations are affected as little as possible while preventing unintended consequences (Rozdilsky, 2001).

Community Resilience

The term *resilience* is derived from the Latin word *resilio*, meaning "to jump back" or "to spring back." The definition of resilience varies in different disciplines, as there is not one universally accepted definition and it has become more of a concept than a concrete description. In engineering, resilience is seen as an attribute that allows a system to quickly bounce back to its original state, whereas ecological resilience refers to the ability to return to a new normal through flexibility and adaption (de Bruijne, Boin, & van Eeten, 2010). According to the UN Office for Disaster Risk Reduction, **resilience** is considered to be "the ability of a system, community or society exposed to hazards to resist, absorb, accommodate to, and recover from the effects of a hazard in a timely and efficient manner, including through the preservation and restoration of its essential basic structures and functions" (UNISDR, 2009).

In social science, Aaron Wildavsky was one of the first to work with the resilience concept. He defined resilience as "the capacity to cope with unanticipated dangers after they have become manifest, learning to bounce back" (de Bruijne et al., 2010). Wildavsky (1988) provides a

Table 4.1 Appropriate Strategies for Different Risk/Information Conditions

		Amount of Knowledge	
		Small	**Large**
Predictability of Risk	**High**	More resilience, less anticipation (Cell 4)	Anticipation (Cell 1)
	Low	Resilience (Cell 2)	More resilience, less anticipation (Cell 3)

Concept adapted from Wildavsky (1988).

matrix of strategies for handling different risk conditions, as shown in Table 4.1. Anticipatory strategies (Cell 1) are best suited for risks that "can be predicted and are well understood" (de Bruijne et al., 2010). On the other end of the spectrum, where both risk knowledge and predictability are low, decision makers should rely on strategies of resilience (Cell 2). A mixed strategy that emphasizes resilience should be utilized when preventive measures are available, but predictability remains low (Cell 3). Conditions of high predictability, coupled with poor understanding and lacking preventive measures (Cell 4) may warrant anticipation in some cases. Nonetheless, Wildavsky (1988) insists that decision makers should forgo anticipation in these conditions and instead rely on resilience "because otherwise they are likely to do more harm than good."

Decision makers must not only address obvious or known threats through a mix of preventive or anticipatory measures, but also build greater flexibility and response capacity within the sociotechnical system to better detect, improvise, and adapt to potential and unforeseen hazards and threats, as well as response-generated demands (Perry & Lindell, 2007). This broader conception of risk management also makes a distinction between reactive and proactive resilience. *Reactive resilience* is when a society approaches the future by ensuring the status quo is heightened and making sure the current system remains resistant to change. On the other hand, *proactive resilience* anticipates that change and tries to develop a system that is capable of adapting (de Bruijne et al., 2010). Proactive resilience is what can help prepare an affected community to accept the new normal and flourish.

According to McEntire (2005), risk management efforts have predominately focused on the physical aspects of community hazards while downplaying the social, political, and economic determinants of disasters. This traditional approach, often referred to as the *natural hazards perspective*, offers little utility in catalyzing positive community change or enhancing adaptive capacity—the core elements of proactive resilience. Burby (2006) argues that the traditional approach can negatively affect community resilience by encouraging hazardous development under a veil of false security, cultivating dependence on higher-level government assistance, or both. Such problems have led many researchers to demand a "broader view of the disaster problem and even a revolution in approach" (Mileti, 1999).

As a result, the attention of policy makers and scholars has shifted from creating anticipatory policies and strategies to organizing rescue services to prevent and deal with crisis, toward making communities more capable of handling a disaster or emergency (de Bruijne et al., 2010). This paradigm shift became more evident after Hurricane Katrina, as there have been efforts since then to shift the focus from protecting critical infrastructure to building resilient communities. This involves using local knowledge and collaborations to make sure that the community becomes more resilient. This new paradigm in disaster management consists of a more holistic definition of risk management, in which communities are adapting to climate change, hazard mitigation, and sustainable development.

CRITICAL THINKING

As the emergency manager for your community, what strategy would you employ or activities would you engage in to make your community sustainable and hazard resilient?

Sustainable Livelihood

Livelihood can be best defined as the methods and means of making a living in the world. The concept revolves around resources such as land/property, crops, food, knowledge, finances, social relationships, and their interrelated connection with the political, economic, and sociocultural characteristics of an individual community. A livelihood consists of capabilities, assets, and activities that are required for living. A sustainable livelihood is defined by the UN Economic and Social Commission for Asia and the Pacific (UN-ESCAP) as having "the ability to cope and recover from unexpected events, while at the same time enhancing current and future capabilities" (UN-ESCAP, 2008). This definition interlinks the definitions of resilience, sustainability, and livelihood, as each affects the others and highlights how DRR or mitigation strategies

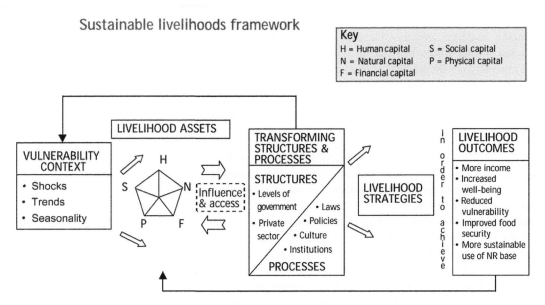

■ **FIGURE 4.3** Sustainable livelihoods framework and the Pentagon model. *Image courtesy of UN-ESCAP.*

directly affect sustainable livelihood. This means that there needs to be a heavy focus on reducing vulnerabilities of the community, including reducing poverty levels, building capacities and coping mechanisms, and focusing on community resilience (UN-ESCAP, 2008).

There are five primary assets or capitals in the sustainable livelihoods framework (Figure 4.3) that can influence sustainability and community resilience, as they can all be affected during disasters. These assets are human, social, natural, physical, and financial capital. Collectively, this is referred to as the *Pentagon model. Human capital* includes the skills, knowledge, labor ability, and good health that collectively allow people to pursue livelihood. *Social capital* consists of the specific social resources that are necessary to pursue one's own unique livelihood. These can be fostered via establishment of networks, trusting relationships, and membership of formalized groups. *Natural capital* consists of the natural resource stocks from which resource flows and sources are derived; these natural resource stocks include such elements as nutrient cycling and erosion protection, both which are useful for maintaining livelihood. *Physical capital* represents the resources available to support viable livelihood. This may include clean water, adequate sanitation, and effective shelter; these items are often encompassed by basic infrastructure. *Financial capital* consists of the financial resources that are required if people want to fulfill their livelihood objectives (UN-ESCAP, 2008).

There have been examples that show how sustainable livelihood and DRR are interrelated. For example, in post-tsunami research, it is noted that disasters represent both a crisis and an opportunity; it depicted how the disaster helped raise awareness of the gaps in strategy that had been present, thus further highlighting the importance of reducing vulnerabilities. Components of risk/vulnerability reduction include relief and rehabilitation, and it was stressed that these two elements should actually help reduce risk instead of just reconstructing current risks (UN-ESCAP, 2008). The American Red Cross sees the relationship between sustainable livelihood and DRR from an economic standpoint and emphasizes that helping people gain a stable income allows them to handle disasters more effectively and make them less vulnerable to facing livelihood losses; this, in turn, increases resiliency and mitigates the disastrous effects of hazards. The Red Cross also recommends using a community-inclusive approach, in which the community has a say in building their resiliency levels and identifying plans that can help with DRR. This allows the community to gain more control of their own lives, protection, and livelihood sustainability, along with the opportunity to produce an accurate needs assessment on how to achieve their resiliency goals.

Whole Community Approach

FEMA introduced the whole community approach in 2011 to bring together state, local, tribal, and territorial partners, along with private-sector organizations such as faith-based and nonprofit groups and industries. FEMA recognizes that it takes all aspects of a community, not just governmental organizations, to effectively prepare for, protect against, respond to, recover from, and mitigate against any disaster (Lombardo & Ryan, 2013).

FEMA has three primary principles that build the foundation for a whole community approach to emergency management (FEMA, 2011):

- *Understand and meet the actual needs of the community.* This involves community engagement in order to better understand their needs, wants, social infrastructure, etc. The more knowledgeable we are about our communities, the better we can develop preparedness plans and understand their motives to participate in EM-related preparedness activities.
- *Engage and empower all parts of the community.* Allowing and empowering the entire community to fully participate ensure that all voices will be heard, enable stakeholders to meet expectations, and strengthen the adaptive capability and resilience capacities of the

community. This means that all different types of stakeholders need to have a voice: public sector, private sector, nonprofit organizations/ nongovernmental organizations (NPOs/NGOs), academia, religious and cultural affiliations, and vulnerable population representatives.

■ *Strengthen what works well in a community on a daily basis.* This means finding ways to support and strengthen institutions, assets, and connections that are already running smoothly and are working on current issues that the community faces. Also, one can strengthen existing daily structures and organizations in a way that ensures that they are empowered to handle any future disturbances.

The whole community approach also establishes the following six strategic themes:

■ Understand community complexity.
■ Recognize community capabilities and needs.
■ Foster relationships with community leaders.
■ Build and maintain partnerships.
■ Empower local action.
■ Use and strengthen social infrastructure, networks, and assets.

Threat and Hazard Identification and Risk Assessment (THIRA) is a four-step risk assessment process based on the whole community approach designed to help all community partners. It is described in detail in Chapter 8.

IMPORTANCE OF BUSINESS CONTINUITY AND DEVELOPING A BUSINESS CONTINUITY PLAN (BCP)

Natural or manmade hazards can cause staggering economic losses as businesses are interrupted following a disaster. For instance, during Superstorm Sandy in 2012, the total cost of property damage and lost business was estimated to run between $10 billion and $20 billion, as businesses ranging from corner stores to the New York Stock Exchange shut down for an extended period (Whiteside, 2012). In 2010, the Deepwater Horizon oil spill in the Gulf of Mexico, which by most estimates was leaking 5000 barrels of crude oil a day from April 20 to July 15, heavily affected the fishing industry and other business sectors. The fishery closures that occurred due to the oil spill decreased commercial fishing production by as much as 20% and created an immediate economic hardship for fishers in the region (Figure 4.4). While the long-term damage estimates vary, researchers determined that the oil spill could have had an $8.7 billion impact on the economy of the Gulf of Mexico

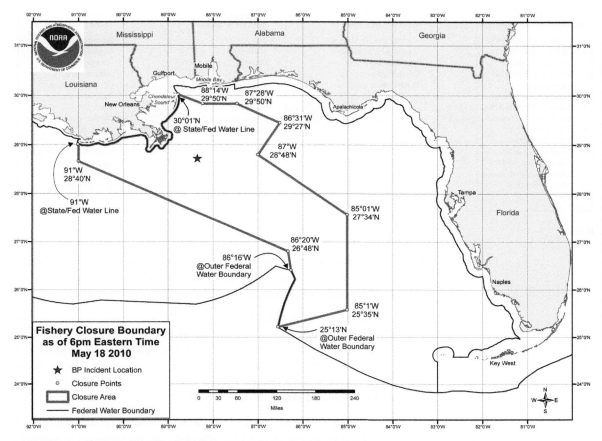

■ **FIGURE 4.4** Fishery closures imposed by the National Oceanic and Atmospheric Administration (NOAA) to ensure seafood safety, effective May 18, 2010. The closed areas changed daily as NOAA sampled seafood in the area and the geographical extent of the detected oil changed. *Image courtesy of NOAA.*

alone in the fishing sector, including losses in revenue, profit, wages, and close to 22,000 jobs (Sumaila et al., 2012). Protecting businesses and infrastructure, therefore, should be a priority.

Business Continuity Planning

The term **business continuity** refers to maintaining business functions or resuming business operations quickly in the event of a disaster or a major disruption. One study shows that up to 40% of businesses affected by a natural or manmade disaster never reopen (FEMA, n.d.h). Small businesses (generally defined as those employing less than 50 people) suffer the most during a disaster, with about 30% of them being completely demolished when disaster

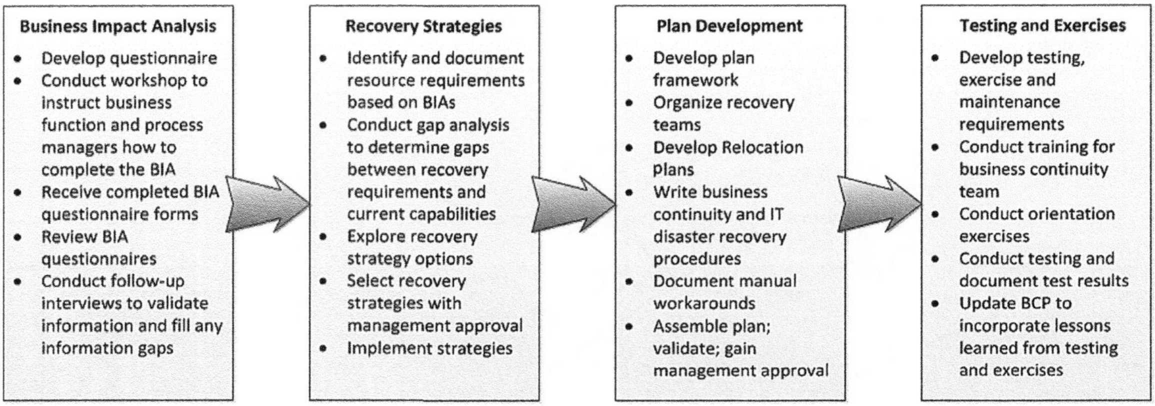

Business Impact Analysis	Recovery Strategies	Plan Development	Testing and Exercises
• Develop questionnaire • Conduct workshop to instruct business function and process managers how to complete the BIA • Receive completed BIA questionnaire forms • Review BIA questionnaires • Conduct follow-up interviews to validate information and fill any information gaps	• Identify and document resource requirements based on BIAs • Conduct gap analysis to determine gaps between recovery requirements and current capabilities • Explore recovery strategy options • Select recovery strategies with management approval • Implement strategies	• Develop plan framework • Organize recovery teams • Develop Relocation Plans • Write business continuity and IT disaster recovery procedures • Document manual workarounds • Assemble plan; validate; gain management approval	• Develop testing, exercise and maintenance requirements • Conduct training for business continuity team • Conduct orientation exercises • Conduct testing and document test results • Update BCP to incorporate lessons learned from testing and exercises

■ **FIGURE 4.5** Process diagram of business continuity planning. *Image courtesy of FEMA.*

strikes (Schwab, Eschelbach, & Brower, 2007). According to the Small Business Administration, small businesses employ about half of all private-sector employees and represent 99.7% of all firms (FEMA, n.d.h).

A business continuity plan (BCP) is essential to continue business during a disaster. However, a survey conducted by the Advertising Council in 2011 reported that nearly two-thirds (62%) of business owner respondents said they do not have an emergency plan in place for their business (FEMA, n.d.h). According to FEMA (n.d.a), development of a BCP includes the following four steps (Figure 4.5):

1. Conduct a business impact analysis (BIA) to identify time-sensitive or critical business functions and processes and the resources to support them.
2. Identify, document, and implement recovery strategies for critical business functions and processes.
3. Organize a business continuity team and compile a BCP to manage a business disruption.
4. Conduct training for the business continuity team and testing and exercises to evaluate recovery strategies and the plan laid out in the previous two steps.

BIA

A **business impact analysis (BIA)** involves calculating the consequences of the disruption of business operations and processes and collecting the information needed to develop recovery strategies (FEMA, n.d.b). The disruption of business operations can occur not only from disasters, but also from the failure of suppliers of goods or services or delayed deliveries. All potential hazards should be identified and analyzed through a risk assessment process, which involves hazard identification, vulnerability assessment and impact analysis, which are described in detail in Chapters 5, 6, and 7 of this book.

The risk assessment provides the basis for investment in recovery strategies, as well as investment in mitigation strategies. Examples of mitigation strategies include selecting a building site that is not located in a hazard-prone area such as a floodplain, an earthquake fault zone or an area near a hazardous facility. Construction of the building should comply with all building codes, including the requirements of fire protection and life safety. The computer network should be secured to protect sensitive information. Electrical systems should be outfitted with uninterruptible power supplies (UPSs) and backup generators. Purchasing insurance is also another effective mitigation strategy that reduces financial impact due to business interruption or loss of or damage to a facility or equipment. Insurance companies provide coverage for property damage, business interruption, workers' compensation, general liability, automobile liability, and many other losses (FEMA, n.d.k). However, insurance does not cover all losses and pays only when the hazard that caused the loss is specified by the policy. For instance, you need to purchase flood insurance separately through the National Flood Insurance Program (NFIP) if the facility is located within a flood zone. Similarly, earthquake, terrorism, and pollution coverage are not covered by standard property insurance policies.

The BIA should identify the impacts of the disruption of business functions and processes, which may include lost or delayed sales and income, increased expenses (e.g., overtime labor, outsourcing, and expediting costs), regulatory fines, contractual penalties or loss of contractual bonuses, customer dissatisfaction or defection, and delays in implementing new business plans (FEMA, n.d.b). The steps for conducting a BIA are as follows:

1. Develop a BIA questionnaire.
2. Conduct a workshop to instruct business function and process managers how to complete the BIA.
3. Receive the completed BIA questionnaires,
4. Review the questionnaires.
5. Conduct follow-up interviews to validate information and fill any information gaps.

A sample worksheet for considering the operational and financial impacts to a business during an emergency, which can be used to develop the BIA questionnaire, is shown in Figure 4.6.

Department / Function / Process _____

Operational & Financial Impacts

Timing / Duration	Operation Impacts	Financial Impact

Timing: Identify point in time when interruption would have greater impact (e.g., season, end of month/quarter, etc.)

Duration: Identify the duration of the interruption or point in time when the operational and or financial impact(s) will occur.

- < 1 hour
- >1 hr. < 8 hours
- > 8 hrs. <24 hours
- > 24 hrs. < 72 hrs.
- >72 hrs.
- > 1 week
- > 1 month

Considerations (customize for your business)

Operational Impacts
- Lost sales and income
- Negative cash flow resulting from delayed sales or income
- Increased expenses (e.g., overtime labor, outsourcing, expediting costs, etc.)
- Regulatory fines
- Contractual penalties or loss of contractual bonuses
- Customer dissatisfaction or defection
- Delay executing business plan or strategic initiative

Financial Impact
Quantify operational impacts in financial terms.

ready.gov/business

■ **FIGURE 4.6** BIA worksheet for operational and financial impacts. *Image courtesy of FEMA.*

Recovery Strategies

Recovery strategies require a variety of resources, including people, facilities, equipment, materials, and information technology (IT) (FEMA, n.d.k). A gap analysis should be conducted to determine the resources that are required to execute recovery strategies. For instance, if one piece of production equipment is rendered inoperable by an event but other machines are readily available to make up lost production, then there is no resource gap. Examples of recovery strategies include IT recovery plans, use of alternate facilities such as a cafeteria and conference or training rooms as office space during an emergency, a telecommuting strategy (i.e., staff can work from home through remote connectivity or temporary relocation to an alternate site that is not affected by the same event), and many others. An IT disaster recovery plan (IT DRP) is also a major component of the BCP, and this is described in the "IT DRP" box.

IT DRP

Almost all businesses, large and small, use IT to store important data and process information effectively. The **IT Disaster Recovery Plan (IT DRP)** focuses mainly on restoring IT infrastructure and operations after a crisis. Since BCPs look at the continuity of an entire organization, the IT DRP is only a part of a complete BCP and should be developed in conjunction with the BCP. So priorities and recovery objectives for the IT DRP should also be developed during the BIA for consistency.

The IT DRP begins with creating an inventory of hardware (e.g., servers, desktops, laptops, and wireless devices), software, and data. The plan should have definitive strategies to back up critical information that might include employee data/payroll/financial records, strategic plans/research data, formulas/trade secrets, inventory lists, supplier contacts, customer/client/patient/student records, building plans/blueprints/engineering drawings, and property lease/insurance records (Schwab et al., 2007).

IT systems require integration of hardware, software, data, and connectivity, and the systems may not function if any of these components do not operate properly. Therefore, recovery strategies should be developed in anticipation of the loss of one or more of the following system components:

- The computer environment (secure computer room with climate control, backup power supply, etc.)
- Hardware (networks, servers, desktop and laptop computers, wireless devices, and peripherals)
- Connectivity to a service provider (fiber, cable, wireless, etc.)

- Software applications (electronic data interchange, electronic mail, enterprise resource management, office productivity, etc.)
- Data and restoration (FEMA, n.d.e).

Recovery strategies for the IT DRP could be internal. For example, hardware can be placed at an alternate site to run similar hardware and software applications when needed, and data can be mirrored between the two sites. Alternatively, it could be managed externally by a third-party vendor who would be responsible for providing hardware, software, and data backup. In such cases, the vendor automatically holds data if an outage is detected on the client side and provide support for detecting malware and computer virus threats, thereby enhancing cybersecurity.

Plan Development

The third step of developing a BCP involves organizing a business continuity team and compiling the plan. This plan should define the roles and responsibilities of each member of the planning team, including the lines of authority, succession of management, and delegation of authority. Also, it should provide contact information of all team members, including contractors and vendors. An example of a business continuity team organization chart is shown in Figure 4.7.

The steps for this area of plan development are:

1. Develop the plan framework.
2. Organize business continuity teams.
3. Develop relocation plans.
4. Write business continuity and IT DRPs based on the BIA.
5. Document manual workarounds (e.g., forms and resource requirements).
6. Assemble the plan, including incident management [e.g., BCP activation, emergency operations center (EOC) activation, training curricula for team members, testing schedules and procedures for recovery strategies, orientation, and tabletop and full-scale exercises] (FEMA, n.d.a).

Testing and Exercises

As part of the BCP, training and exercises should be conducted to evaluate its effectiveness. This element should include the following steps:

1. Develop testing, exercise, and maintenance requirements.
2. Conduct training for the business continuity team.

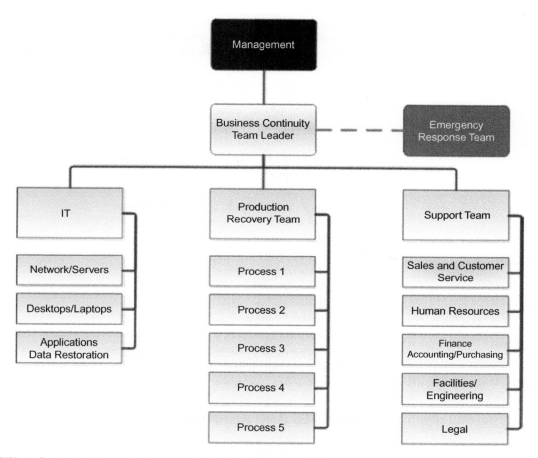

■ **FIGURE 4.7** Example of a business continuity team organization chart. *Image courtesy of FEMA.*

3. Conduct orientation exercises.
4. Conduct testing and document test results.
5. Update the BCP to incorporate lessons learned from the testing and exercises.

■ CONCLUSION

This chapter described the role of the private sector in hazard mitigation. Several important concepts highlight the private sector's involvement in building sustainable and resilient communities for hazard mitigation purposes. These include PPPs, sustainability, community resilience, the sustainable livelihood approach, the Pentagon model, and the whole community approach. The chapter also provided a step-by-step description of developing a BCP, including the BIA and IT DRP.

DISCUSSION QUESTIONS

1. What is the private sector? Discuss briefly the role of the private sector in community hazard mitigation.
2. What are PPPs? How does PPP contribute to emergency management? Find an example of an existing PPP and define its scope and history.
3. What is sustainable development? Discuss the concept of sustainability in relation to hazard mitigation.
4. What is resilience? How does the concept of resilience evolve in emergency management?
5. Define the following terms:
   a. Sustainable livelihood
   b. Pentagon model
   c. Human capital
   d. Physical capital
6. What are the principles of the whole community approach? How can this approach be implemented in your community?
7. What is business continuity? Discuss the steps of developing a BCP.
8. What is a BIA? What are the steps involved in making a BIA?

WEBSITES AND RESOURCES

FEMA Private Sector Resources
www.fema.gov/privatesector
DHS Private Sector Resources
www.dhs.gov/privatesector
Ready Campaign
www.ready.gov
National Preparedness Month
www.community.fema.gov/connect.ti/READYNPM
Stop. Think. Connect.
www.stopthinkconnect.org
FEMA Models of Public-Private Partnerships
www.fema.gov/privatesector/ppp_models.shtm
Comprehensive Preparedness Guide
www.fema.gov/pdf/about/divisions/npd/CPG_101_V2.pdf
Standard on Disaster/Emergency Management and Business Continuity Programs
www.nfpa.org/assets/files/pdf/nfpa1600.pdf
Emergency Management Accreditation Program
www.emaponline.org

REFERENCES

Anderson, R., & Pearce, I. (2013). Public-private partnerships in mitigation initiatives. In A. Jerolleman, & J. J. Kiefer (Eds.), *Natural hazard mitigation* (pp. 59–82). Boca Raton, FL: CRC Press.

Burby, R. (2006). Hurricane Katrina and the paradoxes of government disaster policy: Bringing about wise governmental decisions for hazadous areas. *Annals of the American Academy of Political and Social Science, 604*, 171–191.

ChicagoFIRST. (n.d.). History of ChicagoFIRST. Retrieved from <https://www.chicagofirst.org/about/about_us.jsp>. Accessed February 07, 2015.

de Bruijne, M., Boin, A., & van Eeten, M. (2010). Resilience: Exploring the concept and its meanings. In L. Comfort, A. Boin, & C. Demchak (Eds.), *Designing resilience: Preparing for extreme events* (pp. 13–32). Pittsburgh: University of Pittsburgh Press.

Federal Emergency Management Agency (FEMA). (n.d.a). Business continuity plan. Retrieved from <http://www.ready.gov/business/implementation/continuity>. Accessed February 07, 2015.

Federal Emergency Management Agency (FEMA). (n.d.b). Business impact analysis. Retrieved from <http://www.ready.gov/business-impact-analysis>. Accessed February 07, 2015.

Federal Emergency Management Agency (FEMA). (n.d.c). Citizen corps. Retrieved from <https://www.fema.gov/are-you-ready/citizen-corps>. Accessed February 07, 2015.

Federal Emergency Management Agency (FEMA). (n.d.d). IS-660: Introduction to public-private partnerships.

Federal Emergency Management Agency (FEMA). (n.d.e). IT disaster recovery plan. Retrieved from <http://www.ready.gov/business/implementation/IT>. Accessed February 07, 2015.

Federal Emergency Management Agency (FEMA). (n.d.f). Planning for a sustainable future: The link between hazard mitigation and livability. Retrieved from <http://www.fema.gov/media-library-data/20130726-1454-20490-3505/fema364.pdf>. Accessed February 09, 2015.

Federal Emergency Management Agency (FEMA). (n.d.g). Private sector. Retrieved from <https://www.fema.gov/private-sector>. Accessed February 07, 2015.

Federal Emergency Management Agency (FEMA). (n.d.h). Program management. Retrieved from <http://www.ready.gov/program-management>. Accessed February 03, 2015.

Federal Emergency Management Agency (FEMA). (n.d.i). Public-private partnerships. Retrieved from <https://www.fema.gov/public-private-partnerships>. Accessed February 07, 2015.

Federal Emergency Management Agency (FEMA). (n.d.j). Public private partnership models. Retrieved from <https://www.fema.gov/public-private-partnership-models>. Accessed February 04, 2015.

Federal Emergency Management Agency (FEMA). (n.d.k). Risk mitigation. Retrieved from <http://www.ready.gov/risk-mitigation>. Accessed February 03, 2015.

Federal Emergency Management Agency (FEMA). (2011). A whole community approach to emergency management: principles, themes, and pathways for actions. FEMA.

Lombardo, J., & Ryan, J. R. (2013). Building public health preparedness and food, and agriculture defense capabilities using whole community and one health concepts. *Journal of Homeland Security and Emergency Management, 10*(1), 77–93.

McEntire, D. (2005). Why vulnerability matters: Exploring the merit of an inclusive disaster reduction concept. *Disaster Prevention and Management, 14*(2), 206–222.

Mileti, D. (1999). *Disasters by design: A reassessment of natural hazards in the United States.* Washington, DC: Joseph Henry Press.

Oviatt, K., & Brett, J. (2010). The intrinsic link of vulnerability to sustainable development. In B. Phillps, et al. (Eds.), *Social vulnerability to disasters.* Boca Raton, FL: CRC Press.

Perry, R., & Lindell, M. (2007). *Emergency planning.* Hoboken, NJ: John Wiley & Sons.

Ready Campaign. (n.d.) Ready campaign. Retrieved from <http://www.ready.gov/>. Accessed February 06, 2015.

Rozdilsky, J. L. (2001). Second hazards assessment and sustainable hazards mitigation: Disaster recovery on Monsterrat. *Natural Hazards Review, 2*(2), 64–71. Retrieved from <http://ascelibrary.org/doi/abs/10.1061/%28ASCE%291527-6988%282001%292%3A2%2864%29>.

Schneider, R. O. (2006). Hazard mitigation: A priority for sustainable communities. In D. Paton, & D. Johnston (Eds.), *Disaster resilience: An integrated approach* (pp. 66–87). Springfield, IL: Charles C Thomas Publisher, Ltd.

Schwab, A. J., Eschelbach, K., & Brower, D. J. (2007). *Hazard mitigation and preparedness.* Hoboken, NJ: John Wiley & Sons.

Schwab, J.C. (Ed.) (2010). Hazard mitigation: Integrating best practices into planning. APA Planning Advisory Service Report Number 560. Washington, DC: American Planning Association. Retrieved from <http://wyohomelandsecurity.state.wy.us/pubs/haz_mit_png_best_practices.pdf>.

Sumaila, U. R., Cisneros-Montemayor, A. M., Dyck, A., Huang, L., Cheung, W., Jacquet, J., et al. (2012). Impact of the Deepwater Horizon well blowout on the economics of U.S. Gulf fisheries. *Canadian Journal of Fisheries and Aquatic Sciences, 69*, 499–510. Available from http://dx.doi.org/10.1139/f2011-171.

Tobin, G.A. (1999). Sustainability and community resilience: The Holy Grail of hazards planning? *Global Environmental Change Part B: Environmental Hazards, 1*(1), 13–25. Retrieved from <http://www.sciencedirect.com/science/article/pii/S1464286799000029>.

UN Economic and Social Commission for Asia and the Pacific (UN-ESCAP) (2008). *Building community resilience to natural disasters through partnership: sharing experience and expertise in the region.* New York: United Nations Publication.

UN Office for Disaster Risk Reduction (UNISDR). (n.d.) Private sector. Retrieved from <http://www.unisdr.org/partners/private-sector>. Accessed February 04, 2015.

UN Office for Disaster Risk Reduction (UNISDR). (2009). Terminology: "Resilience," UNISDR. Retrieved from http://www.unisdr.org/we/inform/terminology. Accessed February 04, 2015.

U.S. Department of Homeland Security (DHS). (2013). National Infrastructure Protection Plan. Retrieved from <http://www.dhs.gov/national-infrastructure-protection-plan>. Accessed May 14, 2015.

Whiteside, L. (2012). Sandy's economic impact. *CNN Money Report.* Retreived from <http://money.cnn.com/2012/10/30/news/economy/sandy-economic-impact/>.

Wildavsky, A. (1988). *Searching for safety.* New Brunswick, NJ: Transaction Books.

Thematic Section

2

Assessing Risk—Know Thy Enemy!

PREFACE

The second thematic section of this book introduces the full spectrum of natural and manmade hazards that we must contend with. As the saying goes, you must *know thy enemy*. In fact, Sun Tzu, in his epic book *The Art of War*, stated: "Know your enemy and know yourself and you can fight a hundred battles without disaster" (Tzu, 2003). Surely, this simplistic statement has profound implications for a general preparing his troops for war. If a commander knows the full extent of the resources his enemy has and how he intends to use them tactically, he has a tremendous advantage. Furthermore, he must also know his enemy well enough to estimate what strategic moves he may make.

> *Know your enemy and know yourself and you can fight a hundred battles without disaster.*
>
> **Sun Tzu, *The Art of War***

How can we apply this profound quote to the profession of emergency management and business continuity? In the first setting, our enemy is viewed as Mother Nature. There are few places on Earth that are immune from atmospheric, hydrological, and geologic hazards. Chapter 5 will detail those hazards, including wildfires and the putative effects of climate change. Students of the profession of emergency management must have a grasp on the terminology used to describe these hazards and some of the mechanics and science related to their occurrence.

In 1813, Commodore Oliver Hazard Perry wrote to his commanding officer, General William Henry Harrison, to tell him of a recent naval victory on Lake Erie. He said, "We have met the enemy and they are ours." In 1953, cartoonist Walt Kelly (the creator of the *Pogo* strip) paraphrased this popular quote and made it more apropos to this discussion: "We have met the enemy and he is us." The context is believed to be political, probably a reference to the fears of McCarthyism at that time. But the same quote appeared later, in the early 1970s, to commemorate Earth Day and refer to the evils of pollution (Liberman, 2009).

> *We have met the enemy and he is us.*
>
> **Walt Kelly, 1953**

Human beings are one of the few creatures on the earth to change their environment to their own liking. They do so in dramatic fashion, by extracting from the Earth all things that allow them to build structures, adjust temperature settings, feed the body, and fashion every implement to meet their needs and desires. They often do so at a cost to the environment, and sometimes to ourselves. Amassing and concentrating the substances that make it possible to do all these things bring us in close proximity to their inherent dangers.

Chapter 6 is a thorough discussion of manmade, or technological, hazards. All classes of hazardous materials are discussed here. In addition, the threat of civil unrest, terrorism, weapons of mass destruction (WMD), and cyberterrorism are covered in this hefty chapter.

We all wish that knowing our enemy would be enough. However, knowing the threats we face is just the beginning; it continues as a process. Once we understand a problem, we can then do something about it. The second thematic section of this book aims to provide the reader with an understanding of the threats we face from the natural world and the world that we create through the manipulations of humans and our manmade, technological hazards. Looking at these hazards regionally and locally allows us to study them historically and then rank-prioritize them. We should tackle those that have the potential to do us the greatest harm and occur more than rarely. This is the business of vulnerability assessment and impact analysis, which are discussed in Chapter 7. Finally, the THIRA process is detailed in Chapter 8.

Assessing risk is a starting point for progressive emergency management professionals. Having a thorough understanding of the threats and hazards we face leads to a better understanding of what we are vulnerable to. Vulnerability must be measured and measures must be applied to mitigate those hazards.

REFERENCES

Liberman, M. (2009). We've met the enemy, and that would be in the modal auxiliary, Bob. Blog. Retrieved from <http://languagelog.ldc.upenn.edu/nll/?p=1245>. Accessed February 10, 2015.

Tzu, S. (2003). *The art of war*. New York: Barnes & Noble Classics.

Hazard Identification—Natural Hazards

OBJECTIVES

The study of this chapter will enable you to:

1. Describe the types of natural hazards that can affect our environment and may lead to disaster

2. Discuss the formation and characteristics of atmospheric hazards

3. Discuss the formation and characteristics of hydrologic hazards

4. Discuss the formation and characteristics of geologic and other types of natural hazards

5. Understand key terms associated with natural hazards and relate them to emergency management

Essential Terminology: Tropical cyclone, Coriolis force, hurricane, Saffir-Simpson Hurricane Wind Scale (SSHWS), major hurricane, tornado, Enhanced Fujita (EF) scale, thunderstorm, watches, warnings, extreme heat, avalanche, snowstorm, blizzard, wind chill, flooding, drought, coastal erosion, earthquake, Richter scale, landslide, subsidence, tsunami, wildfire

Even with all our technology and the inventions that make modern life so much easier than it once was, it takes just one big natural disaster to wipe all that away and remind us that here on Earth, we're still at the mercy of nature.
Neil deGrasse Tyson, American astrophysicist

INTRODUCTION

This chapter provides a substantive overview of various natural hazards that can affect our environment. Based on geographic location, a community can face individual or multiple natural hazards. Some of these natural hazards are weather related or caused by the actions of Earth's atmosphere. These are known as *atmospheric hazards*, and they include tropical cyclones, hurricanes, tornadoes, thunderstorms and lightning, heat from extreme summer weather, avalanches, and severe winter storms. Other hazards are related to water or the Earth's hydrology cycle and are called *hydrologic hazards* (e.g., floods, drought, coastal erosion, etc.). Similarly, hazards that are related to the geology of the Earth are referred to as *geologic hazards*; these include earthquakes, landslides, and land subsidence. Tsunamis are mainly caused by earthquakes, but they displace a large volume of water, generally from the ocean. Also, wildfire hazards can be caused by a number of factors that include weather conditions and hydrology.

Risk assessment begins by identifying hazard events that potentially occur in the planning area. It is necessary for emergency managers and mitigation planners to have a clear understanding of various natural hazards—their characteristics, formation, and all pertinent information in order to develop an effective mitigation plan. In this chapter, natural hazards are classed into four categories:

Atmospheric Hazards:
- ❏ Tropical cyclones/hurricanes/typhoons
- ❏ Tornadoes
- ❏ Thunderstorms, lighting, and hailstorms
- ❏ Heat
- ❏ Avalanches
- ❏ Severe winter storms

Hydrologic Hazards:
- ❏ Floods
- ❏ Drought
- ❏ Coastal erosion

Geologic Hazards:
- ❏ Earthquake
- ❏ Landslides
- ❏ Subsidence

Other Hazards:
- ❏ Tsunami
- ❏ Wildfire

ATMOSPHERIC HAZARDS
Tropical Cyclones, Hurricanes, and Typhoons

Communities adjacent to tropical and subtropical waters are susceptible to violent coastal storms known as tropical cyclones. A **tropical cyclone** is a rotating, organized system of clouds and thunderstorms that originates over warm water and has a closed, low-level circulation (NHC, n.d.c). Cyclones are low-pressure systems; in the Northern Hemisphere, the winds rotate counterclockwise, while it is the opposite in the Southern Hemisphere. A typical tropical cyclone is about 300 mi (483 km) wide, although they can vary considerably in size. The main parts of a tropical cyclone are the rain bands on its outer edges, the eye, and the eyewall. The center of a cyclone is a relatively calm, clear area approximately 20—40 mi (32—64 km) across known as the *eye*. The eyewall is surrounded by dense clouds that contain the highest winds in the storm. The outer rain bands are composed of thunderstorms and can extend a few hundred miles from the center (NOAA, 1999). A cyclone can also produce storm surges and tornadoes. Since cyclones in the Northern Hemisphere rotate counterclockwise (see Figure 5.1), the right side of a storm is the most dangerous in terms of storm surge, winds, and tornadoes.

■ **FIGURE 5.1** In the Northern Hemisphere, hurricane winds circulate around the center in a counterclockwise fashion. Hurricane Katrina (2005) satellite image showing the movement of hurricane winds in a counterclockwise direction. *Image courtesy of NOAA.*

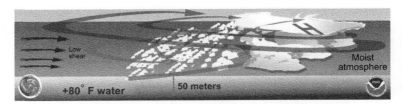

■ **FIGURE 5.2** The environmental conditions required for tropical cyclone development, which include ocean water temperature (minimum 80°F [26.5°C]) and its depth (min. 150 feet/50 m), moist atmosphere, thunderstorm activity, low wind shear, etc. *Image courtesy of NOAA.*

Tropical Cyclone Formation

In order to form a tropical cyclone, several environmental conditions (Figure 5.2) must be in place (Gray, 1968, 1979):

- Warm waters act as a fuel for tropical cyclones, and the temperature of the ocean water should be at least 80°F (26.5°C) and up to a sufficient depth, which should be at least 150 feet (50 m).
- Atmospheric instability is another necessary condition. Thunderstorm activity allows heat to be released from warm ocean waters, which contributes to cyclone development.
- High humidity near the mid-troposphere (3 mi/5 km) is required, as dry conditions are not conducive to thunderstorm activity.
- Tropical cyclones generally occur between 10° and 30° on both sides of the equator and do not form between 0° and 5°, as the **Coriolis force** due to the Earth's rotation is weak near the equator, which is needed to maintain the low pressure.
- Tropical cyclones cannot be developed spontaneously, so a preexisting disturbance is required near the surface.
- Low vertical wind shear (i.e., difference in wind speed and direction) is required so that it cannot prevent the tropical cyclone formation.

There are seven tropical cyclone basins worldwide, where tropical cyclones form on a regular basis (Figure 5.3). These are:

- Atlantic basin: Includes the North Atlantic Ocean, the Gulf of Mexico, and the Caribbean Sea
- Northeast Pacific basin: Extends from Mexico to about the International dateline
- Northwest Pacific basin: Extends from the international dateline to Asia, including the South China Sea
- North Indian basin: Includes the Bay of Bengal and the Arabian Sea

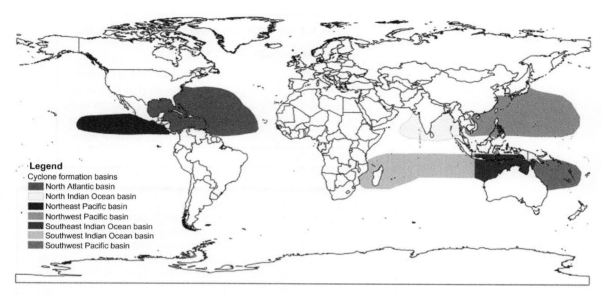

■ FIGURE 5.3 Seven tropical areas worldwide in the ocean where tropical cyclones are generally found. These areas are commonly known as *basins*. *Image is taken from Roy and Kovordányi (2012).*

- Southwest Indian basin: Extends from Africa to about 100°E
- Southeast Indian/Australian basin: Extends from 100°E to 142°E
- Australian/Southwest Pacific basin: Extends from 142°E to about 120°W

Tropical cyclone activity usually peaks in the late summer; however, each tropical cyclone basin has its own seasonal pattern. In the Atlantic basin, tropical cyclones are commonly known as **hurricanes;** in the Pacific region, they are known as **typhoons**. Hurricane season in the Atlantic basin officially begins on June 1 and ends on November 30. In the United States, the National Hurricane Center (NHC) uses the following classifications to categorize storms:

- **Tropical depression:** A tropical cyclone with maximum sustained winds of 38 mph (33 knots) or less.
- **Tropical storm:** A tropical cyclone with maximum sustained winds of 39 to 73 mph (34 to 63 knots).
- **Hurricane:** A tropical cyclone with maximum sustained winds of 74 mph (64 knots) or higher. In the western North Pacific, hurricanes are called *typhoons*; similar storms in the Indian Ocean and South Pacific Ocean are called *cyclones*.
- **Major hurricane:** A tropical cyclone with maximum sustained winds of 111 mph (96 knots) or higher, corresponding to a Category 3, 4, or 5 on the Saffir-Simpson Hurricane Wind Scale (SSHWS; Table 5.1).

Table 5.1 The Saffir-Simpson Hurricane Wind Scale

Hurricane Strength	Wind Speed
Category 1	74—95 mph (119—153 km/h)
Category 2	96—110 mph (154—177 km/h)
Category 3	111—129 mph (178—208 km/h)
Category 4	130—156 mph (209—251 km/h)
Category 5	157 mph (252 km/h) or more

Source: NHC (n.d.b).

Saffir-Simpson Hurricane Wind Scale

Civil engineer Herbert Saffir and meteorologist Robert Simpson developed the first version of the Saffir-Simpson Hurricane Wind Scale (SSHWS) in 1971 (Williams, 2005). Saffir initially devised a 1—5 scale based on wind speed mirroring the Richter magnitude scale used to describe earthquake intensity. Later, Simpson, the director of the NHC from 1967 to 1974, included the effects of storm surge and flooding into the scale. The NHC and the National Oceanic and Atmospheric Administration (NOAA) recently revised the scale to eliminate storm surge, flooding, rainfall, and location information; and a pure wind scale has been operational since 2010 (OFCM, 2013). The scale was found to be inaccurate regarding storm surge and other information for a number of hurricanes, including Hurricane Katrina in 2005 and Hurricane Ike in 2008, which prompted the agency to remove other information from the scale except the wind speed.

Naming of Tropical Cyclones

The World Meteorological Organization (WMO) is the main authority for issuing names to tropical cyclones worldwide. An international committee of the WMO solely maintains and updates the names. For the North Atlantic Basin, the six lists in Table 5.2 are used in rotation and recycled every six years, which means that the 2015 list will be used again in 2021. However, if a major hurricane that causes significant casualties or costs occurs, its name is retired from the list, and a new name adopted by the WMO committee (NHC, n.d.d). Usually, a name is assigned in alphabetical order from the current year's list when a storm intensifies into a tropical storm in the Atlantic basin.

Hurricane Watches and Warnings

In the United States, National Weather Service (NWS) watches and warnings are critical to being prepared for any dangerous weather hazard,

Table 5.2 Atlantic Tropical Storm/Hurricane Names

2015	2016	2017	2018	2019	2020
Ana	Alex	Arlene	Alberto	Andrea	Arthur
Bill	Bonnie	Bret	Beryl	Barry	Bertha
Claudette	Colin	Cindy	Chris	Chantal	Cristobal
Danny	Danielle	Don	Debby	Dorian	Dolly
Erika	Earl	Emily	Ernesto	Erin	Edouard
Fred	Fiona	Franklin	Florence	Fernand	Fay
Grace	Gaston	Gert	Gordon	Gabrielle	Gonzalo
Henri	Hermine	Harvey	Helene	Humberto	Hanna
Ida	Ian	Irma	Isaac	Ingrid	Isaias
Joaquin	Julia	Jose	Joyce	Jerry	Josephine
Kate	Karl	Katia	Kirk	Karen	Kyle
Larry	Lisa	Lee	Leslie	Lorenzo	Laura
Mindy	Matthew	Maria	Michael	Melissa	Marco
Nicholas	Nicole	Nate	Nadine	Nestor	Nana
Odette	Otto	Ophelia	Oscar	Olga	Omar
Peter	Paula	Philippe	Patty	Pablo	Paulette
Rose	Richard	Rina	Rafael	Rebekah	Rene
Sam	Shary	Sean	Sara	Sebastien	Sally
Teresa	Tobias	Tammy	Tony	Tanya	Teddy
Victor	Virginie	Vince	Valerie	Van	Vicky
Wanda	Walter	Whitney	William	Wendy	Wilfred

Source: NHC (n.d.d).

including hurricanes. A *watch* means that weather conditions are favorable for a hazard to occur. During a severe weather watch, it is important for people to continuously monitor the weather and discuss emergency/evacuation plans with their families in the case of threatening conditions. The NWS issues a tropical storm or a hurricane watch 48 h in advance of the anticipated onset of tropical-storm-force winds.

Consequently, a *warning* is issued when a weather hazard is imminent and requires immediate action. In the case of tropical storms or hurricanes, warnings are issued 36 h in advance of the anticipated onset of tropical-storm-force winds. A tropical storm warning means that tropical-storm conditions are expected within the specified area. Similarly, a hurricane warning means that hurricane conditions are expected within the specified area. So storm preparations need to be taken, and people should leave the threatened area immediately if directed by local officials (NHC, n.d.a).

Tornadoes

A **tornado** is a violently rotating column of air in contact with the ground that extends from a thunderstorm (see Figure 5.4). Although tornadoes dissipate within a very short time after formation, they are capable of making large-scale destructions as wind speeds may reach more than 300 mph (480 kmph). Tornadoes can be seen in many shapes and sizes, but typically, they appear as a funnel encircled with dust and debris. If the violently rotating column of air has not touched the ground, it is called a *funnel cloud* (NWS, n.d.a). Tornadoes on water are known as *waterspouts*. Tornadoes are more common in the United States than any other country. About 1200 tornadoes hit the United States each year on average. Most of these occur in a particular region known as

■ **FIGURE 5.4** Tornadoes are one of nature's most violent storms. In an average year, about 1200 tornadoes are reported across the United States, resulting in 80 deaths and more than 1500 injuries. In this image, a funnel cloud of a violent tornado touches the ground extending from a thunderstorm. *Image courtesy of NOAA.*

"Tornado Alley" (see Figure 5.5). Besides the United States, tornadoes occur in many parts of the world, including Australia, Europe, Africa, Asia, and South America. Bangladesh and Argentina experience the highest concentration of tornadoes outside the United States (NSSL, n.d.).

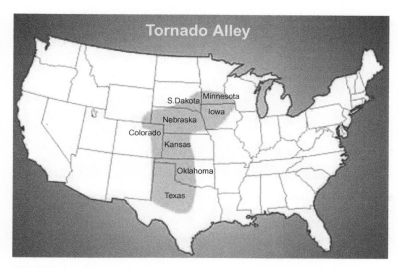

■ **FIGURE 5.5** A diagram of the so-called Tornado Alley, which makes up the plains states in the center of the United States. Tornadoes in this region are the most dangerous and happen most often in April, May, and June. *Image courtesy of NOAA.*

Tornado Formation

Scientists do not fully understand all the mechanics behind the formation of tornadoes. By far, the best-studied and the most common process of tornado formation is associated with supercell thunderstorms (Bryant, 2006). A *supercell* is a thunderstorm characterized by the presence of a high-level, rotating storm known as a *mesocyclone* (Glickman, 2000). When warm, moist air rises and mixes with cold air, it makes the weather unstable and creates thunderstorms. Then if winds change their speed and direction, it starts to rotate and produces a mesocyclone. Although not all tornadoes form mesocyclones, most of the larger and stronger ones are spawned from supercell storms with mesocyclones.

Tornadoes that are formed through supercells or mesocyclones usually follow a particular pattern or life cycle. The back of a mesocyclone is wrapped in a region of dry, descending air known as the *rear flank downdraft (RFD)*. This RFD also drags the mesocyclone toward the ground with it. The rainfall from the storm cools the air, and the mesocyclone, as

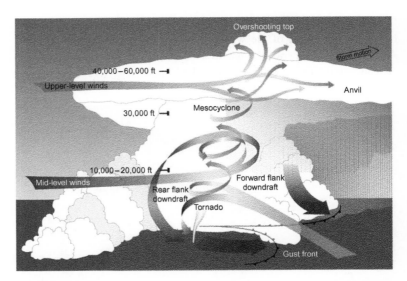

■ **FIGURE 5.6** This diagram shows the tornado formation process. Severe thunderstorms called *supercells* provide the ideal spawning ground for tornadoes. Warm, moist air colliding with cool, dry air causes a swirling updraft called a *mesocyclone*, and as the mesocyclone becomes more compact and intensifies, it may extend all the way to the ground in the form of a tornado. *Image courtesy of NOAA.*

it travels toward the ground, takes in cool, moist air. The convergence of this cool and warm air in the updraft causes a rotating wall cloud to form. The RFD also focuses the mesocyclone's base, causing it to siphon air from a smaller and smaller area on the ground. As the updraft intensifies, it creates an area of low pressure at the surface. This pulls the focused mesocyclone down in the form of a visible condensation funnel (NWS, n.d.b). This funnel cloud becomes a tornado as it touches the ground (see Figure 5.6).

Sometimes multiple tornadoes can be formed from a single weather system and lead to a tornado outbreak. The largest tornado outbreak on record occurred on April 25–28, 2011, which produced as many as 358 tornadoes and affected a number of U.S. states (*NOAA News*, 2012).

F and EF Scale

In 1971, Dr. T. Theodore Fujita of University of Chicago in collaboration with Allen Pearson of the National Severe Storms Forecast Center (currently known as the Storm Prediction Center) introduced a rating system to measure tornado intensity called the *Fujita scale*, commonly known as the *F-scale* (Longshore, 2009). The original F-scale was a 13-level scale (F0–F12) designed to correlate with the Beaufort scale and the Mach

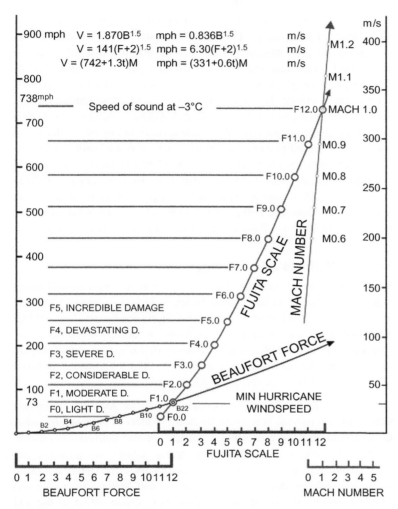

$V = 1.870B^{1.5}$ $mph = 0.836B^{1.5}$

$V = 141(F+2)^{1.5}$ $mph = 6.30(F+2)^{1.5}$

$V = (742+1.3t)M$ $mph = (331+0.6t)M$

■ FIGURE 5.7 The original F-scale as derived by Fujita (1971) was a theoretical 13-level scale (F0—F12) designed to smoothly connect the Beaufort scale and the Mach number scale. Dr. Ted Fujita published this diagram in *Satellite Mesometeorology Research Program Research Paper Number 91*, 1971, for public use.

number scale (SPC, n.d.). The lower level (F0 specifying little or no damage) is placed close to the eighth level of the Beaufort scale, as a Beaufort's level of zero indicates little or no wind. F1 corresponds to the twelfth level of the Beaufort scale, and F12 connects to the Mach number 1.0 (see Figure 5.7).

The scale was intended to use only F0–F5, though, as they covered all possible levels of damage to structures. Since its implementation in 1973,

NOAA updated its tornado database retrospectively, applying the F-scale to measure tornado strength. However, the wind speeds associated with the damage to each category in the F-scale was found higher than the actual wind speeds required to incur such damage. According to NOAA, "precise wind speed numbers are actually guesses and have never been scientifically verified. Different wind speeds may cause similar-looking damage from place to place—even from building to building. Without a thorough engineering analysis of tornado damage in any event, the actual wind speeds needed to cause that damage are unknown" (SPC, 2013). As a result, the Wind Science and Engineering Center (currently the National Wind Institute) at Texas Tech University undertook the Enhanced Fujita Scale project with a team of expert meteorologists and civil engineers and developed the Enhanced Fujita (EF) scale based on a number of engineering studies. In 2007, the F-scale was replaced by the EF scale (Figure 5.8).

Tornado Watches and Warnings

Similar to hurricane watches and warnings, tornado watches and warnings are also issued in the United States to protect citizens. A tornado watch is generally released by the NOAA Storm Prediction Center (SPC) when conditions are favorable for tornadoes. A tornado watch can cover parts of a state or several states, and citizens in that region should prepare for severe weather and stay tuned to radio or local TV channels to know when a warning is issued (NSSL, n.d.).

A tornado warning is issued for a certain area by the local NWS Forecast Office, when a tornado is reported by storm spotters or indicated by radar. Besides radio and TV broadcasts, warnings are also delivered to citizens by their local emergency management agency (EMA) through sirens and other means (e.g., wireless messages, social media, etc.). During a tornado warning, people in the affected area (defined and depicted by a polygon) should immediately take shelter, as there is a serious threat to life and property to those in the path of the tornado (NSSL, n.d.).

Thunderstorms, Lightning, and Hailstorms

A **thunderstorm** is defined as a local storm produced by a cumulonimbus cloud and accompanied by lightning and thunder (NWS, n.d.c). Thunderstorms usually occur in areas where masses of cold and warm air meet; these are known as *fronts*. A thunderstorm, which is sometimes referred to as a *thunder event*, is composed of lightning and rainfall, but it can intensify into a severe thunderstorm with damaging hail, high winds, tornadoes, and flash flooding (FEMA, 1997).

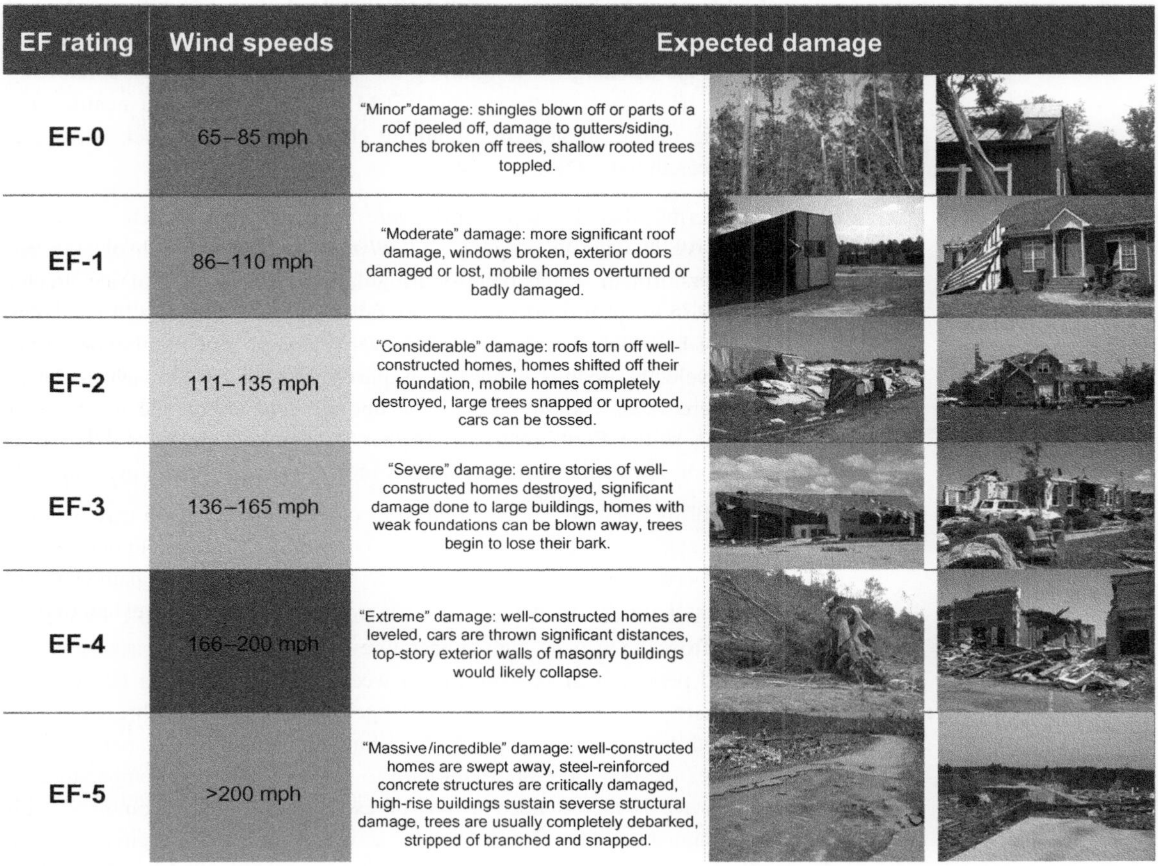

EF rating	Wind speeds	Expected damage		
EF-0	65–85 mph	"Minor"damage: shingles blown off or parts of a roof peeled off, damage to gutters/siding, branches broken off trees, shallow rooted trees toppled.		
EF-1	86–110 mph	"Moderate" damage: more significant roof damage, windows broken, exterior doors damaged or lost, mobile homes overturned or badly damaged.		
EF-2	111–135 mph	"Considerable" damage: roofs torn off well-constructed homes, homes shifted off their foundation, mobile homes completely destroyed, large trees snapped or uprooted, cars can be tossed.		
EF-3	136–165 mph	"Severe" damage: entire stories of well-constructed homes destroyed, significant damage done to large buildings, homes with weak foundations can be blown away, trees begin to lose their bark.		
EF-4	166–200 mph	"Extreme" damage: well-constructed homes are leveled, cars are thrown significant distances, top-story exterior walls of masonry buildings would likely collapse.		
EF-5	>200 mph	"Massive/incredible" damage: well-constructed homes are swept away, steel-reinforced concrete structures are critically damaged, high-rise buildings sustain severe structural damage, trees are usually completely debarked, stripped of branched and snapped.		

■ **FIGURE 5.8** EF Scale chart explaining the range of damage caused by tornadoes. *Image courtesy of NOAA.*

Besides the most dangerous supercell thunderstorms that produce tornadoes, the other two common types of thunderstorms include single cell thunderstorms and squall line (multicell) thunderstorms. Single-cell thunderstorms are individual or clusters of thunderstorms that are not usually severe. These are slow-moving storms, with the main hazards being lightning strikes and possible flooding that follows heavy rainfall. This type of thunderstorm usually occurs in the summer when the atmosphere is warm and unstable, but winds are weak (JSU, 2012). Squall-line or multicell thunderstorms consist of a line of storms that are often severe and cover large areas. Multicell storms may produce hail, strong winds, brief tornadoes, flooding, or any combination (NSSL, n.d.).

Lightning, which occurs during all thunderstorms, can kill people and damage property. Generated by the buildup of charged ions in a thundercloud, the discharge of a lightning bolt interacts with the best conducting object or surface on the ground (FEMA, 1997). The rapid heating and cooling of the air near the lightning channel causes a shock wave that produces thunder (NWS, 1994).

Hailstorms also develop from severe thunderstorms, which can cause extensive damage to property. A *hailstorm* is an outgrowth of a severe thunderstorm in which balls or irregularly shaped lumps of ice greater than 0.75 in. (1.91 cm) in diameter fall with rain (Gokhale, 1975). The size of hailstones is related to the severity and size of the thunderstorm. High-velocity updraft winds are required to keep hail in suspension in thunderclouds. The strength of the updraft depends on the intensity of heating at the Earth's surface. Higher temperature gradients relative to elevation above the surface result in increased suspension time and hailstone size (Bryant, 2006).

Heat

Extreme **heat** can be defined as a temperature that is over 10°F (5.5°C) or more from the average high temperature for a region and persists for a prolonged period, such as more than a week (City of Columbia EMA, n.d.). Exposure to extreme heat can be dangerous and even life threatening, as the high temperature along with high humidity slowdown evaporation and requires the body to work extra hard to maintain a normal temperature. A *heat wave* is an extended period of extreme heat, often combined with very high humidity. Due to human activities and built-up environments, urban areas, especially large metropolitan areas, are significantly warmer than its surrounding rural areas, a phenomenon known as the *Urban Heat Island (UHI) effect* (National Geographic, n.d.). Thus, the effect of a prolonged heat wave may be greater for people who live in urban areas than people living in rural areas.

Heat waves cause casualties, catastrophic crop failures, and severe power outages due to excessive use of air conditioning. More than 1250 people died in the United States from the disastrous heat wave of 1980, and about 700 people died during the 1995 Chicago heat wave (NWS, n.d.f). An infamous heat wave that occurred in 2003 killed more than 70,000 people in several countries in Europe (Robine et al., 2008).

Heat waves are easier to predict than other short-lived and localized weather events, such as tornadoes. A heat wave can be predicted several days ahead of its arrival. NOAA's heat alert forecasts are based on heat

NOAA's National Weather Service
Heat Index
Temperature (°F)

Relative Humidity (%)	80	82	84	86	88	90	92	94	96	98	100	102	104	106	108	110
40	80	81	83	85	88	91	94	97	101	105	109	114	119	124	130	136
45	80	82	84	87	89	93	96	100	104	109	114	119	124	130	137	
50	81	83	85	88	91	95	99	103	108	113	118	124	131	137		
55	81	84	86	89	93	97	101	106	112	117	124	130	137			
60	82	84	88	91	95	100	105	110	116	123	129	137				
65	82	85	89	93	98	103	108	114	121	128	136					
70	83	86	90	95	100	105	112	119	126	134						
75	84	88	92	97	103	109	116	124	132							
80	84	89	94	100	106	113	121	129								
85	85	90	96	102	110	117	126	135								
90	86	91	98	105	113	122	131									
95	86	93	100	108	117	127										
100	87	95	103	112	121	132										

Likelihood of Heat Disorders with Prolonged Exposure or Strenuous Activity

Caution | Extreme Caution | Danger | Extreme Danger

■ **FIGURE 5.9** The Heat Index Chart is used by weather forecasters and emergency preparedness professionals to measure how hot it really feels when relative humidity is factored in with the actual air temperature. For example, if the air temperature is 96°F (35.5°C) and the relative humidity is 65%, the heat index is 121°F (49°C). *Image courtesy of NOAA.*

index values. The heat index is also called the "apparent temperature." Heat index measures how hot the actual temperature of the air feels to a person when relative humidity is considered (NWS, n.d.g). Figure 5.9 shows the NOAA Heat Index Chart, from which the heat index temperature is measured. For instance, if the air temperature is 96°F (35.5°C) and the relative humidity is 65%, then based on the Heat Index Chart, the actual temperature would feel like 121°F (49°C).

Avalanches

An **avalanche** is a layer or mass of snow that slides or falls down a sloping surface. Avalanches are generally of three types—slab avalanches, loose snow avalanches, and wet avalanches (USDA, n.d.).

- *Slab avalanches*: When a more cohesive or harder slab of snow sits on top of a less cohesive or weaker layer of snow, the weaker layer can barely support the harder slab. Any additional weight or stress on the harder layer causes the weaker slab to collapse, which fractures the snowpack and causes an avalanche.
- *Loose snow avalanches*: This type of avalanche occurs when the slope of the terrain cannot hold the powdery grains of the snow.

- *Wet avalanches*: This type of avalanche occurs when temperatures above freezing persist for a prolonged period of time. That melts the surface snow and saturates the layers with water, which weakens the bond between the layers of snow (USDA, n.d.).

The factors that contribute to the occurrences of avalanches are the slope of the terrain, snowpack conditions, and the trigger. Avalanches are most common on slopes steeper than 30 deg (Washington EMD, n. d.). But a slope of such magnitude is not liable to cause an avalanche by itself. The snow on inclined terrain must be unstable for an avalanche to occur. Snow accumulated on the surface forms different layers due to the varying temperature, wind, and humidity during storm events throughout the winter. These layers are called *snowpack*. Weather conditions such as rain, temperature, pressure, and wind cause changes in the surface and subsurface layers. An unstable snowpack is developed when a slab (i.e., strong layer) sits on top of a weak layer. The lower weak layer can just barely hold up the upper slab. In such a situation, only slight additional weight on the upper slab causes the lower layer to collapse. As a result, avalanche occurs. A trigger is the source of stress that overloads the weak layer, causing it to collapse and the snowpack to avalanche. Triggers can be natural or due to human activities. Natural triggers include new snow, wind-driven snow, and rain, as well as rising temperatures that cause the snow to thaw. Human activity triggers include snowboarding, skiing, snowmobiling, and the use of explosives (CAC, n.d.).

The Avalanche Danger Scale is an ordinal, five-level warning system developed in Europe in 1993 to provide avalanche information to the public. The system was introduced to North America in 1994 and adopted by the United States and Canada with different descriptors of the danger levels (Statham et al., 2010). Figure 5.10 shows the front portion of the North American Public Avalanche Danger Scale Card.

Severe Winter Weather

During winter, severe storms can create several hazardous weather conditions, such as snowstorms, blizzards, freezing rain, extreme cold, and wind chill. Each type of hazard is defined in the following sections.

Snowstorm

A **snowstorm** is described as any storm marked by heavy snowfall. Snows are nothing but precipitation in frozen form, which occur

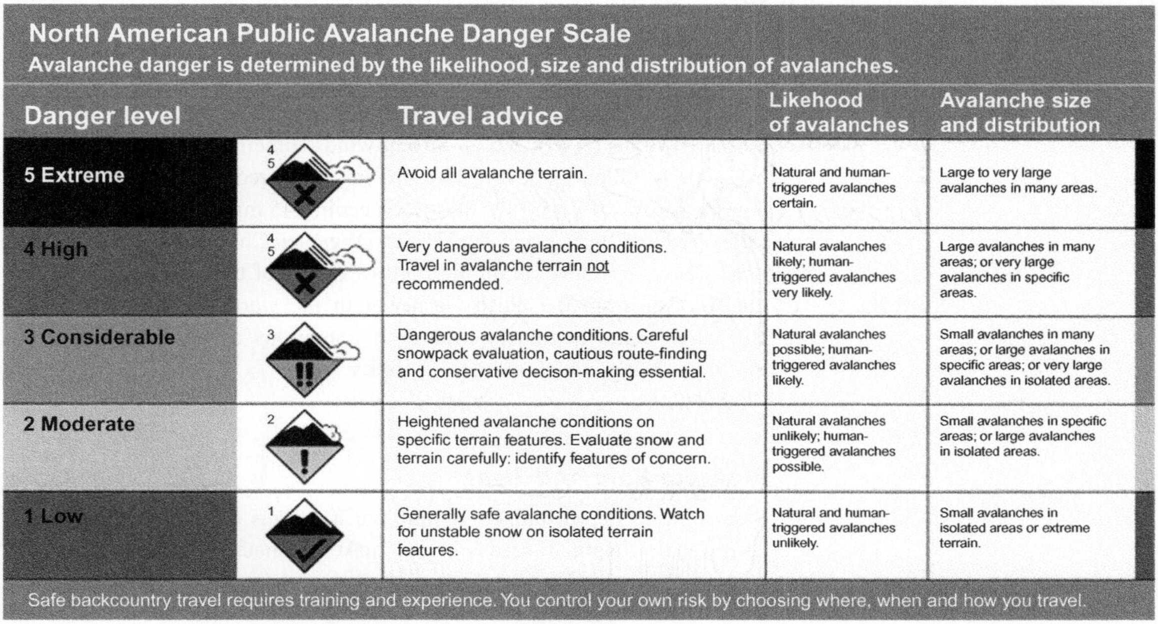

North American Public Avalanche Danger Scale
Avalanche danger is determined by the likelihood, size and distribution of avalanches.

Danger level		Travel advice	Likelihood of avalanches	Avalanche size and distribution
5 Extreme		Avoid all avalanche terrain.	Natural and human-triggered avalanches certain.	Large to very large avalanches in many areas.
4 High		Very dangerous avalanche conditions. Travel in avalanche terrain not recommended.	Natural avalanches likely; human-triggered avalanches very likely.	Large avalanches in many areas; or very large avalanches in specific areas.
3 Considerable		Dangerous avalanche conditions. Careful snowpack evaluation, cautious route-finding and conservative decison-making essential.	Natural avalanches possible; human-triggered avalanches likely.	Small avalanches in many areas; or large avalanches in specific areas; or very large avalanches in isolated areas.
2 Moderate		Heightened avalanche conditions on specific terrain features. Evaluate snow and terrain carefully: identify features of concern.	Natural avalanches unlikely; human-triggered avalanches possible.	Small avalanches in specific areas; or large avalanches in isolated areas.
1 Low		Generally safe avalanche conditions. Watch for unstable snow on isolated terrain features.	Natural and human-triggered avalanches unlikely.	Small avalanches in isolated areas or extreme terrain.

Safe backcountry travel requires training and experience. You control your own risk by choosing where, when and how you travel.

■ **FIGURE 5.10** North American Avalanche Danger Scale. Avalanche danger is determined by the likelihood, size, and distribution of avalanches. *Image courtesy of Northwest Avalanche Center.*

generally when the temperature in the atmosphere is below the freezing point. Frequent snowstorms can totally disrupt day-to-day activities. In the United States, the Northeast Snowfall Impact Scale (NESIS) ranks the severity of an East Coast snowstorm based on the snowfall amount and affected population (Silverman, 2007). NESIS was jointly developed by Paul J. Kocin of the Weather Channel and Louis W. Uccellini of the NOAA National Centers for Environmental Prediction (refer to Table 5.3).

Table 5.3 Categories for the NESIS

Category	NESIS Value	Description
1	1–2.499	Notable
2	2.5–3.99	Significant
3	4–5.99	Major
4	6–9.99	Crippling
5	10.0+	Extreme

Blizzard

According to the NWS, a **blizzard** is a weather condition that persists more than 3 h with large amounts of falling or blowing snow, wind speed greater than 35 mph (56 kmph), and visibility of less than one-quarter of a mile (0.4 km) (NWS, n.d.e). Strong winds sometimes pick up snow that has already fallen. A severe blizzard is considered to have temperatures near or below 10°F (5.5°C), winds exceeding 45 mph (72 kmph), and visibility reduced by snow to near zero (Weather Channel, n.d.b). Blizzard conditions often develop on the northwest side of the storm system when the cold air from the north clashes with the warm air from the south. Blizzards create extremely hazardous conditions as the high winds get the snow flying, which reduces visibility.

Freezing Rain and Sleet

Freezing rain is precipitated as rain, but it freezes upon the impact of the cold surface. Rain freezes when it makes contact with frozen surfaces such as the ground, trees, roofs, and cars. Even small accumulations of freezing rain over surfaces can create a significant hazard. Typically, this results in downed power lines, impassable roads, and closure of businesses and schools. Raindrops that freeze before hitting the surface is referred to as *sleet*. Sleet does not stick to the surface; rather, it accumulates like snow and causes hazardous conditions for driving and other forms of transportation.

Extreme Cold and Wind Chill

Winter storms often accompany periods of extreme cold. Extreme cold can also happen after a windstorm. Extreme cold and its effects can vary in different regions. In the southern United States, near-freezing temperatures can be considered as extreme cold. Such conditions can cause severe damage to crops and vegetation, which is harshly affected by freezing temperatures. In the north and the mountainous regions, subzero temperatures are normally considered extreme cold.

Wind chill is defined as the temperature that the human body feels outdoors due to the combined effect of air temperature and wind speed (NWS, n.d.d). In the same temperature conditions, we feel colder when the wind speed is higher. The heat emitted from the human body forms a layer of warm air adjacent to the skin. High winds rapidly move the heat away from the body, which makes humans feel colder. Frostbite or hypothermia can occur due to exposure to low wind chill.

COLD INJURIES — FROSTBITE AND HYPOTHERMIA

Frostbite occurs when body tissue freezes in extreme cold. The most susceptible parts of the human body are fingers, toes, earlobes, or the tip of the nose. Symptoms include a loss of feeling in the extremities and a white or pale appearance.

Hypothermia occurs when body temperature falls below 95°F. Young children under 2 years of age and the elderly over 60 years of age are the most susceptible to hypothermia. Symptoms include uncontrollable shivering, memory loss, disorientation, incoherence, slurred speech, drowsiness, and exhaustion (NWS, n.d.d). Immediate medical attention is required for frostbite and hypothermia conditions.

Figure 5.11 shows the wind chill for various temperatures and wind speeds.

Wind Chill Chart

Wind (mph)	\ Temperature (°F) 40	35	30	25	20	15	10	5	0	-5	-10	-15	-20	-25	-30	-35	-40	-45
5	36	31	25	19	13	7	1	-5	-11	-16	-22	-28	-34	-40	-46	-52	-57	-63
10	34	27	21	15	9	3	-4	-10	-16	-22	-28	-35	-41	-47	-53	-59	-66	-72
15	32	25	19	13	6	0	-7	-13	-19	-26	-32	-39	-45	-51	-58	-64	-71	-77
20	30	24	17	11	4	-2	-9	-15	-22	-29	-35	-42	-48	-55	-61	-68	-74	-81
25	29	23	16	9	3	-4	-11	-17	-24	-31	-37	-44	-51	-58	-64	-71	-78	-84
30	28	22	15	8	1	-5	-12	-19	-26	-33	-39	-46	-53	-60	-67	-73	-80	-87
35	28	21	14	7	0	-7	-14	-21	-27	-34	-41	-48	-55	-62	-69	-76	-82	-89
40	27	20	13	6	-1	-8	-15	-22	-29	-36	-43	-50	-57	-64	-71	-78	-84	-91
45	26	29	12	5	-2	-9	-16	-23	-30	-37	-44	-51	-58	-65	-72	-79	-86	-93
50	26	19	12	4	-3	-10	-17	-24	-31	-38	-45	-52	-60	-67	-74	-81	-88	-95
55	25	18	11	4	-3	-11	-18	-25	-32	-39	-46	-54	-61	-68	-75	-82	-89	-97
60	25	17	10	3	-4	-11	-19	-26	-33	-40	-48	-55	-62	-69	-76	-84	-91	-98

Frostbite Times [ ] 30 minutes [ ] 10 minutes [ ] 5 minutes

$$\text{Wind Chill (°F)} = 35.74 + 0.6215T - 35.75(V^{0.16}) + 0.4275T(V^{0.16})$$

Where, T = Air Temperature (°F) V = Wind Speed (mph)   *Effective 11/01/01*

■ **FIGURE 5.11** The Wind Chill chart shows the difference between actual air temperature and perceived temperature, and amount of time until frostbite occurs. For instance, if the temperature is 0°F and the wind is blowing at 15 mph, the wind chill is −19°F. At this wind chill temperature, exposed skin can freeze in 30 min. *Image courtesy of NOAA.*

Sperry-Piltz Ice Accumulation Index

In 2007, Sid Sperry, director of public relations, communications, and research for the Oklahoma Association of Electric Cooperatives, and Steven Piltz, meteorologist in charge at the NWS office in Tulsa, Oklahoma, developed the Sperry-Piltz Ice Accumulation Index (SPIA Index™; Erdman, 2013). The goal of this system is to categorize the potential impacts of impending ice storms, making it easier for the public to understand the potential for damage and take appropriate protective actions. The system is similar to the way that the Saffir-Simpson scale categorizes hurricanes and generalizes the type and level of damage to be expected for each category.

The developers describe the SPIA Index™ as "a forward-looking ice accumulation and ice damage prediction index that uses an algorithm of researched parameters that, when combined with National Weather Service forecast data, predicts the projected footprint, total ice accumulation, and resulting potential damage from approaching ice storms" (Sperry and Piltz, n.d.). Similar to other index tools, the SPIA Index™ uses forecast information to rate an upcoming ice storm's impact from 0 (minimal impact to exposed utility systems) to 5 (catastrophic damage) (Figure 5.12).

The Sperry-Piltz Ice Accumulation Index, or SPIA Index – Copyright, February, 2009

Ice Damage Index	DAMAGE AND IMPACT DESCRIPTIONS
0	Minimal risk of damage to exposed utility systems; no alerts or advisories needed for crews, few outages.
1	Some isolated or localized utility interruptions are possible, typically lasting only a few hours. Roads and bridges may become slick and hazardous.
2	Scattered utility interruptions expected, typically lasting 12 to 24 hours. Roads and travel conditions may be extremely hazardous due to ice accumalation.
3	Numerous utility interruptions with some damage to main feeder lines and equipment expected. Tree limb damage is excessive. Outages lasting 1–5 days.
4	Prolonged & widespread utility interruptions with extensive damage to main distribution feeder lines & some high voltage transmission lines/structures. Outages lasting 5–10 days.
5	Catastrophic damage to entire exposed utility systems, including both distribution and transmission networks. Outages could last several weeks in some areas. Shelters needed.

(Categories of damage are based upon combinations of precipitation totals, temperatures and wind speeds/directions.)

■ **FIGURE 5.12** The SPIA Index™, developed by Sid Sperry and Steven Piltz, to categorize the potential impacts of impending ice storms. Image is used with permission from the developers.

Sperry notes that the elements incorporated into the SPIA Index™ ranking go beyond just simple ice accumulation to include related phenomena, such as wind and temperature, as well. In a discussion with the Weather Channel, Sperry described how these two phenomena greatly influence the potential damage that an ice storm can cause to power lines (and tree limbs).

Sperry described a phenomenon on power lines called *galloping*, which can occur with relatively little ice accumulation but high winds. Providing lift similar to that over an aircraft's wing, power lines in this scenario can rise and fall 6 to 8 feet (1.8 to 2.4 m), leading to outages. Temperature also plays a role in an ice storm's destructive power, but not simply by determining what conditions will be too warm for ice. "You can have ice accretion on power lines, then warming (above freezing), followed by more freezing rain. When that happens, ice falls off (the power line), causing the line to bounce," Sperry said (Erdman, 2013).

HYDROLOGIC HAZARDS
Floods

Flooding is defined as the accumulation of water within a body of water and the overflow of excess water onto adjacent floodplain lands. A *floodplain* is the land adjoining the channel of a river, stream, ocean, lake, or other watercourse or water body that is susceptible to flooding (FEMA, 1997). According to the Federal Emergency Management Agency (FEMA), most floods fall into one of three major categories: riverine flooding; coastal flooding, and shallow flooding (FEMA, n.d.). Each is described next:

- *Riverine flooding*: This is flooding that occurs along a channel. *Channels* are defined as features (e.g., river, stream, creeks, etc.) that carry water through and out of a watershed, also known as a *basin* or *catchment area* (Figure 5.13). When downstream channels receive more rain than normal or a channel is blocked by an ice jam or debris, the resultant excess water overflows adjacent to the floodplain. This is referred to as *overbank flooding*. This is the most common type of flood event (FEMA, n.d.).
- *Coastal flooding*: This type of flooding occurs in coastal areas when storm surge results from coastal storms such as hurricanes. Tsunamis may also cause flooding in coastal areas. According to the Intergovernmental Panel on Climate Change (IPCC), sea level rise from climate change could be a significant factor for coastal flooding in the next 100 years, as it may cause permanent

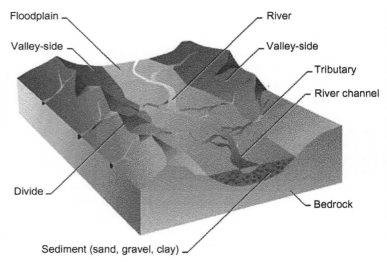

Floodplain
River
Valley-side
Valley-side
Tributary
River channel
Divide
Bedrock
Sediment (sand, gravel, clay)

U.S. Army Corps of Engineers

■ **FIGURE 5.13** Floodplains perform an important function of storing floodwaters and sediment produced by the riverine watershed under conditions of heavy rain or snowfall. In an unaltered watershed, large volumes of water can remain in a floodplain for a long period of time and gradually are released through the river channel. *Image courtesy of the U.S. Army Corps of Engineers.*

inundation of low-lying areas. Also, climate change would increase the frequency and intensity of hurricanes, and as a result, storm surge would become more frequent (Nicholls et al., 2007).

■ *Shallow flooding*: This flooding occurs in flat areas where water cannot drain away easily, mainly due to lack of channels. In areas where there are no defined channels, floodwaters drain out at a uniform depth over a large area known as *sheet flow*. This usually occurs during extended periods of rainfall, as the ground cannot absorb all the rainwaters. In some areas, it can create a ponding effect (i.e., floodwaters do not drain off, but remain in the temporary ponds until they evaporate or infiltrate the soil. Urban drainage systems can also cause shallow flooding. An urban drainage system (comprising of ditches, storm sewers, retention ponds, and other facilities) is typically designed to handle the amount of water expected during a 10-year rainstorm (describes a greater rainfall event that is likely to occur once every 10 years). When the system is overloaded by a larger storm, it creates shallow flooding in the area (FEMA, n.d.).

Flash Flooding

Flash flooding primarily occurs due to extensive rainfall from an intense rainstorm in a very short time frame. Flash floods cause most flood-related deaths in the United States (FEMA, n.d.). Hilly areas or areas with steep slopes are highly vulnerable to flash floods because of the high-velocity flows and short warning time. Banks of small streams and drainage channels can also be dangerous as they can be flooded suddenly. Flash floods can also occur from a dam or levee failure, or a sudden release of ice-jam flooding. Flash flooding frequently occurs in urban areas, as much of the ground is covered by an impermeable surface that does not allow rainwater to be absorbed. As a result, the water flows over the surface as runoff and can result in a flash flood. During a flash flood, cars can be swept away quickly in just 2 feet (0.6 m) of rushing water. Walking is also dangerous as 6 in. of moving water can make someone fall. People should move immediately to higher ground if there is any possibility of flash flooding.

Drought

Drought is usually defined as a water shortage for an extended period of time caused by a deficiency of rainfall. During severe droughts, agricultural crops do not mature, wildlife and livestock are undernourished, land values decline, and unemployment increases (FEMA, 1997). As drought involves a severe shortage of water, it affects industrial production, hydroelectric power, recreation, navigation, and even day-to-day human consumption. Water quality declines and severity of wildfires may increase during a drought. Drought occurs almost everywhere in the world. In the United States, it is one of the costliest natural disasters, as the average cost of losses due to drought each year exceeds $1 billion (NCDC, n.d.a).

Although drought is mainly a water-related hazard, it has been studied and defined by a number of disciplines from different perspectives. Wilhite and Glantz (1987) categorized the definitions of drought into four major types:

- *Meteorological drought*: Meteorologists define drought on the basis of the degree of dryness and the duration of the dry period. It is defined by comparing the current precipitation or dryness to the average or normal precipitation or dryness. Since meteorological conditions that result in drought vary greatly from region to region, the definition of a meteorological drought must be region specific. For instance, the average or normal precipitation of a high-rainfall area is not similar to that of a low-rainfall area, so the baselines are different.
- *Agricultural drought*: Refers to a situation where the deficiency of moisture in the soil hinders the growth of a particular crop and results

in substantial loss of yield. Agricultural drought links various characteristics of meteorological drought to agricultural impacts focusing on rainfall shortage, departure from normal meteorological factors such as evapotranspiration, soil moisture shortage, and reduced ground water level.

■ *Hydrological drought*: Occurs when the deficiency of precipitation contributes to inadequate surface or subsurface water supplies such as lower than normal stream flow, groundwater level, and reservoir level. The influence of hydrological drought on watershed or river basin is the determinant of its severity. While the effects of precipitation deficiencies can immediately create the situations that can be defined as meteorological or agricultural drought, it takes more time to manifest the effects of precipitation deficiency in the components of hydrological cycle.

■ *Socioeconomic drought*: Socioeconomic drought associates the supply and demand of a particular economic good with drought conditions. It occurs when the shortage of water supply causes demand to exceed the supply of an economic good. In other words, it is a situation where the physical water shortage affects people (Wilhite & Glantz, 1987).

Many indices attempt to define the severity of different types of drought. These include the Palmer Drought Severity Index, Percent of Normal Index, Standardize Precipitation Index, Crop Moisture Index, Surface Water Supply Index, and Reclamation Drought Index (FEMA, 1997). According to Redmond (1991), a single index cannot describe everything about the original data, and an index can only give an approximation of the real event. However, in the United States, the **Palmer Drought Severity Index (PDSI)** has been used frequently in research studies, as well as in operational drought monitoring (NCDC, n.d.b). Many U.S. government agencies and states rely on the PDSI to initiate the drought relief program.

The PDSI, developed by Wayne Palmer in 1965, compares the amount of precipitation in an area during a specified time period with the average or normal amount of precipitation for the same timeframe (see Figure 5.14). This index is based on a supply-and-demand concept of the water balance equation, using not only precipitation, but also temperature, evaporation, soil runoff, and soil recharge data to measure drought (Weather Channel, n.d.a).

Coastal Erosion

Coastal erosion is defined as the wearing away of land surfaces and loss of beach, shoreline, or dune material as a result of natural or coastal processes or human-induced influences (Skaggs & McDonald, 1991). Natural processes that cause coastal erosion include the actions of winds, waves,

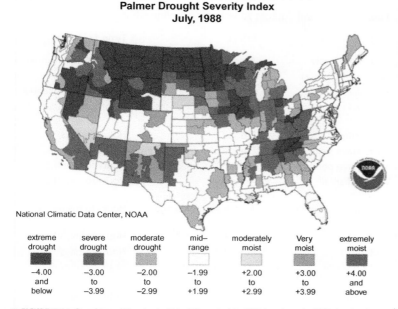

Palmer Drought Severity Index
July, 1988

National Climatic Data Center, NOAA

extreme drought	severe drought	moderate drought	mid–range	moderately moist	Very moist	extremely moist
−4.00 and below	−3.00 to −3.99	−2.00 to −2.99	−1.99 to +1.99	+2.00 to +2.99	+3.00 to +3.99	+4.00 and above

■ **FIGURE 5.14** Drought conditions in the United States in July 1988 based on the PDSI classifications. The darkest green areas represent extremely moist areas, and the purple areas represent extreme drought conditions. *Image courtesy of NOAA.*

and currents, while human influences include the construction of seawalls, groins, and jet ties, navigation of inlets and dredging, and other interruptions of physical processes (FEMA, 1997). Coastal erosion can occur from rapid, short-term, daily, seasonal, or annual episodic events, such as storm waves, storm surge, overwash, and rip currents. This can occur within a short term (e.g., hours to days) or over a long-term period. Table 5.4 provides a detailed list of natural factors that affects shoreline changes (NAS, 1990).

The average annual erosion rate is used in land-use and hazard management to define areas where development should be limited and special measures should be used for construction. Many coastal U.S. states have setback rules in place based on the average annual erosion rate along the shoreline (Schwab, Eschelbach, & Brower, 2007).

GEOLOGIC HAZARDS

Earthquake

An **earthquake** or a seismic activity is a sudden, rapid shaking of the Earth caused by the breaking and shifting of rock beneath the surface (American Red Cross, n.d.). In Greek, the word *seismos* means to quake, so *seismology* refers to the study of earthquakes.

Table 5.4 Natural Factors Affecting Shoreline Changes

Factor	Effect	Time Scale
Sediment supply (sources and sinks)	Accretion/erosion	Decades to millennia
Sea level rise	Erosion	Centuries to millennia
Sea level change	Erosion (for increases in sea level)	Months to years
Storm surge	Erosion	Hours to days
Large wave height	Erosion	Hours to months
Short wave period	Erosion	Hours to months
Waves of small steepness	Accretion	Hours to months
Alongshore currents	Accretion, no change, or erosion	Hours to millennia
Rip currents	Erosion	Hours to months
Underflow	Erosion	Hours to days
Inlet presence	Net erosion; high instability	Years to centuries
Overwash	Erosional	Hours to days
Wind	Erosional	Hours to centuries
Subsidence	Erosion	Years to millennia

The outermost shell of the Earth is comprised of the crust and upper mantle (see Figure 5.15) and is known as the *lithosphere* (*lithos*, rocky; and *sphaira/sphere*, rigid). The lithosphere is broken up into a number of tectonic plates (see Figure 5.16). These tectonic plates are able to move because the lithosphere is cooler and more rigid than the layer beneath it (known as the *asthenosphere*). Earthquakes are largely caused by the movement of these thin tectonic plates (Kious & Tilling, 1996). However, earthquakes can also be generated by volcanic activity, landslides, or human activity such as nuclear tests.

The action of plate tectonic forces cause fractures on the Earth's crust, with the largest forming the boundaries between the plates. The process by which one tectonic plate moves under another plate and sinks into the mantle at convergent boundaries is known as *subduction*, and the area is called a *subduction zone* (Defant, 1998). Energy releases associated with active faults are the cause of most earthquakes. The surface where the fracture happens or two blocks slip is called the *fault* or *fault plane* (see Figure 5.17). The location below the Earth's surface where the earthquake starts is called the *hypocenter*, and the location directly above it on the surface of the earth is called the *epicenter* (USGS, n.d.e).

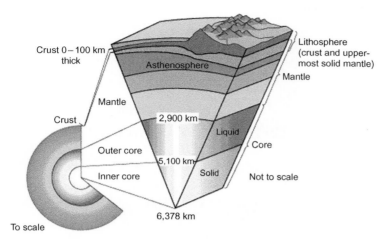

■ **FIGURE 5.15** Image depicts the lithosphere of the Earth. Cutaway diagram of Earth's internal structure (to scale) with inset showing a detailed breakdown of structure (not to scale). The lithosphere remains rigid for very long periods of geologic time, in which it deforms elastically and through brittle failure. *Image courtesy of the U.S. Geological Survey.*

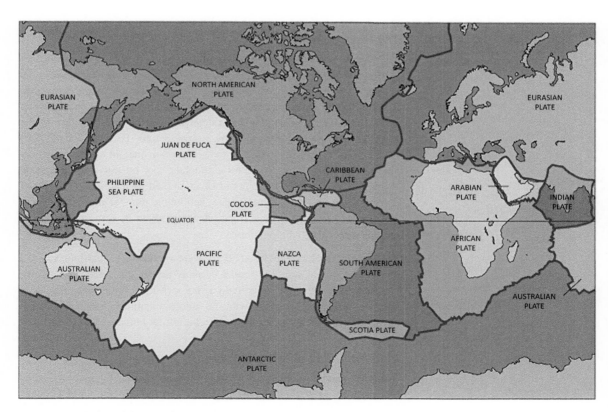

■ **FIGURE 5.16** The layer of the Earth is broken into a dozen or so rigid slabs (called *tectonic plates* by geologists) that are moving relative to one another. The map shows the locations of the Earth's plates. *Image courtesy of the U.S. Geological Survey.*

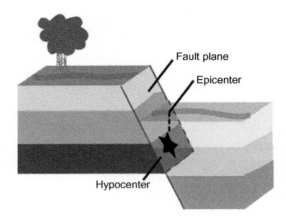

■ **FIGURE 5.17** The diagram depicts the fault plane and epicenter/hypocenter of an earthquake. An earthquake is what happens when two blocks of the earth suddenly slip past one another. The surface where they slip is called the *fault* or *fault plane*. The *epicenter* is the point on the Earth's surface vertically above the *hypocenter* (or focus), the point in the crust where a seismic rupture begins. *Image courtesy of the U.S. Geological Survey.*

The Richter Scale

The Richter scale, developed by Charles Francis Richter of the California Institute of Technology in 1935, uses a logarithmic scale to measure the energy released during an earthquake. Seismic waves, or the vibrations from earthquakes, are recorded by an instrument called a *seismograph*. The magnitude of an earthquake is determined from the logarithm of the amplitude of waves recorded by seismographs (USGS, n.d.d). The Richter scale assigns a number to express the magnitude of an earthquake. For instance, a moderate earthquake can be rated as magnitude 5.1, and a strong earthquake could be computed as magnitude 6.1. Since it is based on the logarithmic scale, each whole number represents a tenfold increase in magnitude and the release of about 31 times more energy than the preceding whole number.

The Richter scale is not used to measure damage. An earthquake in a densely populated area that results in many deaths and considerable damage may have the same magnitude as a shock in a remote area that does nothing more than frighten wildlife. Large-magnitude earthquakes that occur beneath the ocean may not even be felt by humans (USGS, n.d.d).

Modified Mercalli Intensity Scale

There are numerous intensity scales that measure the intensity or effect (damage) of an earthquake on the Earth's surface. In the United States,

Perceived shaking	Not felt	Weak	Light	Moderate	Strong	Very strong	Severe	Violent	Extreme
Potential damage	None	None	None	Very light	Light	Moderate	Moderate/Heavy	Heavy	Very heavy
Peak ACC (%g)	<0.17	0.17–1.4	1.4–3.9	3.9–9.2	9.2–18	18–34	34–65	65–124	>124
Peak vel (cm/s)	<0.1	0.1–1.1	1.1–3.4	3.4–8.1	8.1–16	16–31	31–60	60–116	>116
Instrumental intensity	I	II-III	IV	V	VI	VII	VIII	IX	X+

■ **FIGURE 5.18** Classifications of the Modified Mercalli Intensity Scale. The scale is composed of 12 levels that represent increasing intensity based on observed effects. The lower numbers on the intensity scale generally deal with the manner in which the earthquake is felt by people. The higher numbers of the scale are based on observed structural damage. Structural engineers usually contribute information for assigning intensity values of VIII or above. *Image courtesy of the U.S. Geological Survey.*

the Modified Mercalli Intensity Scale has been used for this purpose. American seismologists Harry Wood and Frank Neumann developed this scale in 1931. The scale is composed of 12 levels that represent increasing intensity based on observed effects (USGS, n.d.c). The scale has no mathematical basis; the lower numbers in Roman numerals generally deal with the manner in which the earthquake is felt by people, and the higher numbers are based on observed structural damage (Figure 5.18).

The following is an abbreviated description of the 12 levels of the Modified Mercalli Intensity Scale:

I. Not felt except by a few people under special conditions.
II. Felt by persons at rest, on upper floors of buildings.
III. Felt indoors. Vibrations similar to the passing of light trucks.
IV. Felt indoors by many, and outdoors by few people during the day. Vibrations similar to the passing of heavy trucks.
V. Felt outdoors. Small, unstable objects displaced or overturned.
VI. Felt by all. Furniture moved; a few instances of fallen plaster. Slight damage.
VII. Difficult to stand. Damage to masonry and chimneys.
VIII. Partial collapse of masonry. Frame house moved.
IX. Masonry seriously damage or destroyed.
X. Many buildings and bridges destroyed.
XI. Rails bent greatly. Pipelines severely damaged.
XII. Damage nearly total.

Ring of Fire

A large number of earthquakes and volcanic eruptions occur in a zone surrounding the Pacific Ocean basin known as the *Ring of Fire* (see Figure 5.19). This area, also called the *Circum-Pacific belt*, is a direct result of plate tectonics and movement of lithospheric plates. About 90% of the world's earthquakes occur here (USGS, n.d.a), and 75% of the

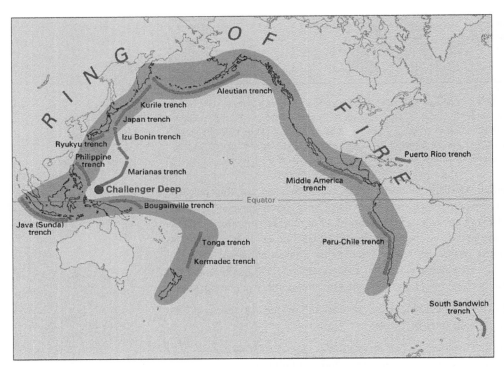

■ **FIGURE 5.19** Volcanic arcs and oceanic trenches partly encircling the Pacific Basin form the so-called Ring of Fire, a zone of frequent earthquakes and volcanic eruptions. The trenches are shown in blue-green. The volcanic island arcs (not labeled here) are parallel to, and always landward of, the trenches. For example, the island arc associated with the Aleutian Trench is represented by the long chain of volcanoes that make up the Aleutian Islands. *Image courtesy of the U.S. Geological Survey.*

world's active and dormant volcanoes are found in this region (Rosenberg, n.d.). The area is comprised of a series of oceanic trenches, volcanic arcs, belts, and plate movements.

Landslide

"Landslide is the movement of a mass rock, debris, or earth down the slope" (Cruden, 1991). The primary reason for **landslides** is the action of gravity as it exceeds the strength of the Earth's materials. However, there are other contributing factors (either natural or human-induced) that can affect slope stability and cause landslides. According to the USGS (2004), factors that can cause landslides include:

- Geological causes
    a. Weak or sensitive materials
    b. Weathered materials

Type of movement		Type of material		
		Bedrock	Engineering soils	
			Predominantly coarse	Predominantly fine
Falls		Rock fall	Debris fall	Earth fall
Topples		Rock topple	Debris topple	Earth topple
Slides	Rotational	Rock slide	Debris slide	Earth slide
	Translational			
Lateral spreads		Rock spread	Debris spread	Earth spread
Flows		Rock flow (deep creep)	Debris flow	Earth flow
			(soil creep)	
Complex		Combination of two or more principal types of movement		

■ **FIGURE 5.20** Types of landslides and materials involved; adapted from Varnes (1978). *Image courtesy of the U.S. Geological Survey.*

   c. Sheared, jointed, or fissured materials
   d. Adversely oriented discontinuity (bedding, schistosity, fault, unconformity, contact, etc.)
   e. Contrast in permeability and stiffness of materials
■ Morphological causes
   a. Tectonic or volcanic uplift
   b. Glacial rebound
   c. Fluvial, wave, or glacial erosion of slope toe or lateral margins
   d. Subterranean erosion (solution, piping)
   e. Deposition loading slope or its crest
   f. Vegetation removal (by fire, drought)
   g. Thawing
   h. Freeze-and-thaw weathering
   i. Shrink-and-swell weathering
■ Human causes
   a. Excavation of slope or its toe
   b. Loading of slope or its crest
   c. Drawdown (of reservoirs)
   d. Deforestation
   e. Irrigation
   f. Mining
   g. Artificial vibration
   h. Water leakage from utilities

There are different types of landslides based on the materials involved (see Figure 5.20) and the type of movement (Varnes, 1978):

■ *Falls*: Falls are sudden movements of geologic materials, such as rocks and boulders, that become detached from steep slopes or cliffs.

Falls are highly influenced by gravity, mechanical weathering, and the presence of interstitial water.

- *Topples*: Topples are forward rotation of a unit under the actions of gravity and forces exerted by adjacent units or by fluids in cracks.
- *Flows*: There are five basic categories of flows, which differ from one another in fundamental ways.
  a. *Debris flow*: A debris flow is a form of rapid mass movement in which a combination of loose soil, rock, organic matter, air, and water mobilizes as a slurry that then flows downslope. Debris flows are commonly caused by intense surface-water flow due to heavy precipitation or rapid snowmelt.
  b. *Debris avalanche*: This is a variety of very rapid to extremely rapid debris flow.
  c. *Earthflow*: Earthflows have a characteristic hourglass shape. The slope material liquefies and runs out, forming a bowl or depression at the head and also widening at the base.
  d. *Mudflow*: A mudflow is an earthflow consisting of material that is wet enough to flow rapidly and that contains at least 50% sand-, silt-, and clay-sized particles. In some instances, such as in newspaper reports, mudflows and debris flows are commonly referred to as *mudslides*.
  e. *Creep*: Creep is the imperceptibly slow, steady, downward movement of slope-forming soil or rock. Movement is caused by shear stress that is sufficient to produce permanent deformation, but too small to produce shear failure. There are generally three types of creep: (i) seasonal, where movement is affected by seasonal changes in soil moisture and soil temperature; (ii) continuous, where shear stress continuously exceeds the strength of the material; and (iii) progressive, where slopes are reaching the point of failure as other types of mass movements.
- *Lateral spreads*: Lateral spreads usually occur on gentle slopes or flat terrain. The dominant mode of movement is lateral extension accompanied by shear or tensile fractures. The failure is caused by liquefaction, the process whereby saturated, loose, cohesionless sediments (usually sands and silts) are transformed from a solid into a liquefied state. Failure is usually triggered by rapid ground motion, such as that experienced during an earthquake, but it can also be artificially induced. The failure starts suddenly in a small area and spreads rapidly.

Combination of two or more of these types is known as a *complex landslide* (USGS, 2004).

Subsidence

Land subsidence, commonly known as *subsidence*, is a gradual settling or sudden sinking of the Earth's surface due to subsurface movement of the Earth's materials. The main causes of subsidence include underground mining; extraction of natural gas; earthquakes; dissolution of limestone, which can result in sinkholes; and groundwater-related events (e.g., aquifer-system compaction, drainage of organic soils, and hydrocompaction).

Subsidence is a global problem. In the United States, more than 17,000 sq. mi. (44,000 sq. km) in 45 states (an area roughly the size of New Hampshire and Vermont combined) have been directly affected by subsidence (USGS, n.d.b).

Sinkholes

A **sinkhole** is a natural depression in the ground caused by some form of collapse or natural processes (Robertson, 2013). Sinkholes are common in "karst terrain" (named after the Karst Plateau, a region in Slovenia where this occurs regularly), where rock below the land surface can be dissolved by groundwater circulating through it. Soluble rocks include salt beds, gypsum, limestone, and other carbonate rock. When it rains, water moves down through the soil, and the rocks begin to dissolve and spaces and caverns develop underground. When the space becomes too big, it cannot hold the land surface above it, which can lead to a sudden collapse and create a sinkhole. Places with such topography are highly susceptible to sinkholes. For instance, Florida is largely underlain by limestone and therefore is highly vulnerable to damage from sinkholes. About 20% of the United States is underlain by karst terrain and hence susceptible to sinkholes (Robertson, 2013).

OTHER HAZARDS

Tsunami

A **tsunami** is a series of water waves generated by any disturbance that displaces a large water mass (Boyarsky & Shneiderman, 2002). *Tsunami* is a Japanese word that translates in English to "harbor wave." Although a tsunami is a water-related hazard, most of them (about 90–95%) are caused by earthquakes, and the remainder occur due to volcanic eruptions, landslides, explosions, meteorites, and other disturbances (refer to Figure 5.21). Tsunamis are different from storm surges in that they are not wind-generated and do not resemble a normal sea wave. Wind-generated waves typically have high frequencies and short wavelengths (i.e., distance between wave crests) as compared to the low frequencies and long wavelengths of tsunami waves (Keim, 2013).

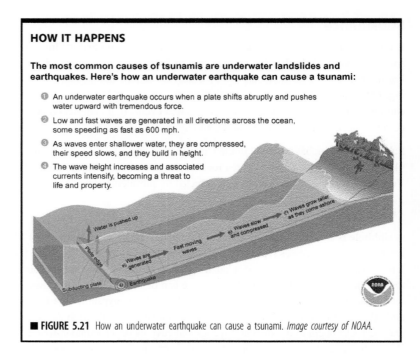

HOW IT HAPPENS

The most common causes of tsunamis are underwater landslides and earthquakes. Here's how an underwater earthquake can cause a tsunami:

① An underwater earthquake occurs when a plate shifts abruptly and pushes water upward with tremendous force.

② Low and fast waves are generated in all directions across the ocean, some speeding as fast as 600 mph.

③ As waves enter shallower water, they are compressed, their speed slows, and they build in height.

④ The wave height increases and associated currents intensify, becoming a threat to life and property.

■ **FIGURE 5.21** How an underwater earthquake can cause a tsunami. *Image courtesy of NOAA.*

Tsunamis have been reported since ancient times. The Global Historical Tsunami Database at the NOAA National Geophysical Data Center contains a worldwide tsunami database spanning from 2000 B.C. to the present (http://www.ngdc.noaa.gov/hazard/tsu_db.shtml). About 80% of tsunamis occur in the Pacific Ocean due to earthquakes and volcanic activity in the Ring of Fire. However, they can occur anywhere near large water bodies, including lakes. The Indian Ocean tsunami that occurred on December 26, 2004, was one of the deadliest natural disasters on record, killing more than 200,000 people in 14 countries. On March 11, 2011, a powerful earthquake of 9.0 magnitude hit the coast of Japan, which also caused tsunami and nuclear accidents in the Fukushima Daiichi nuclear power plant. According to the World Bank estimates, it caused about $235 billion in losses (Kim, 2011) and killed more than 15,000 people.

Wildfire

A **wildfire** is an uncontrolled fire that spreads quickly over a large wild area, such as grasslands and primary forests. It differs from other fires in that it takes place in the wilderness or in an outdoor wooded area that acts as a source of fuel for the wildfire (FEMA, 1997). Although wildland fires (i.e., fires fueled by natural vegetation) are the most common form, there can be other types of wildfires as well. The following four categories of wildfires are experienced in the United States and throughout the world:

- *Wildland fires*, which typically occur in parks, forests, savannah, or in large areas of natural vegetation
- *Interface or intermix fires*, combining wildland and urban areas, where both vegetation and the built-up environment provide fuel
- *Firestorms*, which usually occur because of extreme weather and where suppression is virtually impossible
- *Prescribed fires*, which are intentionally set fires for beneficial purposes

Either natural conditions or humans can cause wildfires with little effort. A lightning strike or the sun's heat can spark a fire in dry conditions. Human carelessness can also cause wildfires during campfires, fireworks, smoking, or trash burning (Discovery Channel, n.d). According to experts (IRIN, 2011) "Fire activity is increasing in many global regions, for many different reasons, including climate change, changes in vegetation, and changing impacts of people."

Wildfires occur all over the United States, but they are a common occurrence in the western parts of the country because of arid conditions. In southern Australia, wildfires (commonly also known as *bushfires*) happen frequently during the summer months due to the hot and dry climate. Wildfires also occur in Israel, Russia, Botswana, Greece, Brazil, Indonesia, and in many other countries around the world (IRIN, 2011).

Keetch-Byram Drought Index

The Keetch-Byram Drought Index (KBDI) is used to estimate the potential risk of wildfire (see Figure 5.22) based on soil moisture and other conditions related to drought (i.e., temperature and rainfall). Keetch and Byram (1968) developed and published the index for the U.S. Department of Agriculture—Forest Service. The KBDI is based on 8 in. (20 cm) of available moisture and expresses moisture deficiency in hundredths of an inch, thus the scale ranges from 0 to 800. Zero is the point

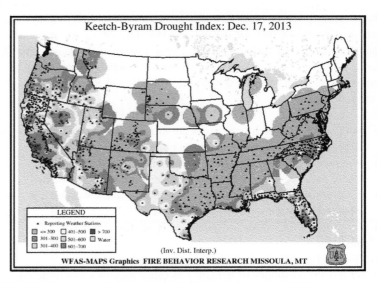

Keetch-Byram Drought Index: Dec. 17, 2013

LEGEND
▲ Reporting Weather Stations

(Inv. Dist. Interp.)
WFAS-MAPS Graphics FIRE BEHAVIOR RESEARCH MISSOULA, MT

■ **FIGURE 5.22** The potential wildfire risks in the United States on December 17, 2013, based on the KBDI. Hot and dry weather across the western United States and Florida in December contributed to an increase in observed fire danger. *Image courtesy of the U.S. Forest Service.*

of no moisture deficiency and 800 is the maximum drought that is possible. Based on the index, there are seven drought stages:

Index	Stage
0–99	0
100–199	1
200–299	2
300–399	3
400–499	4
500–599	5
600–699	6
700–800	7

As weather is an important factor to initiate wildfires, and moisture content influences fire intensity, the KBDI index is a useful tool for firefighters, emergency managers, and mitigation planners to mitigate the risk of wildfires.

CRITICAL THINKING

Which natural hazards strike with little or no warning, allowing the least amount of time for emergency managers in terms of decision-making?

■ CONCLUSION

Emergency managers and mitigation planners need to have a clear under-standing of all natural hazards. Hazard identification is the first step of the risk assessment process to develop a hazard mitigation plan. This chapter provides the reader a substantive overview of various natural hazards that can affect our communities and often lead to disasters. Atmospheric hazards are weather related phenomena caused by the actions of our atmosphere, which include tropical cyclones or hurricanes, tornadoes, thunderstorms and lightning, heat from the extreme summer weather, avalanches and severe winter storms. Hydrologic and geologic hazards include floods, drought, coastal erosion, earthquake, landslides, and land subsidence. Tsunamis are mainly caused by earthquakes, but they displace a large volume of water generally from the ocean. Wildfire hazards can be caused by a number of factors that include weather condi-tions and hydrology. The formation, characteristics, and other relevant information of these natural hazards are discussed in this chapter.

DISCUSSION QUESTIONS

1. What environmental conditions are required for a tropical cyclone to form?
2. Why is extreme heat as a weather condition a concern for emergency managers?
3. Describe hazardous weather conditions that occur in the winter months.
4. What is drought? Discuss the four major types of drought defined by Wilhite and Glantz (1987).
5. Why is drought a concern for emergency managers?
6. What causes earthquakes? Discuss the importance of the Richter scale and the Modified Mercalli Intensity Scale? How do the two scales differ?
7. Explain the following terms:
   a. Watches and warnings
   b. Saffir-Simpson Hurricane Wind Scale (SSHWS)
   c. Enhanced Fujita Scale (EFS)
   d. Supercell
   e. Squall line thunderstorms
   f. Hypothermia
   g. Flash flooding
   h. Ring of Fire
   i. Sinkhole
   j. Keetch-Byram Drought Index (KBDI)

WEBSITES

Hurricane: The NOAA provides more information on hurricanes in the e-book *Hurricane Basics*, available through the NOAA website:
http://hurricanes.noaa.gov/pdf/hurricanebook.pdf

Tornado: To learn more about tornado myths, facts, and safety tips, visit:
http://www.ncdc.noaa.gov/oa/climate/severeweather/tornadosafety.html

Severe Weather 101: NOAA National Severe Storms Laboratory questions and answers about weather phenomena, including tornadoes, thunderstorms, lightning, hail, floods, damaging winds, and winter weather, can be found at:
http://www.nssl.noaa.gov/education/svrwx101/

Volcanic Eruption: Although volcanic eruption was not discussed separately in this chapter, it can pose serious threat to areas that are prone to volcanic activity such as lava flows, volcanic ash, volcanic mudflows, etc. Mount St. Helens in Washington State erupted on May 18, 1980, killing 57 people, including a USGS geologist. The USGS scientists recorded their experiences before, during, and after the Mount St. Helens eruption in this video: http://gallery.usgs.gov/videos/234

REFERENCES

American Red Cross. (n.d.). Earthquake safety checklist. Retrieved from <http://www.redcross.org/images/MEDIA_CustomProductCatalog/m4240216_Earthquake.pdf>. Accessed January 11, 2015.

Boyarsky, I., & Shneiderman, A. (2002). Natural and hybrid disasters—Causes, effects, and management. *Topics in Emergency Medicine, 24*(3), 1–25.

Bryant, E. (2006). *Natural hazards* (2nd ed.). Cambridge, UK: Cambridge University Press.

Canadian Avalanche Center (CAC). (n.d.). Online avalanche course: Common triggers. Retrieved from <http://www.avalanche.ca/cac/training/online-course/avalanche-formation/common-triggers>. Accessed January 21, 2015.

City of Columbia EMA. (n.d.). Extreme heat. Retrieved from <http://www.gocolumbiamo.com/EM/Natural_Disasters/extreme_heat.php>. Accessed January 20, 2015.

Cruden, D. M. (1991). A very simple definition for a landslide. *IAEG Bulletin* 27–29.

Defant, M. (1998). Voyage of discovery: From the Big Bang to the ice age. Tampa, FL: Mancorp, 325.

Discovery Channel. (n.d.). What are some common causes of wildfires? Retrieved from <http://curiosity.discovery.com/question/some-common-causes-of-wildfires>. Accessed January 17, 2015.

Erdman, J. (2013). Category 5 ice storm? A new index rates ice storm impacts. The Weather Channel. Retrieved from <http://www.weather.com/news/weather-winter/rating-ice-storms-damage-sperry-piltz-20131202>. Accessed October 04, 2014.

Federal Emergency Management Agency (FEMA). (1997). Multi-hazard risk identification and assessment: A cornerstone of the National Mitigation Strategy, prepared in support of the International Decade for Natural Disaster Reduction. Retrieved from <http://www.fema.gov/media-library-data/20130726-1545-20490-4487/mhira_in.pdf>. Accessed January 11, 2015.

Federal Emergency Management Agency (FEMA). (n.d.). IS-9: Managing flood plain development through the National Flood Insurance Program. Independent Study Course. Retrieved from <https://www.fema.gov/pdf/floodplain/is_9_complete.pdf>. Accessed January 06, 2015.

Fujita, T. (1971). *Proposed characterization of tornadoes and hurricanes by area and intensity*. Chicago: University of Chicago Press.

Glickman, T. S. (Ed.), (2000). *Glossary of meteorology* (2nd ed.). Cambridge, MA: American Meteorological Society.

Gokhale, R. (1975). *Hailstorms and hailstone growth*. Albany, NY: State University of New York Press.

Gray, W. (1968). A global view of the origin of tropical disturbances and storms. *Monthly Weather Review*, *96*, 669–700.

Gray, W. (1979). Hurricanes: Their formation, structure, and likely role in the tropical circulation. In D. B. Shaw (Ed.), *Meteorology over tropical oceans* (pp. 155–218). Bracknell, U.K: Royal Meteorological Society.

IRIN. (2011). Developing countries hardest hit by wildfires. Retrieved from <http://www.irinnews.org/report/93072/global-developing-countries-hardest-hit-by-wildfires>. Accessed October 04, 2014.

Jacksonville State University (JSU). (2012). Disaster-resistant university: Hazard mitigation plan. Jacksonville, AL: JSU.

Keetch, J., & Byram, G. (1968). A drought index for forest fire control. USDA Forest Service Research Paper SE-38, Southeastern Forest Experiment Station, Asheville, NC, pp. 33.

Keim, M. (2013). Health-related impacts of tsunami disasters. In S. Mambretti (Ed.), Tsunami: from fundamentals to damage mitigation. Billerica, MA: WIT Press.

Kim, V. (2011). Japan damage could reach $235 billion, World Bank estimates. *LA Times*. Retrieved from <http://www.latimes.com/business/la-fgw-japan-quake-world-bank-20110322,0,3799976.story>. Accessed October 04, 2014.

Kious, W., & Tilling, R. (1996) The dynamic earth: The story of plate tectonics. USGS publication. Retrieved from <http://pubs.usgs.gov/gip/dynamic/dynamic.html>. Accessed October 04, 2014.

Longshore, D. (2009). Encyclopedia of hurricanes, typhoons, and cyclones (New ed.). New York: Checkmark Books.

National Academy of Sciences (NAS) (1990). *Managing coastal erosion*. Washington, DC: National Academy Press. Retrieved from <http://www.nap.edu/catalog/1446/managing-coastal-erosion>. Accessed October 4, 2014.

National Climatic Data Center (NCDC). (n.d.a). Drought termination and amelioration. Retrieved from <http://www.ncdc.noaa.gov/temp-and-precip/drought/recovery.php>. Accessed January 14, 2015.

National Climatic Data Center (NCDC). (n.d.b). North American drought: A paleo perspective. Retrieved from <http://www.ncdc.noaa.gov/paleo/drought/drght_alleve.html>. Accessed January 14, 2015.

National Geographic. (n.d.). Urban Heat Island: Encyclopedia entry. Retrieved from <http://education.nationalgeographic.com/education/encyclopedia/urban-heat-island/?ar_a=1>. Accessed October 04, 2014.

National Hurricane Center (NHC). (n.d.a). Hurricane preparedness: Watches and warning. Retrieved from <http://www.nhc.noaa.gov/prepare/wwa.php>. Accessed October 04, 2014.

National Hurricane Center (NHC). (n.d.b). Saffir-Simpson Hurricane Wind Scale. Retrieved from <http://www.nhc.noaa.gov/aboutsshws.php>. Accessed October 04, 2014.

National Hurricane Center (NHC). (n.d.c). Tropical cyclone climatology. Retrieved from <http://www.nhc.noaa.gov/climo/>. Accessed October 04, 2014.

National Hurricane Center (NHC). (n.d.d). Tropical cyclone names. Retrieved from <http://www.nhc.noaa.gov/aboutnames.shtml>. Accessed October 19, 2014.

National Oceanic and Atmospheric Administration (NOAA). (1999). Hurricane basics. Retrieved from <http://hurricanes.noaa.gov/pdf/hurricanebook.pdf>. Accessed October 04, 2014.

National Severe Storms Laboratory (NSSL). (n.d.). Severe Weather 101: Tornado basics. Retrieved from <http://www.nssl.noaa.gov/education/svrwx101/tornadoes/>. Accessed October 04, 2014.

National Weather Service (NWS). (1994). Thunderstorms and lightning: The underrated killers. Brochure No. NOAA/PA 92053. Washington, DC: NWS.

National Weather Service (NWS). (n.d.a). A comprehensive glossary of weather terms for storm spotters. Retrieved from <http://www.srh.noaa.gov/oun/?n=spotterglossary>. Accessed October 04, 2014.

National Weather Service (NWS). (n.d.b). Advanced spotters' field guide. Retrieved from <http://www.crh.noaa.gov/oax/skywarn/adv_spotters.pdf>. Accessed October 04, 2014.

National Weather Service (NWS). (n.d.c). Glossary. Retrieved from <http://w1.weather.gov/glossary/index.php?letter=t>. Accessed October 04, 2014.

National Weather Service (NWS). (n.d.d). Wind chill terms and definitions, Retrieved from <http://www.nws.noaa.gov/om/windchill/windchillfaq.shtml>. Accessed October 04, 2014.

National Weather Service (NWS). (n.d.e). Winter weather terms. Retrieved from <http://www.weather.gov/bgm/WinterTerms>. Accessed October 05, 2014.

National Weather Service (NWS). (n.d.f). Severe weather awareness—heat waves. Retrieved from <http://www.weather.gov/mkx/taw-heat_waves>. Accessed October 09, 2015.

National Weather Service (NWS). (n.d.g). What is the Heat Index? Retrieved from <http://www.srh.noaa.gov/ama/?n=heatindex>. Accessed October 09, 2015.

Nicholls, R. J., et al. (2007). Coastal systems and low-lying areas. In *Climate change 2007: Impacts, adaptation, and vulnerability. Contribution of Working Group II to the Fourth Assessment Report of the Intergovernmental Panel on Climate Change.* Cambridge, UK: Cambridge University Press.

NOAA News. (2012). 2011 tornado information. Retrieved from <http://www.noaa-news.noaa.gov/2011_tornado_information.html>. Accessed October 04, 2014.

Office of the Federal Coordinator for Meteorology (OFCM). (2013). National Hurricane Operations Plan. Retrieved from <http://www.ofcm.gov/nhop/13/pdf/00-front%20matter%20plus%20cover.pdf>. Accessed October 04, 2014.

Redmond, K. (1991). Climate monitoring and indices. In D. A. Wilhite, D. A. Wood, & P. A. Kay (Eds.), *Drought management and planning* (pp. 29–33). International Drought Information Center, Department of Agricultural Meteorology, University of Nebraska—Lincoln, IDIC Technical Report Series 91-1.

Robertson, J. (2013). The science of sinkholes. USGS science features. Retrieved from <http://www.usgs.gov/blogs/features/usgs_top_story/the-science-of-sinkholes/>. Accessed October 04, 2014.

Robine, J.-M., et al. (2008). Death toll exceeded 70,000 in Europe during the summer of 2003. *Comptes Rendus Biologies, 331*(2), 171−178.

Rosenberg, M. (n.d.). Pacific Ring of Fire. Retrieved from <http://geography.about.com/cs/earthquakes/a/ringoffire.htm>. Accessed October 04, 2014.

Roy, C., & Kovordányi, R. (2012). Tropical cyclone track forecasting techniques—A review. *Atmospheric Research, 104−105*, 40−69.

Schwab, A. K., Eschelbach, K., & Brower, D. J. (2007). *Hazard mitigation and preparedness*. Hoboken, NJ: John Wiley and Sons.

Silverman, A. (2007). The Northeast Snowfall Impact Scale (NESIS). National Weather Service. Retrieved from <http://www.erh.noaa.gov/rnk/Newsletter/Fall%202007/NESIS.htm>. Accessed October 04, 2014.

Skaggs, L., & McDonald, F. (1991). *National economic development procedures manual: Coastal storm damage and erosion*. Ft. Belvoir, VA: U.S. Army Corps of Engineers.

Sperry, S., & Piltz, S. (n.d.). What is the Sperry-Piltz Ice Accumulation Index? Retrieved from <http://www.spia-index.com/>. Accessed January 11, 2015.

Statham, et al. (2010). The North American Public Avalanche Danger Scale. *Proceedings of the 2010 International Snow Science Workshop, Squaw Valley, California*. Retrieved from <http://www.fsavalanche.org/NAC/techPages/articles/10_ISSW_Statham_etal_DangerScale.pdf>. Accessed January 23, 2015.

Storm Prediction Center (SPC). (2013). Online tornado FAQ. Retrieved from <http://www.spc.noaa.gov/faq/tornado/>. Accessed October 04, 2014.

Storm Prediction Center (SPC). (n.d.). The Enhanced Fujita Scale. Retrieved from <http://www.spc.noaa.gov/efscale/>. Accessed October 04, 2014.

U.S. Department of Agriculture (USDA). (n.d.). Kinds of avalanches, USDA Forest Service National Avalanche Center, Retrieved from <http://www.fsavalanche.org/Default.aspx?ContentId=4&LinkId=10&ParentLinkId=9>. Accessed October 04, 2014.

U.S. Geological Survey (USGS). (2004). Landslide types and process, Retrieved from <http://pubs.usgs.gov/fs/2004/3072/fs-2004-3072.html>. Accessed October 04, 2014.

U.S. Geological Survey (USGS). (n.d.a). Earthquake glossary—Ring of Fire. Retrieved from <http://earthquake.usgs.gov/learn/glossary/?term=Ring%20of%20Fire>. Accessed October 04, 2014.

U.S. Geological Survey (USGS). (n.d.b). Land subsidence. Retrieved from <http://water.usgs.gov/ogw/subsidence.html>. Accessed October 04, 2014.

U.S. Geological Survey (USGS). (n.d.c). The Modified Mercalli Intensity Scale, Earthquake Hazards Program. Retrieved from <http://earthquake.usgs.gov/learn/topics/mercalli.php>. Accessed October 04, 2014.

U.S. Geological Survey (USGS). (n.d.d). The Richter Magnitude Scale, Earthquake Hazards Program. Retrieved from <http://earthquake.usgs.gov/learn/topics/richter.php>. Accessed October 04, 2014.

U.S. Geological Survey (USGS). (n.d.e). The science of earthquakes, Earthquake Hazards Program. Retrieved from <http://earthquake.usgs.gov/learn/kids/eqscience.php>. Accessed October 04, 2014.

Varnes, D. J. (1978). Slope movement types and processes. In R. L. Schuster, & R. J. Krizek (Eds.), Landslides—Analysis and control. Transportation Research Board, Special Report 176 (pp. 11–33). Washington, DC: National Research Council.

Washington EMD. (n.d.). Hazard profile—Avalanche, State of Washington Emergency Management Department. Retrieved from <http://www.emd.wa.gov/plans/documents/ehmp_5.2_avalanche.pdf>. Accessed October 04, 2014.

Weather Channel. (n.d.a). Palmer Drought Severity Index (PDSI). Retrieved from <http://www.weather.com/encyclopedia/heat/palmer.html>. Accessed October 04, 2014.

Weather Channel (n.d.b). Winter storms. Retrieved from <http://www.weather.com/encyclopedia/winter/types.html>. Accessed October 04, 2014.

Wilhite, D., & Glantz, M (1987). Understanding the drought phenomenon: The role of definitions. In D. Whilhite, & W. E. Easterling (Eds.), *Planning for drought* (pp. 11–27). Boulder, CO: Westview Press.

Williams, J. (2005). Hurricane scale invented to communicate storm danger. *USA Today*. Retrieved from <http://usatoday30.usatoday.com/weather/hurricane/whscale.htm>. Accessed October 04, 2014.

Hazard Identification— Manmade Hazards

OBJECTIVES

The study of this chapter will enable you to:

1. Define technological hazards

2. List and describe the nine classes of hazardous materials as detailed by the U.S. Department of Transportation (DOT)

3. Discuss civil unrest and its potential for general disorder and chaos

4. Discuss the historical perspective of terrorism, select terrorist groups, and international and domestic terrorist threats

5. List reasons why terrorists might use weapons of mass destruction (WMDs) and discuss potential terrorist targets and tactics

6. Define WMDs and chemical, biological, radiological, nuclear, and explosives (CBRNE)

7. Discuss the broad classifications of chemical warfare agents (CWAs) and some of their important physical properties

8. Identify the classification and sources of toxic industrial chemicals (TICs)

9. Identify characteristics, exposure routes, exposure indicators and health effects for exposure to select CWAs

10. Describe technological threats due to radiation, radioactive material and nuclear weapons

11. Define the following terms associated with radiation: external exposure, external contamination, internal exposure, and internal contamination

12. Describe the different types of explosives, devices to trigger and deliver explosives, and the potential damage from explosives to human health and infrastructure.

Essential Terminology: Technological hazards, chemical, biological, radiological, nuclear, and explosives (CBRNE), dirty bomb, Category A agents, chemical warfare agent (CWA), toxic industrial chemical (TIC), toxic industrial material (TIM), hazardous materials (hazmat)

Mankind already holds in its hands too many of the seeds of its own destruction.

President Richard M. Nixon, as he signed an executive order putting an end to the U.S. biological weapons program in November 1969

INTRODUCTION TO TECHNOLOGICAL HAZARDS

The purpose of this chapter is to inform the reader of the wide spectrum of technological hazards that should be considered by every emergency manager planning mitigation strategies for his or her community. Technological hazards, or manmade hazards, are wide ranging and emanate from manufacturing, transportation, and the use of substances such as radioactive materials, chemicals, explosives, flammables, pesticides, herbicides, and disease agents; oil spills on land, coastal waters, or inland water systems; and even debris from space (FEMA, 2001). Cutter (1993) also described them as "... the interaction between technology, society, and the environment" and that they "arise from our individual and collective use of technology."

Given the broad range of hazards, there is a plethora of information presented herein. However, it is not all inclusive or exhaustive. There are far too many individual technical hazards for all of them to be covered here. Detailed information on thousands of chemical, biological, and radiological hazards can be accessed in the numerous references listed at the end of this chapter. Many of the most serious technological hazards are discussed in this chapter.

Instructors using this textbook may wish to break up this chapter into two separate lessons to allow students ample time to review all the materials and consider the implications. Students may ask "Why give us so much technical information about technical hazards?" Well, in the immortal words of Sun Tzu (2002), "Know your enemy." To truly develop effective strategies that will lessen or prevent the effects of technical hazards, you must understand them, know where to find information about them, and possibly even reach out to subject matter experts that can assist you. So, the details here need not be memorized. The reader should come to appreciate how much potential these hazards have for doing harm and how difficult it can be to mitigate their effects, which is especially noteworthy when they are utilized in acts of terrorism.

DOT Classes of Hazardous Materials

Hazardous materials (hazmat) are classified according to their physical state. These materials exist in solid, liquid, or gaseous states. The U.S. Department of Transportation (DOT) has placed hazardous materials into nine classes (DOT Pipeline and Hazardous Materials Safety Administration, 2012). Refer to Figure 6.1 for details. They are as follows:

- *DOT Class 1*—Includes mass explosion hazards, projectiles, blast and insensitive explosives (munitions that are chemically stable enough to withstand mechanical shocks, fire, and impact by shrapnel). Examples include 2'4'6-trinitrotolene (TNT), dynamite, and nitroglycerin.
- *DOT Class 2: Gases*—A gas is a material that has a vapor pressure greater than 300 43.5 psi at 50°C (122°F) or is completely gaseous at 20°C (68°F) at a standard pressure of 14.7 psi. Examples are hydrogen, chlorine, nitrogen, and hydrogen cyanide.
- *DOT Class 3: Flammable liquids; combustible liquids*—A flammable liquid is a liquid with a flash point of 60.5°C (141°F) or lower. A combustible liquid has a flash point greater than 60.5°C (141°F) and below 93°C (100°F). U.S. regulations permit a reclassification of flammable liquids to combustible if the flash point is between 38°C (100°F) and 60.5°C (141°F). Examples include diethyl ether, gasoline, acetone, and diesel.
- *DOT Class 4: Flammable solids; spontaneously combustible materials; and dangerous when wet materials/water-reactive substances*—These are broken down as follows:

   A flammable solid is a self-reactive material that reacts to excessively high temperatures or by contamination without the introduction of oxygen.

   A spontaneously combustible material can ignite within minutes after coming in contact with oxygen.

   Water-reactive substances can react violently, even explosively, with water.

   Examples include nitrocellulose, magnesium, white phosphorous, and sodium.

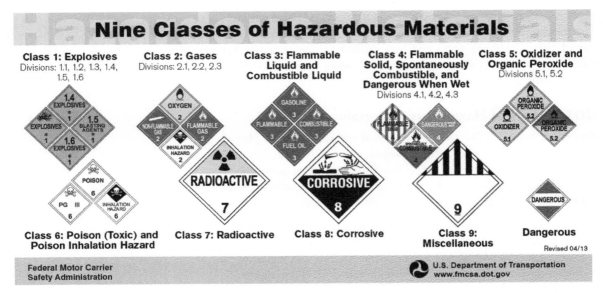

FIGURE 6.1 This image, courtesy of the U.S. DOT, summarizes the nine classes of hazardous materials, which are the most common concerns for day-to-day technological hazards present in any community or work setting.

- *DOT Class 5: Oxidizing substances and organic peroxides*—An oxidizing substance supplies its own oxygen and helps other combustible material burn more readily. Examples are hydrogen peroxide, ammonium nitrate, and benzoyl peroxide.
- *DOT Class 6: Toxic and infectious substances*—This category refers to poisonous materials, other than gases, known to be so toxic that they present a health hazard during transportation (Division 6.1). It also includes infectious materials (Division 6.2). Examples include 6.1 (pesticides, potassium cyanide) and 6.2 (HHS Category A and B agents).
- *DOT Class 7: Radioactive*—All substances that emit ionizing radiation. Examples include uranium and plutonium.
- *DOT Class 8: Corrosive substances*—A corrosive substance is any liquid or solid that causes destruction or alterations in human skin tissue at the site of contact, or a liquid that corrodes steel or aluminum. Examples are strong acids and bases like sulfuric acid, hydrochloric acid, sodium hydroxide, and potassium hydroxide.
- *DOT Class 9: Miscellaneous hazardous materials*—These materials present a hazard during transportation, but do not meet the definition of any of the other hazard classes. Examples are asbestos and dry ice.

Hazardous Materials Incident—Spills, Accidents, and Mishaps

As we go about our busy lives, most of us do not notice the hazardous materials (hazmat) being transported daily via road, rail, waterway, and air. Next time you're out on an interstate highway, take note of some of the hazmat placards on the 18-wheelers that pass you. Then, consider the potential for small- and large-scale disasters that would occur if one of those vehicles were involved in a major accident.

Pure chlorine is a very useful chemical agent—an element that touches our daily lives in many ways. It is used to disinfect water (as in swimming pools) and is part of the process of sanitizing sewage and industrial waste. During the production of paper and cloth, chlorine is used as a bleaching agent. It is also used in cleaning products, including household bleach, which is chlorine dissolved in water. A 90-ton railcar filled with chlorine is a common sight in rail yards all over the world. Chlorine, also transported as a liquid, has a very pungent odor and a yellowish-green color. In its gaseous state, chlorine is approximately twice as heavy as air.

How dangerous would it be if a rail car filled with 90 tons of chlorine were to derail and leak its contents rapidly into a populated area? On a cold morning in January 2005, that exact scenario played out in **Graniteville**, in South Carolina. With a population of a little more than 5000, this small town played host to a major chlorine spill (Figure 6.2). An improperly set switch caused a slow-moving freight train to collide with a parked train on a spur leading to a steam plant. One of the two train cars that were carrying liquid chlorine ruptured. When all was said and done, 9 people were killed and more than 250 people were injured. More than 5000 people had to be evacuated, and it took hazmat crews nearly two weeks to clean up the contaminated area (NTSB Report, 2005).

Another commodity that touches our daily lives is oil and related petroleum products. Oil is what makes the world go around! Indeed, this statement can be taken literally. Our reliance on oil to drive the world's economy through transportation and industry is ever present. This has led to extracting oil from the ground and offshore oil well sites. The inherent risk here is that the oil may escape in a dramatic fashion, such as when the Deepwater Horizon oil rig caught fire and exploded in the Gulf of Mexico on April 20, 2010. This oil spill, which flowed continuously into the ocean for 87 days, is the largest accidental marine oil spill in history, with an estimated discharge of 4.9 million barrels (refer to Figure 6.3).

■ **FIGURE 6.2** Just one of the horrific scenes resulting from the discharge of liquid chlorine that occurred in Graniteville, South Carolina, on January 6, 2005. The accident resulted in the evacuation of more than 2500 people, 9 deaths, and more than 250 injuries. It took hazmat crews nearly two weeks to clean up the spill. *Image courtesy of the U.S. EPA.*

■ **FIGURE 6.3** A skimming operation is used to clean up crude oil that has leaked into the Gulf of Mexico from the Deepwater Horizon oil spill. This was the largest oil spill in history, resulting in an estimated 4.9 million barrels discharged into the sea. *Image courtesy of NOAA.*

As a result, the environment was harmed, businesses lost revenue, people lost their jobs, and local, state, and federal governments all spent billions of dollars on the response and recovery. A major lawsuit against British Petroleum (BP) is helping to recoup the costs to government agencies, businesses, and private individuals affected by the incident (DOI, 2012).

CRITICAL THINKING

Most local emergency response organizations are prepared for small-scale spills of hazardous materials. But what role does the emergency manager play in response and recovery from larger hazmat incidents? Should the local and state emergency management agency (EMA) be a "clearing house" for cleanup resources or a focal point for communications?

CIVIL UNREST

Civil unrest, sometimes referred to as *civil disorder* or *civil strife*, is a term that is used by law enforcement agencies to describe one or more types of conflict generated by a group of people. This typically comes in the form of protests against political or social issues. Some examples of this are reactions to acts of discrimination, immigration reform, opposition to war efforts, and religious persecution. Civil disorder or unrest can turn into uncivil and even criminal activity when the people take to illegal parades, sit-ins, and other forms of obstruction. Rioting, vandalism, and even blatant brutality may ensue. Groups that resort to civil unrest aim to demonstrate their displeasure with government institutions or other agencies, but only rarely do they intend for their actions to degrade into something that requires police action. However, emergency managers and the government officials they serve should realize that the world is a turbulent place, and emotions run high over numerous "hot button" issues. What can start as a peaceful demonstration can soon evolve into general chaos and lawlessness.

Specific Examples of Civil Unrest

In Los Angeles, California, in 1991 a man named Rodney King was arrested by police officers following a high-speed car chase. The beating that he received from four police officers during his arrest was captured on film and showed repeatedly on television. The officers charged with his beating were acquitted of all charges in April 1992. This outraged people all over the country, but in particular, it sparked six days of riots in South Central Los Angeles. The rioting escalated into acts of arson, looting, and civil disturbance throughout Los Angeles County. The Rodney King riots were the largest acts of unrest seen in the United States since the race riots of the 1960s. The military was needed to quell the riots, but not before 53 people were killed and more than 2000 were injured. The only U.S.-based riot to exceed these numbers was the New York City draft riots in 1863, where, after five days of mayhem, an estimated 120 people were killed (CNN, 2014a).

CRITICAL THINKING

When civil unrest turns to general chaos, what role does the emergency manager play in the preparation and response to such an event? In your community, what causes could spark a movement towards civil unrest and chaos? Thinking ahead, what strategies might be employed to quell civil unrest?

In Ferguson, Missouri, in August 2014, 18-year-old Michael Brown, Jr., was shot dead by a police officer. The use of force against this unarmed African American young man sparked weeks of civil unrest and chaos, making national news coverage and drawing protestors from afar. In the end, intervention from the Office of the U.S. Attorney General and the National Guard was necessary to restore peace and general order to that community. The incident brought national attention to this small community of about 21,000 people and renewed the debate about the militarization of police forces in the United States and racial inequality in our communities (CNN, 2014b).

TERRORISM

This section of the chapter covers the potential for terrorist threats. It also addresses and defines international and domestic threat groups through a historical perspective of terrorist acts committed against targets in the United States and terrorist acts against U.S. interests in other parts of the world. It covers the rationale, tactics, techniques, and procedures that a terrorist group may use against a potential target.

Terrorism did not begin on September 11, 2001. Such violent events have been scattered throughout history, with attacks against U.S. domestic and international interests. Consider the assassination of President Abraham Lincoln in 1863 and the assassination of President William McKinley in 1901, and their effects on American actions and policy (Budinsky, 2013). With the continuing daily attacks on U.S. interests

■ **FIGURE 6.4** The wreckage of the Chicago Federal Building after the explosion of a bomb planted by the Industrial Workers of the World in 1918. *Image courtesy of the U.S. National Archives.*

around the world, American history has been marked by terrorism (an example from 1918 is shown in Figure 6.4).

Terrorism has been highly successful as an ideology and even an institution, due to adaptation to the environment it operates within. The development of democratic states resulted in a philosophical change among terrorist groups. Modern governments are designed to be more dependent upon processes and structure than individuals, so the death of an individual, even a president or prime minister, no longer necessarily produces the major disruption that terrorists want. Terrorists have reacted to this development by turning from targeting prominent individuals toward those historically considered immune, such as a country's infrastructure, national landmarks, emergency first responders (i.e., fire, police, and emergency medical service personnel), or the population in general. Terrorists believe that causing death and destruction will bring attention to their causes (Martin, 2012). Yesterday's ideologies have, in many cases, given way to random acts of violence perpetrated by individuals with no real aim beyond causing pain and suffering to a government they feel has wronged them. Some terrorist groups are evolving into new organizational structures that are harder to detect and infiltrate. These groups are often a collection of factions with common interests. Accordingly, they form, change, and regroup in response to specific agendas or

■ **FIGURE 6.5** A Coast Guard rigid-hulled inflatable boat off Manhattan on the morning of September 11, 2001. Photo was taken by Chan Irwin and was provided courtesy of Mike Harmon, U.S. Coast Guard. *Image courtesy of the U.S. DHS.*

planned actions. The large number of these groups, an absence of central direction, and changing organizational structures make them very difficult to track.

Terrorist groups have become increasingly self-sufficient by exploiting the global environment to support their operations. They can now use the advantage of technology to distribute leadership, training, and logistics not just regionally, but globally. The availability of emerging technologies provides the prospect that these trends could result in unprecedented human disasters. For these reasons, terrorism has become a global threat that does not recognize governmental or continental boundaries (Morgan, 2004).

The dark specter of terrorism became starkly apparent to people all over the world as they watched the twin towers of the World Trade Center come down on September 11, 2001 (refer to Figure 6.5). Most people can tell you where they were and what they were doing on that day when they first realized that the United States had been deliberately attacked by a group of terrorists. Terrorism is nothing new, but it became quite personal to most civilized people all over the world on that fateful day.

Few words provoke such fear in the minds of modern society as does *terrorism*. That is part of the point of terrorism. Fear is a powerful emotion, and when manipulated by terrorists, it becomes an effective device for destabilizing social order, creating dispute, and undermining societal cohesion. Throughout history, terrorism has shown itself to be a global threat from which no community is free. Terrorism transcends all geographic and demographic boundaries; all jurisdictions—suburban, urban, and rural—are at risk. Terrorists have demonstrated the capability to strike anywhere in the world.

International Terrorism

International terrorists continue to pose a threat to the interests of the United States and other Western civilizations and developed countries. Many terrorist groups and loosely affiliated extremists view the United States and its allies as enemies. Currently, Syria, Iran, and Sudan are the three current state sponsors of terrorism. Terrorist acts by governments are declining, yet terrorist activity by individuals and independent groups are increasing (DOS, 2013). The following international terrorist groups will be covered in some detail in this chapter:

- Al-Qaeda
- Hezbollah (Party of God)
- Revolutionary Armed Forces of Colombia (abbreviated as FARC, due to its Spanish name, Fuerzas Armadas Revolucionarias de Colombia)

Section 2656f(d) of Title 22 of the United States Code defines some key terms used in this subsection of Chapter 6. *International terrorism* means "terrorism involving citizens or the territory of more than one country." *Terrorism* means "premeditated, politically motivated violence perpetrated against noncombatant targets by subnational groups or clandestine agents." *Terrorist group* means "any group practicing, or which has significant subgroups which practice international terrorism."

Al-Qaeda, Hezbollah, and FARC have demonstrated some of the highest degrees of hostility from international terrorist organizations, as well as the ability to carry out sophisticated, simultaneous attacks; each is considered a formal terrorist group (DOI, 2013). All three receive support from state sponsors of terrorism, which enhances its abilities to receive funding, shelter, and logistical support for their operations.

Al-Qaeda

Al-Qaeda was established in the late 1980s to bring together Arabs who fought in Afghanistan against the Soviet Union. It helped finance, recruit, transport, and train Sunni Islamic extremists for the Afghan resistance. Al-Qaeda became a direct threat to the United States in February 1998, in a

■ **FIGURE 6.6** A worker stands at Ground Zero in New York City after the 9/11 attacks. U.S. National Archives' Local Identifier: P8026-16. Office of White House Management. Photography Office.

series of showdowns between the United States and Iraq over UN weapons inspections, and for the continued U.S. support of Israel. Osama bin Laden, founder of al-Qaeda, issued a fatwa (religious decree) calling for jihad (holy war) against the United States and its interests around the world.

Al-Qaeda members proved its dedication to the fatwa when it conducted the bombings in August 1998 of the U.S. embassies in Nairobi, Kenya, and Dar es Salaam, Tanzania, which killed at least 301 people and injured more than 5000. They also claim to have shot down U.S. helicopters in Somalia in 1993, killing members of the U.S. military, and they were implicated in the attack on the *U.S.S. Cole* in the port of Yemen in October 2000. The attack on the *U.S.S. Cole* killed 17 U.S. Navy service members and injured another 39 (Martin, 2012).

On September 11, 2001, 19 al-Qaeda members hijacked four U.S. commercial jets. Two were flown into the World Trade Center in New York City, one into the Pentagon near Washington, D.C., and a fourth crashlanded in a field in Shanksville, Pennsylvania, in an aborted part of the attack (Figure 6.6). In total, about 3000 individuals were dead or missing. This was the worst terrorist attack in U.S. history (Martin, 2012).

Al-Qaeda's primary goal is to establish an Islamic government throughout the world, working with allied Islamic extremist groups to overthrow regimes it deems "non-Islamic," and expelling Westerners and non-Muslims from Muslim countries. On May 2nd, 2011 Seal Team Six of the U.S. Special Operations Command of the Department of Defense

(DoD), successfully located and killed bin Laden in Abbottabad, Pakistan (White House, 2011). Military operations against al-Qaeda since 2001 have limited the group's scope and reach, but not effectively eliminated it. Al-Qaeda remains one of the most dangerous active terrorist groups in the world.

Hezbollah

Hezbollah is also known as the Islamic Jihad, Revolutionary Justice Organization, Organization of the Oppressed on Earth, and Islamic Jihad for the Liberation of Palestine. The group seeks to create a fundamentalist state modeled on Iran, and it formally advocates the ultimate establishment of Islamic rule in Lebanon and liberating all occupied Arab lands, including Jerusalem. It has named the elimination of Israel as one of its goals. Hezbollah is closely allied with and often directed by Iran, but the group may have conducted several operations not approved by Tehran (Martin, 2012).

Hezbollah's campaigns against the United States include the suicide truck bombing of the U.S. Embassy in April 1983, the bombing of the U.S. Marine barracks in October 1983, and the bombing of the U.S. Embassy Annex in September 1984—all in Beirut, Lebanon. Elements of the group have been responsible for the kidnapping and detention of U.S. and other Western hostages in Lebanon (Martin, 2012).

FARC

FARC was established by the Colombian Communist Party to defend what were then autonomous communist-controlled rural areas. It is Latin America's oldest, largest, most capable, and best-equipped insurgency. There are approximately 9000 to 12,000 armed combatants and several thousand supporters, mostly in rural areas. FARC has well-documented ties to a full range of narcotics-trafficking activities, including taxation, cultivation, and distribution. Cuba provides the group with some medical care and political consultation (FAS Intelligence Resource Program, 2008). FARC targets the United States because it believes that the ideology of the U.S. government has been imposed on the Colombian people by the ruling class. FARC also believes that, in 1964, the Fuerza Armadas Revolucionarias de Colombia—Ejército de Puelbo (FARCEP-EP; Armed Forces of Colombia) was advised and directed by the United States in a large military operation attacking peasants who had settled in the region of Marquetalia.

In March 1999, the FARC executed three U.S. Indian-rights activists on Venezuelan territory after kidnapping them in Colombia. In February 2003, the FARC captured three U.S. contractors, and killed one American and one Colombian when their plane crashed in Florencia (FAS Intelligence Resource Program, 2008).

Domestic Terrorism

Domestic terrorist groups represent interests that span the full spectrum of political and economic viewpoints, as well as social issues and concerns. The Federal Bureau of Investigation (FBI) is the lead federal agency in the United States dealing with domestic terrorism. The FBI views domestic terrorism as "the unlawful use, or threatened use, of violence by a group or individual based and operating entirely within the United States or its territories without foreign direction, and which is committed against people or property with the intent of intimidating or coercing a government or its population in furtherance of political or social objectives." Recent domestic terrorist threat primarily comes from right wing extremist groups, left wing and special interest extremists (Bjelopera, 2013). The following domestic terrorist groupings will be covered in some detail in the next sections:

- Right-wing extremists
- Left-wing extremists
- Special-interest extremists

Right-Wing Extremists

Right-wing terrorist groups often adhere to conservative or reactionary principles. Such groups endorse racial supremacy, embrace antigovernment and antiregulatory beliefs, or both. Patriot movements, militias, and common-law groups fall into the right wing category.

Patriot groups define themselves as being opposed to a so-called New World Order. They often advocate or adhere to extreme antigovernment doctrines. Patriot groups may overlap with the race- or ethnicity-based hate groups. The proliferation of antigovernment conspiracy theories is widely accepted among the Ku Klux Klan, neo-Nazis, skinheads, Christian Identity, Black separatists, and other hate groups. At the same time, the anti-Semitism (anti-Jewish) and racism that underlies most common-law patriot doctrine is becoming more apparent.

Militia group motivations vary widely, from a desire for self-determination at the local governmental level to racism and religious extremism—the common thread is often a right-wing, antifederal government ideology. Militia groups are also known as patriots or minutemen. An estimated 10,000 to 100,000 people belong to right-wing militia groups, but their level of involvement varies, and the extremist core of this movement is small (Martin, 2012).

Left-Wing Extremists

Left-wing groups profess a revolutionary socialist doctrine and view themselves as protectors of the people against the "dehumanizing effects" of capitalism and imperialism. Left-wing terrorists are responsible for bombings, assassinations, robberies, and planned attacks on infrastructure targets. Another threat posed by left-wing groups is their potential support of espionage conducted against the United States from supporting countries such as Cuba. From the 1960s to the 1980s, leftist-oriented extremist groups posed the most serious domestic threat to the United States (Martin, 2012).

A specific difference between right- and left-wing groups is the way they publicize their doctrine. Right-wing organizations are very vocal and openly claim responsibility for their actions. Left-wing organizations are very quiet and often operate underground. This difference makes it very difficult to identify and work against left-wing agencies. Such left-wing groups can exist and evolve for years without the knowledge of law enforcement (Martin, 2012).

Special Interests

This is a category of terrorism recognized by the FBI. Special interest terrorism differs from traditional right-wing and left-wing terrorism in that extremist special interest groups seek to resolve specific issues, rather than effect widespread political change. These groups occupy the extreme fringes of animal rights, pro-life, environmental, antinuclear, and other political and social movements. Since 1990, more than 1200 criminal incidents were claimed by animal and environmental rights extremists. The tactics used range from firebombing condominium complexes to vandalizing university research labs, from spray painting sport utility vehicles to destroying businesses and new homes. Ecoterrorists and animal rights extremists, as they are also known, are considered one of today's most serious domestic terrorist threats by the FBI (Lewis, 2005).

The Earth Liberation Front (ELF) and Animal Liberation Front (ALF) are special-interest groups. ELF has been linked to fires set at sport utility vehicle dealerships and construction sites in various states, while ALF has been blamed for arson and bombings against animal research labs and the pharmaceutical and cosmetics industry (Frieden, 2005). ALF and

ELF incidents often involve active surveillance, careful planning, and detailed operations. It is not uncommon for both ALF and ELF to post joint declarations of responsibility for terrorist actions on their websites, after declaring solidarity of actions in 1993 (PR Newswire, 2005).

ALF is a loosely organized movement committed to ending the exploitation of animals. Members engage in direct action against companies or individuals who utilize animals for research or economic gain. Terrorist campaigns are generally carried out against fur companies, mink farms, restaurants, and animal research laboratories. ALF has become one of the most active extreme special-interest elements within the United States (Lewis, 2005).

ELF was founded in 1992 by members of Earth First!, a group based in England. ELF targets industries and other entities perceived to be damaging to the natural environment. The ELF advocates "monkey wrenching"—acts of sabotage and property destruction that include tree spiking, arson, and sabotage of logging or construction equipment. ELF claimed responsibility for the arson fires set at a ski resort in Vail, Colorado, in October 1998 that destroyed eight separate structures and caused $12 million in damage. The group also set a fire at the Stock Lumber Company in Orem, Utah, on June 14, 2004, that resulted in an estimated $1.5 million in damages.

Domestic Terrorism—Some Examples

Often, lone individuals (or sometimes referred to as a *lone wolf*) are motivated by causes affiliated on the fringes of right-wing interests. The 1995 bombing of the Alfred P. Murrah Federal Building in Oklahoma City was the result of a conspiracy by a couple of individuals, but executed by a lone person, Timothy McVeigh (refer to Figure 6.7). The bombing killed 168 men, women, and children and injured approximately 500 others. McVeigh wrote several letters explaining his reasons for attacking the Murrah Federal Building. He stated that the bombing was a retaliatory strike—a counterattack for the cumulative raids (such as Ruby Ridge and Waco) that federal agents had participated in over the years (McVeigh, 2001).

Eric Robert Rudolph (refer to Figure 6.7), a lone individual, bombed the New Woman All Women Clinic in Birmingham, Alabama, in January 1998. The bombing killed an off-duty Birmingham police officer working as a security guard at the clinic and severely wounded a nurse. Rudolph had associations with the racist fundamentalist group Christian Identity (an extreme right-wing group). Christian Identity describes a religion that is fundamentally racist, anti-Semitic, and opposed to abortion (Rudolph,

■ **FIGURE 6.7** Mug shots of the Oklahoma City Bomber, Timothy McVeigh (left) and Eric Robert Rudolph, the bomber of numerous abortion clinics, Centennial Park in Atlanta. Rudolph is the terrorist who is best known for targeting first responders with secondary devices. Both were convicted of their crimes. McVeigh was executed on June 11, 2001. Rudolph is serving a life sentence in federal prison. *Images courtesy of the U.S. DOJ and FBI.*

2005). Rudolph, after his capture in May 2003, agreed to plead guilty to three other bombings: the Atlanta Centennial Olympic Park bombing in July 1996; the attack on a family planning clinic in Sandy Springs, Georgia, in January 1997; and the bombing of the Otherside Lounge in Atlanta, Georgia, in February 1997. This lone-wolf attacker is also known for planting secondary devices at the scene of his bombings that were intended to target emergency services personnel responding to the initial detonation, and other terrorists have adopted this tactic as well.

CBRNE AND WMD

Chemical, biological, radiological, nuclear, and explosives are referred to by the acronym **CBRNE**. **Weapons of Mass Destruction (WMD)** is another common term used in homeland security and emergency management programs and reference documents. WMD is also inclusive of chemical, biological, nuclear, radiological, and high-yield explosive weapons. The term *WMD* first arose in 1937 in reference to the mass destruction of Guernica, Spain, by aerial bombardment. The bombing of the Basque city was an aerial attack on April 26, 1937, during the Spanish Civil War by the German Luftwaffe squadron known as the Condor Legion. It was the first aerial bombardment in history in which a civilian population was attacked with the apparent intent of producing total destruction. In fact, a *New York Times* description of the carnage stated that the Germans had used "weapons of mass destruction" against the Basque people (Larsen, Wirtz, & Croddy, 2004).

Following the bombing of Hiroshima and Nagasaki, and progressing through the Cold War, the term came to refer more to nonconventional weapons. The terms ABC (atomic, biological, and chemical), nuclear, biological, or chemical (NBC), and CBRNE have been used synonymously with WMD, although nuclear weapons have the greatest capacity to cause mass destruction. The phrase entered popular usage in relation to the U.S.-led 2003 invasion of Iraq.

WMDs cause indiscriminate effects on society because fear of it has shaped political policies and campaigns, fostered social movements, and has been the central theme of many films. Support for different levels of WMD development, and control varies nationally and internationally. Yet understanding of the nature of the threats is not high, in part because of imprecise usage of the term by politicians and the media (Bowman, 2002).

CRITICAL THINKING

What makes an act of terrorism different from an accident? Intent, pure and simple. If an incident is intentional, the site where it occurs is a crime scene. That is likely to impede efforts to stabilize the incident, increase the casualty count, and introduce complications for removing and treating victims and restoring the area to a state of normalcy. So, what does this imply for the emergency manager?

LEGAL DEFINITION OF WMD

(1) any destructive device as defined in section 921 of this title [which reads] any explosive, incendiary, or bomb, grenade, rocket having a propellant charge of more than one quarter ounce, mine or device similar to the above; (2) poison gas; (3) any weapon involving a disease organism; or (4) any weapon that is designed to release radiation or radioactivity at a level dangerous to human life.

The WMD Quagmire

According to the U.S. Department of Justice, almost any explosive device or weapon may be considered a WMD. In addition, 18 U.S.C. 2332a further states that a WMD may include "any destructive device." That in turn is defined in 18 U.S.C. 921 to include almost any type of weapon that is not "generally recognized as particularly suitable for sporting purposes."

WMD can be categorized as belonging to one or more of the following groups: chemical, biological, radiological, nuclear, or explosive. Incendiary devices and cyberterrorism can also be added to this list. Title 18, U.S.C. 2332a, includes the following accepted definition for weapons of mass destruction in the United States.

Explosives have been defined by a variety of sources, ranging from the fire service to the United States Code. Commonly, these definitions focus on chemical reactions that produce a shock wave and heat, so this can include those caused by nuclear fission devices. These and incendiary devices are truly WMD, their purpose being to cause widespread damage to property and injury to people. Definitions of explosives include black powder, pellet powder, initiating explosives, detonators, safety fuses, squibs, detonating cord, igniter cord, and igniters. Incendiary devices include chemicals that may accelerate or initiate fire.

Any individual or combination of the WMD classes listed can be used as booby traps, mines, and bombs and can be directly or remotely detonated or initiated. Increasingly, experts are putting efforts into countermeasures related to cyberterrorism. The global economy's reliance on transactions and communications presents an inviting target to terrorists, who can operate in almost any corner of the globe. Terrorists may consider the use cyberattacks as a force multiplier in a physical incident to impede first responders, spread misinformation, and promote panic in the general population.

Today, *WMD* means different things to different people. The most widely used definition is that of NBC weapons, although there is no treaty or customary international law that contains an authoritative definition (Larsen et al., 2004). Instead, international law has been used with respect to the specific categories of weapons within WMD, not to WMD as a whole.

Reasons Why Terrorists Might Use CBRNE

Why might terrorists consider the use of CBRNE materials in their plan of attack? According to the U.S. Department of Homeland Security (DHS), there are four primary reasons: cost, availability, effectiveness, and difficulty of detection (Bolz, Dudonis, & Schulz, 2005). Each is discussed in the next sections.

Cost

WMD materials are relatively inexpensive to produce or manufacture. This may be especially true for biological materials. Information on how to produce WMD materials is readily available from the Internet. The deadly nature of these agents means that large amounts of nascent material are not required.

Availability

Many of the ingredients needed to produce WMD devices and materials are not strictly monitored and are relatively easy to obtain. For instance, Timothy McVeigh used the common fertilizer Ammonium nitrate to make the bomb that was used in the Oklahoma City bombing (1995). New rules and programs have been put into place to try to control this at the federal level (e.g., the Select Agent Program), and procurement of some chemical precursors may alarm federal agents. Still, given the long list of possibilities, terrorists are only limited by their knowledge of the subject and their imagination.

Effectiveness

WMD materials give users the ability to cause mass casualties from a single weapon—from close up or at a great distance. Chemical agents are excellent weapons for covert dissemination because they can be spread over large areas by the wind. Some biological agents present a significant inhalation hazard, and others are spread through person-to-person contact prior to the onset of serious signs and symptoms of disease.

Difficult to Detect

Biological and chemical agents are difficult to detect without specialized monitoring devices and training. Many of the effects are delayed, allowing the perpetrator to be far from the scene before the act is detected. This also limits situational awareness, making it difficult (if not impossible) to recognize, isolate, and escape the agent.

CRITICAL THINKING

There are many technological hazards in the community that you live or work in. Consider the potential targets in your community that would be of interest to a terrorist. Make a list of the top five technological hazards and the top five targets. Discuss one possible scenario with your classmates.

Examples of the Use of CBRNE by Terrorists

In June 1994, the Aum Shinryko, a religious-based organization in Japan, released vaporized sarin nerve agent within the city of Matsumoto, Japan. The group used a converted refrigeration truck equipped with metal tanks, a heater, and a fan to produce a sarin vapor that was released from the truck while it was parked outside a residential apartment building. Despite releasing the vapor in a populated residential area, only 600 of the city's 200,000 residents were affected. In the incident, 58 people were hospitalized and 7 died (Ryan, 2005).

Following the al-Qaeda attacks of September 11, 2001, discussed earlier in this chapter, anthrax spores were placed in envelopes and sent through the U.S. mail. Now referred to as *Amerithrax* (from the case name assigned to it by the FBI), this act of bioterrorism was perpetrated by a U.S. Army biological defense research scientist, Dr. Bruce Ivins, at Fort Detrick, Maryland. The attack resulted in the deaths of five people and stunned the entire nation (Ryan & Glarum, 2008).

To date, there have been no specific instances where radiological materials were utilized by a terrorist or terrorist group. However, there have been accidents and a couple of instances where a radiological substance was used in a criminal act (i.e., murder). The most notable was the assassination of Alexander Litvinenko, a Russian journalist who was allegedly poisoned with polonium 210 by Russian operatives in 2006 (Goldfarb, 2007).

To date, there have been no specific instances where a nuclear weapon was utilized by a terrorist or terrorist group in an act of terrorism. There are two specific events where a nuclear weapon was used against a population of people in an act of war. To end the war with Japan in World War II, the United States used an atomic weapon to destroy two Japanese industrial cities: Hiroshima (August 6, 1945) and Nagasaki (August 9, 1945).

Explosive materials are a clear choice for terrorists motivated to use WMD. They are relatively cheap, readily available, and easy to deploy, especially in an unstable world where combat operations against terrorists are a daily occurrence. One of the most stunning examples of the use of high-yield explosives by a terrorist was the bombing in Oklahoma City discussed earlier in this chapter (Martin, 2012).

CHEMICAL AGENTS

Chemical agents are classified according to their physical state (DOT Pipeline and Hazardous Materials Safety Administration, 2012). Chemical agents can exist in solid, liquid, or gaseous states. This section of the chapter provides an explanation of chemical agents and toxic industrial chemicals (TICs) and toxic industrial materials (TIMs). Often, when this subject is broached, we tend to look at chemical hazards in a worst-case scenario—for instance, pick some of the most toxic substances and imagine them being disseminated against a large, unsuspecting population of people who are completely exposed and vulnerable.

Frankly, this type of scenario makes us think long and hard about the issues related to mass casualty treatment, fatality management, and contamination avoidance. It is a good exercise and makes for some challenging planning. Fortunately, this is not representative of our day-to-day concerns about chemical hazards in our communities. In real life, we are more likely to be dealing with a small-scale, isolated event involving the transport or storage of a TIC or TIM. In that light, consider the multitude of hazardous chemical substances being used in your community in both the private (manufacturing, fuels, health care, etc.) and public (water sanitization, waste treatment, etc.) sectors. Recognize these everyday chemical hazards for what they are—manageable risks, but with the potential for doing great harm to a community and its populace.

Then again, the dark specter of terrorism changes everything, and we can view chemical hazards as having even more deadly consequences and greater potential for doing harm to a community. Chemical agents were first used in modern warfare on the battlefields of Europe in World War I. Indeed, these agents, when used as weapons, are intended to kill, injure, and incapacitate people through their serious physiological effects. Many chemical agents have been exploited in warfare, and have even been custom-designed to produce a rapid onset of medical symptoms (in minutes to hours). When we discuss chemical agents used in warfare, or chemical warfare agents (CWAs), we include military classifications. Jargon and military acronyms are used to describe and name these CWAs. Since these agents have the greatest potential for doing harm in a criminal or terrorist act, they will be explained in extra detail here.

Characteristics of Chemical Hazards

Before getting into any specific CWA groups or compounds, there are several general characteristics to know. Overall, there are some broad types of groups of CWAs: nerve agents, blister agents, choking agents, blood agents, and riot control agents. In addition, the North Atlantic Treaty Organization (NATO) military organizations use a two-letter designation to identify specific chemical agents (e.g., GB, sarin, a common nerve agent). Chemical names, trade names, synonyms, and military classifications are used interchangeably, which can make this topic confusing to anyone new to it (Ryan, 2005).

Another important consideration for CWAs, TICs, and TIMs is *dissemination*. How the agent is dispersed or is released and its concomitant effect is directly related to a number of elements: vapor pressure of the agent, environmental conditions at the site of release, purity of the compound, and other factors. This also has a direct bearing on how we might adopt appropriate mitigation strategies, respond to the release of an agent, prepare to evacuate or shelter in place, and sample and identify these agents (Ryan, 2005).

Chemical agents have several *routes of entry* into the body—inhalation, ingestion, and absorption. Gases or aerosols can be inhaled. Residue that has settled on food or drink can be ingested. The agent coming into contact with the skin or mucous membranes (nose, mouth, eyes, open sores, or wounds) can be absorbed into the body. Some chemical agents are persistent in the environment because their boiling point is very high. Those with the consistency of motor oil (e.g., VX, methylphosphonothioic acid, a persistent nerve agent) may persist for days, weeks, or months. Those CWAs with a low boiling point may persist for only a few minutes after release. Military chemical weapons experts often refer to the *persistence* of chemical agents to predict their duration in the environment (Ryan, 2005).

TICs

Today's emergency manager and hazmat professional must be aware of chemicals commonly found within their local communities. TICs and TIMs are stored and transported in vast quantities throughout the industrialized world—quite frankly, they are all around us. One only needs to grab a hazardous materials reference book (DOT, 2012) and travel throughout their community to get a sense for what is making its way across the highways and being stored with or without security and containment measures. These chemicals and materials alone constitute a tremendous potential hazard in and of themselves. Chlorine and phosgene are industrial chemicals that are transported in multiton shipments by road and rail. Accidental or intentional rupturing of their containers could easily disseminate these gases. Inhalation effects of chlorine and phosgene are similar to some CWAs (e.g., blister and choking agents). TIC and TIM sources include:

- Chemical manufacturing plants (chlorine, peroxides, industrial gases, plastics, and pesticides)
- Food processing, storage facilities with large tanks, and chemical transportation assets (rail tank cars, tank trucks, pipelines, and river barges)
- Gasoline and jet fuel storage tanks at distribution centers, airports, and barge terminals with compressed gases in tanks, pipelines, and pumping stations

- Pesticide manufacturing and supply distributors, as well as pest control shops where they are stored. Organophosphate pesticides (e.g., parathion) are in the same chemical class as nerve agents. Although most of these pesticides are much less toxic, the inhalation effects and medical treatments are the same as for weapons-grade nerve agents.
- Industries in which cyanide and mercury compounds are used, such as ore processing and metal plating
- Educational, medical, and research laboratories
- Hospitals and medical clinics

CWAs

Chemical agents used in World War I were relatively simple substances. Most were either common industrial chemicals or their derivatives (Brown, 2005). Chlorine was one of the first CWAs (Trumpener, 1975). It is cheap to produce and concentrate; easy to deploy, as it readily goes from a liquid to gaseous state; and, due to its chemical properties, it is heavier than air, so it tends to "hug" the ground when released. This makes it even more of a hazard, since this attribute keeps it in close proximity to exposed people (Figure 6.8 shows military protective gear in World War II for CWAs). Another CWA is phosgene, which is employed to irritate the eyes and respiratory tracts of soldiers. Phosgene is used today throughout industry as a chlorinating material. A second such substance was hydrogen cyanide, a CWA that interferes with the transfer of oxygen in bodily tissues. Today, hydrogen cyanide is used worldwide in the manufacture of acrylic polymers. What follows is a brief summary of some CWAs by category (nerve agents, blister agents, blood agents, and choking agents). Note that most CWAs have a two-letter designation (e.g., Cyanogen chloride − CK).

Nerve Agents

Nerve agents comprise some of the most toxic substances. Most of these were developed from the late 1930s to early 1940s (Figure 6.9 shows a military stockpile of nerve agents). These agents are similar in structure to organophosphate insecticides. Organophosphates are widely used as agricultural insecticides. Malathion, for example, is commercially available in the United States. However, organophosphates developed for military use are approximately 100,000 times more toxic to humans. While they are commonly referred to as nerve gas, *nerve agents* is the preferred term for these poisons, which are dispersed as aerosols and form vapor under normal atmospheric conditions (Ryan, 2005).

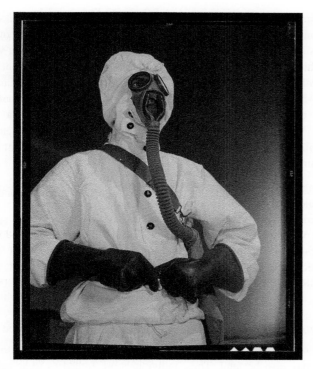

■ **FIGURE 6.8** This image from August 1942 depicts a sailor at a Naval Air Base in Corpus Christi, Texas, wearing protective clothing and a gas mask designed for use in chemical warfare. *Image courtesy of U.S. DoD; Howard R. Hollem, photographer.*

■ **FIGURE 6.9** Sarin-filled 105-mm artillery shells are safely stored in earth-covered "igloos" at Anniston Army Depot, Alabama. *Image courtesy of U.S. DoD.*

The primary agents in this group are tabun (GA), sarin (GB), soman (GD), and methylphosphonothioic acid (VX). G-series nerve agents are nonpersistent and easily dispersed as a liquid or as a vapor. The vapors are highly toxic, resulting in illness and death if untreated. VX behaves differently in that it is oily—similar to baby oil in appearance and viscosity—and persistent. Although nerve agents are liquids, when dispersed, the more volatile ones constitute both a liquid and a vapor hazard. VX is the most toxic nerve agent; it has the consistency of motor oil, deposits primarily as a contact hazard, and is persistent in the environment (Ryan, 2005).

Nerve agents interfere with nerve signal transmission. Exposure indicators could include some or all of the following: pinpointed pupils, respiratory arrest, sweating, weakness, disorientation, diarrhea, slurred speech, nausea, vomiting, drooling, trembling, paralysis, depression, abdominal pain, respiratory failure/depression, vomiting, headache, reduced vision, convulsions, general increase in secretions, tremors, and death (USAMRIID, 2004).

Blister Agents

Blister, or vesicant, agents, produce injuries; however, exposure to these agents may also be fatal. Thus, individuals are forced to wear personal protective equipment (PPE). Vesicants blister the skin and any other part of the body with which they come in contact. Vesicants act on the eyes, mucous membranes, lungs, skin, and blood-forming organs; they can also damage the respiratory tract if inhaled, and may cause vomiting and diarrhea if ingested (Ryan, 2005).

Mustard is a blister agent (not to be confused with the condiment) that poses both a contact and vapor hazard. Its color ranges from clear to dark brown, depending on purity. Mustard is a viscous, oily liquid at room temperature. Its odor is that of garlic, onion, or the mustard condiment (hence its name). To recognize this smell, a person would have to be exposed to the agent; therefore, odor should *not* be relied upon for detection. Under temperate conditions, mustard evaporates slowly and is primarily a liquid hazard, but its vapor hazard increases with increasing temperature.

Mustard agent exposure may elicit no effects for hours. Two other blister agents, lewisite and phosgene oxime, produce immediate pain, severe itching, and blisters (USAMRIID, 2004).

Blood Agents

Blood agents affect the body by being absorbed into the bloodstream and changing red blood cells. Examples of such agents include arsine, carbon monoxide, cyanogen chloride, hydrogen cyanide, potassium cyanide, and sodium cyanide (Ryan, 2005).

The blood agents hydrogen cyanide (AC) and cyanogen chloride (CK) are colorless-to-pale yellow liquids that will turn into a gas near room temperature. AC has a characteristic odor of bitter almonds, and CK has an acrid, choking odor and causes burning pain in the victim's eyes. These signs may provide enough warning to enable evacuation or ventilation of the attack site before the agent reaches a lethal concentration. Sodium or potassium cyanides are white-to-pale yellow salts that can be easily used to poison food or drink (Ryan, 2004).

At high doses, cyanide exposure causes gasping, frothy sputum or vomiting, loss of consciousness, and death; onset of symptoms occurs very rapidly—within seconds. Additional symptoms resulting from exposure to high doses include palpitations, confusion, hyperventilation, anxiety, and vertigo that may progress to agitation, stupor, coma, and death. At high doses, cyanides cause immediate collapse; at lower doses, symptoms may be delayed (USAMRIID, 2004).

Choking Agents

Chemical agents that attack the lung tissue, possibly resulting in pulmonary edema, are classified as lung-damaging, or choking, agents. This classification of CWA includes phosgene, diphosgene, chlorine, and chloropicrin. Phosgene is the most dangerous choking agent; the toxic action of phosgene is typical of most choking agents (FAS, 2004).

Because phosgene and chlorine choking agents are heavier than air, they will settle into low places in the surrounding terrain. Subways, sewers, and manholes, for instance, would be likely concentration areas if phosgene or chlorine were used. Therefore, evacuation to higher floors in buildings, evacuations of subways, and so on would be appropriate (Ryan, 2005).

These agents primarily attack the airway and lungs, causing irritation of the entire airway, from the nose to the lungs. Fluid fills the lungs, and pulmonary edema (commonly referred to as *dry-land drowning*) occurs; onset of symptoms usually occurs immediately (USAMRIID, 2004).

■ **FIGURE 6.10** As part of a three-day demonstration exercise, a California National Guard civil support worker in full chemical protective gear demonstrates rapid-response operations. Personnel trained in chemical response procedures and technologies drive by a portable personal decontamination facility and sample air for chemical warfare agents. *This image is courtesy of U.S. Army National Guard Bureau.*

Chemical Agents Used as Weapons

There are literally thousands of toxic chemicals that could be used as weapons (Figure 6.10). Many of these agents require nothing more than acquisition by purchase or theft—the weapon is already made. Some of the more common types of chemicals that could be used in improvised weapons against communities include:

- Eye, skin, and respiratory irritants (acids, ammonia, acrylates, aldehydes, isocyanates)
- Flammable chemical industry gases (acetone, alkenes, alkyl halides, amines)
- Aromatic hydrocarbons used as water supply contaminants (benzene, carbon tetrachloride)
- Oxidizers for improvised explosives (oxygen, butadiene, peroxides)
- Common chlorinating and choking agents (chlorine, hydrogen sulfide, phosgene)
- Compressed hydrocarbon fuel gases used as incendiaries or simple asphyxiates (liquefied natural gas, propane, isobutane)
- Liquid hydrocarbon fuels used as incendiaries or water supply contaminants (gasoline, jet fuel)

- Industrial compounds that could be used as blister agents (dimethyl sulfate)
- Organophosphate pesticides used as low-grade nerve agents (malathion)
- Aniline, nitrile, and cyanide compounds used as chemical asphyxiates

This is not an all-inclusive list, but it does give an idea of some of the toxic chemicals that may be used as weapons and how they may affect the health and safety of emergency responders and the population (Ryan, 2005).

In warfare, the principal method of disseminating chemical agents has been the use of explosives. Usually, these have taken the form of central bursters that expel the agent laterally. Efficiency is not particularly great, in that much of the agent is lost to incineration in the initial blast and being thrown to the ground. The efficiency of explosives and pyrotechnics for dissemination is limited by the flammable nature of some agents. For flammable aerosols, sometimes the agent cloud is totally or partially ignited (flashing) in the dissemination process (Ryan, 2005).

A spray tank, commercially available for dissemination of agricultural chemicals from aircraft, can be used to disseminate chemical agents. Similarly, ground-based aerosol generators used to disseminate pesticides can be used for chemical agent and TIC dispersal purposes. Chemicals stored or transported in pressurized containers will self-disseminate upon container rupture. This reinforces the fact that a truck trailer or rail tanker car can be an effective dissemination device.

Some Examples of the Potential of Chemical Hazards

One example of a large-scale military chemical release has been well described. In April 1915, the German military released more than 150 tons of chlorine near Ypres, France. The chlorine was stored in thousands of canisters placed within the German trenches and opened when the wind blew toward the Canadian and French troops. Although politically motivated reports have described thousands of deaths, actual French and German accounts from the time refer to 625 casualties and three deaths (Trumpener, 1975).

In 1984, the world's worst industrial disaster occurred in Bhopal, India. Late at night on December 2, approximately 27 metric tons of methyl isocyanate (MIC), and possibly phosgene, hydrogen cyanide, nitrogen oxide, and carbon monoxide, were released in proximity to a highly populated area over a 1- to 2-h period (Ramana & Ramana, 2002). Environmental factors, including low wind speed and a thermal inversion, prevented dissipation of the chemicals and resulted in exposure of 200,000 of the 900,000 residents of Bhopal (Ramana & Ramana, 2002; Singh & Ghosh, 1987). The incident produced more than 80,000 victims, with approximately 3000 deaths (Varma & Guest, 1993). There has been considerable controversy over whether the release was an industrial accident or the intentional act of individuals (perhaps terrorists). In either case, Bhopal is a striking example of the effectiveness of chemical agents. However, it should be noted that the mass fatalities in Bhopal were due to the tremendous volume of chemicals used, the location of the release (populated area), and environmental conditions.

In October 1987, 53,000 pounds of hydrofluoric acid were accidentally released from a petrochemical plant in Texas. The release produced a vapor cloud that covered a community of 41,000 residents, sending 939 citizens to area hospitals. Of the exposed victims, 94 were admitted to hospitals, and there were no reported deaths (Wing et al., 1991).

In March 1988, Iraqi warplanes and helicopters dropped a cocktail of mustard and nerve gas, and possibly blood agents onto a population of 60,000 in Halabja, Iraq, over the course of several days. This chemical drop, directed by Saddam Hussein, resulted in the deaths of over 5000 victims, most of whom were women and children. Thousands more received irreparable injuries to the skin, the eyes, and the membranes of the nose, throat, and lungs. Many of those killed and injured were on the roads leading out of Halabja, where the roadways were showered with chemical munitions by Iraqi pilots who anticipated an evacuation from the city (BBC News, 1988).

BIOLOGICAL AGENTS

We have all experienced illness from a biological agent, right? Yes, of course. everyone has had a cold at one time or another, and most of us have had the flu (brought on by the influenza virus). You may have experienced food poisoning or been exposed to a 24-h "stomach virus." Generally speaking, the cause of these common maladies are bioliogical agents (or pathogenic microorganisms). *Biological agents* are microorganisms or toxins that can kill, incapacitate, and sicken people, animals, and crops. There are three primary types of biological agents that fall into the realm of technological hazards, especially when used intentionally in an act of bioterrorism—bacteria, viruses, and toxins (Ryan & Glarum, 2008).

Bacteria are single-celled organisms capable of causing a variety of diseases in animals, plants, and humans. They may also produce extremely potent toxins inside the human body. These single-celled organisms may be cultured in nutrient media.

Viruses are microorganisms smaller than bacteria. They are incapable of metabolism and completely dependent upon the host cell for reproduction.

Toxins are potent poisons produced by a variety of living organisms, including bacteria, plants, and animals. Some biological toxins are the most toxic substances known.

Characteristics of Biological Agents

Certain characteristics are common to most biological agents. They are obtained from nature, where they cause disease naturally, and they are relatively easy to acquire if you know where to find them and how to recover them. Biological agents are invisible to the senses. Because they cannot be felt, tasted, or smelled, biological agents are not detectable by any human senses, especially when the agent is disseminated in an aerosol form (Ryan & Glarum, 2008).

Biological agents have a wide range of effects, from causing simple flu-like illness and diarrhea to more damaging symptoms like coma, seizures, and death. The effects that appear depend on a number of factors, including the age or general health of the victim, the agent that he or she is exposed to, the dose received, and the route of entry. Generally, bacteria and viruses do not produce immediate effects. They need time to grow within the host to result in illness (Ryan & Glarum, 2008).

Biological agents are relatively easy to produce. If one can obtain a specimen of an organism and knows how to culture it (provide a suitable environment, provide nutrients, and allow it to reproduce), one can increase the quantity using basic procedures and commercially available equipment (Ryan & Glarum, 2008). Some other considerations for biological agents are:

- *Availability*—Biological agents may be commercially available, stored in an authorized laboratory, or recovered from a natural setting.
- *Routes of entry*—There are several ways for biological agents to gain access to the body. These routes of entry include inhalation, ingestion, or injection. Gases or aerosols can be inhaled. Inhalation is the most important route of entry and the one you need to be most

concerned about. Residue that has settled on food or drink products can be consumed. With rare exception, biological agents do not typically enter the body by absorption. One example of an agent that **is** absorbed are mycotoxins.

■ *Incubation periods*—Most biological agents require days to weeks before the effects are experienced. Once the incubation period is completed, victims will begin to exhibit effects of the exposure that occurred days or weeks before. The time required for a biological agent to gain access to the human body and cause harm is highly dependent on the dose a person receives and the pathogenicity of that agent. Periods may vary from a few hours (with a toxin) to many days (with a bacteria or virus).

■ *Signs and symptoms*—A sign indicates the presence of a disease; a symptom is a change from normal function, sensation, or appearance, generally indicating disease or disorder.

■ *Mortality*—Mortality is the potential for death resulting from a biological event.

Biological agents used intentionally to kill and causes illness are the one aspect of the terrorist threat that the United States is least prepared for as a nation. There are two very distinct aspects of this that must be taken into consideration. The first is the reality of this threat, and the other is the potential of it. From the standpoint of reality, the world has faced bioterrorism. The first major use of a biological agent came in 1984 when the Rajneesh cult used *Salmonella typhimurium* to poison the salad bars of several restaurants in a small community called The Dalles in the state of Oregon (Ryan & Glarum, 2008). This attack, intended to influence local elections, managed to put 751 people in the hospital. In addition, recall the "anthrax letters" incident from the fall of 2001, which resulted in 22 cases of anthrax and 5 deaths.

Moving on to the potential, consider this aspect by detailing all the **Category A agents** and one of the **Category B agents**. The Soviets spent more than 40 years developing "superbugs" that were intended to be more lethal, more confounding, more resistant, and more stable than the pathogens from which they were derived (Alibek, 1999). At one point, *Biopreparat* employed more than 60,000 people, working in more than a dozen production facilities, which produced some agents by the ton each year.

Categories of Biological Agents

The following category agent definitions are provided by the Centers for Disease Control and Prevention (CDC).

Category A agents—The U.S. public health system and primary health-care providers must be prepared to address various biological agents, including pathogens rarely seen in the United States. These high-priority agents include organisms that pose a risk to national security because they

- Can be easily disseminated or transmitted from person to person
- Result in high mortality rates and have the potential for major public health impact
- Might cause public panic and social disruption
- Require special action for public health preparedness

Category B agents—The second-highest priority agents include those that have the following characteristics:

- Are moderately easy to disseminate
- Result in moderate morbidity rates and low mortality rates

Anthrax

Anthrax is a disease caused by *Bacillus anthracis*, the bacterium that primarily causes disease in cattle, sheep, and other hoofed animals. This is a Category A pathogen. These bacteria are capable of forming spores in conditions that are not ideal for supporting growth. This inactive stage of the organism makes it more resilient and an ideal candidate for bioterrorism (Ryan & Glarum, 2008).

In spore form, anthrax can be transmitted to humans through the respiratory tract, where it can lead to inhalation anthrax, which is the most lethal form of the disease (90% mortality rate). Inhalation anthrax could occur from inhalation of aerosolized spores released during a biological weapon attack (Figure 6.11). Inhalation anthrax usually occurs when individuals working with animal hides, wool, or bone meal inhale the spores. Although the incubation period is 1—7 days, the disease is not contagious, requiring direct contact with the spores to cause infection (Ryan & Glarum, 2008).

Plague

Once known as the Black Death, plague is a disease caused by the bacterium *Yersinia pestis*, a Category A pathogen. In the United States, the last urban plague epidemic occurred in Los Angeles in 1924—1925. Since that time, human plague in the United States has occurred as mostly scattered cases in rural areas (with an average of 5—15 victims each year). Globally, the World Health Organization (WHO) reports 1000—3000 cases of plague every year. In North America, plague is found in certain animals and their

■ **FIGURE 6.11** Hazmat technicians work outside the U.S. Capitol in 2001 to help contain anthrax spore contamination from the Hart Senate Building following the Amerithrax incident. *This image is courtesy of the U.S. DOJ, FBI.*

fleas from the Pacific Coast to the Great Plains, and from southwestern Canada to Mexico. Most human cases in the United States occur in two regions: (1) northern New Mexico, northern Arizona, southern Colorado, and southern Utah; and (2) California, southern Oregon, and far western Nevada (Ryan & Glarum, 2008).

Plague is normally transmitted to humans from rats through the bite of infected fleas. Infection by flea bite leads to bubonic plague. Plague-causing bacteria can also be aerosolized and transmitted to humans through the respiratory tract, causing pneumonic plague. Pneumonic plague is highly contagious (person-to-person) and, if untreated within 24 h of the victim becoming symptomatic is universally fatal (Ryan & Glarum, 2008).

Tularemia

Tularemia is a disease caused by the bacterium *Francisella tularensis*. This is a Category A pathogen. Known also as *rabbit fever* or *deerfly fever*, tularemia is a zoonosis (i.e., an animal disease that causes disease in humans) found in the Four Corners region of the United States (the point at which Arizona, New Mexico, Utah, and Colorado meet) and Martha's Vineyard, where it affects rodents, rabbits, and hares. Tularemia has great potential as a biological weapon. The Russians worked extensively with this bacterium, and one report suggests that they used it against the German army in World War II during the defense of Stalingrad (Ryan & Glarum, 2008).

F. tularensis is highly infectious. As few as 10 organisms inhaled into the lungs are sufficient to cause a fatal infection. Most human infections arise when the bacterium enters the body through breaks in the skin, or through mucous membranes after the handling of infected animals. Infection can also occur from the bite of infected deerflies, ticks, or mosquitoes. Inhalation of contaminated dust and ingestion of contaminated foods or water are other ways for humans to become infected (Ryan & Glarum, 2008).

Smallpox

Smallpox is a disease caused by the smallpox virus, *Variola major*, a Category A pathogen. Due to a successful global vaccine program, the WHO declared smallpox eradicated in 1980 (see Figure 6.12). Small quantities of live virus are still held in freezers at secure research facilities in the United States and Russia. Despite the WHO's declaration, a potential dissemination threat remains, because there is the possibility that some countries that did not sign the 1972 Biological Weapons Convention may have viral stocks (Ryan & Glarum, 2008).

The mortality rate for the major form of the disease is approximately 30% in unvaccinated populations and 3% in vaccinated populations. The incubation period for smallpox averages 12 days; therefore, those who may have had contact with the virus should be quarantined for a minimum of 16–17 days following exposure. A single case of smallpox would constitute an

■ **FIGURE 6.12** Extreme symptoms of one of the last cases of smallpox in Ghana in the late 1970s. This scourge was eradicated by a successful vaccination program in 1980. The agent, smallpox virus, does not exist in nature anymore. A single case of this emerging today would constitute an international emergency. *Courtesy of the U.S. Department of Health and Human Services Public Health Image Library.*

international emergency. Given the severity of this disease, communities need to have a response plan in place, providing details for surveillance, contact management, quarantine, and treatment (Ryan & Glarum, 2008).

Viral Hemorrhagic Fevers

Viral hemorrhagic fevers (VHFs) are caused by a number of viral agents, primarily Arenaviruses and Filoviruses. All of these are Category A pathogens. Examples are Ebola, Marburg, Lassa, Junin, and Machupo viruses. These viruses were named for places where the first cases of each were reported. Highly contagious and extremely lethal, they are known to occur naturally. Typically, these viruses are spread by person-to-person contact, especially contact with the bodily fluids of sick victims (Ryan & Glarum, 2008).

From several outbreaks that have occurred in parts of West Africa, 80% or more of the fatalities in these outbreaks come from the health-care workers that treated the initial patients (Ryan & Glarum, 2008). A recent outbreak of Ebola virus in 2014 illustrates the deadly nature of this viral pathogen and its potential to disrupt local communities and international travel and trade.

Botulinum Toxin

Botulinum toxin (Botox) is a natural, biological poison produced by the bacteria *Clostridium botulinum*. This is a Category A pathogen. Botulism is mostly associated with the consumption of improperly canned food. Botulinum toxin is the most lethal substance known to humans. It would require approximately 0.08 micrograms to kill an average person (176 lbs or 80 kg). By weight, botulinum toxin is about 10,000 times more toxic than the nerve agent sarin. Botox, which is being used for medical treatments, can be aerosolized and presented as an inhalation threat. Botulism is not transmissible from person to person (Ryan & Glarum, 2008).

Ricin

Ricin is a toxin derived from the water-soluble component of the castor bean (*Ricinus communis*). This agent is in Category B. Ricin is very popular among amateur bioterrorists because it is fairly simple to make a crude extract of the castor bean. Anyone can buy castor beans from a seed supply company. Once you have the beans, you can perform a fairly simple, crude extraction to derive a dirty preparation of ricin. Commercially, the mash from preparing castor oil contains up to 5% ricin. Because of its lethality, very little ricin is needed to cause great harm (a few hundred micrograms of ricin is lethal). Ricin can be transmitted to victims through the respiratory system, ingested in food, or injected. It is not communicable from person to person (Ryan & Glarum, 2008).

Biological Agent Attack Indicators and Dissemination Methods

The effects of a biological attack are not likely to be immediately visible at the scene of the attack. Rather, health-care workers and public health officials would have the first indication of an attack unless the containers used to disseminate the agent are left at the scene, or communications from the perpetrators indicated what occurred (Ryan & Glarum, 2008).

When a terrorist attack involving biological agents occurs, the emergency medical responder will most likely not be able to see the signs of the release of and contamination by an agent. Due to the incubation period, recognizing a biological attack or incident will be more difficult and subtler than a chemical attack; at first, the victims may go unnoticed (Figure 6.13). The onset of symptoms would be gradual and nonspecific; often, signs and symptoms are mistaken for the flu (Eitzen, 1997).

On-site detection of biological agents is currently not practical for emergency responders. Samples are best collected by hazmat teams from the incident site and analyzed using state-of-the-art technologies in a federally certified laboratory (the CDC Laboratory Response Network in Atlanta, Georgia). These technologies include simple culturing techniques and bioassays, immunoassays, and complex nucleic acid-based assays (Ryan & Glarum, 2008).

■ **FIGURE 6.13** A member of a Georgia Army National Guard 4th Civil Support team sheds his hazmat suit with help from Howard County Fire and Rescue hazmat technicians. Behind him, Cobb County hazmat technicians wait their turns to undress during Operation Vigilant Sample III at Fort Detrick, Maryland. *Image courtesy of Georgia Department of Defense. Photo by Sgt. 1st Class Roy Henry, Public Affairs Office.*

Dissemination of Biological Agents

The dissemination of biological agents can occur in many ways. The most effective large-scale means of dissemination is through the use of spraying devices (Eitzen, 1997). The following are possibilities for dissemination:

- *Spraying devices*—Aerosolization of biological agents using spray devices is the method of choice for dissemination. The aim of an aerosol delivery is to generate invisible clouds that can remain suspended for long periods. Spraying devices include crop dusters, sprayers mounted on trucks, smaller aerosol tanks used in pesticides, and many others.
- *Direct-deposit devices*—Biological agents can be disseminated through the use of direct-deposit devices, including injectors such as darts, needles, nails, or anything that penetrates the skin. Biological agents can also be placed on objects such as doorknobs, in packages and letters, and in food and water to be ingested. While some biological agents could be placed in water supplies, water purification systems would be sufficient to kill most pathogens.
- *Exploding devices*—While exploding devices can be used in the dissemination of biological agents, this is a less effective delivery system. Explosive, heat-generating entities can inactivate the organisms or toxins.
- *Vectors*—Vectors (e.g., mosquitoes, ticks, and fleas) transmit diseases naturally. If properly handled, terrorists could also use vectors as a weapon. The capability exists to purposely infect these carriers with certain diseases that are then transmitted to the victims. During World War II, the infamous Japanese Unit 731 experimented with the introduction of plague through the dispersion of infected fleas. They produced millions of infected fleas by feeding the fleas on plague-infected rodents. They mixed these fleas with rice and sand and poured that mixture into small clay bomblets. The bomblets were then dropped into Manchuria. The attacks were effective. Plague took hold in these areas, with estimates of as many as 10,000 deaths.

Modern-Day Example of Bioterrorism

In November 2003, the U.S. Secret Service intercepted a letter addressed to the White House that contained a vial of the toxin ricin, but never revealed the incident publicly and delayed telling the FBI and other agencies. Sources said that the letter contained complaints about trucking regulations and was nearly identical to one discovered a month earlier at a mail-sorting facility in Greenville, South Carolina, that was accompanied by a metal vial that contained powdered ricin. In February 2004, three Senate office buildings were closed after a white powder was found in an office of Senate Majority Leader Bill Frist. Dozens of Senate workers were monitored and health officials urged Senate staff to watch for swiftly developing fever, coughs, or fluid in the lungs over a 2- to 3-day period. Genetic testing by the CDC provided confirmation that the powder was indeed ricin. When inhaled in sufficient quantities or injected, ricin can be fatal, and there is no known vaccine or cure (Starr, et al., 2004).

RADIOLOGICAL AND NUCLEAR THREATS

Radiation is the invisible energy emitted by certain types of unstable or radioactive atoms. This energy travels through the air but cannot be seen, felt, smelled, or tasted. Some types of radiation can penetrate packaging materials, vehicles, and building walls. When radiation energy reaches a person, he or she is exposed to radiation. The amount of radiation energy absorbed by a person is the dose that was received. A small dose of radiation (for example, from a dental x-ray) has a very low risk of health effects. A high dose of radiation (such as sitting near an industrial radiography source for several hours) has a high risk of health effects, including nausea, vomiting, diarrhea, burns, and possibly even death.

The four types of radiation emitted by radioactive material are alpha, beta, gamma, and neutron radiation. When radioactive material is properly contained, it still emits radiation and may be a hazard. The radiation travels from the radioactive material in all directions and the distance it can travel ranges from ¼ inch (5 mm) to hundreds of feet (meters), depending on the specific type of radioactive material. The farther the radiation travels from its source, the weaker (and less hazardous) it becomes. The Emergency Response Guidebook (DOT Pipeline and Hazardous Materials Safety Administration, 2012) recommends isolating a spill, leak, or damaged container of radiological material for at least 25 to 50 meters (80 to 160 feet) in all directions.

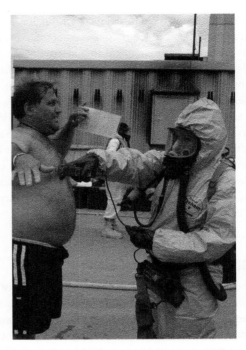

■ **FIGURE 6.14** Homeland Response Force. Pvt. Rosa Ruiz of the 149th Chemical Company, 579th Engineer Battalion, 49th Military Police Brigade, California Army National Guard, scans a civilian for gamma radiation on November 4 during the 2011 Arizona Statewide Vigilant Guard Exercise in Phoenix. *Image courtesy of Army National Guard. Photo by SPC Eddie Siguenza.*

Radioactive contamination is defined as radioactive material in an unwanted place, particularly where its presence may be harmful. Some types of contamination may be readily spread from one surface to another, making decontamination of possible victims necessary (see Figure 6.14). Some contamination may be suspended in the air or in the form of radioactive dust (ceramic or powder). Most radioactive sources (devices or items with radioactive material) in use do not meet the definition of a WMD, as defined in Title 18, U.S.C. 2332a, because they do not "release radiation or radioactivity at a level dangerous to human life." Examples of radioactive sources that do not emit life-endangering amounts of radiation are smoke detectors, tritium night sights on firearms, vials of radiopharmaceuticals (i.e., radioactive drugs), lantern mantles, tungsten welding rods, industrial moisture/density gauges (also called portable nuclear gauges), and most radioactively-contaminated medical waste. As explained in DOT Pipeline and Hazardous Materials Safety Administration (2012), packages (cartons, boxes, drums, etc.) identified as "Type A" by marking on packages or by shipping papers contain non-life-endangering amounts of radioactive material.

■ Radioactive sources that can be life-endangering may be found in the following locations:*Hospitals and cancer treatment facilities:* Blood irradiators, sterilizers, cancer treatment irradiators
■ *Industrial and construction sites:* Radiography cameras, food irradiators
■ *Nuclear power plants:* Used (or spent) fuel rods from a nuclear reactor
■ *In transit:* Material inside metal containers identified as "Type B" (DOT Pipeline and Hazardous Materials Safety Administration, 2012)

Signs and Symptoms of Radiation Exposure

Victims who receive a large dose of radiation may suffer from **acute radiation syndrome** (ARS), also known as *radiation sickness*. Symptoms of nausea, vomiting, and diarrhea may not develop until a few hours after exposure. The larger the dose of radiation a victim receives, the quicker the symptoms appear and the more severe the reaction. Victims who receive a high dose of radiation may die in days to weeks, but proper medical attention may save many of them if the dose is not too high. Victims and individuals who receive lower doses of radiation may have no symptoms, and they have only a very small increase in the risk of developing cancer. Some victims may also receive high enough doses of radiation to increase their risk of developing cancer in the future, but not high enough to suffer from any of the symptoms of ARS (Jarrett, 1999).

Radiation burns may appear on skin exposed to high doses of radiation. Essentially, the skin of victims may turn red and look "puffy" several hours after exposure. Radiation burns are not painful while the damage is occurring. After burns to the skin start to develop, the skin may start to itch and become painful. Radiation burns may seem to heal, then return a day or more later with more severe pain, blistering, and swelling. In some cases where people have found or stolen industrial radioactive sources and taken the containers apart, they suffered burns on their hands (Jarrett, 1999).

RDD

A radiological dispersal device (RDD) or "dirty bomb" is a conventional explosive or bomb containing radioactive material. In these instances, a conventional bomb is used as a means to spread radioactive contamination. It is not a nuclear bomb and does not involve a nuclear explosion. Any type of radioactive material could be used in a dirty bomb, but in general, these devices would be unlikely to cause serious health effects beyond those caused by the detonation of conventional explosives (Zimmerman & Loeb, 2004). An RDD may be as simple as a pipe bomb or explosives attached to a shipping container of radiological material. Because of the wide availability of radiological material throughout the world and the ease of building simple explosives, the probability of the use of an RDD is much higher than that of a nuclear weapon. The probable effects of a dirty bomb detonation would be the potential for panic in the general public and contamination areas near the blast site (Musolino and Harper, 2006).

Examples Where Radiological Hazards Occurred

In March 1979, an accident at the Three Mile Island nuclear facility near Harrisburg, Pennsylvania, led the U.S. Food and Drug Administration (FDA) to arrange emergency provisions of potassium iodide for 1 million residents to block thyroid uptake in the event of accidental release of radioactive iodine. The accident was caused by either a mechanical or electrical failure that affected the nuclear reactor's cooling system. This led to a partial meltdown of the core (Walker, 2004) (see Figure 6.15).

In April 1986, the Chernobyl nuclear power plant in the USSR underwent a catastrophic explosion due to a power surge. The explosion and fire released large quantities of radioactive particles into the atmosphere, which spread over much of the western part of the then−Soviet Union and Europe. The Chernobyl disaster is the worst nuclear power plant accident in history in terms of cost and resulting deaths, and is one of only two classified as a level 7 event (the maximum classification) on the International Nuclear Event Scale (the other being the Fukushima Daiichi nuclear disaster in 2011). The battle to contain the contamination and avert a greater catastrophe ultimately involved over 500,000 workers and cost an estimated 18 billion rubles. During the accident itself, 31 people died, and long-term effects such as cancers and deformities are still being accounted for (World Nuclear Association, 2014).

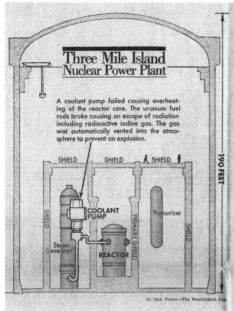

Three Mile Island Nuclear Power Plant

A coolant pump failed causing overheating of the reactor core. The uranium fuel rods broke causing an escape of radiation including radioactive iodine gas. The gas was automatically vented into the atmosphere to prevent an explosion.

SHIELD   SHIELD   SHIELD

190 FEET

SHIELD

COOLANT PUMP

PRIMARY SHIELD

Pressurizer

SHIELD

Steam Generator

REACTOR

By Dick Furno—The Washington Post

Radiation Spreads 10 Miles From A-Plant Mishap Site

By Thomas O'Toole
Washington Post Staff Writer

In what federal regulators called one of the nation's most serious nuclear accidents, a cooling system failure early yesterday at Pennsylvania's Three Mile Island power plant spread radiation as far as Harrisburg, 10 miles northwest of the plant.

The Nuclear Regulatory Commission described the radiation over Harrisburg as "quite low" and not dangerous to humans, but it was detected by instruments carried above Harrisburg by helicopter last night, more than 12 hours after the accident that triggered the radioactive release.

At 10 p.m., NRC spokesman Frank Ingram said that radiation was "continuing" to escape in "detectable levels" from the Three Mile Island plant.

Apparently, uranium fuel rods that had broken up earlier in the day from overheating were continuing through the night to release radiation that seeped through the four-foot-thick walls surrounding the reactor building.

Officials of Metropolitan Edison Co., part owner of the plant, said some radioactive steam also escaped during efforts to cool the overheated fuel rods with water. They conceded that some employes had been exposed to radiation but that there was no evidence of injury.

The radioactive release apparently occurred when an operator mistakenly turned off the pumps driving the plant's emergency water cooling system, allowing the uranium fuel to overheat and rupturing an unknown number of the 36,000 fuel rods that generate heat for the plant.

By 7 o'clock last night, the uranium fuel was still so hot that the plant's managers had to vent radioactive steam into the atmosphere to prevent an explosion inside the thick concrete dome protecting the nuclear reactor.

"The situation is still not stabilized," Edison Case, deputy director of the Nuclear Regulatory Commission, said last night. "The reactor core is not cooling down as fast as we'd like."

He said radiation levels inside the plant's reactor building registered 1,000 times normal.

Case said that more than 60,000 gallons of water had been flooded into the room housing the reactor, which was still as hot as 550 degrees 12 hours after being shut down. Some of the water was flashing into steam, the reason the radioactive steam had to be periodically vented to the atmosphere.

Radioactive iodine was found on the ground around the plant, suggesting it had escaped as a gas from the broken fuel bundles in the reactor. Gamma and beta radiation was detected as far as a mile from the plant in the nearby townships of Middletown and Londonderry.

The NRC's Case described this as "direct radiation" escaping from the broken fuel bundles through the 4-foot-thick concrete walls surrounding the reactor building. This radiation was measured at three milliroentgens per hour, a measure of radiation less than the exposure a patient receives from an x-ray.

The sequence of events that led to the accident was unclear but what happened was an event that the nuclear power industry long has said was unlikely or even impossible.

■ **FIGURE 6.15** In March 1979, an accident at the Three Mile Island nuclear facility near Harrisburg, Pennsylvania, led the FDA to arrange emergency provisions of potassium iodide for 1 million residents to block their thyroid uptake in the event of accidental release of radioactive iodine. *Image courtesy of the U.S. FDA.*

In 1987, several people handled highly radioactive cesium powder released from a metal capsule inside an abandoned cancer treatment machine in Goiânia, Brazil. Some of them intentionally rubbed this powder on their bodies because it glowed with what they thought was a pretty blue color. After eating food with contaminated hands, the victims showed radiation burns on their tongues and mouths. For most victims of this incident, the symptoms did not appear immediately after the contamination (IAEA, 1988).

Chechen guerrillas in Russia have used radiological material, but they have not detonated an RDD. In 1995, Chechen guerrillas buried a container of radioactive cesium-137 in a park in Moscow. The guerrillas notified the authorities and warned them that next time, they would use an RDD with explosives. In 1998, an RDD consisting of a container of radioactive material with explosives and an anti-tampering device was found near a railway east of Grozny, Russia (PBS, 2003).

■ **FIGURE 6.16** Nuclear detonation in the Bikini Atoll, circa 1958. The destructive force of a single, small nuclear weapon is enough to destroy a small city. *Courtesy of the U.S. National Archives.*

Nuclear Weapons

The most sophisticated and deadly weapon is a nuclear weapon. It derives its great explosive potential from the energy gained from splitting atoms (fission) of special nuclear material (e.g., uranium and plutonium). The use of a nuclear device would produce devastating effects, including thermal (heat) impulse, blast wave, penetrating neutron and gamma radiation, and radioactive fallout with radiological contamination; and would have a tremendous psychosocial impact on a community, a nation, and perhaps even the World (Bowman, 2002). There is a very low probability that an act of terrorism or modern warfare will result in the detonation of a nuclear weapon.

> *If I had known they were going to do this, I would have become a shoemaker.*
>
> **Albert Einstein**

The size of a nuclear explosion is much larger than conventional explosives (Figure 6.16). The size of nuclear explosions is measured in kilotons (kt). The energy of 1 kt is equivalent to the explosion of 1000 tons of trinitrotoluene (TNT) explosives. Nuclear weapons have been fashioned to be small enough to be carried by one person (often referred to as a "backpack" or "suitcase" nuclear device). Although a nuclear device with a yield similar to the atomic bombs used in World War II in Hiroshima and Nagasaki, Japan (16 and 23 kt, respectively) may devastate the center of a city, a supposedly small nuclear detonation of less than 1 kt may be mistaken for a large truck bomb. The area of destroyed buildings may be less than a city block.

HIGH-YIELD EXPLOSIVES

According to the FBI Bomb Data Center, approximately 70% of all terrorist incidents involve the use of explosives and incendiary agents (DOJ, 2014). Because of the prevalence of use, individuals need to understand explosives. Energetic materials can be divided into three categories. The first, pyrotechnics, has the least explosive potential and are produced to create smoke, light, heat, and sound. Examples of pyrotechnics are fireworks, road flares, smoke grenades, and thermites. Second, there are propellants, which are also referred to as *low explosives*. Propellants are designed to provide a controlled release of gas to perform useful work. This gas can be used to push something (such as a bullet from a gun or a rocket into space). The vast majority of improvised explosive devices (IEDs) in the United States has historically incorporated propellants. Examples of propellants are black or smokeless powders and solid and liquid rocket fuel. Finally, there are explosives, also referred to as *high explosives*, which are designed to yield a near-instantaneous release of energy. Explosives are normally used for destructive purposes. A bomb designed to cause maximum dispersion of shrapnel is intended to kill and cause property destruction. Common examples of explosives are TNT, Composition C-4 (C4), and dynamite (DHS, 2004).

Categories of High Explosives

There are three high-explosive categories: primary, secondary, and tertiary. Each category designates a different level of sensitivity to stimuli (DHS, 2004):

- *Primary explosives*—Extremely sensitive and, as a consequence, extremely dangerous. Very small quantities—a single, salt-grain-sized silver azide crystal, for example—can undergo deflagration to detonation transfer (DDT). Simply breaking such a crystal can cause detonation. Almost all detonators contain primary explosives.
- *Secondary explosives*—Generally far less sensitive than primary explosives, they are the explosive materials more commonly used in bulk. Most people are familiar with these materials, which include TNT, C4, and dynamite. Secondary explosives are made to withstand

rough handling. Detonating a secondary explosive requires the tremendous energy levels created by another explosion, usually created by a primary explosive found in a blasting cap.

- *Tertiary explosives*—Based on ammonium nitrate, which is a very insensitive substance, these explosives typically require initiation from a secondary explosive to cause detonation. A blasting cap will not generally initiate them. Usually, a large mass (one-half-pound or 225 gms range) of secondary explosive (referred to as a *booster*) is needed for this purpose. For example, a stick of dynamite can be used to initiate a tertiary explosive.

Improvised Explosives

Most improvised explosives are comprised of chemical constituents easily found in any home or local community, even in large quantities. Improvised explosives, such as military and commercial explosives, are typically mixtures of an oxidizer and a fuel. Regardless of type, all are extremely hazardous. Most improvised explosives are based on formulations used in commercial applications or research. Legitimate users do not use improvised explosives very often today. This is due to their sensitivity and unsuitability to be handled in a safe manner. Improvised explosives can be as effective as manufactured explosives in many applications. Terrorists employ these in all sizes of devices. The following sections describe common types of improvised explosives being utilized today, mainly by terrorists (DHS, 2004).

Potassium Chlorate

Potassium chlorate has approximately 83% of the power of TNT. It is a common ingredient in some fireworks and can be purchased in bulk form from fireworks/chemical supply houses. Potassium chlorate normally appears in white crystal or powder form.

Peroxide-Based Improvised Explosives

Peroxide-based improvised explosives are currently an emerging threat domestically. However, they have been commonly used by international terrorists for some time before now. Hexamethylenetriperoxidediamine (HMTD) and triacetonetriperoxide (TATP) were initially developed 100 years ago. They are both extremely sensitive and are used as an explosive by bombers as both an initiator (blasting cap) and as a main charge. TATP is commonly found as the main charge employed by Middle East terrorists in suicide bombings (DHS, 2004).

HMTD has between 60% and 116% of the power of TNT and is comprised of peroxide (ideally 30% or more), citric acid, and hexamine (heat tabs). TATP has 88% of the power of TNT and is comprised of peroxide, acetone, and sulfuric (battery) acid.

Powdered Ammonium Nitrate and Aluminum Powder

Ammonium nitrate can be procured in powdered form—one example is a common cold pack. These use either ammonium nitrate in prill or powder form. If ammonium nitrate is in prill form, such as in fertilizer, it is a simple task to grind it into a powder. The aluminum powder can be procured at a professional paint store or simply filed from an ingot. The explosive has 75% the power of TNT and is sensitive to friction impact. It requires only a blasting cap for initiation.

While this is only one-half pound (225 gms) of explosive, consider that this mixture of readily available constituents has been used in very large devices. In 1997, there were three apartment complex bombings in Moscow, each of which consisted of ammonium nitrate in amounts equivalent to 500 pounds (225 kgs) of TNT. The devastating effects from each of those devices resulted in over 100 casualties per incident (DHS, 2004).

Urea Nitrate

Urea nitrate is also considered a type of fertilizer-based explosive; in this case, the two constituents are nitric acid (one of the 10 most produced chemicals in the world) and urea. A common source of urea is prills used for deicing sidewalks. Urea can also be derived from concentrated urine. This is a common variation used in South America and the Middle East by terrorists. Often, sulfuric acid is added to assist with catalyzing the constituents. A bucket containing the urea is used surrounded by an ice bath. The ice assists with the chemical conversion when nitric acid is added. The resulting explosive can be sensitive to a blasting cap. Urea nitrate has a destructive power similar to ammonium nitrate (DHS, 2004).

Hypergolic Devices

Some improvised explosives are hypergolic in nature. This means when two particular chemical constituents are brought together, they can violently react with each other, with the surrounding atmospheric temperature often being the catalyst; they are highly unstable and unpredictable. This reaction will result in either an incendiary effect or an explosion.

■ **FIGURE 6.17** A man who lost a family member in the Oklahoma City bombing in April 1995 is comforted by an FBI agent at the scene. This horrendous act of terrorism was perpetrated by Timothy McVeigh. He and an accomplice, Terry Nichols, utilized a rental truck filled with explosives. As a result, there were 168 deaths and more than 680 injuries. *Images courtesy of the U.S. DOJ, FBI.*

An example is sulfuric acid (oxidizer) and sugar (fuel) in a Styrofoam® cup. The acid slowly eats through the Styrofoam and mixes with the sugar, causing a hypergolic reaction within seconds and resulting in an explosion (DHS, 2004).

Examples of Incidents Involving Explosives

On April 19, 1995, just after 9 a.m., a truck, containing a 5,000-pound ammonium nitrate/fuel oil (ANFO) bomb, pulled into a parking area outside the Alfred P. Murrah Building. The driver, Timothy McVeigh, stepped down from the truck's cab and walked away. A few minutes later, at 9:02, the truck's deadly cargo blasted the building with enough force to shatter one-third of the seven-story structure (see Figure 6.17).

In March 11, 2004, 10 bombs were detonated on Madrid's commuter train system. The bombs, made of dynamite, were packed into sports bags with cell phones set to ring at different times to ignite the puttylike explosives. With 191 dead and 1800 wounded, it was the worst attack in Spain's history. The Basque terrorist group, Euskadi Ta Askatasuna (ETA, which translates as "Basque Fatherland and Liberty"), is said to be responsible for the bombings; however, there is much debate over who actually originated the attack. There have been suggested links to al-Qaeda, and it has been proven that ETA does have past connections with that terrorist group. Whoever they were, the terrorists succeeded in shutting down commuter, regional, intercity, and international train traffic, and created chaos with the attack (DHS, 2004).

In April 2013, a fertilizer storage and distribution facility in West, Texas, caught fire and exploded. A total of 15 emergency services personnel responding to the fire were killed, and more than 160 were injured. In addition, more than 150 buildings were damaged or destroyed. Investigators have affirmed that ammonium nitrate was the material that exploded, but the cause of the initial fire is unknown. A recent report states that the loss of life from this disaster was preventable because firefighters and community officials were not aware of what the facility stored, so they did not take the proper precautions when responding to the fire (McLaughlin, 2014). This serves as a prime example of why emergency management officials and first responders need to have complete awareness of the technological hazards in their communities.

CYBERTERRORISM

We live in the information age. Computing and information services have become a mainstay of our professional and personal lives. Economically, there isn't a single commodity that isn't touched in some way by information systems (production, inventory, transport, and sales). Businesses and individuals alike are extremely vulnerable to the theft or manipulation of sensitive information. National defense and government depends on the protection of critical information and systems. In February 2014, President Obama stated that cyberterrorism was the biggest threat to the United States (Harress, 2014). It is well known that there are numerous state-sponsored programs to steal government and corporate secrets. In addition, there are a number of groups (such as a "hacktivist" group known as *Anonymous*) that aim to undermine the integrity and daily operations of some corporations and government agencies. Some groups or individuals have succeeded in breaching the firewalls of sensitive government systems, resulting in a denial of service (DOS) for a network (Lewis, 2002). Cybersecurity has become a top priority to counter this threat. Current methods for hacking into a system and strategies for countering those methods are often classified, so they are impractical to discuss in a general textbook on hazard mitigation. Defense groups like Cyber Command in the United States are fighting cyber warfare attempts on a daily basis.

> **CRITICAL THINKING**
>
> What community information systems related to emergency management and emergency services are vulnerable to computer hacking or an act of cyberterrorism? How might this affect the emergency manager?

■ CONCLUSION

Technological hazards has been defined for us as manmade hazards from manufacturing, transportation, and the use of substances such as radioactive materials, chemicals, explosives, flammables, pesticides, herbicides, and disease agents. The U.S. DOT has categorized technological hazards into nine classes of hazardous materials, which truly helps reveal the wide-ranging spectrum of these hazards. In this chapter, TICs, TIMs, CWAs, civil unrest, biological agents, radiological materials, and nuclear weapons were discussed. The information presented was not all inclusive (and in some cases it could not be because much of the information on cyberterrorism is classified), but it was given in sufficient depth to communicate an appreciation for all the technological hazards that are present in communities and how emergency management programs need to be aware of what hazards are present and where they are stored. Accidents do happen. When they do, we must be prepared to respond properly. But, more important for the focus of this textbook, our awareness of these threats can lead to mitigation strategies that may either prevent an incident or lessen the impact of one.

But this chapter also addressed the reality that not all incidents are accidents. Terrorism, or the intentional use or threat of force to advance a cause or coerce a people or its government through fear, was discussed. Terrorist threats can come from both domestic and international terrorist organizations, which mobilize in order to initiate acts of violence to further or publicize their beliefs.

It is important for emergency managers and first responders to understand the interdependence of critical infrastructure and their vulnerability to attack. Vulnerability reduction of critical infrastructure and key assets should always be a focus of the mitigation strategies. Should an incident involving CBRNE occur, emergency managers and responders who understand the threat and are prepared for the response are more likely to reduce the overall consequences.

Chemical agents can be formidable weapons, which may have overwhelming effects. This is due to the toxicity of these agents and the special actions that emergency managers, first responders, and medical professionals will have to perform to respond should they be released into the environment. With this in mind, it is clear that an understanding of the physical characteristics, health effects, and dissemination methods of chemical agents is important for individuals to consider.

Biological agents are natural, but when used against people or animals, they have great potential for doing harm. There are many ways to look at this subject. To do justice to it, you should be mindful of the realities of the threat, as well as the potential for it. The Category A agents and one of the Category B agents were covered in this chapter. Often, when the subject of bioterrorism comes up, some professionals are quick to point out how simple it would be to acquire these materials. Hence, the assumption is that biological terrorism is easy to accomplish.

However, it is the author's opinion that there is really nothing easy about turning these agents into weapons. Certainly, government programs involving thousands of talented, bright scientists did produce these agents, and some materials may be available for purchase on the black market. To start a program from scratch, acquire the pathogens, propagate the materials, separate and purify the agents, stabilize them, and put them into a weaponized format is no easy task, though. Outbreaks of anthrax, plague, tularemia, and one of the VHF agents would be devastating to our communities. But given the difficulty of perpetrating a large-scale act of bioterrorism, this is a low-probability event.

Radiological material is any material that spontaneously emits ionizing radiation. Four types of radiation were addressed: alpha, beta, gamma, and neutrons. Alpha and beta radiation are primarily internal threats to body organs, while gamma rays and neutrons can be either an external or an internal threat to any part of the body, due to their ability to penetrate. The primary route of entry into the body for alpha and beta radiation is the respiratory tract or through open wounds. Ingestion or inhalation of alpha or beta particles can result in tumors that may not become evident for several years. Gamma rays and neutrons act more quickly to produce burns and radiation sickness.

Radiological threats posed by terrorists could include an RDD or a nuclear weapon. Most of the physical damage to the general population from an RDD would come from inhalation or ingestion of the radiological material. Nuclear weapons could be obtained and used by terrorists, but it is widely believed that an RDD is the more likely weapon for use by terrorists. Detonation of a nuclear weapon produces a blast effect, resulting in large amounts of heat and scattered radioactive material.

Of all the technological hazards discussed, the most likely CBRNE material to be used by a terrorist is high-yield explosives. There are many examples to illustrate their great potential for doing harm and the relative ease of obtaining the ingredients for making a large and effective bomb. In addition, cyberterrorism is something that occurs daily at the national and international levels; it is a transparent evil with great potential for destroying information systems that we have come to rely on.

In summary, technological hazards are present in our communities. Your task as an emergency manager is to identify and locate them. From there, you need to adopt specific strategies for mitigating their effects whether they are the result of an accident or an intentional incident. Remember that intentional acts often lead to situations where response and recovery can be hindered by crime scene considerations. Your task is daunting given the wide-ranging spectra of manmade threats.

DISCUSSION QUESTIONS

1. Technological hazards saturate our communities. What locations in a community are many of these hazards found? What areas or sites within your own community might there be a concentration of these materials?
2. Why would a terrorist want to utilize CBRNE?
3. CBRNE materials are readily available—or are they? Which of these materials would be difficult to acquire, and why?
4. What makes an act of terrorism involving a manmade hazard different from an accident involving the same agent (use TNT as an example)?
5. Discuss challenges to situational awareness when responders and emergency managers are confronted with an incident involving an unknown hazardous substance.

WEBSITES

U.S. Central Intelligence Agency (CIA). Terrorist CBRN: Materials and effects
https://www.cia.gov/library/reports/general-reports-1/terrorist_cbrn/terrorist_CBRN.htm.
U.S. Department of Justice (DOJ). Bureau of Alcohol, Tobacco, Firearms, and Explosives. U.S. Bomb Data Center
https://www.atf.gov/content/explosives/explosives-enforcement/us-bomb-data-center
U.S. Central Intelligence Agency (CIA). *Chemical/biological/radiological incident handbook* (October 1998)
https://www.cia.gov/library/reports/general-reports-1/cbr_handbook/cbrbook.htm
Memorial Institute for the Prevention of Terrorism (MIPT). MIPT Terrorism Knowledge Base
https://www.mipt.org

U.S. Department of Transportation (DOT). Pipeline and Hazardous Materials Safety Administration. 2012 *Emergency Response Guidebook* and other useful tools and information
http://phmsa.dot.gov/hazmat/library/erg

REFERENCES

Alibek, K. (1999). *Biohazard: The chilling true story of the largest covert biological weapons program in the world—Told from the inside by the man who ran it.* New York: Random House.

BBC News. (1988). BBC ON THIS DAY | 16 | 1988: Thousands die in Halabja gas attack. Retrieved from <http://news.bbc.co.uk/onthisday/hi/dates/stories/march/16/newsid_4304000/4304853.stm>. Accessed August 20, 2014.

Bjelopera. J. (2013). The domestic terrorist threat: Background and issues for congress. CRS report written by Jerome P. Bjelopera. January 17, 2013. Congressional Research Service Report #R42536. Retrieved from <http://fas.org/sgp/crs/terror/R42536.pdf>. Accessed August 20, 2014.

Bolz, F., Dudonis, K., & Schulz, D. (2005). *The counterterrorism handbook: Tactics, procedures, and techniques* (3rd ed.). Boston: CRC Press.

Bowman, S. (2002). *Weapons of mass destruction: The terrorist threat.* CRS Report for Congress. March 7, 2002. Congressional Research Service Report #RL31332. Retrieved from <http://www.mipt.org/pdf/CRS_RL31332.pdf>. Accessed August, 2014.

Brown, F. (2005). *Chemical warfare: A study in restraints.* New Brunswick, NJ: Transaction Publishers.

Budinsky, S. (2013). Protection of the President: Changing views of the Secret Service and the American executive, 1901–1951. An honors thesis submitted to the history department of Rutgers, The State University of New Jersey, New Brunswick, NJ.

CNN. (2014a). Los Angeles riots fast facts. Retrieved from <http://www.cnn.com/2013/09/18/us/los-angeles-riots-fast-facts/>. Accessed August 2014.

CNN. (2014b). Did media make the Ferguson Riots Worse? Retrieved from <http://www.cnn.com/videos/us/2014/11/30/rs-did-media-make-ferguson-riots-worse.cnn>. Accessed May 15, 2015.

Cutter, S. L (1993). *Living with risk: The geography of technological hazards.* London and New York: Edward Arnold.

Eitzen, E., & Takafuji, E. (1997). Historical overview of biological warfare. In F. Sidell, E. Takafuji, & D. Franz (Eds.), *Medical Aspects of Chemical and Biological Warfare* (pp. 415–423). Washington, DC: Office of the Surgeon General, Borden Institute, Walter Reed Army Medical Center.

Federation of American Scientists (FAS) Intelligence Resource Program. (2008). Revolutionary armed forces of Colombia. Fuerzas Armadas Revolucionarios de Colombia—FARC. June 18, 2008. Retrieved from <http://fas.org/irp/world/para/farc.htm>. Accessed August 2014.

Frieden, T. (2005). FBI, ATF address domestic terrorism. CNN Online. May 19, 2005. Retrieved from <http://www.cnn.com/2005/US/05/19/domestic.terrorism/>. Accessed August 2014.

Goldfarb, A. (2007). *Death of a dissident: The poisoning of Alexander Litvinenko and the return of the KGB.* New York: Free Press.

Harress, C. (2014). Obama says cyberterrorism is country's biggest threat, U.S. government assembles "cyber warriors." *International Business Times.* February 18, 2014.

International Atomic Energy Agency (IAEA). (1988). The radiological accident in Goiania. Retrieved from <http://www-pub.iaea.org/mtcd/publications/pdf/pub815_-web.pdf>. Accessed August 2014.

Jarrett, D. (1999). *Medical management of radiological casualties handbook.* Bethesda, MD: Armed Forces Radiobiology Research Institute.

Larsen, J., Wirtz, J., & Croddy, E. (2004). *Weapons of mass destruction: An encyclopedia of worldwide policy, technology, and history* (2 vols), Santa Barbara, CA: ABC-CLIO.

Lewis, J. (2002). Assessing the risks of cyber terrorism, cyber war, and other cyber threats. Center for Strategic and International Studies. Retrieved from <http://csis.org/files/media/csis/pubs/021101_risks_of_cyberterror.pdf>. Accessed August, 2014.

Lewis, J. (2005). When talk turns to terror: Homegrown extremism in the U.S. FBI Internal Report. FBI Archives. No longer accessible.

Martin, C. (2012). *Understanding terrorism: Challenges, perspectives, and issues* (4th ed.). Thousand Oaks, CA: Sage Publications.

McLaughlin, E. (2014). West, Texas, fertilizer plant blast that killed 15 "preventable," safety board says, CNN online. April 22, 2014 Retrieved from <http://www.cnn.com/2014/04/22/us/west-texas-fertilizer-plant-explosion-investigation/>. Accessed August, 2014.

McVeigh, T. (2001). *Letter.* Fox News on the Web. April 26, 2001. Retrieved from <http://www.foxnews.com/story/0,2933,17500,00.html>. Accessed August, 2014.

Morgan, M. (2004). The origins of the new terrorism. Parameters. Retrieved from <http://Carlislewww.army.mil/usawc/Parameters/04spring/morgan.htm>. Accessed August 2014.

Musolino, S., & Harper, F. (2006). Emergency response guidance for the first 48 hours after the outdoor detonation of an explosive radiological device. *Health Physics, 90* (4), 377−385.

PR Newswire. (2005). PETA, Humane society of the United States providing support to ALF, ELF. Retrieved from <http://www.thefreelibrary.com/PETA,+Humane+Society+of+the+United+States+Providing+Support+to+ALF,...-a0132539592>. Accessed August, 2014.

Public Broadcasting Service (PBS). (2003). Dirty bomb. *NOVA.* February 25, 2003. Retrieved from <http://www.pbs.org/wgbh/nova/dirtybomb/chrono.html>. Accessed August 2014.

Ramana, D. V., & Ramana, D. R. (2002). The union carbide disaster in Bhopal: A review of health effects. *Environmental Health, 57*(5), 391−404.

Rudolph, E. (2005). Statement of Eric Robert Rudolph. April 15, 2005. Retrieved from <http:// www.vanguardnewsnetwork.com/2005/Rudolphtext.htm>. Accessed August 20, 2014.

Ryan, J. (2005). Hazardous Materials Technicians Course, Chemical Agents Module. Department of Homeland Security, Center for Domestic Preparedness. Anniston, AL.

Ryan, J. R., & Glarum, J. F. (2008). *Biosecurity and bioterrorism: Containing and preventing the biological threat.* Boston, MA: Butterworth-Heinemann, Elsevier.

Singh, M., & Ghosh, S. (1987). Bhopal gas tragedy model simulation of the dispersion scenario. *Journal of Hazardous Materials, 17*, 1−22.

Starr, B., Carroll, J., Feig, C., Barrett, T., Ahlers, M., Madden, M. (2014). Frist: Ricin confirmed, but no illness reported. CNN.com, February 4, 2004. Retrieved from <http://www.cnn.com/2004/US/02/03/senate.hazardous/>. Accessed August 20, 2014.

Trumpener, U. (1975). The road to Ypres: The beginnings of gas warfare in World War I. *Journal of Modern History, 47*(3), 460−480.

Tzu, S. The art of war. (2002, October 25). In WriteWork.com. Retrieved from <http://www.writework.com/essay/sun-tzu-art-war>. Accessed August 20, 2014.

U.S. Army Medical Research Institute of Infectious Disease (USAMRIID). (2004). *Medical management of biological casualties handbook* (5th ed.). Retrieved from <http://www.usamriid.army.mil/education/bluebook.htm>. Accessed August 20, 2014.

U.S. Department of Homeland Security (DHS). (2004). Awareness level WMD training. Explosive devices module. Center for Domestic Preparedness. *Technical Emergency Response Training (TERT) Student Manual.*

U.S. Department of Interior (DOI) (2012). Natural resource damage assessment, April 2012 status update for the Deepwater Horizon oil spill. Retrieved from <http://www.doi.gov/deepwaterhorizon/upload/FINAL_NRDA_StatusUpdate_April2012-2.pdf>. Accessed August 20, 2014.

U.S. Department of Justice (DOJ). (2014). Bureau of Alcohol, Tobacco, Firearms and Explosives. U.S. Bomb Data Center. Retrieved from <https://www.atf.gov/content/explosives/explosives-enforcement/us-bomb-data-center>. Accessed August 20, 2014.

U.S. Department of State. (2013). Patterns of global terrorism, Retrieved from <http://www.state.gov/j/ct/rls/crt/>. Accessed August, 2014.

U.S. Department of Transportation (DOT) Pipeline and Hazardous Materials Safety Administration. (2012). *2012 emergency response guidebook.* Retrieved from <http://phmsa.dot.gov/hazmat/library/erg>. Accessed August 20, 2014.

U.S. National Transportation Safety Board (NTSB). (2005). Collision of Norfolk Southern Freight Train 192 with Standing Norfolk Southern Local Train P22 with subsequent hazardous materials release, Graniteville, South Carolina. January 6, 2005. NTSB Number: RAR-05-04. NTIS Number: PB2005-916304. Retrieved from <http://www.ntsb.gov/investigations/AccidentReports/Pages/RAR0504.aspx>. Accessed May 15, 2015.

Varma, D. R., & Guest, I. (1993). The Bhopal accident and methyl isocyanate toxicity. *Journal of Toxicology and Environmental Health, 40*, 513−529.

Walker, J. (2004). *Three Mile Island: A nuclear crisis in historical perspective.* Berkeley, CA: University of California Press.

White House. Official Press Release. (2011). Osama Bin Laden dead. May 2, 2011. Retrieved from <http://www.whitehouse.gov/blog/2011/05/02/osama-bin-laden-dead>. Accessed August 20, 2014.

Wing, J. S., Brender, J. D., Sanderson, L. M., Perrotta, D. M., & Beauchamp, R. A. (1991). Acute health effects in a community after a release of hydrofluoric acid. *Archives of Environment Health, 46*(3), 155−160.

World Nuclear Association (2014). Chernobyl accident 1986. Retrieved from <http://www.world-nuclear.org/info/safety-and-security/safety-of-plants/chernobyl-accident/>. Accessed August, 2014.

Zimmerman, P., & Loeb, C. (2004). Dirty bombs: The threat revisited. National Defense University. Retrieved from <http://hps.org/documents/RDD_report.pdf>. Accessed May 15, 2015.

Vulnerability Assessment and Impact Analysis

OBJECTIVES

The study of this chapter will enable you to:

1. Define the terms *hazard*, *risk*, *vulnerability*, and *impact*. Discuss their interrelatedness and the general process used to determine the priorities for hazard mitigation.

2. Describe the processes used to conduct vulnerability assessment and impact analysis.

3. List and discuss elements of a community that are considered to be parts of its critical infrastructure.

4. Discuss the concept of key assets.

5. Describe hazard mapping and how this might be accomplished by the emergency manager in a community.

Essential Terminology: Asset, base map, vulnerability assessment, critical infrastructure, hazard, impact, key asset, magnitude, probability, risk, vulnerability

There can be no vulnerability without risk; there can be no community without vulnerability; there can be no peace, and ultimately no life, without community.

M. Scott Peck, author of *The Road Less Traveled*

INTRODUCTION

Chapters 1 through 6 helped lay down a foundation of knowledge about comprehensive emergency management (CEM), key disaster-related legislation, milestones in the CEM timeline, and natural and technological hazards. Now that you have all that information, what can and should you do with it? Well, you should employ some specific processes in your professional settings to mitigate those hazards. This chapter will look at the community setting and considerations for the assessment of natural and technological hazards and focus on critical infrastructure and key assets. Following that, it will discuss and apply a specific process needed for you to assess vulnerability to natural and technological hazards.

Community Setting

Regardless of where you live, you are part of a community. Some communities are large and urban, others are small and rural, and there is everything in between. Busy, bustling, opulent, quiet, sleepy, industrial, agricultural, poor, run-down—there are many words that can be used to describe the communities we live in and serve as emergency managers. Consider the many pieces within each community and how they are interrelated. Not only are they interrelated, they also depend very much on each other for the normalcy that has been achieved in the evolution of that community. Natural and technological disasters disturb community normalcy. They may obliterate an entire community or destroy a very specific slice. Either way, we have to examine our communities in their entirety and imagine how we are vulnerable to any one natural or technological disaster and then how that hazard might affect us given its varying magnitudes. Such is the essence of vulnerability assessment and impact analysis.

Refer to Figure 7.1 for an overview of the process that should lead the emergency manager to determine what the priorities for hazard mitigation should be in his or her community. There are some key terms used in this chart: *asset, hazard, hazard analysis, impact, impact analysis, magnitude, probability, risk*, and *vulnerability*. Review the definitions for these key terms listed at the end of the chapter if they are not familiar to you.

How one might interpret the chart in Figure 7.1 is as follows: Hazard analysis involves identifying and investigating both the hazard location and its geographical extent. It further examines the identified hazard's strength (scale, magnitude, intensity) and probability of occurrence. The many methods and instruments available for hazard analysis operate on the basis of available scientific data. Vulnerability assessment is the next step in the process, where assets at risk are pitted against the hazards, the probability that they will

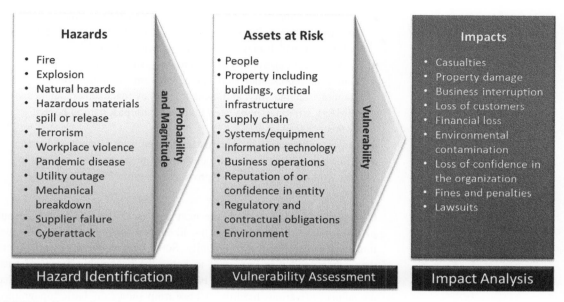

■ FIGURE 7.1 The general process used in a community or other professional setting to consider hazards, vulnerability to them, and their impact. *Courtesy of FEMA.*

occur, and the magnitude that one might expect. This will then lead to impact analysis, where we can consider the consequences of the hazards should they affect us. The process should enable us to identify those hazards that are most likely to occur and have the greatest impact (Cannon, 1994). Given that resources for mitigation efforts can be scarce, one should be working off of a prioritization list that best serves the community.

What follows in this chapter is a discussion of the process utilized to conduct hazard analysis, vulnerability assessment, and impact analysis, especially concerning natural hazards, and then considerations for incorporating technological hazard vulnerability assessment into the overall picture are given.

HAZARD ANALYSIS

In terms of hazard identification, FEMA (2001b) suggested the following techniques that should provide a good starting point to identify hazards:

■ Research newspapers and other historical records, which often contain dates, magnitudes of the events, damages, and other information about previous natural disasters that occurred in the area.

- Review existing plans and reports such as local comprehensive plans, land use plans, capital improvement plans, building codes, and flood ordinances, which may indicate the presence of local hazards.
- Talk to local experts in your community, such as floodplain managers, representatives of the department of public works, planning, engineering, and local emergency management agencies (EMAs), who may have been involved with past natural hazard events.
- Collect information on hazards in the area from relevant websites.
- After preliminary research, focus on the most prevalent hazards in your community. Figure 7.2 provides a sample FEMA worksheet of tasks to identify the hazards.

Once hazards are identified, the next step is to develop **hazard event profiles**, which help determine the likelihood, magnitude, and potential impact of hazards in the community. Some hazards affect the area more than others, and it is important to know the geographic extent of each hazard. Obtaining or creating a base map is essential to show areas that are subject to various hazards. A **base map** shows the basic topography, physical elements and infrastructure, political boundaries such as city limits, streets and roads, rivers, etc. (Schwab et al., 2007). The base map is also very important when conducting vulnerability assessment.

The potential impact of a hazard can be determined by its location, how large an area within the community is affected, magnitude or maximum probable extent, and the probability or likelihood of future events. FEMA (2013) uses the following classifications for location, magnitude, and probability of hazards and then rank each hazard based on overall significance.

- *Location (Geographic area affected):* Can be classified as negligible (less than 10% of planning area affected), limited (10 to 25% of planning area affected), significant (25 to 75% of planning area affected), or extensive (75 to 100% of planning area affected).
- *Maximum probable extent:* Can be classified as weak, moderate, severe, or extreme, based on history and probability, speed of onset, duration, and potential damage.
- *Probability of future events:* The history of previous hazard events in each category helps estimate the likelihood or probability of future events, so they can be classified as highly likely, likely, occasional, and unlikely. FEMA (2013) defines this classification as follows:
   - *Unlikely:* Less than 1% probability of occurrence in the next year, or a recurrence interval of greater than every 100 years

Task A. List the hazards that may occur.

1. *Research newspapers and other historical records.*
2. *Review existing plans and reports.*
3. *Talk to the experts in your community, state, or region.*
4. *Gather information on websites.*
5. *Next to the hazard list below, put a check mark in the Task A boxes beside all hazards that may occur in your community or state.*

Task B. Focus on the most prevalent hazards in your community or state.

1. *Go to hazard websites.*
2. *Locate your community or state on the website map.*
3. *Determine whether you are in a high-risk area. Get more localized information if necessary.*
4. *Next to the hazard list below, put a check mark in the Task B boxes beside all hazards that pose a significant threat.*

	Task A	Task B
Avalanche	☐	☐
Coastal Erosion	☑	☐
Coastal Storm	☑	☑
Dam Failure	☐	☐
Drought	☐	☐
Earthquake	☑	☑
Expansive Soils	☐	☐
Extreme Heat	☐	☐
Flood	☑	☑
Hailstorm	☑	☐
Hurricane	☑	☐
Land Subsidence	☐	☐
Landslide	☑	☑
Severe Winter Storm	☑	☐
Tornado	☑	☑
Tsunami	☑	☑
Volcano	☐	☐
Wildfire	☑	☑
Windstorm	☐	☐
Other———	☐	☐
Other———	☐	☐
Other———	☐	☐

Use this space to record information you find for each of the hazards you will be researching. Attach additional pages as necessary.

Hazard or event description (type of hazard), date of event, number of injuries, cost and types of damage, etc.)	Source of information	Map available for this hazard?	Scale of map
Flood – June 1936. 500-year flood. One death, some corn & crop losses.	• Members of community • Newspaper • Floodplain manager	FIRM	1 : 6000
Hurricane Camille – Nov. 1969. One death. Flooding & wind caused $1.5 million in damages.	• Newspaper • Internet research	FIRM & storm surge map	1 : 6000 1 : 6000
Severe strom caused flooding & landslides – May 1973. $2 million in damages.	• Newspaper • State geologist	Topo-graphic & soils maps	1 : 24000
Severe strom & tornadoes – April 1980. Wind & flash floods caused $1.5 million in damages.	• Newspaper	No	
Wildfires – April 1981. 1,050 acres burned.	• Newspaper • State fire marshal	Topo-graphic USDA & fuel model maps.	1 : 24000

■ **FIGURE 7.2** FEMA sample worksheet for identifying hazards in your community. It is important to keep records of what you have found and where you found it. Your records may include copies of documents or maps, notes on whom you talked to and when you talked to them, website references, and so forth. This information will also be useful later in loss estimations and the rest of the mitigation planning process. *Image courtesy of FEMA.*

Table 7.1 Example of a Natural Hazards Profile for an Area

Hazard	Location (Geographic Area Affected)	Maximum Probability Extent (Magnitude/ Strength)	Probability of Future Events	Overall Significance Ranking
Flood	Significant	Weak	Likely	Medium
Severe weather (lightning, strong wind, hail)	Extensive	Moderate	Highly likely	High
Tornado	Significant	Moderate	Likely	Medium
Winter weather (snow, ice, extreme cold)	Significant	Weak	Likely	Medium

❏ *Occasional:* 1–10% probability of occurrence in the next year, or a recurrence interval of 11–100 years
❏ *Likely:* 10–90% probability of occurrence in the next year, or a recurrence interval of 1–10 years
❏ *Highly likely:* 90–100% probability of occurrence in the next year, or a recurrence interval of less than 1 year

Next, each hazard can be ranked as low, medium, or high based on overall significance. Table 7.1 shows an example of a natural hazards profile for an area; this profile can be used for both natural and manmade hazards. Note the overall significance ranking for each hazard.

VULNERABILITY ASSESSMENT FOR NATURAL HAZARDS

Vulnerability assessment involves identifying structures and areas of a community that are vulnerable to hazards using current knowledge or some degree of existing building stock (FEMA, n.d.a). It helps answer the question: "What assets in the community will be affected by the hazard event?" *Assets* are the features of a community that have value, such as buildings, facilities, infrastructure, historic and cultural landmarks, and other local resources (Schwab et al., 2007). The first task for compiling an inventory list is to determine the number and value of the buildings and the total estimated population within the hazard areas. You may decide to end your inventory at this point if time, money, or other resources are scarce. Even a truncated inventory such as this can be useful to provide a broad picture of the potential extent of damage likely from a hazard event and to convince decision makers of the need for further study to determine potential losses (FEMA, 2001b). The procedures and techniques to create this inventory are described in the next sections.

Estimate or Count the Total Number of Buildings, Value of Buildings, and Number of People in Your Community

Information about the total number of buildings in your community can be obtained from the local tax assessment report, aerial photographs, or the local planning department. This information can be grouped by occupancy class, such as residential, commercial, and industrial. HAZUS, loss estimation software developed by FEMA, is a great tool to use to collect this information. Once you gather this data, the next thing to do is to establish the total approximate replacement value of the buildings located inside the hazard area. Again, this information can be obtained from HAZUS or from the tax assessment values of individual buildings. The population data can be found or estimated from census data, HAZUS, or local resources.

Estimate the Total Number of Buildings, Total Value of Buildings, and the Number of People in Each of Your Hazard Zones

Using a geographic information system (GIS), maps of hazard areas and locations of community assets can be overlaid on top of the base map to determine the number and value of the buildings and the populations that are vulnerable to the hazard events (refer to Figure 7.3). This can also be done using HAZUS.

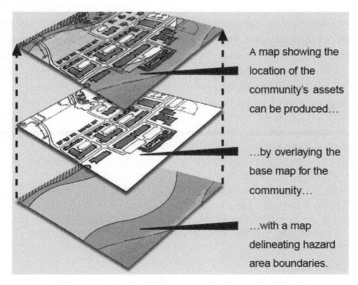

A map showing the location of the community's assets can be produced...

...by overlaying the base map for the community...

...with a map delineating hazard area boundaries.

■ **FIGURE 7.3** Using GIS, hazard-specific information and locations of community assets can be overlaid onto a base map to analyze the impact of hazards. *Image courtesy of FEMA.*

Calculate the Proportion of Assets Located in Hazard Areas

To determine the proportion of buildings or assets located in hazard areas, you can divide the number or value in your hazard area by the total number or value in your jurisdiction. For instance, if your community has 20 residential buildings, and 10 of those are located in the 100-year floodplain, then 50% of your residential buildings are located in the flood hazard area of the community.

Determine the Location of Expected Growth in Your Community

The location of expected growth in the community can be determined by reviewing your local comprehensive plan or by talking with your local community officials where the future growth is expected to occur. Note if these areas lie within the hazard areas of your community.

If you decide to develop a more detailed inventory, you can collect data on other types of assets located in hazard areas and the characteristics of these assets. This will help determine the losses to these assets from different hazards. Types of assets include critical facilities that are important to your community; vulnerable populations, such as non-English speaking people or elderly people; economic elements, such as major employers and financial centers in your area; areas with special needs, such as high-density residential or commercial development; historic, cultural, and natural resource areas; and other important facilities such as government buildings of a particular size, type, and quality (FEMA, 2001). Besides the structure's replacement value, you can determine the content value, function use or value, displacement cost, and occupancy or capacity to calculate detailed potential losses from different hazards.

Replacement Value
The replacement value is the current cost of returning a physical asset to its predamaged condition (FEMA, 2001a). In the U.S., this is usually expressed in terms of cost per square foot and reflects the present-day cost of labor and materials to construct a building of the size, type, and quality of the original building. Information about replacement value can be obtained from HAZUS or from local sources, and the historic dollar figures should be adjusted for inflation.

Content Value
Content value is expressed as the percentage of the replacement value, which can also be found in HAZUS. Table 7.2 shows the estimated

Table 7.2 Content Value as Percentage of Replacement Value

Type	Content Value (%)
Residential (including homes, apartment buildings, temporary lodging, dormitories, and nursing homes)	50
Commercial (including retail, wholesale, professional, services, financial, entertainment, and recreation)	100
Commercial (including hospital and medical offices and clinics)	150
Commercial parking	50
Industrial (including heavy and light)	150
Industrial construction	100
Agriculture	100
Religion/nonprofit	100
Government emergency response	150
Government general services	100
Education (schools/libraries)	100
Education (colleges/universities)	150

Source: HAZUS.

content value (in terms of percentage) for different type of buildings. Find the type of building that you are assessing and determine the percentage of the content replacement value. Multiply this percentage by the building replacement value to calculate the content replacement value. Note that some contents, such as antiques or other special types of objects, may be worth more than the average values.

Function Use or Value

Function use or value represents the value of a building's use or function that would be lost if it were damaged or closed altogether. A standard way to calculate the monetary damage from losing public functions is to use the budget of the service as a proxy for its value to the community (FEMA, 2001b). For private entities such as businesses, it can be determined using the average annual sales or production.

Displacement Cost

The displacement cost is the dollar amount that it would cost for a function (business or service) to be relocated to another structure because of a hazard event. These costs include monthly rent for temporary building space, one-time displacement costs to set up operations in the new space, lost rent per month from all tenants, and other costs of displacement (FEMA, 2001b).

> **CRITICAL THINKING**
>
> Based on your community resources, would it be better for you to do a truncated or a detailed inventory of assets for your vulnerability assessment?

IMPACT ANALYSIS

Impact analysis is done by estimating losses in terms of the expected losses from hazard events to people, buildings, and other important assets that are compiled during inventory assets. Comprehensive loss estimation should assess the level of damage, including to the contents and functions of the buildings or assets, in addition to the risk to the structure itself (FEMA, 2001b). For instance, suppose that a particular building could suffer damage from a 100-year flood event at a level equal to 50% of its total value. The loss estimation should calculate the potential loss by multiplying the value of structure, contents, or use by the percentage of damage expected from the hazard event.

Loss estimation from floods, earthquakes, and hurricanes for any region in the United States can be done using HAZUS software. Chapter 11 provides a tutorial on using HAZUS during a flood, an earthquake, and a hurricane. The procedures and techniques used by FEMA (2001b) for conducting loss estimation are described in the next sections.

Determine the Extent of Damages

A loss estimate assesses the level of damage from each type of hazard event to each individual asset in the inventory of a community (Schwab et al., 2007). This involves combining structural loss, content loss, and use or function loss, as follows:

> Total estimated loss = Structural loss + Content loss
> + Use and Function loss

Structural loss can be determined by multiplying the structure replacement value identified in the previous equation by the expected percent damage from a hazard event. Information about the estimated percent damage can be obtained from the loss estimation tables developed by FEMA for HAZUS or benefit-cost analysis (Figure 7.4), or from other publications. For instance, if the city hall's structure replacement value equals $100,000

Flood Building Loss Estimation Table

Flood Depth (feet)	One Stories No Basement (% Building damage)	Two Stories No Basement (% Building damage)	One or Two Stories With Basement (% Building damage)	Manufactured Home (% Building damage)
-2	0	0	4	0
-1	0	0	8	0
0	9	5	11	8
1	14	9	15	44
2	22	13	20	63
3	27	18	23	73
4	29	20	28	78
5	30	22	33	80
6	40	24	38	81
7	43	26	44	82
8	44	29	49	82
>8	45	33	51	82

Source: FEMA Benefit-Cost Analysis Full Data Module 3/10/99

■ **FIGURE 7.4** The Flood Building Loss Estimation Table depicts the extent of damage from various flood depths on different kinds of structures. This table is from the FEMA Benefit-Cost Analysis Module and has been compiled based on flood damage across the country. *Image courtesy of FEMA.*

and the expected damage from a 100-year flood is 40% of the structure, then the estimated structural loss for the city hall from a flood is $40,000.

If loss estimation tables are not available for a particular hazard, you can use the full value of the assets that are in the hazard area or assume the percentage based on the past occurrences of such hazard events in the planning area (FEMA, 2001b). Similarly, content loss can be estimated by multiplying the replacement value of the contents by the expected percent damage for a particular hazard event. For example, if the city hall's content replacement value equals $200,000 and the expected damage from a 100-year flood is 10% of the contents, then the estimated content loss from a flood would be $20,000.

Also, you may need to calculate functional downtime of some assets (e.g., businesses or services), as those might not be operational due to a hazard event. For instance, if a convenience store has daily sales of $2500 and is forced to shut down for two weeks due to a hazard event, their function loss would be $35,000 ($2500 × 14 days). If it is a public facility, such as the city hall, with an annual budget of $600,000 and an average daily budget of $1644 ($600,000/365), then the cost for the loss of use of this building for two weeks would be $23,016.

In addition, sometimes a function may need to operate from a temporary location due to a hazard event. For example, if the city hall was closed for two weeks (functional downtime) and had to operate from a temporary location for the next 90 days until the damages to the existing building could be repaired, then the displacement time would be 90 days. When you multiply the displacement cost determined during inventory by the displacement time, you will find the total displacement cost for 90 days. The sum of functional downtime cost and displacement cost will give the total losses as a result of losing the function in a particular hazard event. For example, if the functional downtime cost for two weeks for the city hall is $23,016 and the displacement cost for 90 days is $34,000, the total functional loss for the city hall would be $57,016. Therefore, the total estimated losses for the city hall from a 100-year flood event would be $117,016 [$40,000 (structural loss) + $20,000 (content loss) + $57,016 (functional loss)].

Calculating Human Losses

Human losses from hazard events are difficult to calculate. There are credible estimates available from HAZUS and other sources estimating the number of people that may be hurt or killed in various types of buildings under various hazard conditions. In conducting risk or vulnerability assessment, it is important to note that the likelihood of people being injured or killed depends upon factors such as warning time and the characteristics of the hazard itself (FEMA, 2001b). Although it is very complicated to place a dollar value on human lives; the mitigation planning process should consider areas that can be improved to help save lives and reduce injuries in future hazard events.

Calculate the Loss from Each Hazard Event

To determine which hazard event could have the largest economic losses in your community, calculate the total loss for all assets in the hazard area from each hazard event. For instance, if there are three buildings located in the 100-year floodplain of your community with estimated total flood losses of $10,000, $5000, and $2500, the total estimated loss from floods would be $17,500.

Next, you can find out which hazard event would likely affect the greatest proportion of your community assets by dividing the total hazard loss by the total value of the assets that you determined during inventory. For instance, if the total estimated flood loss is $17,500 and the value of three buildings you assessed is $100,000, then the flood losses would be approximately 17% of the value of the assets. Finally, you can create a composite loss map showing areas affected by multiple hazards as your high loss potential areas, and the areas with few or no hazards as moderate or low loss potential areas.

Addressing Repetitive Loss Properties and Development Trends

A hazard mitigation plan also requires including information about repetitive loss structures and Severe Repetitive Loss (SRL) structures inrisk assessment and how repetitive loss structures will be addressed in the mitigation strategy portion of the plan. For instance, repetitive loss properties can be identified during inventory for participation in an acquisition and demolition program.

While it is not required, the Disaster Mitigation Act (DMA) 2000 regulations suggest that local plans discuss vulnerability in terms of a general description of land uses and development trends within the community. This can include:

- Existing land uses in the identified hazard areas
- Development densities in the identified hazard areas
- Anticipated future/proposed land uses
- Anticipated new development
- Anticipated redevelopment
- Anticipated annexation areas

Also, risk assessment can incorporate a review of local capital improvement programs and local infrastructure plans. Scheduled infrastructure is a good predictor of future development because once public services such as roads, water lines, sewer lines, schools, and other community facilities are extended into undeveloped areas, development will usually follow soon afterward (Schwab et al., 2007).

> **CRITICAL THINKING**
> Why is scheduled infrastructure a good predictor of future development?

TECHNOLOGICAL HAZARD ASSESSMENT

Technological hazard assessment or *hazard vulnerability analysis (HVA)* for technological hazards is accomplished in much the same way as one would perform an HVA for natural hazards. As with natural hazards, the variables include the probability of occurrence, the magnitude, and the potential impact on people, property, operations, the environment, and perhaps the agency or organization. Probabilities for many of the natural hazards are available from a number of government sources. Data for manmade hazards can be obtained from local industry (for fixed-site hazards), pipeline operators, railroads, or truck carriers (Waugh & Tierney, 2007) to name just a few possible sources.

One significant difference between natural hazards and technological hazards is that we look *internally* to community assets, transportation nodes, industry, public and private agencies, and companies to locate the sources of those hazards, the threats they pose, and subsequent risk. In essence, the threat (risk) is within the community. Where does it exist? How potentially dangerous is it? What accidents have occurred previously and where? What are potential targets for an intentional incident, and how likely is an act of terrorism? These are some of the questions that one could use to begin the process of technological hazard mapping.

To begin to answer the questions posed here, the process is heavily reliant on the collection of data from the community. Collection of technological hazard data from multiple sources can be used to generate multilayered hazard maps, which can be very useful in mitigation and preparedness planning.

Hazard mapping is the process of identifying and displaying the spatial variation of hazard events or physical conditions. Important variables involved in mapping hazards and interpreting hazard maps include the size (scale) of the area to be mapped, the availability and completeness of data, the cost of collecting and mapping data (Noson, 2012).

When you conduct an HVA, you identify, using current knowledge or some degree of existing building stock, those structures and areas that are vulnerable to hazards. In addition, a community growth plan or flat map superimposed on the hazard map will help you identify areas vulnerable to natural hazards. Vulnerability identification determines the facilities at risk and to what degree they might be affected, as well as how they might affect other surrounding structures (FEMA, n.d.b). Assessing the technological hazard risk for an entire community with its many structures, improved areas, and facets is a daunting task. Technological hazards are all around us, and many of them move throughout the community (e.g., 90 ton rail tanker car filled with chlorine). One should examine the hazards present and then consider the probability, risk, and subsequent impact of each one. Conversely, one might chose to look more carefully at the most important features of a community and then determine which technological hazards would affect them. As such, critical infrastructure and key assets must be considered.

Critical Infrastructure

When it comes to vulnerability assessment, the emergency manager should consider the entire community. But, as previously stated, hazard mitigation programs are costly and hazard mitigation funds are scarce. Therefore, the emergency manager might want to focus his or her attention for technological hazards on critical infrastructure.

Critical infrastructure is defined as assets, systems, and networks, whether physical or virtual, that are so vital to the United States, your State or local community that the incapacity or destruction of such assets, systems, or networks would have a debilitating impact on security, national economic security, public health or safety, or any combination (DHS, 2006).

The critical infrastructure that keeps your community running includes, but is not limited to, the electrical grid, telecommunications networks, natural gas network, and key transportation nodes. Threats or hazards of all types may render those critical systems or key assets inoperable or dysfunctional. If we view critical infrastructure as targets of opportunity, then some carry value for both their disruption impact and the potential for a mass casualty incident. Much of each community's critical infrastructure is dangerously exposed and therefore exceedingly vulnerable.

The following is a listing and short descriptions of critical infrastructure sectors (refer to Figure 7.5) provided from the National Strategy for the Physical Protection of Critical Infrastructure and Key Assets.

Agriculture and Food

The agriculture/food sector is a source of essential commodity and accounts for close to one-fifth of the gross domestic product (GDP) of the United States. A significant percentage of that figure also contributes to its export economy. The United States exports approximately one-quarter of its farm and ranch products. The remainder is used to feed its own people.

Water

The water sector consists of two basic, yet vital, components: freshwater supply and wastewater collection and treatment. The public water systems depend on reservoirs, dams, wells, and aquifers, as well as treatment facilities, pumping stations, aqueducts, and transmission pipelines. Wastewater utilities collect and treat sewage and process water from domestic, commercial, and industrial sources. It also includes systems collecting and sometimes treating stormwater runoff. Clean water is

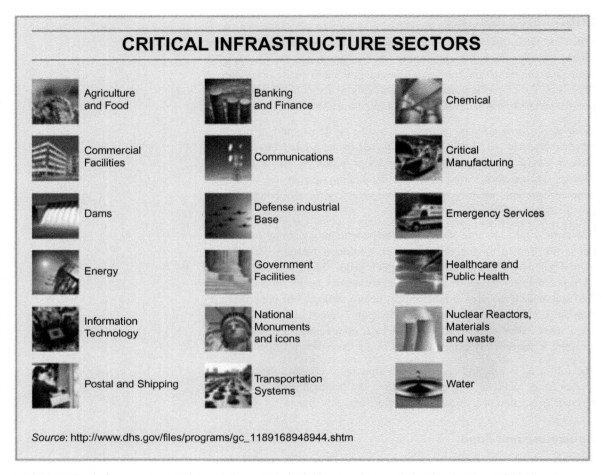

■ **FIGURE 7.5** Critical infrastructure sectors and key assets. The 18 sectors identified here are in keeping with the U.S. National Strategy for the Physical Protection of Critical Infrastructure. *This image provided by DHS.*

essential for sustaining communities and agricultural production. In addition, water has become a precious commodity in parts of the world affected by drought and climate change.

Healthcare and Public Health

The public health sector consists of state and local health departments, hospitals, health clinics, mental health facilities, nursing homes, blood-supply facilities, laboratories, mortuaries, and pharmaceutical stockpiles.

The ability to protect the health of residents is not only one of the greatest qualities of a nation's life, but the pharmaceutical industry also can be a major element of the economy.

Emergency Services

The emergency services sector consists of highly mobile teams of specialized personnel and equipment. It includes fire, emergency medical services (EMS), governmental administration, HazMat units, law enforcement, public health, health care, public safety communications, public works, and EMAs that support technological and natural disasters.

Defense Industrial Base

The defense industrial base sector consists of the private-sector defense industry and some supporting military facilities. Private industry manufactures and provides a majority of the equipment, materials, services, and weaponry used by a nation's armed forces. National defense is highly dependent upon the private sector to contribute to the effective execution of its core defense missions, including mobilization, deployment, and sustainment of a nation's military forces abroad.

Communications

The telecommunications sector provides communications through voice and data services to public and private users through a complex and diverse public-network infrastructure encompassing the Public Switched Telecommunications Network (PSTN), the Internet, and private enterprise networks. The PSTN provides switched circuits for telephone, data, and leased point-to-point services. Enterprise networks are dedicated networks supporting the voice and data needs and operations of large companies or industries.

Energy

The energy sector is divided into two segments: electricity and oil and natural gas. The electricity industry services almost every household and institution in the developed world. Almost every form of productive activity—whether in businesses, manufacturing plants, schools, hospitals, homes, or agriculture—requires electricity. Oil and natural gas facilities and assets are widely distributed. In the United States, this consists of more than 300,000 producing sites, 4000 offshore platforms, 600 natural gas processing plants, 150 refineries, 1400 product terminals, and 7500 bulk stations. Other oil- and natural gas-producing nations could post equally impressive numbers.

Transportation

The transportation sector consists of several key modes: aviation, maritime traffic, rail, pipelines, highways, trucking, busing, and public mass transit. The diversity and size of the transportation sector makes it vital to the economy and national security of any developed nation.

Banking and Finance

The banking/finance sector consists of a variety of physical structures, such as buildings and financial utilities. The financial utilities infrastructure includes electronic devices such as computers, storage devices, and telecommunications networks. Many financial service employees have highly specialized skills and are therefore considered essential elements of the industry's critical infrastructure. The financial industry relies heavily on continued public confidence and involvement to maintain normal operations; financial stability is dependent on these areas. Disasters that have the potential to disrupt this sector may create significant changes in the economic status of essential market areas.

Chemical Industry

The chemical industry and hazardous materials sector provides products essential to the economy and standard of living of most nations. The chemical industry manufactures products that are fundamental elements of other economic sectors. For example, it produces fertilizer for agriculture and chlorine for water purification. In the United States, more than $100 billion of the sector's products go to health care. Currently, the chemical sector in the United States is the nation's top exporter, accounting for 10 cents of every export dollar.

Postal and Shipping

The postal/shipping sector is relied on heavily for the delivery of billions of pieces of mail and packages all over the world daily. Any nation's postal system is highly dependent on and interconnected with other key infrastructure systems, especially the transportation sector. The postal service depends on a fleet of both service-owned and contractor-operated vehicles and equipment. Mail and packages also travel daily by commercial aircraft, truck, railroad, and ship. This sector is essential for commerce to function and for people to communicate.

Key Asset Categories

The following sections list key assets, according to the National Strategy for the Physical Protection of Critical Infrastructure and Key Assets.

National Monuments and Icons

Protection of national monuments and icons typically combines the authorities, responsibilities, and resources of federal, state, and local jurisdictions, and, in some cases, private foundations. Imagine the importance of preserving the Washington Monument or Statue of Liberty in the United States. Also, imagine the importance of Eiffel Tower to France, the Taj Mahal to India, Buckingham Palace to the United Kingdom, the Coliseum to Italy, and so on. These national treasures and iconic buildings must be preserved at all cost. It should go without saying that mitigation planning for these structures should be extremely proactive and a very high priority.

Nuclear Power Plants

Currently, there are 31 countries with nuclear power plants: United States, France, Japan, Russia, South Korea, Canada, Ukraine, China, Germany, United Kingdom, Sweden, Spain, Belgium, Taiwan, India, Czech Republic, Switzerland, Finland, Bulgaria, Hungary, Brazil, South Africa, Slovakia, Mexico, Romania, Argentina, Iran, Pakistan, Slovenia, Netherlands, and Armenia. In some cases (i.e., France, Belgium, and Slovakia), this capability may represent more than 50% of a nation's electrical generation capacity. The United States has more than 100 commercial nuclear reactors in 31 states. Nuclear power plants are among the most strongly constructed structures in a country. However, they are not impervious to natural or technological hazards. Recent disasters in Japan (Fukushima) and Ukraine (Chernobyl) are illustrative of this (refer to Chapter 6, which discusses these events in detail). Furthermore, nuclear power plants make an attractive target to would-be terrorists.

Dams

This category consists of larger and symbolic dams that are major components of other critical infrastructure systems that provide water and electricity to large populations, cities, and agriculture complexes. In the United States, there are approximately 80,000 dam facilities identified in the national inventory. Most of these are small, privately owned dams on farm property. The federal government is responsible for roughly 10% of the dams in the country, and their failure could cause significant property damage, have public health and safety consequences, or both.

Government Facilities

This category is composed of buildings that governments own and others lease from the private sector. Government organizations also occupy buildings used by a variety of nongovernmental tenants, such as shops and restaurants.

Commercial Key Assets

This category consists of prominent commercial centers, office buildings, sports stadiums, theme parks, and other sites where large numbers of people congregate to pursue business activities, conduct personal commercial transactions, or enjoy recreational activities. Day-to-day protection of such facilities is the responsibility of their commercial owners and operators, in close cooperation with local law enforcement. At the national level, the government is normally responsible for providing timely threat indicators and warnings. This includes the inherent responsibility to protect large gatherings of citizens. The threat of severe weather or credible threat of terrorism to a stadium complex on game day is a prime example of this.

TERRORISM AND TECHNOLOGICAL HAZARDS

The potential for terrorism is nearly unlimited, which is especially true when one imagines a terrorist group utilizing deadly manmade substances against soft targets (e.g., schools, churches, etc.). A successful attack on critical infrastructure and key assets could have tremendous impact beyond the immediate target, and could continue to resurface through other related or interdependent infrastructures long after the immediate damage is done.

Terrorists are inventive and resourceful in terms of target selection, as well as in their use of specific instruments of violence and intimidation. To achieve their objectives, terrorists may choose to target critical infrastructures and key assets as a low-risk means to generate mass casualties, shock, and panic.

The immediate damage to facilities and disruption of services that resulted from the attacks on September 11, 2001, on the World Trade Center towers, which housed critical assets of the financial services sector, as well as on the Pentagon, a major military complex, is a prime example of a terrorist attack on critical infrastructure and key assets.

The attacks led to public disengagement from air travel and other facets of the economy. Terrorists proved that they could exploit elements of the transportation infrastructure and hoped that this might have a spreading effect into other critical infrastructures within the United States, such as participation in and reliance on global economic markets. Terrorists target crucial infrastructure, and key assets to achieve effects that fall into three general categories (National Strategy for the Physical Protection of Critical Infrastructure and Key Assets, 2008):

- *Direct infrastructure effects*—Disruption or arrest of the functions of critical infrastructure or key assets through direct attacks on a critical node, system, or function
- *Indirect infrastructure effects*—Cascading disruption and financial consequences for a government, society, and economy through public- and private-sector reactions to an attack
- *Exploitation of infrastructure*—Exploitation of elements of a particular infrastructure to disrupt or destroy another target

Vulnerability of Targets

Government security officials and emergency first responders have no higher purpose than to ensure the security of their people and preserve their way of life. The more we understand and identify our vulnerability to terrorist attacks, the better we can protect ourselves. *Vulnerability* is defined as the characteristics of an asset's design, location, or operation/use that render it susceptible to damage, destruction, or incapacitation by terrorist or other intentional acts, mechanical failures, and natural hazards (Figure 7.6).

Intelligence gathering over the past 20 years has shown that numerous terrorist groups have been and are working to obtain chemical, biological, radiological, and nuclear weapons for the stated purpose of killing large numbers of people. But terrorists also continue to employ conventional means of attack, such as bombs and guns. Explosives are a weapon that is easy to procure, assemble, and deliver; they give terrorists maximum effect with minimum resources. Approximately 80% of all terrorist acts within involve incendiary and improvised explosive devices (IEDs). At the same time, they are gaining expertise in less traditional means, such as cyberattacks on Information Technology and computer systems. The knowledge, technology, and materials needed to build weapons of mass destruction are spreading. Terrorists can conceivably steal or obtain chemical, biological, radiological, nuclear, and explosives (CBRNE) materials or related technology from states with such capabilities.

Vulnerability Assessment

Vulnerability is a weakness, an inadequately protected exposure, or susceptibility to damage or harm. A vulnerability assessment is a process to identify, evaluate, and assess:

- ▶ Susceptibility of a site to natural or artificial hazards
- ▶ Weaknesses in buildings, systems, equipment, management programs, and the capabilities of people
- ▶ Lack of, or inadequate protection from a hazard
- ▶ Dependencies and interdependencies

■ **FIGURE 7.6** Key points about HVA.

Terrorists will also seek to cause widespread disruption and damage, including casualties, by attacking computer and electronic networks. Computer and electronic networks are linked to other critical infrastructure, such as energy, financial, and security networks. Terrorist groups are already exploiting new information technology and the Internet to plan attacks, raise funds, spread propaganda, collect information, communicate securely, and manage global resources.

The sites and structures making up the key assets category typically draw large amounts of tourism and frequent media attention—factors that impose additional protection challenges. A terrorist attack on such assets could profoundly affect national public confidence, and could represent a great boon to the terrorists' organization and recruitment.

Using an Assessment Process for Critical Infrastructure

Vulnerability assessment is a process to identify, evaluate, and assess susceptibility to natural and technological hazards (Figure 7.7). Through a vulnerability assessment, areas of weakness and potential actions that would exploit those weaknesses are identified, and the effectiveness of additional security measures is assessed (DHS, 2006). Next, we lay out a simple, six-step HVA process that can be used when planning for

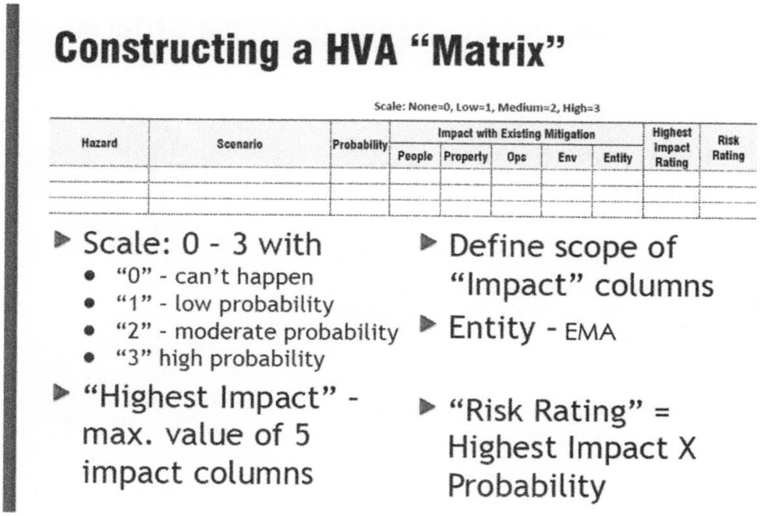

Constructing a HVA "Matrix"

Scale: None=0, Low=1, Medium=2, High=3

Hazard	Scenario	Probability	Impact with Existing Mitigation					Highest Impact Rating	Risk Rating
			People	Property	Ops	Env	Entity		

▶ Scale: 0 - 3 with
- "0" - can't happen
- "1" - low probability
- "2" - moderate probability
- "3" high probability

▶ "Highest Impact" - max. value of 5 impact columns

▶ Define scope of "Impact" columns

▶ Entity - EMA

▶ "Risk Rating" = Highest Impact X Probability

■ **FIGURE 7.7** A sample HVA Matrix. Also, some notes for completing the matrix following steps 3—6 as described in the text are included.

technological hazards in general, as well as the protection of critical infrastructure and key assets.

Step 1:
Form an assessment team made up of key personnel who can identify critical infrastructure and key assets and are knowledgeable of manmade hazards.

Step 2:
Construct a blank Hazard Vulnerability Assessment matrix with columns for each hazard, a possible scenario, the probability of an event, and the impact of such an event is for people, property, operations, the environment and the entity making the assessment. In addition, add a column for the highest impact rating and risk rating.

Step 3:
Begin filling out a matrix for identifying technological hazards and pit those against critical infrastructure or key assets found within the community to create a hazard and scenario combination. Ultimately, this should enable the team to evaluate the potential vulnerability of the critical infrastructure and key assets against a broad range of identified threats.

Probability of Occurrence (Example Criteria)

HVA

0. **Zero:** Not possible.

1. **Low:** Less than 10% annual probability or on average less than once every 10 years

2. **Medium:** Greater than or equal to 10% annual probability or on average at least once every 10 years

3. **High:** 100% annual probability of occurrence (expected to occur on average at least once each year)

Caution
For most types of hazard, probabilities will vary with magnitude.

■ **FIGURE 7.8** The assessment team should assign relative probabilities. For each hazard, there are many combinations of probability and severity.

Note that multiple sources of data and team deliberations will be needed to complete the analysis for this matrix.

Step 4:

The assessment team should assign relative probabilities (with values ranging from 0 to 3) for each hazard and scenario combination. Refer to Figure 7.8 for a description of how to rate occurrence or frequency probabilities.

Step 5:

Impact values are subjectively ranked on a scale of 1−5, with 5 being the highest impact. The team should rank each of the five impact areas (people, property, operations, environment, and entity). More detail about this step is presented in the following subsection of this chapter.

Step 6:

Calculate the risk rating, which is the value of the probability figure for a hazard/scenario combination multiplied by the highest impact rating for any of the five areas assessed.

Figure 7.9 shows an example of a partial HVA conducted for a small town. HVA analyzes the threat, critical infrastructure/key asset value, and vulnerability to ascertain the level of risk for each critical infrastructure/key asset against each applicable threat. In this example, the two scenarios shown at

			Impact with Existing Mitigation					Highest Impact Rating	Risk Rating
Hazard	Scenario	Probability	People	Property	Opns	Environ	Entity		
Fire and Explosion	Major fire in ABC plastics factory	3	2	3	2	3	1	3	9
HazMat Incident	Derailment of chlorine tanker car at industrial park railhead	2	3	3	2	2	1	3	6
Nuclear Power Plant Incident	Coolant tower failure at XYZ Station	1	3	2	2	2	1	3	3
Radiological Incident	Cesium detected in County landfill site	1	1	1	1	1	1	1	1
Civil Unrest	Protest turns violent at city hall	1	2	2	2	1	1	2	2
Act of terrorism	High yield explosives used at high school football stadium	1	3	2	2	1	1	3	3

■ **FIGURE 7.9** A simple example of an HVA matrix for a small town. The two boxes highlighted in gray (upper right corner) have been rated as the highest hazard/scenario combinations and should get our attention for mitigation efforts.

the top of the matrix produced the highest risk rating. Community attention and assets for mitigation measures should be placed there. In the simple HVA matrix shown in Figure 7.9, impact analysis was assessed on a scale of 1–5. So, for example, *Major fire in the ABC plastics factory* would have a *moderate to high* effect (3) on Property and the Environment, a *low to moderate* effect (2) on People and Operations, and a *low* effect (1) on the Entity (in this case, the EMA). The assessment team may use any reasonable approach or scale to quantitatively determine the impact of any hazard on the community and entity making the assessment. FEMA gives more detailed guidance for business impact analysis, which is performed in business continuity planning activities. Business continuity professionals should visit the FEMA website listed at the end of this chapter for that information.

■ CONCLUSIONS

HVA is the basis for developing a comprehensive emergency management program. It evaluates what events could happen, the likelihood of these events occurring, and the magnitude of problems created because of a given event. By identifying potential events that could occur, efforts can be directed toward mitigation activities and developing needed response plans. Although this is not a complex task, it does require a comprehensive review of the natural and technological (manmade) hazards of the region. Consideration must be given to the possibility of damage or failure of facilities, loss of basic utilities, and multiple casualty events, to name just a few possibilties. The organization must also consider the effect of a loss of trust from the community, as well as legal ramifications, if it fails to respond properly. Consulting with local emergency planners, public health, fire, police, public works, and utility company officials is essential to the process of identifying current hazards and historical events that have occurred in the region. Examples of this would be obtaining information on the region's 100-year flood plain record, hurricane or severe storm experience, earthquake potential, utility outage records, and hazardous material concerns in the area.

Vulnerability assessment (natural hazards) helps to inventory assets in the community that will be affected by hazard events. The first task for compiling an inventory list is to determine the number and value of the buildings and the total estimated population within the hazard areas. If resources are available, a detailed inventory of assets can be compiled. Impact analysis is done by estimating the expected losses from hazard events to people, buildings, and other important assets that are compiled during inventory. Comprehensive loss estimation should assess the level of damage from natural hazards, including the contents and functions of the buildings or assets and the risk to the structure itself. The hazard mitigation plan should also address repetitive loss properties and development trends, including scheduled infrastructure, while conducting risk and vulnerability assessment.

HVA for manmade (technological) hazards begins by looking within a community for where these hazards exist. Multiple sources of data must be collated to determine the threat of these hazards and the relative risk they bring to a community.

Protecting critical infrastructure and key assets represents an enormous challenge since they are a highly complex and interdependent mix of facilities, systems, and functions that are vulnerable to a variety of threats. Critical infrastructure's continued reliability, robustness, and resiliency create a sense of confidence and form an important part of national identity and strategic purpose. Key assets represent individual targets whose destruction could cause large-scale injury, death, or destruction of property. An attack on a key asset could profoundly damage national prestige and confidence. Such assets and activities alone may not be vital to the continuity of critical services on a national scale, but an attack on one of them could produce significant loss of life, public health and safety consequences, or both.

In this chapter, a simple process was applied to assessing the threat of technological hazards. This process can be used for incidents due to man-made hazards that are the result of accidents and intentional acts. The process is the same; however, the magnitude and probabilities are likely to be different for accidents and incidents due to terrorism. This means that accidents are more likely to occur, but of a smaller magnitude than something that is designed to cause mass casualties. In most communities, terrorist events have a low probability of taking place. Regardless of your community's profile, technological hazards have tremendous potential to disrupt normalcy and do considerable damage. Mitigation strategies for these types of hazards must be prioritized based upon a process created by a team of highly knowledgeable professionals. The HVA matrix product proposed in this chapter can be easily adopted in any community.

DISCUSSION QUESTIONS

1. Describe the hazard analysis process, including hazard identification and event profiles.
2. Discuss the process of conducting HVAs for natural hazards
3. Discuss the procedures and techniques used by FEMA (2001b) for conducting comprehensive loss estimation.
4. What is critical infrastructure, and what are key assets? Explain how they differ and give some examples of each from your community. Discuss how they can be interrelated.
5. Technological hazards can cause accidental incidents, and they also can be used to carry out an act of terrorism. Compare and contrast these two mechanisms (accident versus intentional) with respect to probability and magnitude and the overall effects of each.
6. Use the HVA Matrix to produce one plausible technological hazard/ scenario assessment for your community.

WEBSITES

FEMA Business Impact Analysis
http://www.ready.gov/business-impact-analysis
FEMA Risk Assessment
http://www.ready.gov/risk-assessment
Department of Homeland Security (DHS) Critical Infrastructure Sectors
http://www.dhs.gov/critical-infrastructure-sectors

REFERENCES

Cannon, T. (1994). Vulnerability analysis and the explanation of "natural" disasters. In A. Varley (Ed.), *Disasters, development and environment*. London: Wiley. Chapter 2, pp. 13−30.

Federal Emergency Management Agency (FEMA). (n.d.a). *Emergency planning* (IS-235). Washington, DC.

Federal Emergency Management Agency (FEMA). (n.d.b). Facilitator guide—Unit 2: hazard vulnerability analysis and risk assessment, EMI, independent study, May 24, 2007 update. Retrieved from <http://worldbank.mrooms.net/file.php/356/2234/Introduction%20Reading%20-%20VulnerabilityAndRiskAssessmentGuide.pd>. Accessed May 18, 2015.

Federal Emergency Management Agency (FEMA). (2001a). *Disaster dictionary*, 58, citing Robert T. Stafford Act, 602.

Federal Emergency Management Agency (FEMA). (2001b). Mitigation planning how-to guide #2. Understanding your risks: Identifying hazards and estimating losses (FEMA 386-2). Retrieved from <http://www.fema.gov/media-library/assets/documents/4241>. Accessed October 30, 2014.

Federal Emergency Management Agency (FEMA). (2013). Local mitigation planning handbook. Retrieved from <http://www.fema.gov/mitigation-planning-laws-regulations-guidance>.

Noson, L. (2012). Hazard mapping and risk assessment. Regional workshop on best practices in disaster mitigation. Retrieved from <http://www.adpc.net/audmp/rllw/PDF/hazard%20mapping.pdf>. Accessed September 10, 2014.

Schwab, A., Eschelbach, K., & Brower, D. (2007). *Hazard Mitigation and Preparedness*. Hoboken, NJ: John Wiley and Sons.

U.S. Department of Homeland Security (DHS). (2006). National infrastructure protection plan. Washington, DC: June 30. Retrieved from <http://www.dhs.gov/xprevprot/programs/editorial_0827.shtm>. Accessed October 30, 2014.

Waugh, W. L., & Tierney, K. (Eds.), (2007). *Emergency management: Principles and practice for local government* Washington, DC: International City/County Management Association/ICMA Press.

Threat and Hazard Identification and Risk Assessment

OBJECTIVES

The study of this chapter will enable you to:

1. Discuss the purpose of THIRA.

2. List the agencies that are required to complete the THIRA process.

3. Discuss in detail the four-step process used in THIRA.

4. List and describe the five core capabilities (Mission Areas) referenced in the National Preparedness Goal (NPG).

Essential Terminology: Core capabilities, impact, impact analysis, mission areas, state preparedness report (SPR), threat and hazard identification and risk assessment (THIRA)

The world we have created today as a result of our thinking thus far has problems which cannot be solved by thinking the way we thought when we created them.

Albert Einstein

THE 5 Ws OF THIRA

In the previous chapter, we discussed the virtues of hazard assessment and impact analysis. We also presented a simple method for addressing natural and manmade hazards within an agency or small community. The purpose of this short chapter is to introduce the reader to a much more thorough process used in the United States for assessing hazards, projecting capabilities needed to counter those hazards, and performing gap analysis. The process, which originates from the U.S. Department of Homeland Security (DHS) and the

Federal Emergency Management Agency (FEMA) is called the **Threat and Hazard Identification and Risk Assessment (THIRA)**. The following THIRA-related questions will be answered in this chapter:

- What is THIRA?
- Who must complete it?
- Where is THIRA used at the regional and national level?
- When is it applied and completed?
- Why do we do it?

What Is THIRA?

Essentially, THIRA is a four-step process that enables emergency managers to evaluate their most important hazards and threats and then understand how their impacts may vary in relation to a number of factors. This process helps emergency management programs establish capability targets, see the gaps they have in necessary resources, and begin taking steps to address their shortfalls (DHS, 2013).

The four-step process for developing a THIRA is as follows (shown in Figure 8.1):

1. *Identify the threats and hazards of concern.* Based on a combination of experience, forecasting, subject matter expertise, and other available resources, identify a list of the threats and hazards of primary concern to the community.
2. *Give the threats and hazards context.* Describe the threats and hazards of concern, showing how they may affect the community.
3. *Establish capability targets.* Assess each threat and hazard in context to develop a specific capability target for each core capability identified in the National Preparedness Goal (DHS, 2011; PPD 8, 2011). The capability target defines success for the capability.

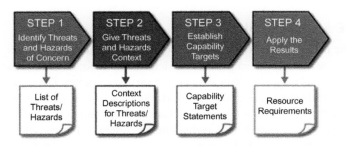

■ **FIGURE 8.1** The four steps necessary to complete the THIRA process. The corresponding box below each step indicates a product that results at the completion of each step. *Image courtesy of FEMA (DHS, 2013).*

4. *Apply the results.* Estimate the resources required for each core capability to achieve the capability targets through the use of community assets and mutual aid, while also considering preparedness activities, including mitigation opportunities.

Who Must Complete the Process?

The THIRA requirement, as it applies to FEMA preparedness grants, is that the following entities must complete a THIRA by December 31 of each year as a condition of their federal grant funding:

- All State administrative agencies (SAAs) receiving federal funding from the Homeland Security Grant Program (HSGP) and the Emergency Management Performance Grant (EMPG) program.
- All urban areas receiving funding from the Urban Areas Security Initiative (UASI) grant program.
- *Note*: All tribal nations that receive Tribal Homeland Security Grant Program (THSGP) funding are encouraged, but *not required*, to complete the THIRA.

Other jurisdictions, such as local units of government and regional planning groups, are highly encouraged, but *not required*, to complete a THIRA in conjunction with the SAA. The SAA is expected to engage the whole community, including tribal nations, to ensure that the entire scope of statewide risk is incorporated into a state's THIRA.

Where Is THIRA Used at the Regional and National Level?

The primary goal of THIRA is to help community planners understand the risks that confront them. Through the THIRA process, communities identify and prioritize their hazards and threats and then make better decisions about managing the associated risks. They do so through better planning and the development of needed core capabilities and mitigation strategies. The latter is more the focus of this textbook. The ultimate outcome of the THIRA process is a set of capability targets. The state preparedness report (SPR) assesses current capability against these targets and documents any gaps that exist. The capability targets generated through the THIRA process are used as the basis for the SPR assessment. The SPR is an annual capability assessment. The Post-Katrina Emergency Management Reform Act of 2006 (PKEMRA) is required to have a current SPR on file before it receives federal preparedness assistance administered by DHS. Each state submits an SPR to FEMA.

When Is It Applied and Completed?

The THIRA requirement, as it applies to the FEMA preparedness grant recipients, must be completed by December 31 of each year as a condition of their federal grant funding. Jurisdictions must allow considerable time for the process to be completed by a capable team of knowledgeable professionals.

Why Do We Do It?

Emergency management agencies participate in THIRA because they are mandated to do so when we receive federal preparedness grants. The process best serves both individual states and the nation as a whole when it trickles down to the local level and is initiated with good guidance and support. States will collate the results of local governments when they generate their own products. The better the process is implemented at the local level, the better the product will be at the state and national levels. In addition, FEMA regional offices will collate the results of the states they serve to generate their own products.

THIRA BY THE NUMBERS

Step 1

In Step 1 of the THIRA process, emergency managers need to develop a list of community-specific threats and hazards. These include natural hazards, technological hazards (accidents or systems failures), and human-caused incidents (such as terrorism). Refer to Table 8.1 for some examples of each of the three categories.

Emergency managers should consult a number of different sources when attempting to identify community specific hazards and threats. These sources include other documents or assessments, historical data, intelligence from fusion centers, and whole community partners. They should include only those threats and hazards that are of specific concern to them. The two factors that must be considered here are **likelihood of the incident** and **significance of threat/hazard effects**. In other words, to include specific hazards and threats, the emergency manager must consider what may be plausible and, at the same time, would have a significant effect on their community. Hazards and threats that are not plausible, possible, or serious should not be considered in a community's THIRA. The output of Step 1 is a list of a community's plausible and significant threats and hazards.

Table 8.1 Examples of Hazards and Threats by Subcategory*

Natural	Technological	Human-Caused
Avalanche	Airplane crash	Biological attack
Animal disease outbreak	Dam failure	Chemical attack
Drought	Levee failure	Cyber incident
Earthquake	Mine accident	Explosives attack
Epidemic	Hazardous materials release	Radiological attack
Flood	Power failure	Sabotage
Hurricane	Radiological release	School and workplace violence
Pandemic	Urban conflagration	
Tornado		
Tsunami		
Volcanic eruption		
Wildfire		
Winter storm		

*Note that human-caused *refers to intentional actions of an adversary (act of terrorism).* Technological hazards, *in this instance, refers to incidents with manmade hazards that result from accidents or system failures. Table courtesy of FEMA.*

Step 2

In Step 2 of the THIRA, emergency managers need to add context descriptions for each threat and hazard identified in Step 1. Context descriptions outline conditions, including time and location, under which a threat or hazard might occur. We can use expert judgment and analysis to provide us with better descriptions of the conditions we might expect. Threats and hazards are likely to have different impacts depending on the time, place, and conditions in which they occur. Emergency managers should develop more than one context description for each hazard or threat listed. Community planners should take into account past experiences, but they should realize that the past may not be a good predictor of the future. Refer to Table 8.2 for an example of a typical context description from an actual THIRA.

The product from Step 2 of the THIRA is a description for each hazard/threat shown in Step 1 that shows context.

Step 3

The third step in the THIRA process is probably the most difficult for any emergency manager. In this step, communities need to establish capability targets for each core capability. Where do these core capabilities come from in the first place? They were described in the NPG, which comes

Table 8.2 A context description for two hazards to the Dallas-Fort Worth, Texas area

Natural	
Tornado	A multiple-strike tornado event occurs on a Saturday afternoon in mid-May. The tornadoes range from EF-2 to EF-4 and impact densely populated urban areas, including the cities of Arlington, Dallas, Ft. Worth, Irving and Richardson. Significant structural damage occurs to residential and business areas, significantly damaging an estimated 75,000 households and causing 30,000 people to be in need of short-term public shelter.
Technological	
Dam or Levee Failure	A weakness in a lake's dam system reaches failure point, releasing millions of gallons of water "toward" regional cities. Immediately power systems, major thorough fares, and water delivery systems are heavily impacted or completely inoperable. Citizens with little or no warning of the event Immediately, require swift water rescue from homes or businesses. Estimated economic losses are expected to be in the billions, with recovery operations lasting multiple years.

This image taken from the 2013 Dallas-Fort Worth Area (DFWA) UASI THIRA.

■ **FIGURE 8.2** Flow chart for how the NPG (DHS, 2011) describes the needs for capabilities in the five Mission Areas of Prevention, Protection, Mitigation, Response, and Recovery. *Image courtesy of FEMA.*

from DHS and FEMA (DHS, 2011). The NPG was mandated by Presidential Policy Directive (PPD) 8: "National Preparedness," which was released in April 2011, and it was originally published the following October. In the NPG, capabilities were detailed within five distinct **Mission Areas (Prevention, Protection, Mitigation, Response** and **Recovery**). The Mission Areas are defined in the Glossary of this chapter (also refer to Figure 8.2).

The NPG defines what it means for a whole community to be prepared for all types of disasters and emergencies. The goal itself is succinct:

> A secure and resilient nation with the capabilities required across the whole community to prevent, protect against, mitigate, respond to, and recover from the threats and hazards that pose the greatest risk.

These risks include events such as natural disasters, disease pandemics, chemical spills and other manmade hazards, terrorist attacks, and cyberattacks. In addition to stating the goal, the document describes 31 activities, called *core capabilities*, which address the greatest risks to the nation. Each of these core capabilities is tied to a capability target (see Table 8.3). These targets recognize that everyone needs the flexibility to determine how they apply their resources based on the threats that are most relevant to them and their communities. Note that within the Mission Area of Mitigation, there are four specific

Table 8.3 Core Capabilities Identified for Each of the Mission Areas

Prevent	Protect	Mitigate	Respond	Recover
Planning	Planning	Planning	Planning	Planning
Public Information and Warming	Public Information and Warming	Public Information and Warming	Public Information and Warming	Public Information and Warming
Operation Coordination	Operation Coordination	Operation Coordination	Operation Coordination	Operation Coordination
Forensics and Attributes	Access Control and Identity Verification	Community Residence	Critical Transportation	Economic Recovery
Intelligence and Information Sharing	Cybersecurity	Long-Term Vulnerability Reduction	Environmental Response/Health and Safety	Health and Social Services
Screening, Search, and Detection	Intelligence and Information Sharing	Risk and Disaster Residence Assessment	Fatality Management Services	Housing
	Interdiction and Disruption	Threats and Hazard Identification	Infrastructure Systems	Infrastructure Systems
	Physical Protective Measures		Mass Care Services	Natural and cultural Resources
	Risk Management for Protection Programs and Activities		Mass Search and Rescue Operations	
	Screening, Search, and Detection		On-Scene Security and Protection	
	Supply Chain Integrity and Security		Operational Communications	
			Public and Private Services and Resources	
			Public Health and Medical Service	
			Situational Assessment	

Note that there are three core capabilities (Planning, Public Information and Warning, and Operation Coordination) that fall into all five Mission Areas. Image courtesy of FEMA.

core capabilities: Community Resilience, Long-Term Vulnerability Reduction, Risk and Disaster Resilience Assessment, and Threats and Hazard Identification.

To continue with the lengthy process in Step 3, capability targets must be specific and measureable. To do this, a community must consider the impacts and the desirable outcome for each threat and hazard. In keeping with what was covered in the last chapter, impacts describe how a threat or hazard might affect us. Now, extend this effect to each core capability. Since impacts are linked to the size and complexity of the hazard and threat, one should realistically estimate the magnitude of that threat/hazard to gauge the effect. The larger and more complex the hazard or threat, the more dramatic the impact will be on that community. In addition, the effects on core capabilities will be greater.

Consider this example from one THIRA (DFWA UASI, 2013): The hazard/threat from Step 1 is a hazardous materials incident. The context from Step 2 is a chemical spill of sulfuric acid being transported on a 90-ton railway car, which occurs during the morning rush hour in a large metropolitan area in mid-March. High winds generate a corrosive plume moving due east from the accident site into areas with a high daytime population. Prior to projecting the impact of this hazard in the context described here, the THIRA team addressed desired outcomes for core capabilities in each of the five Mission Areas. Focusing on Mitigation, let's look at what the team came up with for the four critical core capabilities (refer to Table 8.4). These

Table 8.4 Part of Step 3 in the THIRA Process Requires the Jurisdiction to Address Each Core Capability in all Five Mission Areas and Describe Their Desired Outcome

Community Resilience	Implement hazard mitigation plans for communities with highest risk through partnerships with whole community representatives. Identify opportunities to mitigate risk through public education, effective code policies and enforcement, project development, and implementation.
Long-term Vulnerability Reduction	Achieve decrease in the long-Term vulnerability posed by an increased risk to a similar incident. Ensure that long-Term community development plans and design incorporate hazards and risk information into consideration and encourage development of appropriate ordinances and resources to implement risk reduction activities for similar future events.
Risk and Disaster Resilience Assessment	Provide technical assistance to the whole community and to regional jurisdictions to identify, analyze, and maintain a risk assessment that includes information about localized vulnerabilities and consequences.
Threats and Hazard Identification	Identify threats and hazards in collaboration with whole community partners and incorporate findings into analysis and planning process for all Mission areas.

In essence, these goals will be applied to each threat and hazard scenario with their likely impact. The table above shows how the four Core Capabilities for Mitigation have been addressed in one jurisdiction's THIRA. Image taken from the 2013 DFWA UASI THIRA.

descriptions of desired outcomes or end states basically reiterate the description for each core capability with organizational goals or specifications incorporated.

Desired Outcomes

Desired outcomes describe the time frame or level of effort needed to successfully deliver core capabilities. Capabilities are useful only if communities can deliver them in a timely and effective manner. For example, success in the Response and Recovery mission areas often requires communities to deliver capabilities within a certain time frame (e.g., complete search and rescue operations within 72 h). When considering desired outcomes, communities should not be constrained by their current ability to meet time frames or other conditions of success (DHS, 2013). Refer to Table 8.5 for an example of how the Dallas Fort Worth Area (DFWA) Urban Area Security Initiative (UASI) assessed the Mission Area for the same HazMat incident described here.

The output of Step 3 is a minimum of one capability target for each core capability listed in the NPG. These capability targets will be used to identify resource requirements in Step 4. Additionally, communities can begin to identify preparedness activities to reduce future resource requirements.

Step 4

In this step of the THIRA process, emergency managers will apply the results of Step 3. So, in summary, Steps 1–3 listed the threats and hazards, provided a context description for each, stated the capability targets, and then examined the impacts of each hazard and threat to see what resources would be needed to counter the incident. Applying the results is also viewed as gap analysis, where we will look at existing resources, compare them to what is needed, and try to determine what the shortfalls are and how to counter them.

CRITICAL THINKING

The results of the THIRA process clearly show what hazards and threats confront a community and its leaders. The process also shows what capabilities the emergency manager feels are needed to counter these same hazards and threats. Gap analysis shows where the community is vulnerable. When it comes to an act of terrorism, doesn't this information make the community more vulnerable? Should these documents be kept from public view?

Table 8.5 Example of Desired Outcomes for Specific Core Capabilities That Relate to the Mission Area of Response for a HazMat Incident

				Response				
	Critical Transportation	Environmental Response/ Health and Safety	Fatality Management Services	Mass Care	Mass Search and Rescue Operations	On-Scene Security and Protection	Operational Communications
Hazardous Materials Incident	Identify possible response routes for potential responders to gain access to the incident.	Assess the environmental issues/health and safety issues, then provide the resources to address the incident.	Five (5) fatalities	Sheltered in place for most of this incident. Travelers will need to be rerouted away from the areas affected.	There will be a need for several SAR terms to assist. Consideration of a long-term search and rescue needs to be understood.	A large area of the incident will need on-scene security and protection for an extended period of time. Coordinate with ICP as incident progresses.	Interoperable radio Communications in effect.

Taken from the 2013 DFWA UASI THIRA.

Capability Estimation

Capability estimation begins when THIRA team members identify the major actions needed to achieve their capability targets. Mission-critical activities can be gleaned from current community-level plans, as well as from the National Planning Frameworks. Team members should consider the quantity and types of resources needed to complete each mission-critical activity in support of the capability targets. To identify quantity and types of resources, communities can use existing tools and information sources, such as:

- Strategic, operational, and tactical plans
- Resource typing data, including standardized resource characteristics
- Existing capacity analysis and capability calculators

THIRA team members should avoid developing very detailed, tactical-level task lists. Rather, they should strive to identify resources at a management level of detail. An example of the level of appropriate detail is found in Table 8.6.

Step 4 of the THIRA process enables emergency managers to estimate how many resources—including FEMA's Tier I National Incident Management System (NIMS) typed resources—are needed to achieve capability targets. In this step, communities develop a list of resource requirements to meet the capability targets, while also considering preparedness activities that may reduce future resource requirements (Table 8.7).

At the end of this journey, the THIRA team comes to discover the core capability, capability target and desired outcome for each Mission Area. Refer to Table 8.8 for an example of what this product looks like.

Table 8.6 Level of Resource Detail Recommended for Meeting a Core Capability Requirement from a Typical THIRA Process

Too Broad	Recommended	Too Detailed
All adequate personnel to meet the outcome	1 Type 3 Case Management Team	1 operations manager 1 team leader 1 case management supervisor 1 case manager 1 community coordination Specialist

Courtesy of DHS (2013).

Table 8.7 Final Product for the Mission Area of Mitigation

	Core Capability	Desired Outcome
Mitigation	**Community Resilience**	Implement hazard mitigation plans for communities with highest risk through partnerships with whole community representatives. Identify opportunities to mitigate risk through community education, effective code policies and enforcement, project development, and implementation.
		Greatest Estimated Impacts: Emergency event impacts community centers such as: hospitals, faith-based facilities, shopping centers, and entertainment venues. Creating a strain on citizens and the local economy.
		Capability Target:
		Work with Local Jurisdictions to ensure Vulnerability Assessment Plans are in place, and use findings to develop plans for long term recovery.
	Long-term Vulnerability Reduction	Achieve decrease in the long-term vulnerability posed by an increase risk to a similar incident. Ensure that long term community development plans and design incorporate hazards and risk information into consideration and encourage development of appropriate ordinances and resources to implement risk deduction activities for similar future events.
		Greatest Estimated Impacts: Current Hazard Vulnerability assessments and hazard mitigation plans do not adequately detail steps for long term mitigation or recovery.
		Capability Target:
		Achieve consistently integrated long-term risk reduction culture in impacted community. Provide technical assistance to update hazard mitigation plans, utilize federal grant opportunities, produce studies (as appropriate), work together to determine resources available to communities, provide guidance for recovery programs and policies.
	Risk and Disaster Resilience Assessment	Provide technical assistance to the whole community and to regional jurisdictions to identify, analyze, and maintain a risk assessment that includes information about localized vulnerabilities and consequences.
		Greatest Estimated Impacts: Assessments completed to ensure reconstitution of normal activities do not adequately identify weaknesses for risk reduction action and take inadequate action has been taken.
		Capability Target:
		Evaluate ability to withstand similar incident and take appropriate action to mitigate that risk, create defensible space for all hazards, and implement smart growth policies.
	Threats and Hazard Identification	Identify threats and hazards in collaboration with whole community partners and incorporate findings into analysis and planning process for all mission areas.
		Greatest Estimated Impacts: Results from THIRA process are not applied to existing capabilities and create gaps in mitigation and response planning.
		Capability Target:
		Ensure all probable threats and hazards are identified, assessed, and prioritized and integrated into each hazard mitigation plan.

The table shows each of the four specific core capabilities, the capability target, and the greatest estimated impacts for each of the four areas. Taken from DFWA UASI THIRA (2013).

Table 8.8 How Specific Mitigation Activities May Be Identified After the THIRA Process and Their Putative Effects and Potential Outcomes

Mitigation Activity	Effect	Outcome
Seismic retrofitting on utility buildings	Increased utility resilience	Key emergency services retain 100% power during incidents
Installing safe rooms in residential and commercial buildings for areas affected by tornadoes	Increased ability for individuals to Shelter in place during disasters	100% preservation of life safety for occupants taking shelter in Safe rooms designed to FEMA P-320/361 standards

Courtesy of DHS (2013).

As previously mentioned, THIRA is a process mandated by DHS, and it feeds into an overall process that enables government organizations to comply with and achieve the NPG. Preparedness can be viewed as the steps we take to having a "good disaster." In other words, preparedness paves the way for effective response and recovery. In some people's view, preparedness can also encompass the identification and implementation of mitigation strategies. As such, THIRA, which is primarily a preparedness tool, identifies threats and hazards and then gets us to address our capabilities to functionally prepare for, protect against, respond to, recover from, and mitigate dangerous events. Table 8.8 provides an example of structural mitigation activities identified in the THIRA process and discusses their putative effects and possible outcomes.

■ CONCLUSIONS

THIRA is a process that allows organizations at all levels of government to identify, assess, and prioritize their natural and manmade risks. These assessments are meant to facilitate the identification of capability and resource gaps and allow organizations to track their year-to-year progress to address those gaps.

The purpose of the THIRA process is to build unity of effort and a common strategic understanding among all levels of government. THIRAs should employ existing hazard mitigation processes, but in a reasonably standard manner so that results may be incorporated into state-, regional-, and national-level assessments. Using these assessments, emergency managers can develop planning assumptions and, working with its regional partners, identify and implement priority actions to address the identified shortfalls.

Understanding the risks faced by communities and the nation as a whole is essential to national preparedness. The THIRA process provides a common and consistent approach for communities to support the first two components of the National Preparedness System: (i) identifying and assessing risk and (2) estimating capability requirements. It expands on existing local, state, tribal, and territorial hazard identification and risk assessment processes.

THIRA contributes to a much broader approach that helps the United States achieve its NPG of "a secure and resilient nation with the capabilities required across the whole community to prevent, protect against, mitigate, respond to, and recover from the threats and hazards that pose the greatest risk." THIRA is not a substitute for comprehensive hazard mitigation planning. On the other hand, the products of THIRA may be useful in hazard mitigation planning.

DISCUSSION QUESTIONS

1. THIRA is a requirement for some jurisdictions receiving certain types of federal funding. What federal funding programs require a community to follow the THIRA process?
2. Should THIRA be used to guide a community's actions in hazard mitigation?
3. What are the features and benefits of THIRA?
4. List the four steps of THIRA and briefly explain each one.
5. Review your state's THIRA product and SPR. Discuss the product with a special focus on Mission Area mitigation. Are the desired outcomes realistic and achievable? Are the resource requirements specific enough to guide mitigation efforts?

WEBSITES

California Office of Emergency Services; examples of THIRA and related forms.
http://www.calema.ca.gov/InfrastructureProtection/Pages/THIRA.aspx
DHS FEMA Core Capabilities
http://www.fema.gov/core-capabilities
DHS FEMA NPG
http://www.fema.gov/national-preparedness-goal
DHS FEMA THIRA
http://www.fema.gov/threat-and-hazard-identification-and-risk-assessment
FEMA National Planning Frameworks
http://www.fema.gov/national-planning-frameworks

REFERENCES

Dallas—Fort Worth Area (DFWA) Urban Area Security Initiative (UASI) THIRA. (2013). Retrieved from <http://nctcog.org/ep/uasi/fy14_uasi/DFWA_UASI_THIRA_DEC2013.pdf>. Accessed September, 2014.

Presidential Policy Directive (PPD) 8. (2011). Retrieved from <http://www.dhs.gov/presidential-policy-directive-8-national-preparedness>. Accessed October 30, 2014.

U.S. Department of Homeland Security (DHS). (2011) National Preparedness Goal. October 2011. Retrieved from <http://www.fema.gov/national-preparedness-goal>. Accessed September, 2014.

U.S. Department of Homeland Security (DHS). (2013). Threat and hazard identification and risk assessment (THIRA) comprehensive preparedness guide (CPG) 201. Retrieved from <http://www.fema.gov/media-library/assets/documents/26335>. Accessed September, 2014.

3

Mitigation Strategies, Tools, and Techniques— What Can Be Done?

PREFACE

So you now have the knowledge to identify and understand all the natural and artificial hazards that confront you and your community or organization. Furthermore, you've been given a process that allows you to assess risk and vulnerability. What is the next step and what can be done to mitigate those hazards? That's what the final section of this textbook is about.

In the third thematic section of this book, you will be introduced to mitigation strategies, tools and techniques for natural (Chapter 9) and artificial hazards (Chapter 10). Like most treatments of the broad subject of mitigation strategies, we break them up into two broad categories: structural and non-structural. Both strategies have their merits and both have their drawbacks.

> Structural mitigation strategies can be very effective, but they are often quite costly. It can be very difficult to convince a politician that the money spent today will benefit someone in the future.

Structural mitigation strategies can be very effective at holding back floodwaters and storm surge. In addition, many things can be done in new construction and to modify existing structures so that they are resistant to the effects of wind, water, and vibration. But these measures are often very costly to build; and once they are built or employed, there may be maintenance costs. Also, there is no guarantee that these costly measures will weather the storm or sustain the quake. Storm surge from a powerful hurricane or tsunami can easily top 8–10 m (25–30 ft) or more. Few structures on Earth could sustain a category 5 hurricane, an Enhanced Fujita (EF) 5 tornado, or an earthquake measuring 8.0 on the Richter scale.

> Nonstructural mitigation strategies may be very inexpensive to employ, but they are not always easy to get approved. Remember that the devil is in the details: social, political, and economic details.

Nonstructural mitigation strategies are thought to be very inexpensive to enact. Essentially, you propose an idea, put it on paper, put it up for a vote, and, then put it into action after it passes. This seems very simple, right? But it is not so simple in many cases. Legislative measures may be very effective at keeping people from building homes and businesses in hazard-prone areas. However, changes to existing laws, codes, and regulations can be real "hot button" issues at a local level. You may be in for the political fight of your life. You may learn that a simple idea or solution to a real problem is not so simple after all. As we've often heard ... the devil is in the details! Changing laws, rules, regulations, or codes may dramatically increase the cost of construction or impede commerce. It could be the reason why a community fails to grow economically or is outcompeted by a neighboring community.

Whenever we envision the enactment of some new nonstructural measure, be certain that your social, economic, and political analyses are complete. A thorough Social, Technical, Administrative, Political, Legal, Environmental, and Economic (STAPLEE) analysis should be very helpful for reaching that end, but do not underestimate the opposition to these measures.

There are many tools that can be employed to assist emergency management practitioners and business continuity professionals. We delve into only a few of these tools in this textbook. Specifically, we discuss Computer-Aided Management of Emergency Operations (CAMEO), geographic information system (GIS), Hazards United States (HAZUS), and HAZUS-MH. There is a HAZUS-MH tutorial at the end of Chapter 11. In Chapter 12, the final chapter of this book, we discuss best practices for hazard mitigation and some resources that are available to those seeking to improve their communities or organizations with a comprehensive hazard mitigation program.

Mitigation Strategies for Natural Hazards

OBJECTIVES

The study of this chapter will enable you to:

1. Identify various structural and nonstructural mitigation measures against natural hazards.

2. Understand and discuss structural projects related to flood control, shoreline protection, and sediment-trapping structures.

3. Understand and discuss various regulatory mitigation measures related to prevention.

4. Understand and discuss property protection measures that require modifying or strengthening structures.

5. Understand the importance of mitigation measures related to natural resource protection.

6. Understand the role of public education and awareness programs.

7. Understand the role of emergency services.

8. Discuss the advantages and disadvantages of structural and nonstructural mitigation measures.

9. Understand the process of incorporating mitigation strategies into a hazard mitigation plan (HMP).

Essential Terminology: Structural mitigation, nonstructural mitigation, dam, reservoir, levee, dike, floodwall, seawall, bulkheads, revetments, groin, jetty, zoning, overlay zone, amortization, subdivision regulations, setback regulations, Capital Improvement Program (CIP), eminent domain, taking law, building code, retrofitting, floodproofing, windproofing, seismic retrofitting, the law of nuisance, storm safe room, acquisition/buyout, fee simple acquisition, easement, purchase of development rights (PDR), transfer of development rights (TDR), relocation, wetland, buffer zone, erosion, community outreach projects, real estate disclosure, warning systems, emergency response services, critical infrastructure, simple listing

We can't control forces of nature. But we can control what comes afterward. We have a chance to start fresh.

Jim Hunt, former governor of North Carolina

INTRODUCTION

Once risk assessment for your community is completed, it is important to identify appropriate mitigation actions or measures before developing a hazard mitigation plan (HMP). In this step, information revealed in hazard identification and risk assessment is used to develop clear mitigation goals (general guidelines that explain what you want to achieve) and objectives (statements that detail how these goals will be achieved). Mitigation actions are specific measures or strategies that help you achieve these community goals and objectives. Such measures can either be structural or nonstructural. **Structural** measures are those that involve physical construction to avoid possible impacts of hazards or application of engineering techniques to achieve hazard resistance and resilience in structures or systems (UNISDR, 2009). In contrast, **nonstructural** measures seek to reduce the likelihood or consequence of risk through modifications in human action, human behavior, or natural processes (FEMA, n.d.c). Nonstructural mitigation differs most significantly from that of structural mitigation, in that it reduces risk (likelihood and consequences) without requiring the use of engineered structures.

FEMA (2003) has further categorized mitigation strategies for natural hazards into six broad categories: structural projects, prevention, property protection, natural resource protection, public education and awareness, and emergency services. These categories have the following characteristics:

- *Structural projects*: Actions that involve the engineering or construction of structures to lessen the impacts of natural hazards. These include flood control structures (e.g., dams and levees); shoreline protection structures (e.g., seawalls, bulkheads, and revetments); and sediment-trapping structures (e.g., groins and jetties).

- *Prevention*: Government administrative or regulatory actions or processes that influence land development and built environments to completely avoid the hazard or keep existing hazards from worsening. Examples include zoning, subdivision regulations, setback regulations, eminent domain, and building codes.
- *Property protection*: Actions involving modifying or strengthening existing buildings or structures to better withstand hazards or removal from the hazard area. Examples include acquisition, easement, relocation, and structural retrofits.
- *National resource protection*: Actions that preserve or restore the functions of natural systems in addition to minimizing hazard losses. Examples include wetland restoration and preservation, erosion control, and watershed management.
- *Public education and awareness*: Actions to inform and educate citizens, elected officials, and property owners about how to protect themselves and their property. Examples include community outreach projects, in-school hazard education programs, and real estate disclosures.
- *Emergency services*: Actions that protect people and property during and immediately after a disaster or hazard event. These include warning systems, emergency response services, and protection of critical infrastructure.

This chapter will first describe some of the mitigation strategies for natural hazards in each category, and then also discuss how to incorporate mitigation strategies into the HMP.

STRUCTURAL PROJECTS
Flood Control Structures
Dams and Reservoirs

A **dam** is an artificial barrier designed to hold back water or other liquid-borne materials for any of several reasons, such as human water supply, irrigation, livestock water supply, energy generation, containment of mine tailings, recreation, and pollution or flood control. Many dams fulfill a combination of these functions. They can be used as effective flood control devices by retaining water and releasing it at a controlled rate that does not overwhelm the capacity of downstream channels (Schwab, Eschelbach, & Brower, 2007).

A **reservoir** is an artificial lake formed by the construction of a dam. Reservoirs are located behind dams and reduce flooding by storing water

■ **FIGURE 9.1** The Garrison Dam on Lake Sakakawea in North Dakota. *Courtesy of FEMA.*

during peak runoff periods. For instance, Lake Sakakawea in North Dakota, the third-largest artifical lake in the United States, is a body of water created and contained by the Garrison Dam.

Dams are classified by a number of factors, including the type of construction material used, the methods used in construction, the slope or cross section of the dam, the way the dam resists the forces of the water pressure behind it, the means used for controlling seepage, and, occasionally, according to the dam's purpose (FEMA, 2013). Materials used for constructing them include soil, rock, concrete, masonry, steel, timber, miscellaneous materials (e.g., rubber, plastic), and any combination of these materials. Embankment dams are the most common type of dams that are mainly made of natural materials. Embankment dams that are constructed mostly of compacted earth are known as *earth-fill dams*, whereas the ones comprised of mostly compacted or dumped rock are called *rock-fill dams*. The Garrison dam in Figure 9.1 is an example of an earth-fill embankment dam. Concrete dams are categorized as either arch or gravity dams, depending on how they resist water pressure from the reservoir. Arch dams, as their name indicates, are curved in the shape of an arch so that the water pressure presses against the arch (Figure 9.2). Arch dams are thinner, require less material, and are usually constructed in narrow, steep valleys (British Dam Society, n.d.).

Gravity dams are the most common type of concrete dams. The name *gravity dam* comes from the fact that gravity holds it down to the ground, keeping the water reservoir from pushing it over. A buttress dam is a

■ **FIGURE 9.2** At 564 feet (172 m) high, Hungry Horse Dam in Montana is one of the largest concrete arch dams in the United States. *Courtesy of the U.S. Bureau of Reclamation.*

specific type of gravity dam, where the large mass of concrete is reduced and the buttresses are spaced at intervals on the downstream side. This design resists the force of the reservoir water and prevents the dam from tipping over (Figure 9.3).

Dams provide many vital benefits to people and local economies, including flood protection, water supply, hydropower, irrigation, and recreation. However, dam failure is a significant threat to people and property downstream. Storm events are not usually the cause of dam failure. Most of these failures fall into one or more of the following categories: structural failures, such as foundation defects, slope instability, or damage caused by earthquakes; mechanical failures, such as malfunctioning gates, conduits, or valves; and hydraulic failures, such as overtopping of a dam due to inadequate spillway design and debris blockage of spillways.

The owners are solely responsible for the safety of their dams. In the United States, most dams (69%) are privately owned, although the state agencies regulate more than 80% of them (FEMA, 2013). Most states have a dam safety program that monitors dams and carries out inspections on a regular basis. Although dam failures are infrequent, the impacts can be catastrophic and can far exceed that of typical flood events.

■ **FIGURE 9.3** The Spillway section of the Pueblo Dam in Colorado, as seen from downstream. This is an example of a buttress dam. *Photo by the U.S. Bureau of Reclamation/Stanley Core.*

Historically Significant Dam Failures in the United States
May 31, 1889—Johnstown, Pennsylvania

The deadliest dam failure in U.S. history, caused by the breaking of the South Fork Dam on the Little Connemaugh River, took the lives of more than 2200 people.

February 26, 1972—Buffalo Creek Valley, West Virginia

The failure of a coal-waste impoundment owned by the Buffalo Mining Company killed 125 people and caused more than $400 million worth of damage.

June 9, 1972—Rapid City, South Dakota

The failure of the Canyon Lake Dam killed an undetermined number of people (estimates range from 33 to 237) and caused more than $60 million worth of damage.

June 5, 1976—Eastern Idaho

Failure of the Teton Dam in two counties in Idaho killed 11 people and caused more than $1 billion worth of damage. The failure flooded at least six communities, encompassing tens of thousands of acres.

July 19–20, 1977—Laurel Run, Pennsylvania

The Laurel Run Dam (also near Johnstown, Pennsylvania) failed, killing more than 40 people and causing $5.3 million worth of damage.

November 5, 1977—Toccoa Falls, Georgia

Kelly Barnes Dam, in Stephens County, failed, killing 39 students and staff at Toccoa Falls College and causing about $2.5 million worth of damage.

Following the Toccoa Falls tragedy, President Jimmy Carter directed the U.S. Army Corps of Engineers (USACE) to inspect the nation's nonfederal high-hazard dams.

CRITICAL THINKING

Suppose that a privately owned dam is located in your community. As the director of emergency management, you are charged with protecting public safety. What mitigation strategies would you implement with regard to this dam?

Levees, Dikes, and Floodwalls

A **levee** is a manmade structure, usually an earthen embankment, built parallel to a waterway or a river in order to protect lives and properties behind it from some level of flooding. These are often referred to as **dikes**, which are usually earthen or rock structures built partially across a river to maintain the depth and location of a navigation channel (Schwab et al., 2007). **Floodwalls** are also similar to levees, but they are usually found in more urban areas and are made of stone or reinforced concrete. A levee system is a flood risk reduction system that consists of levees and associated structures (FEMA, n.d.e). These measures are inexpensive and effective as a barrier against floodwaters.

Levees were first built in the United States more than 150 years ago. No entity was solely responsible for levee design, construction, operation, and maintenance. Some were built by citizens to protect their properties from flooding. Others were built by various federal, state, or local agencies. The U.S. Army Corps of Engineers (USACE) has designed and built many levee systems and is responsible for the maintenance of federally owned levees (FEMA, n.d.e).

Hurricane Katrina: The Failure of Levee System in New Orleans, Louisiana

Hurricane Katrina is the costliest disaster in the history of the United States; it which caused about $108 billion in damage and killed 1833 people. On August 29, 2005, the hurricane hit the city of New Orleans as a Category 3 hurricane. Much of New Orleans is located below sea level, which makes the city prone to flooding from Lake Pontchartrain, Lake Borgne, the Mississippi River, and the Gulf of Mexico. It has one of the largest levee systems in the world, built by USACE, consisting of 350 miles (563 km) of levees, which are mostly earthen embankments that serve as flood barriers. The system also includes floodwalls, bridges, closable gates, culverts, and canals. It is comprised of four main compartmented basins designed to limit the flooding impacts on the entire system resulting from individual failures of levees and floodwalls (White House, 2006). Although Katrina's wind speed was lessening when it reached New Orleans, the storm surge caused more than 50 breaches in the city's levee system, making it the worst engineering disaster in the history of the United States (Figure 9.4).

The overtopping of levees and subsequent flooding in New Orleans from a major hurricane was predicted before Hurricane Katrina occurred in 2005. In 2004, FEMA funded the Southeast Louisiana Catastrophic Hurricane Project to analyze what would happen if a catastrophic hurricane struck the coast of Louisiana. In July 16–23, 2004, as many as 300 federal, state, and local emergency response officials participated in a meeting where a hypothetical

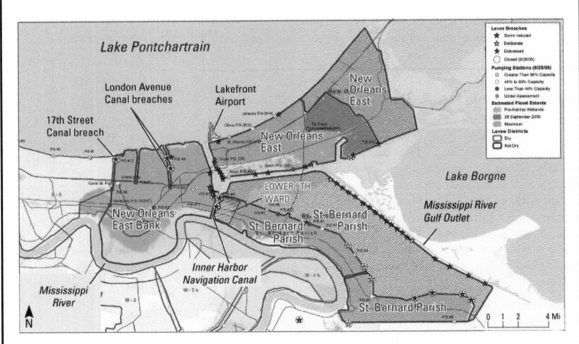

■ **FIGURE 9.4** Locations and levee breaches in New Orleans. Three of the four main protected units that make up the New Orleans flood protection system are labeled: the New Orleans East Bank section, the New Orleans East section, and the Ninth Ward and St. Bernard Parish section. A fourth protected unit, southeast of this map, is a thin, protected strip along the Mississippi River heading southward from St. Bernard Parish to the river mouth. Blue hatching indicates pre-Katrina wetlands. Pink shading shows estimated maximum extent of urban flooding; blue shading shows areas still flooded on September 28, 2005. *Courtesy of the US Geological Survey.*

catastrophic hurricane scenario (Hurricane Pam) was used as an exercise to identify and assess the needs for responding to such hurricanes. Hurricane Pam was laid out as a slow-moving Category 3 storm with sustained winds of 120 mph, and the study showed that such a storm would cause overtopping of the levee system by the storm surge. But these results were not considered further prior to Katrina—there were no efforts to shore up the levee system. The USACE later admitted that faulty design and substandard construction contributed to the failure of its levee system in New Orleans. According to a report published by the American Society of Civil Engineers (ASCE), two-thirds of the flooding in the city could have been avoided if the levees had held (ASCE, 2007).

Shoreline Protection Structures
Seawalls, Bulkheads, and Revetments

Seawalls are "hard" engineering structures built on the shoreline to protect areas from the action of tides and waves, as well as from shoreline erosion. Vertical seawalls are built in exposed areas to deflect wave energy away from the coast. However, seawalls can also be curved or stepped to dissipate smaller waves and reflect larger storm waves (FEMA, n.d.c). In a curved seawall, the curve helps prevent waves from overtopping the wall and provides extra protection for the toe of the wall.

Seawalls should be constructed with durable, immovable materials to withstand the extreme wave attacks that result from powerful hurricanes and other storms. Materials commonly used for seawall construction include reinforced concrete, boulders, steel, or gabions. Additional seawall construction materials may include vinyl, wood, aluminum, fiberglass composite, and large biodegradable sandbags (made of jute and coir) (Clarke, 1994).

The Galveston seawall was built in Galveston, Texas, after the deadliest 1900 storm that killed more than 8000 people with winds in excess of 130 miles per hour (209 km/h) and a 15-foot (4.6 m) storm surge (NOAA, 2000). At that time, Galveston was only 8.7 feet (2.65 m) above sea level. After the devastation of the 1900 hurricane, the people of Galveston made an unprecedented response, supporting the erection of a 16-foot-thick (4.88 m), 17-foot-high (5.18 m) seawall (Figure 9.5). Construction began in September 1902, and the initial segment was completed on July 29, 1904. From 1904 to 1963, the seawall was extended from 3.3 miles (5.3 km) to over 10 miles (16 km). They also raised the entire island by as much as 8 feet (2.4 m) with sand dredged from Galveston Bay.

Bulkheads are vertical walls similar to seawalls on the shoreline, but they are designed to retain loose fill and sediment behind them. They are often constructed of wood or steel. Since the purpose of bulkheads is to maintain the material behind them rather than provide protection from the action of tides and waves, they are usually do not afford good protection from storms or other flood events.

■ **FIGURE 9.5** Construction of the No. 3 Galveston Seawall, west of the Rapid Fire Battery, Fort Crockett, in Galveston, Texas. *Courtesy of the U.S. National Archives and Records Administration.*

Revetments

Revetments are sloping structures placed on river banks or cliffs designed to protect the backshore from high tides and surges (FEMA, n.d.c). They are constructed from a number of types of material, including stone, concrete-mat, willow plantings, and gabions. The USACE also uses trench-fill revetments when the channel is poorly aligned, and concrete mattress revetments cannot be used. In a trench-fill revetment, the river is used as a dredge to remove silt and sand in front of the trench. Once the sand and silt has eroded, the stone is launched into the river and paves a new riverbank (USACE, n.d.). In revetment construction with concrete mats, the process starts with the smoothing of the bank to a stable slope from the top to the bottom of the water surface. Then, concrete mats are placed in the water along the base of the river. The USACE built 361 miles of revetments along the Mississippi River in the New Orleans district. An example of a revetment project in Indiana is shown in Figure 9.6.

Although seawalls and other shoreline protection structures are designed to control coastal land loss, they can accelerate land loss to adjacent beaches and block public access to the shoreline. Beaches would become

■ **FIGURE 9.6** Shoreline revetment project in Indiana. Image by the National Park Service, Indiana Dunes National Lakeshore. *Courtesy of EPA.*

narrower as the shoreline retreats due to these structures. The also contribute to incomplete storm beach recovery as natural dune restoration after a storm is prevented or prolonged by limiting the onshore transportation and deposition of sand. Seawalls are very costly to build and far more expensive than planting natural vegetation to secure the shoreline.

Sediment-Trapping Structures

Groins

Groins (which are known as *groynes* outside the United States) are shore-perpendicular structures designed to interrupt or slow the movement of sediment along the shore (refer to Figure 9.7). Groins are built of timber, concrete, metal sheet piling, or rock. They are usually built in groups called *groin fields*, where each groin is connected to land and extend into the sea or lake. The length and the spacing of the groin system are an important factor for trapping sediment. Usually, shorter groins are used for larger grain size, and vice versa. Groins are effective to trap sand near to shore and reduce the need for sand replacement on beaches (Schwab et al., 2007). Groins can help create wider beaches for recreational purposes, which in turn slow the erosion process as storm waves break further out to sea.

■ **FIGURE 9.7** Groin constructed of rocks stopping the longshore flow of sand in Cape May, New Jersey. Note a buildup of sand to the left of the groin. Image by Sheri Phillips, NOAA/NESDIS/NODC, archived at NOAA's America's Coastlines Collection.

Jetties

Similar to groins, **jetties** are also wall-like structures built perpendicular to the coast (see Figure 9.8). Although the primary function of jetties is to protect navigation channels, they also trap sediment by restricting the movement of materials transported by longshore currents. Jetties help stabilize channels, inlets, and outlets. The critical factors for channel stabilization are the width of the channel and management of sediment (FEMA, n.d.c). The width of the channel should be in balance, as it has to be wide enough to reduce current velocity within the channel, but narrow enough to restrict shoaling.

MITIGATION MEASURES RELATED TO PREVENTION
Zoning Ordinances

Zoning is one of the most powerful regulatory instruments that local governments possess for land use control and management. Zoning

■ **FIGURE 9.8** A father and son fishing at sunrise on a jetty in South Padre Island, Texas. *Courtesy of NOAA.*

ordinances regulate development in a community by dividing areas into different zones (or districts) within the jurisdiction (Figure 9.9) and set criteria for each zone how land should be developed. It is also a part of the community's comprehensive plan to guide future development. In terms of hazard mitigation, zoning can limit development or restrict inappropriate uses in designated hazard areas. One effective method is by down-zoning (decreasing density), which can be accomplished by increasing the minimum lot size or reducing the number of dwelling units permitted per acre, thereby decrease the number of people and structures in high hazard areas (Schwab et al., 2007). On the other hand, safer areas can also be zoned, decreasing the lot size and increasing the number of dwelling units per acre including residential houses, apartments, and commercial buildings. Besides down-zoning, hazard areas can also be designated for low-intensity uses such as parks, open space, and agriculture.

Overlay Zones

Along with the standard zoning ordinances, some communities may have **overlay zones** for a certain area such as floodplains or historic districts that allow communities to isolate and protect areas not covered by the rest of the ordinance. Overlay zones are effective for use in high-hazard areas (e.g., coastal areas) or to protect environmentally sensitive areas such as wetlands. Such zones coexist with other zones, operating like a transparency overlaying existing land-use controls, where development is

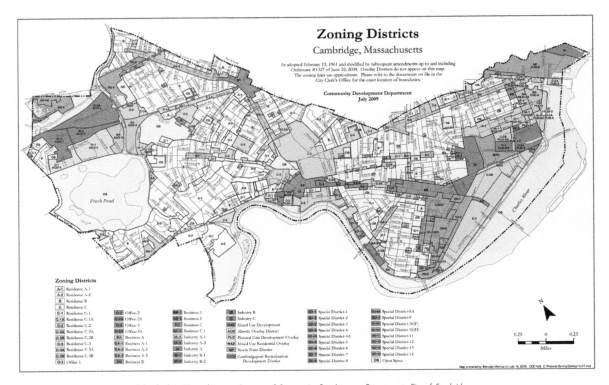

FIGURE 9.9 A zoning map of Cambridge, Massachusetts. *Courtesy of Community Development Department, City of Cambridge.*

regulated by the standard zoning ordinance and the unique requirements of the overlay zone. They can also be triggered by a certain event, such as a hurricane or a tornado. For instance, overlay zones remain transparent until a hurricane causes substantial damage in the designated area. The requirements for these zones will be in effect after the disaster, which might include restriction of reconstruction until a thorough damage assessment can be performed.

Disadvantages of Zoning

Zoning ordinances primarily affect future development rather than existing buildings and properties, and thus, they are less useful in hazard mitigation for current development. Most zoning codes allow continuing prior uses as *nonconforming uses* even changes are made in the ordinance. However, communities can require nonconforming structures to be replaced within a certain time, as the former uses become illegal once the structures are replaced or destroyed. This process is called **amortization**, which may take years to become effective. Zoning is also influenced by local politics as administrative or leadership change in the community can bring changes in local zoning ordinances. Moreover, zoning if not examined carefully, can be a subject to legal challenges and can come at a significant financial cost. The *Lucas v. South Carolina Coastal Council* case (1992), discussed later in this chapter, is one such example of arbitrary zoning challenged by the taking clause of the Fifth Amendment.

Subdivision Regulations

Subdivision regulations or ordinances govern how land will be divided into small parcels for development and set construction standards for developers. These standards typically address lot layout and infrastructures such as roads, utilities, drainage systems, sidewalks, and storm sewers. Subdivision regulations are important in hazard mitigation, as they also set standards for firefighting equipment and snowplows on the road, minimum water pressure needed for firefighting, and installation of adequate drainage and storm water management facilities. The ordinances can also require constructing buildings above the flood level, increased the distance between structures and hazard areas, or even can be used to limit development on hazardous land. The local government must approve the subdivision plat before the lots are ready for sale. Subdivision ordinance can require the final plat to show hazard areas and set provisions to keep minimum distance between the hazard areas and construction sites. If needed, the ordinances can enforce a buffer to limit development or activity within a certain area. For instance, subdivision ordinances in the state of Maryland require a 25-foot buffer next to all wetlands (Schwab et al., 2007).

Setback Regulations

In land use planning, the term **setback** is used to delineate the distance that a building or a structure is away from a street or other feature such as a river or shoreline. In hazard mitigation, setback regulations can establish a minimum distance between the building or lot and a hazard area. In coastal areas, ocean shoreline setbacks are implemented to prevent damages to structures from coastal storms or erosion. Similarly, fault zone setbacks are used in earthquake-prone areas as effective measures to keep buildings and structures from fault lines.

Capital Improvement Programs

Capital Improvement Programs (CIPs) are put in place by local governments to implement large-scale projects in a community, such as schools, bridges, police stations, recreation centers, and other public facilities. Governments can set requirements to implement these major public expenditures for the next 5–20 years, which may include incorporating mitigation measures such as retrofitting, acquisition of open space, and using setback or preventing development altogether in hazard areas. In most cases, CIP funding is augmented with FEMA mitigation grants, along with local or state funding for the projects.

Eminent Domain

Eminent domain is defined as "the right of the government to take (condemn) private property for public use; however, the owner must be given just compensation for the taking" (Schwab et al., 2007). The Bible refers to one of the first instances of eminent domain, as Naboth was compensated for his vineyard being taken by King Ahab of Samaria. Much later, in the 1700s, France implemented a similar decree, which ultimately prompted the United States to follow suit under the Fifth Amendment of the Constitution. The Fifth Amendment stipulates that four conditions shall be met before the government can usurp private land: "(1) private property (2) must be taken (3) for public use (4) and with just compensation" (Gale Group, 2008).

Traditionally, local and state governments commonly use eminent domain for the purpose of creating important infrastructure for public use (e.g., roadways and schools). Projects of this nature are clearly seen for their "public use" and rarely get bogged down in litigation. In some hazard-prone areas (floodplain or coastal areas), this principle can be used for the safety and well-being of the public in an effort to minimize the effects on life and property.

When a state or local government wants to purchase land from an individual, they must provide fair and just compensation for that property, which is defined as "fair market value." However, if the landowner does not want to sell his or her land, the government has the right to seize their land by condemnation. Although eminent domain cannot be used to take private property for private use, the 2005 U.S. Supreme Court decision in *Kelo v. City of New London 545 U.S. 469* (2005) raised concerns over exercising the power of eminent domain for economic development. In their ruling, the Supreme Court upheld the city's use of eminent domain authority to condemn private homes to redevelop a neighborhood for residential, commercial, and park development. The Court concluded that such actions would bring economic growth and benefit the community, and thus, is permissible as "public use" under the Takings Clause of the Fifth Amendment (MRSC, n.d.). This decision generated much public criticism, and as a result, many states and local governments have enacted legislation to prohibit the use of eminent domain to condemn private property for purely economic development purposes (Schwab et al., 2007).

Regulatory Takings and *Lucas v. South Carolina Coastal Council (SCCC)*
Taking laws are those regulations that result in actions comparable to eminent domain. It is the duty of property owners to abide by all rules and regulations within their jurisdictions. But sometimes governments can enact legislations that result in the economic loss for the owners or outright ownership of the property. The state courts and the U.S. Supreme Court have developed a range of guidelines for determining if a case involves taking. These include (Schwab et al., 2007):

- The physical occupation of private land by the government is almost always a taking.
- All land-use regulations must serve a valid public purpose.
- There must be a rational connection between the regulation and the purpose.
- Even a temporary loss of use that does not have a valid purpose and a rational connection is a taking.
- A regulation that deprives the owner of all economically beneficial use of the property is a taking.

Lucas v. South Carolina Coastal Council (SCCC) (1992) presents a primary example of the taking law. David Lucas was the owner of two beachfront lots on a barrier island in South Carolina. The SCCC later enacted the Beachfront Management Act, which prohibited construction on any of the lots owned by Lucas; thus, the property became economically worthless. Lucas won the initial case but lost in appeal at the South Carolina Supreme Court. However, he subsequently won his final appeal at the U.S. Supreme Court and was awarded $1.2 million as compensation for the "taking." Subsequently, the SCCC rezoned the land and sold the property to recover their losses. A large house now sits on the property, which was threatened by erosion in 1996 (Schwab et al., 2007). Kanner (1996) summarized the change of heart sparked by this case by writing, "South Carolina promptly executed a neck-snapping, intellectual about-face. The lots, which were only a year earlier depicted as a 'threat to life and property' if built upon, underwent a sudden metamorphosis." *Lucas v. SCCC* signifies the importance of taking laws, as zoning and regulation of property within a municipality can be used arbitrarily. Governments have to pay a large amount of compensation if their regulatory actions are considered as taking by the court.

Building Codes

Building codes are sets of regulations governing the design, construction, and maintenance of structures (FEMA, n.d.a). They specify the minimum acceptable standard required for structural design, integrity, and construction materials used in buildings and structures, thereby reducing casualties, injuries, and property damage.

The Code of Hammurabi, written around the 18th century B.C. by the Babylonian king Hammurabi, is the earliest known example of building codes. One of these codes stated that "if a dwelling collapsed and caused the death of the owner, the builder would be put to death" (IBHS, n.d.a). London passed the Rebuilding of London Act after the Great Fire, a massive blaze in 1666 that destroyed nearly 15,000 buildings. In the United States, all major cities used to have their own building codes. For example, the city of Baltimore passed its first building code in 1859. Later, however, almost all municipalities adopted model building codes due to the increasing cost and complexity of developing building regulations. Prior to 1994, model building codes were developed through three organizations: Building Officials and Code Administrators International, Inc. (BOCA), the Southern Building Code Congress International, Inc. (SBCCI), and the International Conference of Building Officials (ICBO). In 1994, the International Code Council (ICC) was formed combining these three organizations, and it released its first set of codes in 2000. The ICC's family of international codes includes:

> - International Building Code (IBC): Applies to almost all types of new buildings
> - International Residential Code (IRC): Applies to new one- and two-family dwellings and townhouses of not more than three stories in height
> - International Existing Building Code (IEBC): Applies to the alteration, repair, addition, or change in the occupancy of existing structures (FEMA, n.d.a)

The ICC model building codes are updated every three years to reflect the latest scientific and engineering principles. Most states do have mandatory statewide building codes, but there are still several states where power is given to individual jurisdictions to adopt and enforce building codes. The adoption and enforcement of modern building codes is a major step toward mitigating disasters and becoming hazard resilient for events, such as earthquakes and hurricanes. A massive 2010 earthquake in Haiti killed more than 160,000 people, probably largely because there were no building codes in place to govern construction (Figure 9.10). The New Madrid/

Wabash Valley seismic zone in the United States is prone to earthquake activity; it crosses the states of Arkansas, Illinois, Indiana, Kentucky, Mississippi, Missouri, and Tennessee. Even so, several of these states (Arkansas, Illinois, Mississippi, Missouri, and Tennessee) have inadequate code coverage and enforcement in place (IBHS, n.d.b).

In a comparative assessment of residential building regulations and processes governing construction in the 18 hurricane-prone states along the Atlantic Coast and Gulf of Mexico, it was found that Alabama, Texas, Delaware, and Mississippi had the lowest building code protections and lack many of the residential building code requirements associated with life safety protections (IBHS, 2012). Alabama has now implemented a statewide code for residential buildings after an April 2011 tornado that killed 250 people and damaged or destroyed 23,000 houses; that damage

■ **FIGURE 9.10** Port-au-Prince, Haiti on January 15, 2010, after a magnitude 7 earthquake hit the country on January 12, 2010. The impact was catastrophic, as construction in Haiti was not governed by modern building codes. Many agencies around the world, including the U.S. Department of Defense (DoD), dispatched resources to Haiti to assist with humanitarian assistance and disaster relief after the earthquake. U.S. Air Force photo by Master Sgt. Jeremy Lock. *Courtesy of the DoD.*

could have been greatly reduced with better construction, as required by modern building codes.

PROPERTY PROTECTION MEASURES
Structural Retrofit

Strengthening or modifying a building in order to prevent or reduce damages from hazards is called **retrofit**. There are many approaches to retrofitting, described next.

Floodproofing

Flood retrofitting measures known as **floodproofing** can be done in two ways: dry and wet. Dry floodproofing involves sealing the structure against floodwaters by making all areas below the flood protection level watertight. This can be done through coating walls with waterproofing compounds or plastic sheeting and closing all building openings (i.e., doors, windows) with removable shields or sandbags. Dry floodproofing is recommended for areas subject to shallow flooding and limited to 2 or 3 feet above the foundation of a building due to the pressure exerted by deeper water on the walls and floors (Wetmore, 2013). In addition, sufficient advanced warning time is needed for dry floodproofing to close openings, place sandbags and other measures.

In terms of wet floodproofing, floodwaters are allowed to enter a building to reduce the pressure exerted by deep water. Wet floodproofing involves removal of valuable or essential items that could be affected by flood water and replacing the structural components below flood level with water resistant materials. This method can dramatically reduce damage costs by simply removing furniture and electrical appliances out of the flood prone area.

Windproofing

Windproofing focuses on modifying the design and construction of a building to withstand wind damage. This involves the improvement of the aerodynamics of a structure, materials used, and the addition of features such as storm shutters, shatter-resistant window panes, and paneling put in place to cover windows just before a storm (Figure 9.11). Windproofing helps to secure a building from broken glass and flying debris during a tornado or a hurricane. The **law of nuisance**, pertaining to modern property law, requires that private property owners must refrain from using property in a way that interferes with the rights of adjoining property

■ **FIGURE 9.11** A man placing a storm shutter panel on his house before a hurricane. *Courtesy of FEMA.*

owners or causes injury to the general public. These include securing the structures so that they do not become flying debris during a storm, and not undertaking any activities that increase flooding.

Seismic Retrofitting

Seismic retrofitting involves adding braces, removing overhangs, and providing flexible utility connections and tie-downs to reduce damage. Seismic construction techniques, such as adding reinforcing rods to concrete or using brick veneer wall instead of all brick, can be fairly inexpensive but nevertheless they are very effective at reducing damages during an earthquake. Seismic retrofitting also involves nonstructural mitigation techniques, such as securing movable objects such as bookshelves and tall furniture, and covering windows with shatter-resistant panes. In earthquake-prone areas, such as many areas of California (Figure 9.12), codes that require seismic construction and retrofitting are an integral part of building codes, ensuring that structures can adequately resist seismic forces during earthquakes (FEMA, n.d.a).

Storm Safe Rooms

A **storm safe room** is a hardened structure that can be installed in a private residence or business, or in a community to provide a safe shelter during wind events (especially tornadoes). These should be built in accordance to the guidelines specified in FEMA P-320, *Taking Shelter from the Storm: Building a Safe Room for Your Home or Small Business;* and FEMA P-361, *Design and Construction Guidance for Community Safe Rooms* (FEMA, n.d.f). Research by the wind scientists and engineers at the National Wind Institute at Texas Tech University led to the development of specific, FEMA-endorsed criteria for

■ **FIGURE 9.12** The first story of an apartment building in San Francisco, California, leaning to one side after the 1989 Loma Prieta earthquake. *Courtesy of the U.S. Geological Survey.*

constructing safe rooms. Funding for constructing safe rooms are available through a number of federal programs, including Community Development Block Grant Funds by the Department of Housing and Urban Development (HUD), FHA Mortgage Insured Financing, FEMA Hazard Mitigation Grant Program (HMGP) Funds and Predisaster Mitigation (PDM) program funds. Local communities can apply for these grants to build community safe rooms. Residents can also apply through local authorities to build residential safe rooms. During a tornado in Moore, Oklahoma, on May 20, 2013 (which measured at an EF-5 level storm), it was reported that many families survived in the city's underground residential safe room (Figure 9.13).

Property Acquisition

Property acquisition, also known as a *buyout*, is the most permanent form of mitigating hazards. In this case, the government purchases a private property that is located in a hazard area and makes it public property by acquiring the title (FEMA, n.d.b). Since the property is removed from the private market, inappropriate development and potential threats to public are reduced forever.

Acquisition or buyout is very expensive, as it involves real estate transactions, including the appraisal, title search and, if necessary, lot survey.

■ **FIGURE 9.13** A woman opens the door of her family's safe room in Moore, Oklahoma. She and nine family members took refuge in the shelter during an EF-5 tornado on May 20, 2013, that killed 24 people and injured 377 others. *Courtesy of FEMA.*

The community also pays the closing costs. However, the property owner is responsible for any mortgages, liens, or other fees against their property. FEMA provides 75% funding to the community for purchasing property in flood hazard areas (FEMA, n.d.b). Participation in the buyout program is voluntary, so the government does not pay any relocation costs to the property owner.

The government can also acquire the full bundle of rights to a piece of land in a hazard area which is known as *fee simple acquisition.* When a single owner has all the rights associated with a parcel of land, the owner is said to hold the land in fee simple (Schwab et al., 2007). Fee simple acquisition is a relatively less expensive way to acquire undeveloped land and can act as a development management tool for guiding the location of development before a hazard event occurs.

Easement

Easement is an alternative to fee simple acquisition, where the government acquires lesser rights to a property (such as right of access), leaving the other rights to the owner (Schwab et al., 2007). Property owners commonly grant easements for the placement of utility poles, utility trenches, water lines, or sewer lines. In hazard-prone areas, the government can purchase an easement that prevents building on a particular parcel of land, thereby protecting the area from development. One big disadvantage of the easement method is that easements must be policed and the terms enforced, which can be as expensive as acquiring fee simple rights. Thus, governments usually prefer fee simple acquisition over easement, and it has been used less frequently in hazard mitigation.

Purchase and Transfer of Development Rights

Easement is also known as the **purchase of development rights (PDR)**, while **transfer of development rights (TDR)** programs treat development as a commodity separate from the land itself. The government awards development rights based on the value or acreage of land and establishes sending and receiving areas for these rights. The sending areas contain the land that the government would like to protect, and landowners have limited rights to develop their land. However, in receiving areas, they can sell rights to developers. As a result, developers build on receiving areas in the community, which is considered as a safer alternative to sending areas that might be located in high hazard areas. Besides protecting sensitive areas, TDR programs are supposed to reduce the land value shifts of zoning by compensating those who cannot fully develop their land (FEMA, n.d.c).

Relocation

Relocation is a process whereby the housing, infrastructure, and other assets of an entire community or a segment of a community are rebuilt in a new location. Sometime a few residents of a community are relocated. Relocation of communities away from areas subject to repeated disaster is an important disaster mitigation option, as it reduces the chances of death and injury of the residents and government expenses of repeated restoration. In such areas, it is less costly for the government to help disaster victims move to other places than bear the expenses of repeated insurance claims as well as restoration. FEMA funds the relocation of facilities when they are subject to repetitive heavy damage and when relocation is cost effective (FEMA, n.d.d). When any community or part of a community is exposed to a hazard that can cause significant negative impact, and when other mitigation measures are inadequate in terms of safety, efficacy, and feasibility, the only option is physically moving the residents to and rebuilding the necessary infrastructure in a new location. Human settlement in hazardous areas such as in floodplains, earthquake-prone areas, landslide areas, and wildfire prone areas enhance residents' hazard vulnerability. Relocation is a useful strategy for adjusting human settlement patterns to reduce vulnerability to environmental hazards (Perry and Lindell, 1997).

NATURAL RESOURCE PROTECTION
Wetland Restoration and Preservation

Wetlands are valuable natural resources that provide numerous benefits to the people and the environment. They provide habitats for a large number of ecologically and economically important species, hold flood water, absorb wind and tidal forces, provide recreational spaces and so on. According to the Clean Water Act, wetlands are defined as "areas that are inundated or saturated by surface or ground water at a frequency and duration sufficient to support, and that under normal circumstances do support, a prevalence of vegetation typically adapted for life in saturated soil conditions. Wetlands generally include swamps, marshes, bogs, and similar areas" (EPA, n.d.).

Wetlands that are located at the edge of deep bodies of water function as a **buffer zone**. These areas can hold floodwaters that overflow from rivers, lakes, and other bodies of water. Vegetation within the wetlands reduces the speed of the floodwaters and slowly releases the flood water into the floodplain. As a result, wetlands contribute to reducing the amount of floodwater and soil erosion inland. Similarly, inland isolated wetlands that are surrounded by dry land can retain excess surface runoff as a result of increased paving of surfaces. These areas also retain the pollutants, nutrients, and sediments of the runoff from the higher dry land that surrounds them before the water reaches open water sources. Coastal wetlands can abate the impacts of tropical storms, cyclones, and large storm surges and can preserve lives and property. Wetlands at the margin of the water bodies such as rivers, lakes, and oceans protect the lands from erosion, as plants within the wetlands hold the soil and reduce the strength of waves or the speed of the water flow.

In the United States, less than half of the 221 million acres of wetlands that once existed in the late 1700s remain today, and 75% of the remaining wetlands are located on privately owned lands (FWS, n.d.). Federal agencies including the EPA and U.S. Fish and Wildlife Service (FWS), in partnership with state and local governments, have been restoring wetlands to abate the devastating effects of floods, storms, and erosion (Figure 9.14).

Erosion Control

Erosion is a natural process that affects all landforms. The term refers to wearing down of the land surface and transporting the eroded material through the actions of wind, fluvial processes, marine processes, and glacial processes (Figure 9.15). Human activities that break down the

■ **FIGURE 9.14** Wetlands before and after restoration. *Courtesy of the U.S. Fish and Wildlife Service.*

■ **FIGURE 9.15** Soil erosion involves the breakdown, detachment, transport, and redistribution of soil particles by forces of water, wind, or gravity. *Courtesy of the United States Department of Agriculture (USDA).*

land surface, such as farming, construction, logging, mining, or altering the landforms, can greatly accelerate natural erosion. Coastal erosion involves the breaking down and removal of material along a coastline by the forces of wind, waves, and longshore currents and typically causes a landward retreat of the coastline. It results in loss of land and increases the risks of coastal flooding, which can damage building, property, agricultural land, and ecology. Rates of coastal erosion can be affected by human activity, sea level rise, seasonal fluctuations, and climate change (Schwab et al., 2007). Extreme meteorological events such as hurricanes can drastically increase the amount of coastal erosion. During such events, high waves and storm surge act together to erode beaches in a short period of time.

Some structural measures such as groins, jetties, sediment trapping structures, seawalls and bulkheads, construction, and stabilization of sand dunes are used to protect shorelines and prevent coastal erosion. Most of these measures are expensive and subject to negative environmental impact, and some coastal states have passed legislation that prohibits the construction of such structures. For the protection of people and property along the coastal areas, some states have been using a number of regulations, such as regulatory setbacks, wetland regulation, and restriction on poststorm reconstruction.

PUBLIC EDUCATION AND AWARENESS
Community Outreach Projects

Community outreach and awareness projects can be undergone to educate citizens and potential homebuyers about the hazard risks in a community, possible mitigation strategies that can be taken, how to prepare for a disaster, and how to respond after a disaster occurs. Outreach projects might include any or all of the following:

- Newsletters
- Pamphlets
- Brochures
- Presentations
- Meetings
- Seminars
- Workshops
- Essay/poster competitions on hazard mitigation topics
- Educational and training programs

■ **FIGURE 9.16** A FEMA official polls residents of the Bordeaux community, Tennessee, to find out who has registered with FEMA during a community meeting at the Temple Church of Christ after severe storms and flooding that damaged or destroyed many homes and businesses across the state. *Courtesy of FEMA.*

Communities can send newsletters, pamphlets, and brochures regularly to all its members and potential newcomers to disseminate and highlight information about different hazard risks in the community. Presentations can be given on hazard mitigation in community meetings (Figure 9.16). Seminars and workshops on mitigation can be held, targeting the general public, homebuyers, church members, and public officials. Essay and poster competitions can be promoted in the schools to educate children in different age groups on hazard risks and mitigation topics. Educational and training programs can be arranged by governments and private companies on hazard mitigation topics to protect their employees and property against potential disaster.

Real Estate Disclosures

Many times, property owners are not aware of the past or potential future problems when they purchase land that might be located in a hazardous area. In the United States, federally regulated lending institutions are required to disclose to mortgage and other loan applicants whether a property is on a floodplain, as shown on the Flood Insurance Rate Map

(FIRM). However, this requirement has to be met only 10 days prior to closing; hence, an applicant might already have commited to purchase a property before learning about the flood hazard in the area (Wetmore, 2013). State and local laws can be strengthened to overcome this deficiency and provide property owners hazard information earlier in the purchasing process. For instance, the California Geological Survey has mapped areas of potential landslide, liquefaction, or fault rupture hazard in the state that are designated as "special study zones" by the California Alquist-Priolo Earthquake Fault Zone Act of 1972. According to this act, potential buyers of land in these special study zones must sign a form indicating that they are aware of potential hazards in this area and of the fact that additional inspections or work may be required to live on this property in the future (Cutter et al., 2012). However, the Multiple Listing Service (MLS) provided by Realtors currently does not give any information of potential hazards related to properties for sale. Laws can be enacted to require the real estate industry to incorporate hazard information into the MLS. Additionally, local emergency management agencies (EMAs) can provide such information to potential buyers through their websites.

EMERGENCY SERVICES
Warning Systems

Communities must have effective **warning systems** in place so that residents can get enough lead time to prepare and implement protection measures before a hazard event. This may feature monitoring local weather conditions, outdoor warning sirens, weather radio broadcasts (e.g., NOAA weather radio), mass telephone notification, Wireless Emergency Alerts (WEAs), e-mail alerts, notifications through social media platforms (e.g., Facebook and Twitter), weather channes/news on TV, public service announcements (PSAs), door-to-door contacts, or any combination.

In the United States, the National Weather Service (NWS) issues watches and warnings for flooding, thunderstorms, tornadoes, hurricanes, and winter storms. Watches are issued when conditions are favorable to produce these hazards and warnings are given when the hazards are imminent to occur or have been observed. Local EMAs, as well as television and radio channels (including NOAA weather radio), relay these watches and warnings to the general public. In Bangladesh, cyclone warnings are also disseminated door to door in coastal areas using megaphones, hand sirens, and public address systems by volunteers who work in the Cyclone Preparedness Programme (CPP), which is a joint initiative by the government and the Red Cross (Rashid, 1997).

Emergency Response Services

Emergency response services include first responders such firefighters, police, emergency medical services (EMS), and other entities that protect people at the scene of a hazard event. They take appropriate action to contain the hazard, protect property, conduct search-and-rescue operations, provide mass care, and ensure public safety, including cleanup and special precautions for each type of hazard (e.g., draining standing water after a flood and cautioning residents about aftershock or successive tsunami waves) (FEMA, n.d.c).

Protection and Resilience of Critical Infrastructure

Critical infrastructure are "the assets, systems, and networks, whether physical or virtual, so vital to the United States that their incapacitation or destruction would have a debilitating effect on security, national economic security, national public health or safety, or any combination thereof" (DHS, n.d.). It is important to protect critical infrastructure in our communities from hazard events that provide essential needs and help our economy. This involves facilities related to agriculture/food, energy/power, public health, banking/finance, drinking water/treatment, IT/telecommunications, transportation systems, postal and shipping, and emergency services. Also, it includes government facilities, national monuments and icons, defense industrial base, chemical, commercial facilities, dams, nuclear reactors, materials, and waste (DHS, 2013). Critical infrastructure, such as hospitals and other public health facilities, transportation systems, IT/telecommunications, power system, food supply, and drinking water, are vital during emergency periods and disaster situations. This critical infrastructure must be secured and made resilient so that damages can be reduced and their functions can be immediately restored after a hazard event.

State, local, and tribal governments are responsible for implementing the homeland security mission, protecting public safety and welfare, and ensuring the provision of essential services to communities and industries within their jurisdictions. They also play a very important and direct role in enabling the protection of the Nation's CI/KR, including CI/KR under their control, as well as CI/KR owned and operated by other NIPP security partners within their jurisdictions.

Homeland Security Presidential Directive 7 (HSPD-7) issued the National Infrastructure Protection Plan (NIPP) to unify Critical Infrastructure and Key Resource (CIKR) protection and resilience efforts across the country. The document was updated in February 2013 by Presidential Policy Directive 21 (PPD-21), Critical Infrastructure Security and Resilience. According to the National Flood Insurance Program (NFIP), the DHS's authorized duties include "reducing the Nation's vulnerability to terrorist attacks, major disasters, and other emergencies, and ... the responsibility for evaluating vulnerabilities and ensuring that steps are implemented to protect the high-risk elements of America's CI/KR." It also explains the role of state, local, and tribal governments for protecting critical infrastructure as follows.

ADVANTAGES AND DISADVANTAGES OF STRUCTURAL AND NONSTRUCTURAL MITIGATION MEASURES

Based on the discussion of various structural and nonstructural mitigation measures so far in this chapter, they clearly protect us from natural hazards and, most important, save lives. They provide a range of economic, environmental, and social benefits as well. Structural mitigation measures such as dams and reservoirs can be used for irrigation, water storage, navigation, electricity generation, and even for recreational purposes, such as boating, camping, skiing, and picnic areas. A total of 10% of American cropland is irrigated using water stored behind dams. Hydroelectricity produced by dams is considered clean because it does not contribute to global warming. The United States produces more than 103,800 megawatts of renewable electricity using hydroelectric dams and meets 8—12% of its power needs in that way (FEMA, 2013).

However, the benefits of structural mitigation are always offset by some major disadvantages. First, the most common criticism about structural mitigation projects is that they are very expensive, and most of them are technically difficult to build. It is not easy for local communities to afford large-scale structural mitigation projects. For instance, the USACE rebuilt the New Orleans levees after Hurricane Katrina to the tune of about $14 billion (Toreh, 2012). Second, structural mitigation measures reduce nature's ability to mitigate the effects of a storm or flood. For instance, levees can increase flooding upstream or downstream of them by changing the natural flow and volume of a river (Schwab et al., 2007). While levees are good for individual communities in small-scale to mid-size events, they are bad for an overall river system's capacity to deal with flood flows. Third, structural mitigation measures can afford a false sense of security and encourage them to live in hazard-prone areas. Failure of structural projects is very common, and it can make a disaster worse. Prior to the Great Mississippi Flood of 1927, the USACE were committed to the "levees only" policy to control the Mississippi River. The 1927 Mississippi River flood demonstrated several major problems associated with a one-sided approach to flood control. Much of the levee system along the lower Mississippi was breached or overtopped, and the flood torrent fanned out over the flat delta (Figure 9.17). Similarly, the levee and floodwall failures in New Orleans during Hurricane Katrina made the disaster worse, as discussed earlier in this chapter. The potential for dam failure is also a serious hazard in many communities.

■ **FIGURE 9.17** Flood victims camp on a levee at Arkansas City, Arkansas, during the Great Mississippi Flood of 1927. Levee overtopping and failure was so widespread during this event that dry land was hardly found except atop the levees. *Courtesy of the USACE.*

In contrast, nonstructural mitigation measures are always less costly and more affordable than structural measures. The benefits of these measures can be seen in the evolution of floodplain management in the United States. In the past, government agencies used to build massive flood control structures, such as dams, levees, and floodwalls to control the great rivers. After the Great Flood of 1927, the 1936 Flood Control Act alone authorized the construction of some 250 projects aimed at both flood control and relief work. But flood-related expenses were still going up, and people began to question the effectiveness of just a structural approach. In response, federal, state, and local agencies began to develop policies and programs with a nonstructural emphasis, which were not intended not to control or redirect the path of floodwaters (FEMA, n.d.e). Since the 1960s, floodplain management has evolved from heavy reliance on structural measures to one using a combination of many tools, including nonstructural flood protection measures. The creation of the NFIP in 1968 was a landmark step that came out of this process. In addition, nonstructural mitigation measures such as education and outreach projects can have significant impact. For instance, in the case of pandemic planning, educating public about engaging in healthy behaviors can stop a potential outbreak of disease.

CRITICAL THINKING

Suppose that you are on a committee working on adopting a flood control measure in your community. Given the advantages and disadvantages of structural and nonstructural mitigation measures, which mitigation strategy would you recommend?

INCORPORATING MITIGATION STRATEGIES INTO HAZARD MITIGATION PLANS

According to the Disaster Mitigation Act of 2000 (DMA 2000), an HMP "shall include a mitigation strategy that provides the jurisdiction's blueprint for reducing the potential losses identified in the risk assessment." The direction of the mitigation strategy is determined by the results of the risk assessment and the community's current and potential capabilities. It is during this phase that the mitigation goals and objectives identify possible mitigation actions to reduce high-priority risks and develop a prioritized strategy (FEMA, 2006).

Formulating Goals and Objectives

Goals are broad, forward-looking statements that should articulate a community's desire to protect people and structures and the overall improvements that the community wants to achieve. For instance, floods could be identified as a problem for the community based on its risk assessment. So one of the proposed goal statements addressing the flood issue might be "to minimize losses to existing and future structures in hazard areas from flooding."

Objectives are more specific and narrower in scope than goals (FEMA, 2003). *Objectives* expand on goals and provide a road map how to accomplish the goals. For example, to achieve the goal for minimizing losses from flooding, the following objectives might be formulated:

Objective 1.1: Implement activities that pertain to repetitive loss properties due to flooding or other hazards.
Objective 1.2: To minimize damage to public facilities and utilities by continuing to implement land use and building regulations.
Objective 1.3: To continue participation in the NFIP, thus allowing residents and businesses the opportunity to buy flood insurance.

It is important to get public input while developing goals and objectives because the more residents participate in a process, the more likely they are to support any resulting plan. In order to achieve the mitigation goals and objectives, the planning team must be committed to working with all governmental agencies, the community, and other jurisdictions, as well as developing and completing mitigation projects locally.

Identify and Analyze Mitigation Actions

HMPs must identify and analyze a range of mitigation actions that address the goals and objectives of the community. Emphasis should be placed on new and existing buildings and infrastructure. The analysis needs to address multiple mitigation actions, as already discussed in this chapter, for each profiled hazard. In addition to listing multiple actions for each hazard, the HMP should describe how the community decided upon a particular mitigation action, including the parties involved in the analysis and selection (FEMA, 2003). One popular method used to analyze the mitigation actions systematically for consideration is to evaluate the **Social, Technical, Administrative, Political, Legal, Economic, and Environmental (STAPLEE)** opportunities and constraints associated with each mitigation action. The STAPLEE method is discussed in detail in Chapter 10.

Prioritize Mitigation Actions

Once the planning team has a list of acceptable mitigation actions based on STAPLEE or other evaluation criteria, they need to prioritize implementation actions. The community may wish to complete a benefit-cost analysis (BCA) to prioritize mitigation actions. However, a BCA is required only when a community applies for a grant to implement the action. The mitigation plans require only a review of benefits and costs.

A review of benefits and costs is a broad and comprehensive analysis comparing the monetary and nonmonetary benefits and costs of each action. Usually, it considers the number of people that will be affected by an action, the size of the area in question, and which critical facilities will be affected. It also determines if costs are reasonable compared with the size of the problem and probable benefits. The various methods for prioritizing actions using review of benefits and costs include simple listing, relative rating, simple score, and weighted score (Figure 9.18), all of which are described next.

Simple Listing

Here is an example of how the simple listing method can be used to prioritize mitigation actions. A simple listing "evaluates an action by comparing

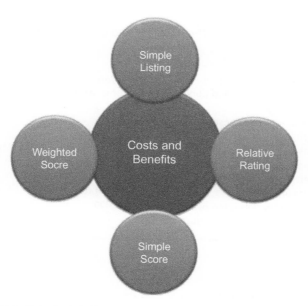

■ **FIGURE 9.18** Various methods for prioritizing mitigation actions using a review of benefits and costs. *Courtesy of FEMA.*

its advantages and disadvantages, and is best used when it isn't possible to quantitatively measure benefits and costs" (FEMA, 2006). The procedure includes three steps:

1. List identified actions.
2. Identify benefits and costs.
3. Assign priority.

The planning team assigns a priority to each action, expressed in different ways. The priority can be high, medium, or low, accompanied by an explanation of what each term means and how the priority was determined. Priorities also can be described as immediate, short term, and long term, accompanied by an explanation of what each category means (e.g., immediate being within a year, short term being within 1–5 years, long term being within 5 or more years). Table 9.1 depicts an example of prioritizing mitigation actions using the simple listing method.

Implementation

The next element of an HMP is to identify how the mitigation actions will be implemented. In this step, the planning team identifies the

Table 9.1 Sample of a Simple Listing Stating Possible Actions, Their Benefits and Costs, and Their Priority

Action	Benefits	Costs	Priority
Expand and reconfigure storm retention ponds on West Hill.	Avoid the loss of life and property. Save monies on private and public property damage. Save monies on road construction and repairs.	Need a year to implement. High construction costs.	High
Repair and/or maintain damaged levees along the Green and White rivers.	Save lives and property. Save monies for rescue and recovery of property.	High cost. Limited funding.	Medium
Develop and adopt changes to the city code to limit tree removal within certain sloped or identified landslide hazard areas.	Saves lives and property. Saves monies for debris removal. Saves monies for road reconstruction.	High cost of road construction.	Low

responsible parties, finding source, and the time frame to implement the selected actions. After the process is completed, the planning team will be ready to document the implementation strategy.

■ CONCLUSION

This chapter describes various structural and nonstructural mitigation measures that can be implemented by communities to protect against natural hazards. Mitigation measures are further categorized by FEMA into six broad categories. Structural projects include flood control devices such as dams, levees, dikes, and floodwalls; shoreline protection structures, including seawalls, bulkheads, and revetments; and sediment-trapping structures (e.g., groins and jetties). Mitigation measures related to prevention include government regulatory actions and processes that discourage land development in hazard-prone areas, reduce damages from hazards, or both. These include zoning, subdivision regulations, setback regulations, eminent domain, and building codes. Protection measures such as structural retrofits, acquisition, easement, and relocation can help property better withstand hazards or be removed from hazard areas. Actions such as wetland restoration and erosion control help communities preserve or restore the functions of natural systems, as well as minimizing disaster damage. Public education and awareness programs such as community outreach projects and real estate disclosures can inform citizens, elected officials, and property owners about potential hazard risks and how to properly protect themselves and their property. Emergency services such as warning systems and emergency response services help protect people and property during and immediately after a disaster or hazard event. Also, it is important to protect critical infrastructure that is essential for emergency services and the nation's economy, security, and public health or safety. The chapter also discusses the advantages and disadvantages of implementing structural and nonstructural mitigation measures. Although government agencies used to undertake massive structural projects, nonstructural mitigation measures have been emphasized since the 1960s. The chapter concludes by describing the process of incorporating mitigation strategies into an HMP, which includes formulating goals and objectives, identifying and analyzing mitigation actions, and prioritizing mitigation actions.

DISCUSSION QUESTIONS

1. Define structural and nonstructural mitigation. What are the six broad categories of mitigation strategies identified by FEMA? Provide two examples from each category.
2. Discuss the importance of dams and reservoirs. When is dam failure a significant threat?
3. Discuss the following shoreline protection structures:
   a. Seawall
   b. bulkheads
   c. revetments
4. Discuss the role of groins and jetties in sediment trapping.
5. What is the purpose of zoning? How can zoning regulations be used in hazard mitigation? What is an overlay zone?
6. What is eminent domain? How it can be misused?
7. Discuss the purpose of building codes. What is the ICC model building code?
8. What is retrofitting? Discuss the following types of retrofitting:
   a. floodproofing
   b. windproofing
   c. seismic retrofitting
9. Discuss the role of property acquisition (buyout) in hazard mitigation. What is the fee simple acquisition?
10. What is easement? What is the purpose of the TDR programs?

11. Define wetlands. What is the purpose of buffer zones? How does wetland restoration help mitigate disasters?
12. Discuss the role of community outreach projects in nonstructural mitigation.
13. Should real estate disclosure be mandatory?
14. Discuss the importance of warning systems and emergency response services in reducing damage from hazard events.
15. Define critical infrastructure. Why should critical structures be protected and resilient?
16. Discuss the advantages and disadvantages of structural and nonstructural mitigation.
17. Discuss the STAPLEE method for evaluating mitigation strategies. How would you evaluate a mitigation action using the STAPLEE method?
18. What is the purpose of a review of benefits and costs? Using the simple listing method, how would you prioritize the mitigation actions considered for an HMP?

WEBSITES

FEMA Dam Safety Publications and Resources
https://www.fema.gov/dam-safety-publications-resources
FEMA Levee Resources Library
https://www.fema.gov/fema-levee-resources-library
FEMA Building Code Resources
https://www.fema.gov/building-code-resources
FEMA P-55, Coastal Construction Manual: Principles and Practices of Planning, Siting, Designing, Constructing, and Maintaining Residential Buildings in Coastal Areas (4th ed.)
https://www.fema.gov/media-library/assets/documents/3293
FEMA P-312, Homeowner's Guide to Retrofitting, 3rd Ed. (2014)
https://www.fema.gov/media-library/assets/documents/480
DHS Critical Infrastructure Security
http://www.dhs.gov/topic/critical-infrastructure-security
Homeowners: Frequently Asked Questions
https://www.fema.gov/frequently-asked-questions/homeowners-frequently-asked-questions
Floodproofing: NFIP Policy Index
https://www.fema.gov/national-flood-insurance-program-2/flood-proofing
History of the Federal Use of the Eminent Domain
http://www.justice.gov/enrd/History_of_the_Federal_Use_of_Eminent_Domain.html
Lucas v. South Carolina Coastal Council
http://web.law.duke.edu/voices/lucas
Intergovernmental Panel on Climate Change (IPCC) Climate Change 2014: Mitigation of Climate Change
http://www.ipcc.ch/report/ar5/wg3/

REFERENCES

American Society of Civil Engineers (ASCE). (2007). The New Orleans hurricane protection system: What went wrong and why. June 4, 2007. pp. 33–46. ASCE: E-book. Available from http://dx.doi.org/10.1061/9780784408933. Accessed January 14, 2015.

British Dam Society. (n.d.). Caring for dams, people, and the environment. Retrieved from <http://www.britishdams.org/BDS_Leaflet_2012.pdf>. Accessed January 11, 2015.

Clarke, J. R. (1994). *Integrated management of coastal zones*. USA: FAO Corporate Document Repository. FAO Fisheries Technical Paper 327. Retrieved from <http://www.fao.org/docrep/003/t0708e/t0708e00.htm>. Accessed January 11, 2015.

Cutter, S. L., Ahearn, J. A., Amadei, B., Crawford, P., Galloway, G. E., Jr., et al. (2012). *Disaster Resilience: A National Imperative*. Washington, DC: National Academies Press. Retrieved from <http://www.nap.edu/catalog/13457/disaster-resilience-a-national-imperative>. Accessed January 11, 2015.

FAO Fisheries Technical Paper 327. Retrieved from <http://www.fao.org/docrep/003/t0708e/t0708e00.htm>. Accessed January 11, 2015.

Gale Group. (2008). Eminent domain. In *West's Encyclopedia of American Law*, 2008. Retrieved from <http://legal-dictionary.thefreedictionary.com/eminent+domain>. Accessed January 11, 2015.

Institute of Business and Home Safety (IBHS). (2012). Rating the states. Retrieved from <http://www.disastersafety.org/wp-content/uploads/ibhs-rating-the-states.pdf>. Accessed January 12, 2015.

Institute of Business and Home Safety (IBHS). (n.d.a). Building code resources. Retrieved from <http://www.disastersafety.org/wp-content/uploads/IBHS_Building_Code_Background.pdf>. Accessed January 12, 2015.

Institute of Business and Home Safety (IBHS). (n.d.b). Importance of strong building codes in earthquake-prone states. Retrieved from <https://www.disastersafety.org/building_codes/the-importance-of-strong-building-codes-in-earthquake-prone-states/>. Accessed January 11, 2015.

Kanner, G. (1996). Not with a bang, but a giggle: The settlement of the Lucas case. In David L. Callies (Ed.), Takings: Land-Development Conditions and Regulatory Takings after Dolan and Lucas, Chicago, IL: Section of State and Local Government Law, American Bar Association, (pp. 308–311).

Municipal Research and Services Center (MRSC). (n.d.). Regulatory taking. Retrieved from <http://mrsc.org/Home/Explore-Topics/Legal/Planning/Regulatory-Takings.aspx>. Accessed January 13, 2015.

National Oceanic and Atmospheric Administration (NOAA). (2000). National Weather Service commemorates 1900 Galveston hurricane. Retrieved from <http://www.nhc.noaa.gov/NOAApr10.htm>. Accessed January 13, 2015.

Perry, R. W., & Lindell, M. K. (1997). Principles for managing community relocation as a hazard mitigation measure. *Journal of Contingencies and Crisis Management, 5*, 49–59.

Rashid, A. K. M. (1997). Cyclone Preparedness Programme in Bangladesh. Retrieved from <http://www.adpc.net/pdr-sea/case/cyclone.pdf>. Accessed January 12, 2015.

Schwab, A. J., Eschelbach, K., & Brower, D. J. (2007). *Hazard mitigation and preparedness*. Hoboken, NJ: John Wiley and Sons.

Toreh, E. (2012). New Orleans' $14 billion levee system holds for now. Retrieved from <http://www.marketplace.org/topics/economy/new-orleans-14-billion-levee-system-holds-now>. Accessed January 12, 2015.

U.S. Army Corps of Engineers (USACE). (n.d.). Revetment types. Retrieved from <http://www.mvn.usace.army.mil/Missions/Engineering/ChannelImprovementandStabilization Program/RevetmentTypes.aspx>. Accessed January 12, 2015.

U.S. Department of Homeland Security. (2013). National Infrastructure Protection Plan (NIPP) 2013: Partnering for critical infrastructure security and resilience. Retrieved from <http://www.dhs.gov/sites/default/files/publications/National-Infrastructure-Protection-Plan-2013-508.pdf>. Accessed January 12, 2015.

U.S. Department of Homeland Security. (n.d.). Critical infrastructure. Retrieved from <http://www.dhs.gov/critical-infrastructure>. Accessed January 12, 2015.

U.S. Environmental Protection Agency (EPA). (n.d.). Water: Wetlands. Retrieved from <http://water.epa.gov/lawsregs/guidance/wetlands/definitions.cfm>. Accessed January 12, 2015.

U.S. Federal Emergency Management Agency (FEMA). (2003). Mitigation planning how-to guide #3. Developing the mitigation plan: Identifying mitigation actions and implementation strategies. FEMA 386-3.

U.S. Federal Emergency Management Agency (FEMA). (2006). Introduction to hazard mitigation. IS-393.A.

U.S. Federal Emergency Management Agency (FEMA). (2013). Living with dams: Know your risks. FEMA P-956. Retrieved from <http://www.fema.gov/media-library-data/20130726-1845-25045-7939/fema_p_956_living_with_dams.pdf>. Accessed January 13, 2015.

U.S. Federal Emergency Management Agency (FEMA). (n.d.a). Building Codes. Retrieved from <https://www.fema.gov/earthquake/building-codes>. Accessed January 13, 2015.

U.S. Federal Emergency Management Agency (FEMA). (n.d.b). Hazard mitigation assistance—Property acquisition (buyouts). Retrieved from <https://www.fema.gov/application-development-process/hazard-mitigation-assistance-property-acquisition-buyouts>. Accessed January 13, 2015.

U.S. Federal Emergency Management Agency (FEMA). (n.d.c). Hazard mitigation planning: Tools and techniques.

U.S. Federal Emergency Management Agency (FEMA). (n.d.d). Permanent relocation. Retreived from <https://www.fema.gov/public-assistance-archived-policies/permanent-relocation>. Accessed January 13, 2015.

U.S. Federal Emergency Management Agency (FEMA). (n.d.e). NFIP and levees: An overview fact sheet. Retrieved from <https://www.fema.gov/media-library/assets/documents/9635>. Accessed January 12, 2015.

U.S. Federal Emergency Management Agency (FEMA). (n.d.f). Safe rooms. Retrieved from <https://www.fema.gov/safe-rooms>. Accessed January 12, 2015.

U.S. Fish and Wildlife Service. (n.d.). Wetland restorations. Retrieved from <http://www.fws.gov/northeast/nyfo/partners/wetland.htm>. Accessed January 12, 2015.

UN International Strategy for Disaster Reduction (UNISDR). (2009). UNISDR terminology on disaster risk reduction. Retrieved from <http://www.unisdr.org/we/inform/publications/7817>. Accessed January 12, 2015.

Wetmore, F. (2013). Tools for hazard mitigation. In A. Jerolleman, & J. J. Kiefer (Eds.), *Natural hazard mitigation* (pp. 291–331). Boca Raton, FL: CRC Press.

White House. (2006). Federal response to Hurricane Katrina: Lessons learned. Retrieved from <http://www.floods.org/PDF/Katrina_Lessons_Learned_0206.pdf>. Accessed January 14, 2015.

Mitigation Strategies for Manmade Hazards

OBJECTIVES

The study of this chapter will enable you to:

1. List and describe some possible structural mitigation strategies for manmade hazards.

2. List and describe some possible nonstructural mitigation strategies for manmade hazards.

3. Discuss how federal and state regulations might be used to mitigate some manmade hazards when it comes to transportation and storage of those materials.

4. Discuss mitigation strategies for acts of terrorism.

5. Discuss mitigation strategies for chemical, biological, radiological, nuclear, and explosives (CBRNE) events.

Essential Terminology: Agroterrorism, biosafety, biosecurity, bioterrorism, Emergency Planning and Community Right-to-Know Act (EPCRA), nonstructural, pathogen, Select Agents Program, Social, Technical, Administrative, Political, Legal, Environmental, and Economic (STAPLEE), structural, toxin

Disasters have a way of making us stronger in the broken places.
James Lee Witt, head of the Federal Emergency Management Agency (FEMA), 1993–2001

INTRODUCTION

This chapter will begin to describe strategies used in the mitigation of manmade hazards and threats. Much in the same way that the previous chapter dealt with natural hazards, technological hazard and threat mitigation strategies can be broadly divided into **structural** and **nonstructural** categories. However, one major difference with manmade hazards is that official hazard mitigation plans (HMPs) at the state and local level seldom address technological hazards or threats.

According to federal regulations on hazard mitigation planning, state and local plans are not required to address manmade hazards [CFR 201.4(c)(2)(i), 201.6(c)(2)(i)]. Indeed, the federal government views the mitigation of many of these hazards that occur accidentally as the responsibility of the private sector, and when it comes to intentional acts, they fall under the purview of the U.S. Department of Homeland Security (DHS) and its programs and directorates.

> The ability to advance structural mitigation projects beyond those that address natural hazards is limited for two reasons: (1) the Robert T. Stafford Disaster Relief and Emergency Assistance Act (Stafford Act) does not require or incentivize state, tribal, and local jurisdictions to prepare and implement HMPs that address technological or manmade hazards, although it does require mitigation plans for natural hazards as a condition of receiving federal mitigation assistance; and (2) the Mitigation Directorate of the Federal Emergency Management Agency (FEMA) has only one program, the National Dam Safety Program, that addresses a technological hazard proactively, and none that is solely dedicated to addressing manmade hazards proactively (FEMA, 2003a).

However, an informal review of some states' HMPs shows that they address technological hazards and threats. These include dam or levee failures, hazardous material spills, acts of terrorism, loss of utilities, transportation incidents, and civil disorder.

From what we've read in this textbook about technological hazards, we know that for the most part, they are a by-product of man's reliance on technology. The Industrial Revolution of the late nineteenth century gave rise to great prosperity and the development of large, relatively unplanned urban centers with dense populations. As a result, increasing numbers of people moved from rural areas to urban areas. In fact, more than 50% of all people in the world now live in urban areas, whereas just

60 years ago, only about 30% of all people did. This trend is likely to continue. It is expected that by the year 2050, more than 70% of the world's population will be living in urban centers (UNFPA, 2014).

The Stafford Act and the National Flood Insurance Act of 1968 specifically require mitigation planning for natural hazards, but not for manmade hazards. However, FEMA supports jurisdictions that choose to consider both technological *and* manmade hazards in their respective mitigation plans. While it is true that a local mitigation plan (LMP) is not required to address manmade hazards in order to be approved, the *Local Multihazard Mitigation Planning Guidance* can be helpful in developing and evaluating plans that include these hazards as part of a comprehensive hazard mitigation strategy. For more information on integrating technological and manmade hazards in mitigation plans, see *Integrating Manmade Hazards into Mitigation Planning* (FEMA 386-7), available at http://www.fema.gov/plan/mitplanning/howto7.shtm (FEMA, 2003b).

When one stops to consider the trends in urbanization, it's easy to see that the challenge for emergency managers is daunting: namely, more and more people are densely configured in and around a variety of serious hazards. Our roads, bridges, and rail lines are all in need of costly maintenance and upgrades. These networks are being used for the transport of hazardous materials and they infiltrate our urban centers.

FEMA MITIGATION FUNDS FOR NATURAL HAZARDS ONLY?

Since the al-Qaeda attacks that occurred in the United States on September 11, 2001, emergency management professionals have challenged the DHS on FEMA's ruling that Predisaster Mitigation (PDM) authorized under Section 203 (b) of the Stafford Act only funds mitigation activities related to natural hazards. The DHS Office of the Inspector General (2009) published a report concluding, "The focus of FEMA guidance for PDM is on addressing the risk from natural hazards that is the primary purpose of the program; however, it is not currently feasible to provide meaningful guidance on cost effectiveness for man-made and technological mitigation projects." This finding implicitly put this issue to rest, at least for the time being.

The Model City

Satellite imagery of any large metropolitan area shows residential areas interspersed with industrial areas. To illustrate this, Figure 10.1 presents an image of Anniston, Alabama. Anniston got its start around the time of

■ **FIGURE 10.1** Satellite image and aerial view of Anniston, Alabama, a typical medium-sized city in the southern United States.

the Civil War. Known for iron and cement production, it had long been a growing and flourishing southern city. The city also was home to Fort McClellan, an Army base that was used originally as a training and deployment area for soldiers going to war. Later, the base became the site of the U.S. Army Military Police Academy and the U.S. Army Chemical School. Adjacent to the base is the Anniston Army Depot, where the army stored chemical weapons and refurbished armored vehicles. All chemical munitions (nerve and blister agents) were destroyed by incineration over an 8-year period (2003–2011) under the army's demilitarization program.

Within this sprawling city of approximately 23,000 people are sources of nearly every known technological hazard: large hospital complexes, industrial parks, chemical storage facilities, an interstate highway, railroad lines with a railhead, an active army depot, a shuttered military base, and even a toxic waste Superfund site (EPA, 2014).

In 2002, an investigation by the television show *60 Minutes* revealed that Anniston was one of the most toxic cities in the United States at that time. The primary source for this toxic contamination came from the Monsanto chemical factory, which was closed in 1971. The description of the site by the Environmental Protection Agency (EPA) appears in the text box to the right.

Therefore, not only does this city have just about every technological hazard known to humanity, it also has a history of long-term accidental releases of toxic substances. Despite all its problems, Anniston is referred to as "the Model City" because due to its careful planning in the late 19th century.

STRUCTURAL MITIGATION STRATEGIES FOR MANMADE HAZARDS

Structural mitigation strategies are one broad category of measures that can be taken to mitigate manmade hazards. As with the natural hazards discussed in Chapter 9, these measures are very costly and must be practical to implement. Furthermore, community emergency managers and their private-sector counterparts need to view these measures holistically and ensure that they are based on risk assessment outcomes and benefit from the support of all stakeholders.

Technological hazards are often concentrated and held in high volumes to facilitate trade, commerce, distribution, and transport. Therein lies the problem: their potential for doing great harm is increased by the fact that they exist and move through and around population centers. Conceptually, we might apply the principle of **time, distance, and shielding (TDS)** from radiological hazards whenever we consider options for broadly mitigating technological hazards. In essence, the less time a human or animal is exposed to an agent, the less harm it can do. The more distance between the agents and people, the less harm it can do. Finally, if shielding or protection can be placed between the offending substance and potential victims, that may lessen or prevent injury altogether.

Limiting the time of exposure is a nonstructural measure that will be addressed in the next section. Increasing distances from hazardous substances may be viewed as a structural measure. Chemical surety, bio-safety, and radiation protection officers will often look for ways to

The Anniston PCB site consists of residential, commercial, and public properties located in and around Anniston, Calhoun County, Alabama, that contain or may contain hazardous substances; including polychlorinated biphenyl (PCB) impacted media. The site is not listed on the National Priorities List (NPL) but is considered to be an NPL-caliber site and is being addressed through the Superfund Alternative Approach. Solutia Inc.'s Anniston plant encompasses approximately 70 acres of land and is located about 1 mile west of downtown Anniston, Alabama. The plant is bounded to the north by the Norfolk Southern and Erie railroads, to the east by Clydesdale Avenue, to the west by First Avenue, and to the south by Highway 202. Polychlorinated biphenyls (PCBs) were produced at the plant from 1929 until 1971.

■ **FIGURE 10.2** Hazmat technicians in Level B Personal Protective Equipment work with an overpack drum of hazardous waste. *Image courtesy of OSHA.*

address the problem of hazardous substance exposures to potential victims and workers (Figure 10.2). These measures are mandated by the Occupational Safety and Health Administration (OSHA) and other federal agencies. Shielding may be accomplished in many ways, including the following:

- Emplacement of barriers and diking
- Hardening of storage and containment areas
- Conducting periodic visual inspections of stored materials to look for leaks
- Using steel or heavy plastic drums
- Overpacking materials to ensure containment
- Using backflow prevention to protect water distribution systems
- Using security fencing, guard force, and instrumentation to impede intruders

A Systems Thinking Approach

It is well known that a major strategy for disaster mitigation stemmed from structural modifications of the human environment. This is best understood if we put the terms *exposure, vulnerability*, and *risk* into context. For emergency managers, these terms are important since they allow for prioritizing and pursuing capability-building measures and improving disaster resiliency. In his seminal book *Disasters by Design*, Denis Mileti helps define these terms and consider systemic approaches to applying them and achieving resilient communities. He defines exposure as "the measure of people, property, or other interests that would be subject to a given risk." Mileti explains that vulnerability is "a degree or measure of the capacity to endure, resist, or recover from the impacts of a hazard in the long term, as well as the short term." He then defines risk as "the probability of an event or condition occurring, and refers to hazards as the product of risk, vulnerability, exposure, and the capacity of humans to respond to extreme events." However, he uses the term *hazard* to mean "the product of risk and vulnerability," essentially considering them extreme phenomena with the potential to cause disasters (Mileti, 1999).

Regardless of how one looks at these terms, the bottom line in emergency management is that we cannot think of each threat or hazard as existing in isolation. By adopting a systems thinking approach, as Mileti proposes, we can consider multiple and interrelated causal factors in the context of the adaptive systems that shape our various communities. Conversely, our traditional ways of looking at risks and hazards are often one-dimensional, meaning that we often focus on pursuing stability rather than the wide array of interrelated factors that we should take into account (Mileti, 1999).

To contextualize this with an example, look at the technological hazard posed by a hazardous material spill from a 90-ton railway car. A simple approach to addressing this dangerous situation might be to focus solely on improving evacuation plans and escape routes for citizens in harm's way. This denotes the acceptance of the incident, which may be helpful, but at the same time, it excludes the idea of addressing other variables. A systems approach might include considerations of passing of legislation to limit or reroute the transport of freight cars carrying bulk containers of specific hazardous materials (e.g., chlorine). In addition, we might install devices to warn approaching trains that they are entering a populated area, post strict speed limits and surveillance cameras to record infractions, or both. We could also get rid of some of the risk factors by working with railroad engineers to identify and remedy dangerous curves or slopes that might contribute to a derailment.

Mileti describes three major systems that contribute to losses and increasing vulnerabilities to hazards, proposing that the interaction among the following systems is what causes losses and significant impacts during and following disasters:

- Earth's physical systems (i.e., natural elements of the planet and atmosphere)
- Human systems (i.e., the characteristics of people and the groups they live in)
- Constructed systems (i.e., the built environment, infrastructure, and technology)

Disaster losses result from the interaction of and changes in the systems described previously. Organizational and community planners need to consider the interactions of these systems for the purposes of effective mitigation and capability building (Mileti, 1999). Through adopting the systemic approach, we are better positioned to achieve resiliency and reduce the impact of the hazards we face.

CRITICAL THINKING

Consider the technological hazards in your community, or even in your workplace. What has been done and what can be done to mitigate those hazards and reduce the risk? To enhance your understanding, you should discuss this topic with an emergency management professional in your community.

NONSTRUCTURAL MITIGATION STRATEGIES

Nonstructural mitigation strategies for technological hazards often come in the form of administrative measures, such as the passing of codes, laws, and regulations. In essence, politicians and community leaders can propose new laws, regulations, and rulings that enable the mitigation of some manmade hazards: that is, a *legislate to mitigate* strategy. Administrative measures may have a significant impact on implementing procedures, protocols, and training, which in turn serve to mitigate manmade hazard incidents. Indeed, many regulations already exist; however, most safety professionals would agree that only those regulations that are enforced can have any impact. Without enforcement, there is no assurance that companies and organizations are taking the necessary steps and that the steps are adequate. After significant incidents (e.g., accidents, spills, and acts of terrorism), further legislation is often proposed in response, but often in haste, which may or may not serve the community well.

Examples of the Legislate to Mitigate Strategy

At a local level and on a large scale, community leaders could move to alter **zoning** restrictions that preclude industrial and business properties from being interspersed with residential areas. This is in keeping with the principle of **distance**. On a much smaller scale, **building codes** for industrial and business properties could be enhanced to compel those organizations that may harbor technological hazards like volatile chemicals and combustible gases to harden their structures and incorporate barriers into their perimeters. This may better protect the areas outside these properties from any sort of incident or accident that could cause harm to the public. Measures such as these are in keeping with the principle of **shielding**.

The federal government has enacted stringent storage, holding, and transport requirements for all hazardous materials. When it comes to addressing technological hazards, a number of federal agencies have their own set of rules and regulations that limit activities involving hazardous materials. Here are only a few prime examples of such legislation:

- Regulations prohibiting and safeguarding hazardous materials transport
- Regulations prohibiting storage of hazmat given specific conditions
  - Disposition of Hazardous Waste under the Resource Conservation and Recovery Act (RCRA)—EPA (Hazardous Waste Operations and Emergency Response, 2007)
  - Federal Insecticide, Fungicide, and Rodenticide Act (FIFRA), governing the storage of pesticides
  - Department of the Army Regulation 50-6, governing the storage of chemical weapons
  - Select Agents Program of the Centers for Disease Control and Prevention (CDC), concerning the storage of biological agents
  - Nuclear Regulatory Commission (NRC) regulations governing the storage of radiological materials
  - Storage of nuclear weapons (DoD is proponent) and materials (refer to 40 CFR)
  - Bureau of Alcohol, Tobacco, and Firearms (ATF), governing the storage of explosive materials

The intended purposes of these regulations are to enhance worker protections, improve overall safety, and ultimately mitigate the risks to people, damage to property, and insult to the environment. Environmental laws enacted in 1986 (i.e., **Emergency Planning and Community Right to Know Act**; or **EPCRA**) and 1990 (i.e., the amendment to the Clean Air Act) gave the EPA oversight of risk management planning at facilities that have higher-than-threshold levels of specified chemicals. Regulatory

HAZARDOUS
MATERIALS
PROHIBITED*
(R14-3)

■ **FIGURE 10.3** Laws banning the transport of hazardous materials through specific high-risk areas may be enforced through the posting of signage and the policing of roads and rails for offenders. An example of such signage is shown here.

standards were enacted in the 1990s in response to several significant accidents in the United States and Bhopal, India (refer to Figure 10.3 for an example). These laws require chemical facility planning for accidental releases of hazardous materials.

MASSIVE CHEMICAL RELEASE IN BHOPAL

The accident at the Union Carbide plant in Bhopal, India, which caused a huge gas leak that killed and sickened hundreds of thousands of people, had a profound effect within the United States. It resulted in a substantial change in U.S. regulations, the formation of the AICHE Center for Chemical Process Safety, and the formation of the Safety and Chemical Engineering (SACHE) program. These initiatives resulted in an emphasis on safety and accountability in the practice and education of chemical engineers in the United States.

Willey, Crowl, and Lepkowski (2005)

A year after the terrorist attacks of September 11, 2001, the U.S. Congress enacted legislation that required DHS to analyze vulnerabilities and enhancements for "critical infrastructure." The Public Health Security and Bioterrorism Preparedness and Response Act of 2002 and the Maritime Transportation Security Act (MTSA, 2002, P.L. 107–295) require vulnerability assessments, security plans, and incident response plans for some chemical facilities that are located in or in close proximity to ports.

Mitigating Chemical Hazards

There have been a number of incidents where first responders were dispatched to the scene of an emergency situation and became the victims of a secondary explosion or chemical release. For instance, a fire at a Kansas City construction site containing explosives in 1988 resulted in the death of six firemen when explosives stored there were ignited by the fire and subsequently detonated (Adams & Miller, 2004). Had that fire department been armed with the information that the site harbored explosives, those deaths would likely have never occurred.

The EPCRA legislation discussed earlier in this chapter was derived from Title III of the **Superfund Amendments and Reauthorization Act (SARA)** of 1986; often referred to as *SARA Title III*. Due to tragic incidents like the 1988 Kansas City explosion, SARA Title III/EPCRA requires information sharing and promotes planning for chemical emergencies at the state and local levels. It is also intended to provide the public with information about the chemicals that are used, stored, and released in their community (Blanksvard, 2007).

EPCRA is organized into four major sections:

- Emergency Planning Notification, §302
- Emergency Release Notification, §304
- Hazardous Chemical Inventory Reporting, §§ 311 & 312
- Toxic Chemical Release Inventory, §313

Those four specific sections of EPCRA apply to a facility based on the type and amount of chemicals that a company produces, processes, uses, stores, or releases. Therefore, which facilities are required to issue reports under EPCRA? Facilities that hold hazardous chemicals above a certain threshold limit are required to submit specific information to the State Emergency Response Commission (SERC), Local Emergency Planning Committee (LEPC), and their local fire department (Protection of Environment, 2007; GSA, 2001). For most hazardous chemicals, the threshold amount is any amount greater than 10,000 pounds (4,500 kg). Chemicals designated by the EPA as extremely hazardous substances are required to be reported in quantities above 500 pounds (225 kg) or the individual chemical threshold planning quantity, whichever is lower (Blanksvard, 2007).

The EPA has two designated forms for chemical inventory submissions. Tier I is simple, while Tier II requires more detailed information (refer to Figure 10.4). Facilities can choose to submit the Tier II form instead of a Tier I form, but community officials can require that the Tier II form be submitted. In either case, facilities required to report under EPCRA must submit their information by March 1 of each calendar year (Blanksvard, 2007).

CRITICAL THINKING

Your sprawling community is interlaced with major thoroughfares and rail lines. You just finished a hazardous materials transport study, and the results are startling. Hundreds of tons of hazardous cargo are moving through your population centers each week. What nonstructural measures might you consider? What is the potential impact of these measures on trade, commerce, and local employment?

Tier Two
EMERGENCY
AND
HAZARDOUS
CHEMICAL
INVENTORY

*Specific
Information
by Chemical*

Facility Identification
Name Acme Chemical Manuf.
Street 8901 N. Flagler Drive
City West Palm Beach   County PALM BEACH   State TX   Zip 33416
NAICS Code 333924   Dun & Brad Number 606072130

FOR
OFFICIAL
USE
ONLY

ID#

Date Received

Owner/Operator Name   **Phone**
Name Acme Chemical Corporation   (561) 387-0134
Mail Address 1450 Main Street, PBG, FL 33418

Emergency Contact
Name Joe Winslow   Title Safety Manager
Phone (561) 365-1211   24 Hr. Phone (561) 222-1212
Name Mary McCarver   Title Asst. Safety Manage.
Phone (561) 123-0012   24 Hr. Phone (561) 222-1222

Important. Read all instructions before completing form   Reporting Period   From January 1 to December 31, 2007   ☐ Check if information below is identical to information submitted last year.

Chemical Description	Physical and Health Hazards (check all that apply)	Inventory	Container Type	Pressure	Temperature	Storage Codes and Locations (Non-Confidential) Storage Locations	Optional
CAS ___ Trade Secret ___ Chem. Name 1020 STRIPPER Check all that apply EHS Name: ☐ Pure ☒ Mix ☐ Solid ☒ Liquid ☐ Gas ☐ EHS	☐ Fire ☐ Sudden Release of pressure ☐ Reactivity ☐ Immediate (acute) ☐ Delayed (chronic)	0 4 Max Daily Amount (code) 0 4 Avg. Daily Amount (code) 2 0 No. of Days On-site (days)	C / B / A	2 / 1 / 1	4 / 4 / 4	Boiler House2 Boiler House2 Boiler House2	☐
CAS ___ Trade Secret ___ Chem. Name 1020 STRIPPER TYPE 2 Check all that apply EHS Name: ☐ Pure ☒ Mix ☐ Solid ☒ Liquid ☐ Gas ☐ EHS	☐ Fire ☐ Sudden Release of pressure ☐ Reactivity ☐ Immediate (acute) ☐ Delayed (chronic)	0 4 Max Daily Amount (code) 0 4 Avg. Daily Amount (code) 1 8 No. of Days On-site (days)	A	1	4	Boiler House2	☐
CAS ___ Trade Secret ___ Chem. Name 198 PAINT Check all that apply EHS Name: ☐ Pure ☒ Mix ☐ Solid ☒ Liquid ☐ Gas ☒ EHS ACETONE, PYRENE	☐ Fire ☐ Sudden Release of pressure ☐ Reactivity ☐ Immediate (acute) ☐ Delayed (chronic)	0 3 Max Daily Amount (code) 0 3 Avg. Daily Amount (code) 1 No. of Days On-site (days)					☐

Certification *(Read and sign after completing all sections)*
I certify under penalty of law that I have personally examined and am familiar with the information submitted in pages one through __2__ and that based on my inquiry of those individuals responsible for obtaining the information, I believe that the submitted information is true, accurate, and complete.

John P. Jones / President
Name and official title of owner/operator OR owner/operator's authorized representative   Signature   Date signed

Optional Attachments
☐ I have attached a site plan
☐ I have attached a list of site coordinate abbreviations
☐ I have attached a description of dikes and other safeguards measures

■ **FIGURE 10.4** A Tier II form required under EPCRA, SARA Title III. The intent of such a form is to keep first responders and the public safe in the event of an emergency or incident. In the example shown here, significant quantities of some volatile substances are being stored in a chemical facility. Should there be a fire in this building, the fire department would now have the information needed to make prudent decisions on how to approach the scene and protect the public. Without such knowledge, they could potentially enter a burning building that is about to explode.

In the post-9/11 environment, concerns grew over the prospect of large stockpiles of dangerous chemicals being used in an act of terrorism. Therefore, in 2003, Homeland Security Presidential Directive (HSPD) 7 transferred to DHS all of the EPA's authority for overseeing the security of chemical facilities, with the single exception of drinking water and water treatment plants. In addition, the HSPD 7 revised the nation's strategy for protecting critical infrastructure by designating DHS the lead agency for the chemical sector.

Chemical accidents do happen and will continue to occur. Accidental spills, releases, and leaks into the environment occur more frequently than most people realize. One database of reportable chemical incidents

■ **FIGURE 10.5** A photo of a hazardous waste site found in New Hampshire. EPA found containers with incompatible wastes of acids and bases stored together, bulging drums, compromised drums and totes, unsecured cardboard boxes, and bags of corrosives. The inspectors also found a similar stockpile of drums, totes, and boxes containing plating waste inside an abandoned room of the mill building directly above a dance studio for children. EPA determined the containers of hazardous substances posed an imminent and substantial danger and called for an immediate cleanup. *Courtesy of EPA.*

suggests that in 2007, an average of 19 events occur each day in the United States. That includes all mishaps, large and small. Therefore, good chemical incident preparedness and well-orchestrated responses play a role in mitigation. Having properly trained and well-equipped hazmat professionals and units are a necessity for all communities. They need to be able to respond quickly and efficiently to contain the substance and protect the public and the environment (refer to Figure 10.5 for an example of response to a hazardous materials incident). They do so in a variety of ways that aim to contain further leakage, absorb the spill, and even neutralize the hazardous materials on site. These professionals need good situational awareness to determine what the substance is, how it might spread, and how to contain it. Crisis management at times like these is what makes the difference in postincident mitigation.

Mitigating Biological Hazards

Biological hazards can be looked at in two main ways. Naturally occurring outbreaks of disease can be widespread on every continent (pandemic) or focused in a well-defined region or nation (epidemic). In some assessments, disease events such as these are considered to be natural hazards because they

Table 10.1 Category A Diseases and Their Causative Agents

Disease	Agent	Type	Primary Concern
Anthrax	*Bacillus anthracis*	Bacteria	Inhalation of spores
Smallpox	*Variola major*	Virus	Person-to-person spread
Plague	*Yersinia pestis*	Bacteria	Person-to-person spread of pneumonic form
Tularemia	*Francisella tularensis*	Bacteria	Highly infectious if inhaled
Viral Hemorrhagic Fever	Several groups of viruses — e.g., Filovirus, Ebola	Virus	Person-to-person spread through contact with bodily fluids
Botulism	Botulinum toxin	Toxin from bacteria	Most deadly toxin known to man

Information presented in this table indicates the type of agent and the primary concern for each (Ryan & Glarum, 2008).

are the very product of nature itself. Then there are those outbreaks that are caused by an accident (e.g., careless laboratory release or exposure) or made possible due to the intentional release of a pathogen or toxin (act of bioterrorism or biocrime). This type of modality is considered a manmade or technological hazard.

Pathogens (bacteria, viruses) and biological toxins of great public health concern have been characterized by the Department of Health and Human Services (HHS) as Category A, B, and C agents. **Category A** contains the agents that have greatest potential for harm (refer to Table 10.1). They have received this dubious distinction because they (i) cause high morbidity and mortality rates, (ii) may be easily dispersed or spread from human to human, (iii) require special public health preparedness needs, and (iv) may lead to panic or social disruption. As a result, HHS requires organizations that store or work with these dangerous pathogens or toxins to follow the rules, guidelines, and reporting requirements of the Select Agents Program (Title 42, Chapter 1, Subchapter F, Part 73). The program follows in the wake of the 2001 Amerithrax incident and the subsequent criminal investigations (discussed later in this chapter). It ensures that the government has visibility on the inventories of those serious pathogens and the activities of the organizations that hold them.

Laboratory workers and researchers that work with dangerous pathogens should report their holdings to local officials, much like with chemical inventories. However, there have been instances where making such inventories or holdings public information is a national security concern because terrorists may target that facility. Much the same point holds true for certain chemical holdings (e.g., nerve agents and other chemical warfare agents).

ADDRESSING CONCERNS FOR THE BIOLOGICAL THREAT

On June 12, 2002, President George W. Bush signed Public Law 107-188, the Public Health Security and Bioterrorism Preparedness and Response Act of 2002. This act specifies that the HHS secretary shall establish and maintain a list of biological agents and toxins that have the potential to pose a severe threat to public health and safety ("select agents") and requires that all facilities and individuals in possession of the select agents register with the department. The act created an analogous program at the U.S. Department of Agriculture (USDA), which is being directed through the Animal and Plant Health Inspection Service (APHIS).

HHS has maintained a list of select agents since April 1997 (see 42 CFR part 72, Appendix A), under the management of CDC. This rule covered the transfer of select agents, including the registration of facilities engaging in transfers and exemptions from such registration.

Rules, regulations, best practices, and special protocols are used in laboratories and diagnostic settings to protect the workers and the public. This is known as *biosafety*. Laboratories that handle dangerous pathogens utilize a ratings system for the level of protection they offer. **Biosafety levels 1–4**, with 4 being the most stringent, are briefly defined as follows:

- **BSL 1** These are common, everyday labs suitable for work with well-characterized agents not known to consistently cause disease in healthy adult humans, and presenting minimal potential hazard to laboratory personnel and the environment (CDC, 1997). Precautions against biohazard materials are minimal and usually involve exam gloves and some sort of facial protection (i.e., goggles).
- **BSL 2** These labs are similar to BSL 1, but they are suitable for work involving agents of moderate potential hazard to personnel and the environment. Lab personnel require training to properly handle the pathogens and must be supervised by scientists with advanced training. Access to the laboratory is limited when work is being conducted. Safety precautions are taken with contaminated sharp items. Also, lab procedures involving infectious aerosols or splashes must be carried out in biological safety cabinets.
- **BSL 3** This level is applicable to clinical, diagnostic, teaching, research, or production facilities where the agents cause serious or potentially lethal disease after inhalation. As with BSL 2, lab personnel require specific training and supervision. All procedures involving the manipulation of infectious materials are conducted within biological safety cabinets, specially designed hoods, or other

physical containment devices, or by personnel wearing appropriate personal protective clothing and equipment. The laboratory has special engineering and design features.

- **BSL 4** Dangerous and exotic agents that pose a high individual risk of aerosol-transmitted laboratory infections and agents that cause severe to fatal disease in humans for which vaccines or other treatments are not available fall into BSL 4. To work with such agents, like the Ebola virus, a BSL 4 laboratory must meet the most stringent criteria. For instance, the use of a positive pressure personnel suit, with a segregated air supply, is mandatory (refer to Figure 10.6). The entrance and exit of a BSL 4 lab will contain multiple showers, an ultraviolet light room, and other safety precautions designed to destroy all traces of the biohazard. Multiple airlocks are employed and are electronically secured to prevent both entrance and exit doors from opening at the same time. All air and water going to and coming from a BSL 4 laboratory will undergo decontamination procedures to eliminate the possibility of an accidental release. In the United States, there are only 15 laboratories rated BSL 4 and equipped to handle such pathogens.

Biosecurity refers to the policies and measures taken for protecting a nation's food supply and agricultural resources from both accidental contamination and deliberate attacks of bioterrorism (Ryan & Glarum, 2008). Biosecurity is big business, and rightfully so. Agriculture is a vital part of the nation's economy, and the systems that make it up as a whole are very vulnerable to plant and animal pathogens. When it comes to food security, we need to adopt a "field to fork" mentality—that is, watching over the entire process of food production, from production to consumption. Our food supply is vulnerable to biological threats (natural or intentional) while the plants or animals are in the field, during processing, packaging, transportation, and while the resulting food products are being sold in a store or market. Our food supply is vulnerable to agroterrorism; therefore, biosecurity efforts to reduce this threat are an ongoing challenge. It has three major components: isolation, traffic control, and sanitation (Ryan & Glarum, 2008).

Isolation refers to limiting access to property where food is grown or produced. It also includes keeping animals separated, not introducing new animals to controlled populations, and closely maintaining feed quality. Traffic control in and around a farm is another important aspect to reducing disease. Visitors should be limited, and foot and vehicle traffic should remain on designated routes. Fences and signs should be in place to keep unwanted persons out of the animal production areas (refer to Figure 10.7).

■ **FIGURE 10.6** Centers for Disease Control (CDC) microbiologists suit up before entering a BSL-4 laboratory. The scientist on the left is attaching a supportive air hose that will provide a supply of filtered, breathable air and maintain positive air pressure inside his airtight orange suit. *Courtesy of the CDC.*

Sanitation of areas where food is processed is critical to biosecurity and safety. All who handle produce must wash their hands, and those entering animal farms should be provided with outerwear to reduce the introduction of pathogens. Vehicles entering and leaving the farms should be

■ **FIGURE 10.7** Signs outside a poultry farm in California warn people outside the facility that biosecurity precautions are in effect to protect the animal population from the introduction of deadly pathogens like avian influenza (AI) virus. *Courtesy of the California Poultry Federation.*

disinfected so as not to transmit diseases into or out of the area. All of these precautions minimize the risk for natural diseases to enter the food chain.

Agroterrorism is a term that refers to the targeting and intentional contamination of food systems by terrorists. Biosecurity exists, but there are many gaps that can be exploited by terrorists. By attacking the nation's food supply, a terrorist could sicken or kill many people. In addition to the people directly affected by such an attack, the entire population could be fearful of retail food consumption. The additional security measures necessary to ease these concerns would cause a financial burden on the U.S. government, as well as individual producers of food products.

People who produce, package, and transport food should be aware of natural and intentional contamination and the procedures for reporting such incidents. The CDC maintains a surveillance system to track foodborne illnesses, but by the time illnesses are detected, many more people may have been exposed. The consequences of foodborne illnesses have severe consequences—thus the importance of biosecurity.

Biological incidents may constitute a public health emergency (Ryan & Glarum, 2008). Public health emergencies precipitate public health measures, such as medical screening, active and passive surveillance, quarantine, contact tracing, social distancing, and monitoring. Whenever we think back to a public health emergency and consider some of these measures used to respond to it, we can easily relate to the Amerithrax incident in 2001 and the Ebola outbreak of 2014. Both can help observers understand the role that public health professionals play in such emergencies.

The first of these events resulted from an intentional act where *Bacillus anthracis* (anthrax) spores were placed in envelopes and mailed to members of the media and Congress. Several cases of inhalation anthrax appeared, and some astute clinicians and diagnosticians quickly realized that they could not be the result of any natural source. That triggered a nationwide alert and investigation to make medical professionals and security experts vigilant for more occurrences. When all was said and done, five people died as a direct result of their exposure to the deadly spores. Public health measures taken during this outbreak included medical screening of exposed people, active surveillance, and monitoring. In addition, some very costly cleanup procedures needed to be carried out in the Hart Senate Building, the Brentwood mail sorting facility, and a few other locations that received secondary cross-contamination from the U.S. postal system. Subsequent to these attacks, the Post Office contracted with industry (Northrop Grumman, Falls Church, VA and Cepheid, Sunnyvale, CA) to develop, produce, and install a biohazard detection system to screen mail in bulk for anthrax spores.

The 2014 Ebola outbreak stemmed from a natural source in West Africa. Ebola virus disease (EVD) is a highly contagious, with person-to-person transmission occurring through contact with the bodily fluids of infected patients. The initial outbreak was not effectively contained, so it quickly spread to other villages, into urban centers, and across national borders. The international response was slow to mount a concerted effort to quell the spread of infection, and some cases spread from West Africa to Europe and North America. When EVD came to the United States with several returning first responders and a Liberian traveler, it resulted in a media feeding frenzy and some very irrational decisions from politicians and government officials. Quickly, the public became introduced to all public health measures necessary to stop the spread of this highly contagious, person-to-person threat. Medical screening was instituted in airport terminals; Health Alert Network messaging was sent to clinicians in the field; contact tracing was implemented for suspect and confirmed cases; and quarantine of contacts, self-monitoring or controlled monitoring of contacts, and isolation of suspect and confirmed patients was carried out.

Another way that we can mitigate biological threats is through medical countermeasures. These include such elements as specific drugs, treatment protocols, and vaccines. Diseases like EVD, which has no specific approved treatment or vaccine, are difficult to control. The only course of action for the clinical community is to provide supportive treatment for the symptoms. In essence, they should try to make the patients comfortable and keep them alive through rehydration and the administration of pain medications. On the other hand, anthrax is a disease that responds to several antibiotic drugs and has an approved vaccine. Both have been used prophylactically to handle the threat to Department of Defense (DoD) personnel and persons exposed in the Amerithrax incident (such as postal workers and congressional staffers).

Mitigating Radiological Hazards

As previously mentioned, radiological hazards are mitigated through the TDS principle (Figure 10.8). The type and rate of emission of the radiological material will dictate how much **time**, **distance**, and **shielding (TDS)** must be applied to achieve the acceptable level of protection. Radiological hazards are readily found in medical imaging and some research laboratories. Radioactive sources must be properly stored and accounted for. Any organization that stores or harbors radiological sources must have a radiation protection officer to monitor the sources and exposure of personnel to those sources. Nuclear power plants are heavily regulated and monitored by the NRC. For more information on this highly technical field, visit the NRC website (http://www.nrc.gov/).

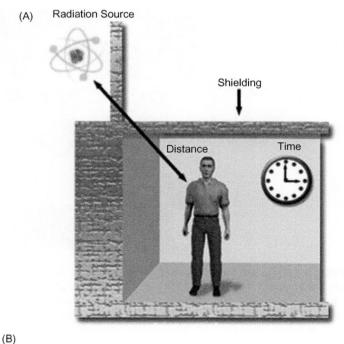

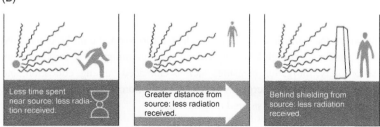

■ FIGURE 10.8 The principle of TDS to mitigate radiological hazards is explained with these simple illustrations. To lessen the effects of radiation spend less time near its sources, put more distance between you and the source, and put a barrier (e.g., lead) between you and the source. *Images courtesy of FEMA (A) and the NRC (B).*

Mitigating Acts of Terrorism

Mitigation planning mandates, such as the Disaster Mitigation Act of 2000 (DMA 2000), grew out of a focus on planning for natural hazards. The events of September 11, 2001, have forced communities to discuss terrorism as a serious possibility. Indeed, for some communities, it is not a low-probability event. In the spirit of an all-hazards approach to our profession, mitigation plans should also address hazards generated by human activities such as

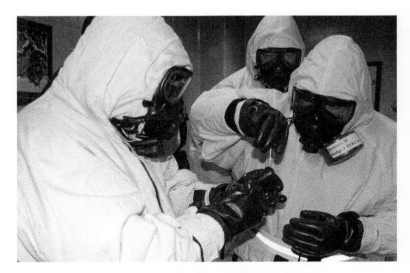

■ **FIGURE 10.9** Three first responders train at the Center for Domestic Preparedness (CDP) in Anniston, Alabama, to practice their response if the area was attacked by a weapon of mass destruction. Here, they work in a nerve agent—contaminated environment to gain expertise in detection procedures and confidence in their equipment. Protective and prevention measures to mitigate manmade hazards, such as acts of terrorism, are authorized and funded by authorities separate and distinct from measures to mitigate against natural hazards. *Image courtesy of FEMA CDP.*

terrorism and hazardous material accidents. Terrorism should be considered as a moderately high-level hazard in any community or organization. Accordingly, mitigation measures such as enhanced training, education, and equipment for local emergency services, law enforcement, and government personnel should be considered (Figure 10.9).

While the term *mitigation* refers generally to activities that reduce loss of life and property by reducing or eliminating the effects of disasters, in the terrorism context, it is often interpreted to include a wide variety of preparedness and response actions. For the purposes of this chapter, the traditional meaning will be assumed; that is, *mitigation* refers to specific actions that can be taken to reduce loss of life and property from manmade hazards by modifying the environment to reduce the risk and potential consequences of these hazards. Good security protocols and the presence of a guard force serve as important deterrents that may preclude or prevent an act of terrorism.

The community or organization should implement strategies that identify and reduce a community's vulnerability to terrorist attacks. They will need to monitor changes in conditions that may make them more vulnerable to these hazard events, such as changes in the flight paths to regional airports. Reducing the risk of terrorism requires partnerships with adjacent communities, local businesses, schools, and federal, state, and county transportation and security agencies.

Here are only a few examples of simple strategies that can be employed to mitigate the threat of terrorism to a community or organization. Police departments, security forces, and emergency management agency (EMA) directors would be primarily responsible for their implementation. Some other examples are shown in Figure 10.10:

- Conduct a discrete inventory of potential terrorist targets within and near the community/organization and implement appropriate security measures.
- Improve security measures at emergency response agencies and other sensitive facilities.
- Improve communication among regional responding agencies and enhance their ability to alert residents.
- Encourage regional response drills on an annual basis.
- Equip the highway department with protective gear.

INCORPORATING TECHNOLOGICAL HAZARDS INTO THE HMP

The overarching mission of the HMP is to identify cost-effective objectives and strategies to reduce the risk to life and property associated with potential high-risk natural hazards and manmade hazards and to improve community response and recovery if these hazards occur. It is important to highlight that the mission emphasizes cost-effective mitigation approaches in recognition of the fiscal limitations of the community. This will likely require that the community develop partnerships and establish priorities (see Figure 10.11), which should be included in their hazard mitigation mission. Partnerships can help overcome financial challenges but also expand possibilities for more effective implementation strategies and identify shared responsibilities in meeting hazard mitigation objectives. In support of this mission, the following hazard mitigation goals are key:

- Protect health and safety.
- Protect property and minimize property losses.

Sample Mitigation Goals and Objectives for Terrorism and Technological Hazard Mitigation

Goal 1: Reduce the community's risk of exposure to hazardous materials.

Objective 1: Install security measures at the anhydrous ammonia transfer and storage facility.

Objective 2: Increase the level of security of the facility using landscape design, lighting, and vehicle barriers.

Objective 3: Assess feasibility of hardening product storage and handling infrastructures.

Goal 2: Protect the community's water supply.

Objective 1: Install security measures at the city water treatment plant.

Objective 2: Secure all remote pump facilities.

Objective 3: Monitor for radiological, biological, and chemical contaminants.

Goal 3: Ensure that the city government has reliable communications systems.

Objective 1: Update the telecommunications capabilities of city government offices.

Objective 2: Create redundant/backup capability for landline telephone system.

Objective 3: Develop off-site backup of information technology systems.

Goal 4: Reduce risk to critical government facilities.

Objective 1: Increase vehicle standoff distance from the Emergency Operations Center.

Objective 2: Restrict parking and vehicle access to the underground parking garage at City Hall.

■ **FIGURE 10.10** Some sample goals and objectives for mitigating acts of terrorism. *From FEMA 386-7.*

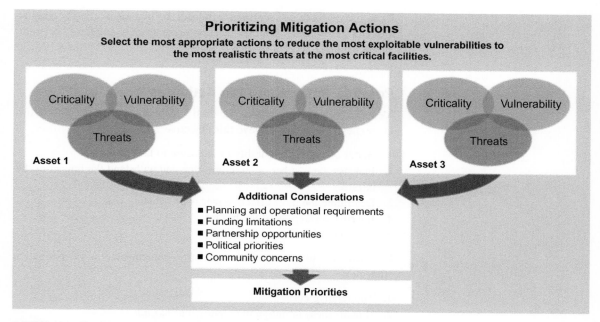

■ FIGURE 10.11 This diagram illustrates the prioritization process. Developing a list of the most important assets to protect will help you focus your loss estimation analysis. *Adapted from FEMA 386-7 (FEMA, 2003b).*

- Promote hazard mitigation strategies consistent with other natural resources, land use planning, quality of life, and other policies of the community/organization.
- Ensure that public funds are used in the most cost-effective and efficient manner.
- Encourage and facilitate partnerships among public agencies, local governments, citizens, nonprofit organizations, businesses, and other interests to advance the implementation of hazard mitigation strategies.

The most preferred goals are those that reduce the number of facilities and structures located within hazard-prone areas as much as possible. Where this cannot be realistically achieved, enhancing the ability of structures to withstand hazard events should be pursued. If efforts to avoid or minimize impacts cannot be practically implemented, communities should seek to improve its response to, recovery from, and preparedness for hazard events. Enhancing community awareness of hazards is also important for effective mitigation planning.

All-hazard mitigation work teams develop mitigation strategies. Hazards requiring similar responses should be grouped together, with the greatest focus placed on those identified as posing the highest risk to the community and its residents. The next section presents an example of how mitigation planning activities might transpire.

Possible Mitigation Plan Activities

Identify mitigation objectives for each hazard and determine the following strategies that will achieve this objective:

1. Better assess the possibility of exposure to hazard events.
2. Increase the number of structures that can withstand the impact of the hazard.
3. Determine the most effective means of reducing risk.
4. Improve awareness of the hazard.
5. Enhance response and recovery.

Consider the following factors for the implementation of mitigation strategies:

1. The relative cost
2. Effectiveness in mitigating a particular hazard
3. The amount of time necessary for implementation
4. Parties responsible for implementing the strategy in question
5. Sources of funding for the strategy

Evaluate the extent to which each strategy supports the goals of the HMP.

Social, Technical, Administrative, Political, Legal, Environmental, and Economic (STAPLEE) criteria (refer to Figure 10.12) are used to formulate a list of priorities for potential projects to be completed within the community (FEMA, 2003a). STAPLEE is a valuable resource for deciding which programs are cost effective and could legitimately be implemented. The STAPLEE criteria is as follows:

- *Social*: Is the project compatible with the present and future community values?
- *Technical*: Is the project feasible with available community/organization resources?
- *Administrative*: Does the community/organization have the capability to implement the project?
- *Political*: Is there public support both for implementing and maintaining the project?
- *Legal*: Does the community/organization have the authority to implement the project?

STAPLEE ACTION EVALUATION TABLE:																								
Alternative Actions	STAPLEE Criteria Considerations + Favorable − Less favorable N Not Applicable																								
	S (Social)		**T** (Technical)			**A** (Administrative)			**P** (Political)				**L** (Legal)		**E** (Economic)				**E** (Environmental)					
	Community Acceptance	Effect on Segment of Population	Technically Feasible	Long-Term Solution	Secondary Impacts	Staffing	Funding Allocation	Maintenance/ Operations	Political Support	Local Champion	Public Support	State Authority	Existing Local Authority	Potential Legal Challenge	Benefit of Action	Cost of Action	Contributes to Economic Goals	Outside Funding Required	Effect of Land/Water	Effect on Endangered Species	Effect on HAZMAT/ Waste Sites	Consistent with Community Environmental Goals	Consistent with Federal Laws	

■ FIGURE 10.12 A potential project list for mitigation strategies should be analyzed using FEMA's STAPLEE method (FEMA 386-3). This is a technique for identifying, evaluating, and prioritizing mitigation actions based on existing local conditions. *(FEMA Blue Book, 2008).*

- *Economic*: Is the project cost effective? Does a cost-benefit analysis show that it offers the greatest benefit from the least amount of money? There are three possible categories for economic benefit:
  - Favorable—Extremely beneficial results for minimal cost to the community/organization, especially if the project is responding to a high-priority hazard
  - Fair—Ratio is neither good nor bad, meaning that the cost is high, but the project is necessary for mitigation against a high-priority hazard; or the cost is low, but the project mitigates against a low-priority hazard
  - Unfavorable—The cost to the community/organization greatly exceeds the expected benefits of the project, or the cost is too great in relation to the priority of the hazard
- *Environmental*: Does the project concern the environment: for example, affecting land, water, or endangered species?

From this type of analysis, community and organizational mitigation planners may determine a few specific projects that could help mitigate potential hazards while improving the response and training of staff, as well as protecting the infrastructure and environment of that entity.

■ CONCLUSION

Technological, manmade hazard mitigation is not typically addressed in community HMPs. This is due to specific language in the Stafford Act and DMA 2000, which stipulate that community planners should focus on natural hazards. FEMA philosophy, supported by a study by the DHS Office of the Inspector General, is that the responsibility for dealing with technological hazards rests with private organizations that harbor dangerous materials. However, more progressive communities are addressing technological hazards, such as dam failures, utility outages, chemical spills and potential acts of terrorism, in their HMPs.

This chapter covered several structural and nonstructural mitigation strategies that can be implemented for chemical, biological, and radiological hazards. In addition, we discussed some basic strategies at the local level to mitigate acts of terrorism. In the context of nonstructural mitigation strategies, we discussed the concept of legislating to mitigate. This included such measures as the passing of laws, guidelines, rules, acts, and codes. A specific example of EPCRA and the sharing of information about hazardous materials inventories were discussed in detail.

In the United States, most chemical hazard issues are regulated by the Department of Transportation (DOT), OSHA, and the EPA. Structurally, chemical hazards are mitigated by the proper positioning, storage, and packaging of these materials.

Biological hazards may come in the form of natural outbreaks, accidents, and intentional releases. In order to respond to such incidents, HHS has the Select Agents Program, which deals administratively with the most serious pathogens and toxins in Categories A, B, and C. Laboratories that handle these pathogens and toxins follow strict guidelines for biosafety to ensure that laboratory workers and the public do not become exposed to these hazards. Biosafety levels 1−4 have been well defined and incorporate nonstructural measures, like training, procedures, and supervision, with structural measures like positive pressure, protective suits, airlocks, and incineration of laboratory waste products. Biosecurity programs and measures were also discussed, which serve to protect a nation's food supply from harmful pathogens that may affect plants, animals, and consumers alike.

In the event of a public health emergency, measures such as medical screening, surveillance, quarantine, contact tracing, social distancing, and monitoring may be utilized to identify and control outbreaks. In addition, medical countermeasures may be employed to provide prophylaxis through vaccines and drugs and specific treatments for the most serious Category A agents.

Protection from the effects of radiation is achieved through a TOS strategy. The type and rate of emission of radiological material will dictate how much TOS must be applied to achieve the acceptable level of protection.

Communities are encouraged to develop actions to mitigate technological hazards that can be implemented by using local tools, such as capital improvement budgets, special district funds, or implementing changes in ordinances, policies, or procedures. In addition, communities are encouraged to consider mitigation actions that may not be currently feasible but may become a realistic possibility following a disaster. Access to state or federal funds may enable communities to accomplish actions during post-disaster recovery that could not otherwise be accomplished pre-disaster. If you're going to build it back, build it back stronger and/or smarter.

DISCUSSION QUESTIONS

1. Why are hazard mitigation strategies for technological hazards ignored in state and local HMPs?
2. Discuss some examples of structural mitigation strategies for a chemical storage facility.
3. Imagine that your community has been proposed as the site of a new BSL 4 laboratory. What concerns might public officials have to address? What steps should be taken to mitigate the threat of an accidental release or act of terrorism involving such a facility?
4. What role might an emergency manager play in addressing concerns for terrorism?
5. Discuss the methodology used by your state or local EMA to evaluate possible mitigation strategies for inclusion in its updated HMP. Did it utilize the STAPLEE method?

WEBSITES

EPA on chemical emergencies: http://www2.epa.gov/regulatory-information-topic/ emergencies OSHA requirements for toxic and hazardous substances: https://www. osha.gov/pls/oshaweb/owadisp.show_document?p_table=standards&p_id=10107 OSHA flammable and combustible liquids:
https://www.osha.gov/dte/library/flammable_liquids/flammable_liquids.pdf
DHS chemical facility antiterrorism standards: http://www.dhs.gov/chemical-facility-anti-terrorism-standards

Information from the EPA on pesticide storage: some guidance, state regulations: http://www.epa.gov/pesticides/regulating/storage_resources.htm

Guide to Chemical Risk Management: New Ways to Prevent Chemical Accidents, from the EPA:

http://www.epa.gov/emergencies/docs/chem/incident.pdf

National Fire Prevention Association (NFPA) diamond for hazardous materials: http://www.pwcgov.org/government/dept/FR/Documents/002867.pdf

REFERENCES

Hazardous materials for first responders. In B. Adams, & L. Miller (Eds.), (3rd ed.). Stillwater, OK: Fire Protection Publications. Oklahoma State University.

Blanksvard, C. (2007). *Identifying requirements for reporting hazardous materials storage to local fire departments. Executive development.* An applied research project submitted to the National Fire Academy as part of the Executive Fire Officer Program.

Hazardous Waste Operations and Emergency Response. (2007). 29 C.F.R. §1910.120.

Maritime Transportation Security Act of 2002 (MTSA). (2002). (Pub.L. 107–295).

Mileti, D. S. (1999). *Disasters by design.* Washington, DC: Joseph Henry Press.

Protection of Environment. (2007). 40 C.F.R. § 370.

Ryan, J., & Glarum, J. (2008). *Biosecurity and Bioterrorism: Containing and Preventing the Biological Threat.* Boston, MA: Butterworth-Heinemann, Elsevier.

UN Population Fund (UNFPA). *Urbanization: A majority in cities.* 2014. Retrieved from <http://www.unfpa.org/pds/urbanization.htm>. Accessed October 2, 2014.

U.S. Department of Homeland Security (DHS) Office of Inspector General. (2009). FEMA's progress in all-hazards mitigation. OIG-10-03.

U.S. Environmental Protection Agency (EPA). (2014). Fact sheet: Anniston PCB site. Retrieved from <http://www.epa.gov/region4/superfund/sites/npl/alabama/anpcbstal.html>. Accessed October 2, 2014.

U.S. Federal Emergency Management Agency (FEMA). (2003a). FEMA 386-3, Developing the mitigation plan: Identifying mitigation actions and implementation strategies. Retrieved from <http://www.fema.gov/media-library-data/20130726-1521-20490-5373/howto3.pdf>. Accessed January 27, 2015.

U.S. Federal Emergency Management Agency (FEMA). (2003b). FEMA 386-7, v2. Incorporating mitigation considerations for manmade hazards into hazard mitigation planning. Retrieved from <http://www.oig.dhs.gov/assets/Mgmt/OIG_10-03_Oct09.pdf>. Accessed January 27, 2015.

U.S. Federal Emergency Management Agency (FEMA). (2008). Blue Book. Multi-hazard Mitigation Planning Guidance Under the Disaster Mitigation Act of 2000. Retrieved from <http://www.fema.gov/media-library-data/1424878409827-c19165ee0d13e65f864b85f8c00546e5/State_Mitigation_Planning_Guidance_2008.pdf>. Accessed May 19, 2015.

U.S. General Services Administration (GSA). (2001). SARA Title III: Community right to know technical guide. (Publication No. E205.0701).

Willey, R. J., Crowl, D. A., & Lepkowski, W. (2005). The Bhopal tragedy: Its influence on process and community safety as practiced in the United States. *Journal of Loss Prevention in the Process Industries, 18*, 365–374.

Mitigation Tools

The study of this chapter will enable you to:

1. Identify and discuss a number of hazard mitigation tools

2. Discuss the Flood Map Modernization (Map Mod) Program and Risk Mapping, Assessment, and Planning (Risk MAP) Program of the Federal Emergency Management Agency (FEMA)

3. Understand the application of the Benefit-Cost Analysis (BCA) tool for submitting mitigation grant proposals

4. List and describe some common tools used to predict contamination profiles for technological hazards

5. Understand the application of Computer-Aided Management of Emergency Operations (CAMEO) for chemical emergencies

6. Discuss the Digital Coast Repository from the National Oceanographic and Atmospheric Administration (NOAA)

7. Discuss the Earthquake Hazards Program of the U.S. Geological Survey (USGS)

8. Understand the application of thegeographic information system (GIS) and Hazus-MH in mitigation

9. Develop skills of using Hazus-MH software with Level 1 expertise

Essential Terminology: Georgraphic information system (GIS), Hazus-MH, Flood Map Modernization (Map Mod) Program, Risk Mapping, Assessment, and Planning (Risk MAP) Program, Benefit-Cost Analysis (BCA) tool, Computer-Aided Management of Emergency Operations

(CAMEO), Areal Locations of Hazardous Atmospheres (ALOHA), Digital Coast, Earthquake Hazards Program, Open Seismic Hazard Analysis (OpenSHA) tool

For a successful technology, reality must take precedence over public relations, for nature cannot be fooled.
Richard P. Feynman, American theoretical physicist

INTRODUCTION

Technology such as **Geographic Information Systems (GIS)** has served all phases of emergency management well, including mitigation. GIS can provide the necessary information needed to support assessment and decision making before, during, and after a disaster. During the preparedness phase, GIS mapping and analysis can help develop an emergency operations plan (EOP) and can be used in operations-level planning, training, and exercises. During the response period that immediately follows a disaster, GIS can be used to enhance damage assessment and can serve as a key intelligence resource that emergency managers can use to make decisions. And as the response moves on to recovery, GIS can identify the greatest needs and capabilities to manage priorities (FEMA, n.d.b).

In terms of mitigation, GIS helps to develop the hazard mitigation plan (HMP) as required by the Disaster Mitigation Act of 2000 (DMA 2000). Using GIS, communities can identify the hazards and critical infrastructure in their jurisdictions. Then, through loss estimation and other analyses, GIS helps with assessment and mitigation of the risks these hazards pose to residents and infrastructure (FEMA, n.d.b). FEMA's Flood Map Service Center (MSC) has developed a number of GIS-based map products and tools, including Hazus (now known as Hazus-MH), which provide excellent support in mitigation activities at all government levels, as well as in the private sector and nongovernmental organizations (NGOs). Besides, there are other mitigation tools, such the Benefit-Cost Analysis (BCA) tool, which can be used to demonstrate cost-effectiveness of mitigation projects.

This chapter describes various mitigation tools and map products that are currently used in the emergency management profession. Then it provides some examples of conducting loss estimation analysis using Hazus-MH software for different hazard models.

HAZARD MITIGATION TOOLS AND MAP PRODUCTS
FEMA Flood Map Modernization (Map Mod) Program

The Flood **Map Modernization (Map Mod) Program** was initiated by FEMA in 2003 as part of the National Flood Insurance Program (NFIP) to update flood maps and provide accurate flood risk data in GIS format on the Digital Flood Insurance Rate Maps (DFIRMs). The program was funded by Congress from fiscal year (FY) 2003 to FY2008 and provided 92% of the population with these digital maps (FEMA, n.d.c). In this process, 95% of the paper flood maps were eliminated and transformed into a GIS-based digital inventory of flood hazard data. Besides reducing the cost of paper map production, this allows community officials and others more flexibility in data sharing, hazard analysis, and risk assessment, as GIS information can be easily integrated with other local GIS data layers.

The Map Mod Program also developed the Mapping Information Platform (MIP) so that stakeholders could access flood hazard data through the Internet. The platform supports integration of multihazard data and provides a greater view for assessing the risks (FEMA, n.d.c).

Risk MAP Program

The Map Mod Program laid the foundation for FEMA's new **Risk Mapping, Assessment, and Planning (Risk MAP) Program** (Figure 11.1), which initiated in 2009. The objectives of the Risk MAP Program are to identify and mitigate flood risk through more precise flood mapping products, risk assessment tools, and planning and outreach support, and to enable communities to make informed decisions about reducing risk (FEMA, 2011). In order to achieve these purposes, FEMA works in collaboration with federal, state, tribal, and local partners across the nation.

Risk MAP focuses on delivering quality products and services that go beyond the traditional Flood Insurance Rate Map (FIRM) and increase public awareness and actions to reduce the risks of flood hazard (FEMA, 2011). The program is implemented by all 10 FEMA regional offices in close collaboration with community partners.

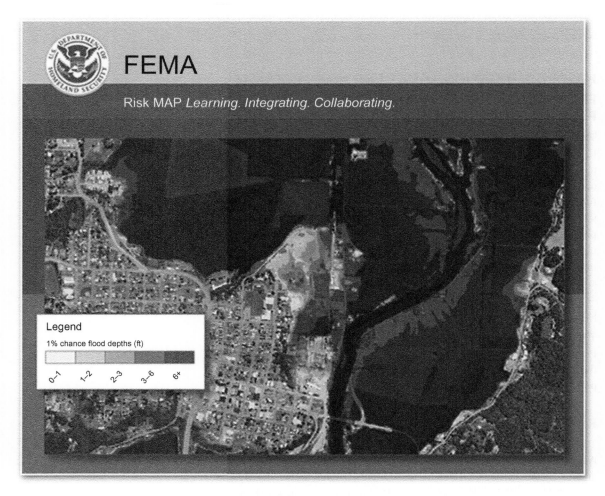

FIGURE 11.1 FEMA Risk Mapping, Assessment, and Planning (Risk MAP) Program (FEMA, n.d.g). *Image courtesy of FEMA.*

Benefit-Cost Analysis (BCA) Tool

FEMA provides hazard mitigation assistance (HMA) grants, such as the Hazard Mitigation Grant Program (HMGP), to states and local governments, enabling the implementation of long-term hazard mitigation measures that are cost effective and designed to reduce the loss of life and property or future damage from natural disasters. Such grant proposals require the inclusion of a benefit-cost analysis (BCA) carried out according to the FEMA-approved methodology to validate the cost-effectiveness of the mitigation project. In the BCA, future benefits of the proposed mitigation projects are estimated and compared to the cost of the projects. The result of this analysis is the benefit cost ratio (BCR), which is derived by dividing a project's net benefits by its total costs (FEMA, n.d.a). Based on the BCA, a project is considered to be cost effective when the net benefit of the project exceeds its total costs or when the BCR is greater than 1. FEMA has developed the **Benefit Cost Analysis (BCA) Tool** software to perform BCAs for applications submitted under FEMA's HMA grant programs.

The BCA tool automates cost-effectiveness analysis and allows the grant applicants to calculate a project BCR. Using this tool, applicants enter data regarding their mitigation projects and structures in the data fields of the program. The cost-effectiveness of the project is determined by built-in calculations using the user-provided data. Default values such as FEMA standard values and the results of previously conducted economic and statistical analyses have been assigned to certain data fields in the BCA tool (FEMA, n.d.a). However, the software allows users to override some of the prefilled standard data inputs, such as the Project Useful Life standard value. In this case, users must justify the value by providing documentation explaining and supporting their new value. The BCA program consists of seven modules covering a range of major natural hazards:

- Flood (Riverine, Coastal Zone A, Coastal Zone V)
- Hurricane Wind
- Hurricane Safe Room
- Damage-Frequency Assessment
- Tornado Safe Room
- Earthquake
- Wildfire

CAMEO

Computer-Aided Management of Emergency Operations (CAMEO) is a "system of software applications used widely to plan for and respond to chemical emergencies" (EPA, n.d.). The tool was developed by the Office of Response and Restoration of the National Oceanic and Atmospheric Administration (NOAA) in collaboration with the Office of Emergency Management (OEM) of the Environmental Protection Agency (EPA) and introduced first in 1986.

The software suite consists of four core programs: CAMEOfm, CAMEO Chemicals, Areal Locations of Hazardous Atmospheres (ALOHA), and MARPLOT, which can be used together or separately to assist first responders and emergency planners access key information quickly. They system integrates data management modules, a chemical database, an air dispersion model, and a mapping platform. Emergency planners and responders can use CAMEO to access, store, and evaluate critical information for developing emergency plans. The software also helps users to comply with the regulatory requirements of the Emergency Planning and Community Right-to-Know Act (EPCRA, also known as SARA Title III) for chemical inventory reporting (EPA, n.d.).

The CAMEOfm application has several data management modules to assist in data management, as required by EPCRA, and to help navigate to other programs. For instance, you can store information here about the chemical facilities of your community and then find out more about the chemicals in CAMEO Chemicals or use ALOHA to predict the threat zones.

The CAMEO Chemicals program contains an extensive database of over 6000 hazardous chemicals, 80,000 synonyms, and product trade names with a powerful search engine (Holderman, 2008). Users can also print customized reports with response recommendations and find out how chemicals would react if they were mixed.

ALOHA and Threat Zone Plot on MARPLOT

ALOHA is a modeling application that predicts threat zones associated with hazardous chemical releases such as toxic gas clouds, fires, or explosions. A *threat zone* is an area that has exceeded a user-specified level of concern (LOC) for a particular hazard (NOAA, n.d.a). ALOHA can also calculate how quickly chemicals are releasing from tanks or pipelines and predict the changes over time. The scenarios and threat zones can be displayed on MARPLOT (Figure 11.2), which is a GIS-based mapping platform for this system.

CRITICAL THINKING

A new chemical manufacturing plant has just opened in your community. As the emergency management director, how would you use the CAMEO software to determine potential risks and develop a response and mitigation plan for the community?

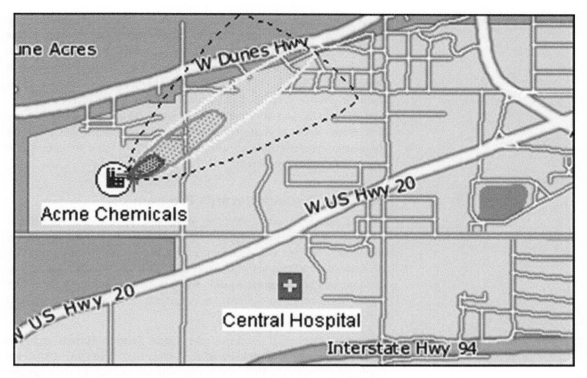

■ FIGURE 11.2 An ALOHA threat zone plot displayed on a MARPLOT map. The red, orange, and yellow zones indicate areas where specific LOC thresholds were exceeded. *Image courtesy of NOAA.*

NOAA's Digital Coast

The Digital Coast (http://coast.noaa.gov/digitalcoast) is a web-based repository developed by the NOAA Office for Coastal Management for the coastal managers, planners, decision makers, and technical users to provide geospatial data, training, case studies, and a number of tools related to coastal hazard issues, including sea level rise, climate change, coastal resilience, hurricanes, and coastal flooding. According to the program's website in early 2015, 4446 coastal communities within the United States utilize the Digital Coast. Furthermore, the most frequently accessed tools include the Sea Level Rise and Coastal Flooding Impacts Viewer, Coastal County Snapshots, Historical Hurricane Tracks, ENOW Explorer (containing economic information), and Land Cover Atlas (NOAA, n.d.b).

The Digital Coast Partnership includes NOAA, the American Planning Association, Association of State Floodplain Managers, Coastal States Organization, National Association of Counties, National Estuarine Research Reserves Association, National States Geographic Information Council, The Nature Conservancy, and Urban Land Institute (NOAA, n.d.b). The partners work together to provide relevant data, tools, and information on key coastal issues, as well as support events such as conferences, webinars, workshops, and meetings for coastal professionals to ensure informed decision making about how to use coastal resources.

USGS Earthquake Hazards Program

The Earthquake Hazards Program developed by the U.S. Geological Survey (USGS) provides earthquake data, including real-time and historic earthquake catalogs, GIS data, and seismic hazard analysis tools that create customized hazard maps to assess individual and overall hazards. The real-time and historical earthquake data and the mapping tools have been a great resource for communities in preparedness, response, recovery and mitigation efforts.

Recently, USGS has developed the Open Seismic Hazard Analysis (OpenSHA) tool in collaboration with the Southern California Earthquake Center (SCEC), which can estimate earthquake risks accommodating both past and future models (USGS, n.d.). As the name suggests, the tool is an open-source project and is currently a work in progress. Although OpenSHA initially focused on California, the project has now been incorporated into the National Sesmic Hazard Mapping (NSHMP) at the USGS, and also into the Global Earthquake Model (GEM) project (OpenSHA, n.d.).

Hazus-MH

Hazus (which is the acronym for Hazards United States) is GIS-based loss estimation software developed by FEMA that contains models for estimating potential losses of a community or a region from earthquakes, floods and hurricanes. The HAZUS Earthquake Model was first released in 1997 as HAZUS97. In 2004, FEMA released the multihazard version of Hazus, Hazus-MH, which has been updated several times. Although the software was developed with a focus on the United States, the Hazus model has been adopted for use by emergency management organizations in Singapore, Canada, Australia, and Pakistan (World Bank, 2014).

Hazus-MH is available for free from the FEMA website. However, it is not a stand-alone program and requires ArcGIS™ software from Esri® (a company in Redlands, California) prior to its installation.

Hazus-MH can be effectively used in all phases of emergency management especially in mitigation. Figure 11.3 shows how Hazus-MH can be applied in all steps of the risk assessment process. Hazus-MH can analyze potential loss estimates of a community based on (i) physical damage to buildings and structures including schools, critical facilities, and infrastructure; (ii) economic losses such as job reduction, business interruption, and repair and reconstruction costs; and (iii) social impacts, including estimates of shelter requirements and displaced households and population affected by floods, earthquakes, and hurricanes (FEMA, 2004).

Hazus-MH comes with data for every census block in the United States. Demographic data from the U.S. Census Bureau include estimates of income, population, demographics, occupancies, and housing unit development. U.S. Census Bureau and Dun & Bradstreet data provide information about the general building stock inventory. U.S. Department of Energy (DOE) data provide regional variations in characteristics such as number and size of garages, types of building foundations, and number of stories within a building. In addition to aggregate data, Hazus contains site-specific data for essential and high-profile facilities (FEMA, n.d.b).

In Hazus-MH, analysis can be done with default hazard, inventory, and damage information, which requires less expertise and is considered as Level 1 or basic estimates. In Level 2, more accurate loss estimates are produced by including detailed information on local hazard conditions and/or by replacing the default inventories with more accurate local inventories of buildings, essential facilities, and other infrastructure. And in Level 3, expert adjustment of analysis parameters and advanced capabilities such as the Advanced Engineering Building Module (AEBM) and the Potable Water System Analysis Model (POWSAM) can be used, which requires a high degree of expertise in Hazus architecture and file structure (FEMA, n.d.b). Figure 11.4 shows a diagram of all three levels.

The following Hazus-MH tutorial subsection of this chapter provides a few examples of a Level 1 estimate using the flood, hurricane, and earthquake models. FEMA's Emergency Management Institute (EMI), located on the National Emergency Training Center campus in Emmitsburg, Maryland, provides advanced training on Hazus-MH at no cost for federal, state, and local community professionals.

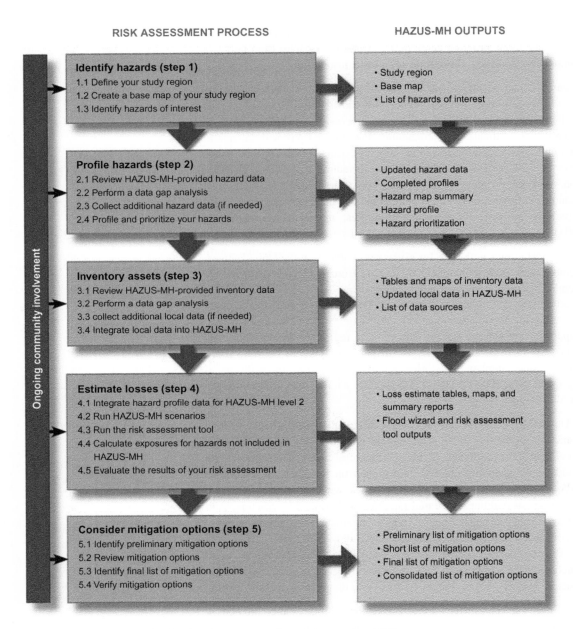

RISK ASSESSMENT PROCESS　　　　　　　　**HAZUS-MH OUTPUTS**

Ongoing community involvement

Identify hazards (step 1)
1.1 Define your study region
1.2 Create a base map of your study region
1.3 Identify hazards of interest

- Study region
- Base map
- List of hazards of interest

Profile hazards (step 2)
2.1 Review HAZUS-MH-provided hazard data
2.2 Perform a data gap analysis
2.3 Collect additional hazard data (if needed)
2.4 Profile and prioritize your hazards

- Updated hazard data
- Completed profiles
- Hazard map summary
- Hazard profile
- Hazard prioritization

Inventory assets (step 3)
3.1 Review HAZUS-MH-provided inventory data
3.2 Perform a data gap analysis
3.3 collect additional local data (if needed)
3.4 Integrate local data into HAZUS-MH

- Tables and maps of inventory data
- Updated local data in HAZUS-MH
- List of data sources

Estimate losses (step 4)
4.1 Integrate hazard profile data for HAZUS-MH level 2
4.2 Run HAZUS-MH scenarios
4.3 Run the risk assessment tool
4.4 Calculate exposures for hazards not included in HAZUS-MH
4.5 Evaluate the results of your risk assessment

- Loss estimate tables, maps, and summary reports
- Flood wizard and risk assessment tool outputs

Consider mitigation options (step 5)
5.1 Identify preliminary mitigation options
5.2 Review mitigation options
5.3 Identify final list of mitigation options
5.4 Verify mitigation options

- Preliminary list of mitigation options
- Short list of mitigation options
- Final list of mitigation options
- Consolidated list of mitigation options

■ **FIGURE 11.3** Application of Hazus-MH in the risk assessment process and outputs. *Image courtesy of FEMA.*

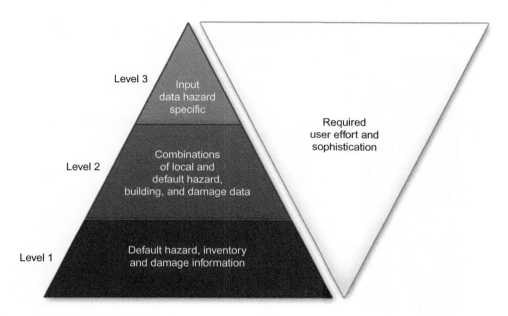

Level 3

Input
data hazard
specific

Required
user effort and
sophistication

Level 2

Combinations
of local and
default hazard,
building, and damage data

Level 1

Default hazard, inventory
and damage information

■ **FIGURE 11.4** Hazus-MH levels of analysis and expertise. *Image courtesy of FEMA.*

HAZUS-MH TUTORIALS
Flood Model

This example will show how to conduct a loss estimation analysis with a flood model using default data. Here, we will estimate the number of people who will evacuate and require short-term shelter during a 100-year flood event for a selected study region.

The first step of conducting a Hazus analysis is to define the study region. Study regions can be created with states, counties, census tracts, or census blocks. After opening the Hazus-MH software, you can create a new region by selecting the option from the startup window (Figure 11.5) to define the study region.

After selecting OK, another pop-up window will open, where you have to enter the name of the study region. For this example, we have selected Calhoun County, AL, as our study region (Figure 11.6).

Next, we have to select the Hazard Type (Figure 11.7). In this case, we should check Flood as the hazard type. In the following window, you have to select the geographic level of the study region, which is called

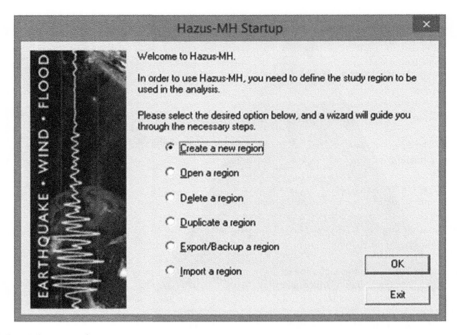

■ **FIGURE 11.5** Hazus-MH startup window.

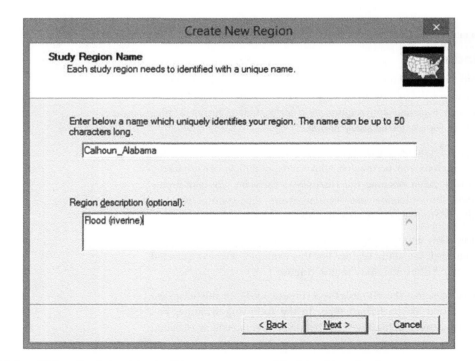

■ **FIGURE 11.6** Hazus-MH Create New Region window, in which you can enter name and description of the study region.

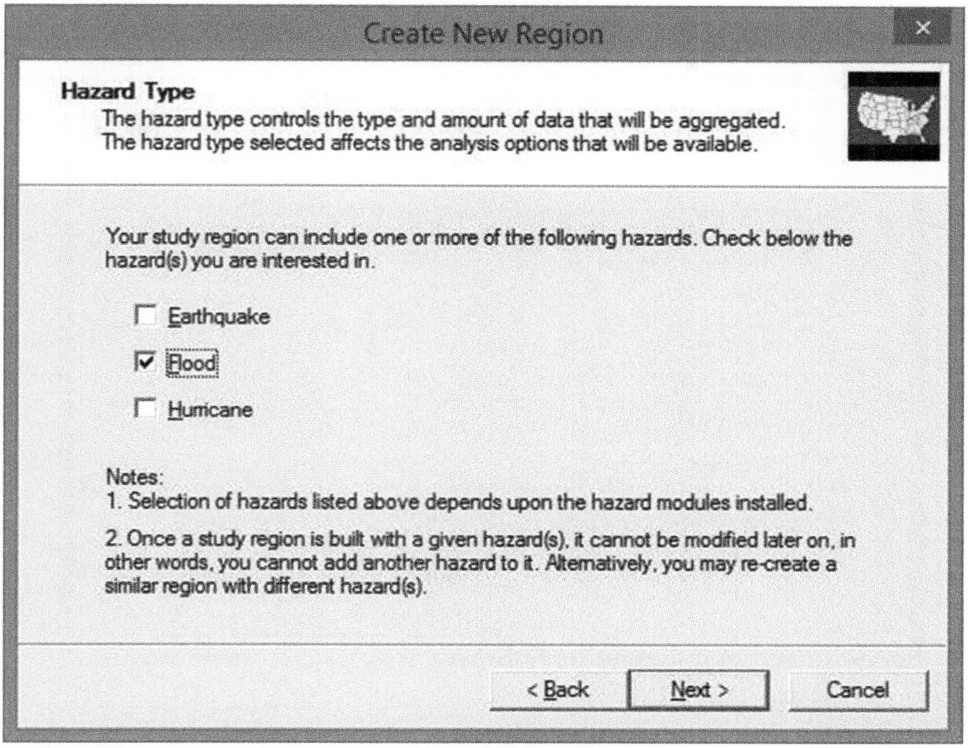

■ FIGURE 11.7 Hazus-MH selection of hazard type.

the Aggregation Level. We have to select County as the Aggregation Level in this case (Figure 11.8).

Then, we select Alabama and Calhoun County from the State and County selection windows, respectively. When you press the Finish button, the program will create the study region, which may take some time. Once the region is created, you can open the region from the Open a Region option in the startup window by entering the name of the study region (e.g., Calhoun_Alabama). Click Next and then Finish to open the study region. Figure 11.9 shows the outline of our study region—Calhoun County, Alabama.

Next, we will select the Flood Hazard Type from the Hazard menu. We will do this analysis for the riverine floods only for this example; thus, the Riverine Only option is selected. Click OK (Figure 11.10).

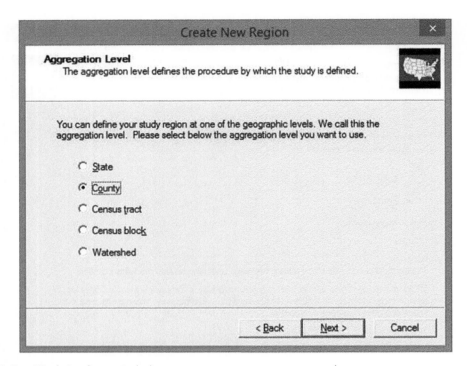

■ **FIGURE 11.8** Hazus-MH selection of aggregation level.

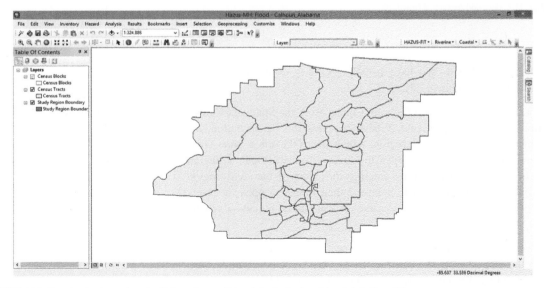

■ **FIGURE 11.9** Map showing the study region (Calhoun County, Alabama) for the flood model analysis in Hazus-MH.

■ **FIGURE 11.10** Hazus-MH selection of flood hazard type.

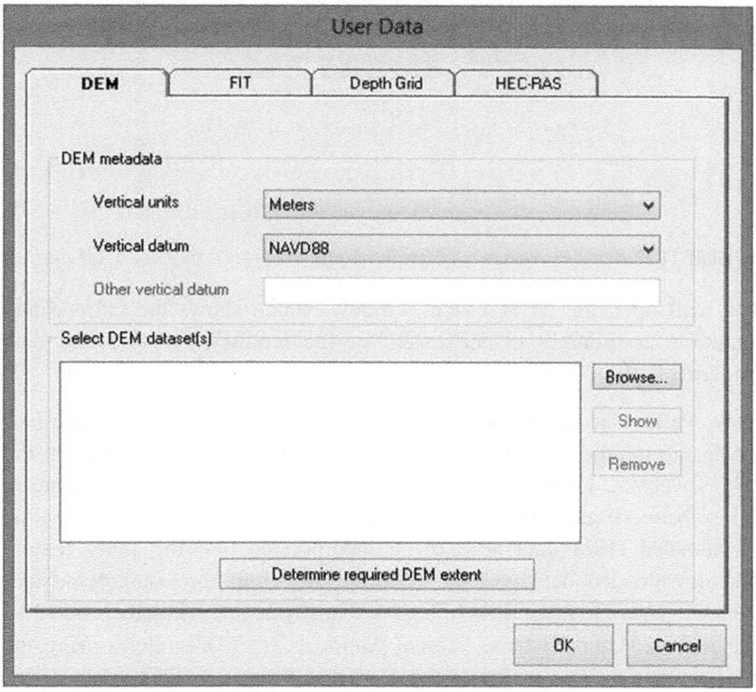

■ **FIGURE 11.11** Hazus-MH User Data window to import the DEM data.

Now, we will import Digital Elevation Model (DEM) data for the study region. We need to select the 'User Data' option from the Hazard menu. It will open the User Data window (Figure 11.11). In this window, select the first tab (i.e., DEM). Then, select the Determine Required DEM Extent button at the bottom.

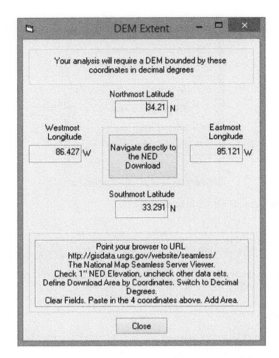

■ **FIGURE 11.12** Hazus-MH DEM Extent window showing the coordinates of the required DEM data.

This will open the DEM Extent window, which shows the latitude and longitude coordinates or the extent of the required USGS DEM data (Figure 11.12).

Now, we have to select the Navigate Directly to the NED Download button in the middle. This will take us to the data download page from the USGS website. Click on the Download button under the USGS icon on the website (Figure 11.13). Close the DEM Extent window. Now the downloaded DEM data need to be incorporated into the study region. The downloaded data will be extracted first into the computer. Next, from the User Data window (refer back to Figure 11.11), select the vertical unit as Meters and the vertical datum as NAVD88. Here, using the Browse button, we can locate the extracted file of the DEM data. Click OK. The computer will process the DEM file for the study region.

The next step is to generate a stream network. Select the Develop Stream Network option from the Hazard menu (Figure 11.14). Specify the appropriate stream drainage area that affects stream density in the box (in units of square miles). For this example, we put 10 square miles. Click OK. Hazus-MH will process the DEM to determine the locations of the stream

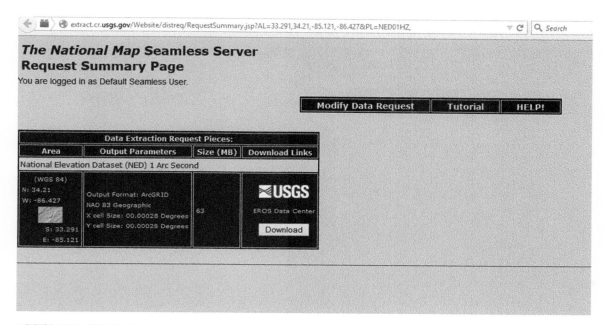

FIGURE 11.13 USGS DEM data download page.

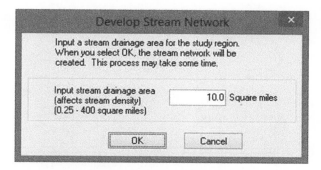

FIGURE 11.14 Hazus-MH Develop Stream Network window.

for the study area. When the process is completed, the identified streams will appear in the study region (Figure 11.15).

Next, we have to define a scenario for the analysis. Click New from the Scenario option under the Hazard menu. The Create New Scenario window will open, where we have to enter a name and a description of the scenario. After clicking OK, another window called New Scenario will pop up. In this window, you can select the streams that you would like to include in the scenario from the River Reaches options. Use the Add to

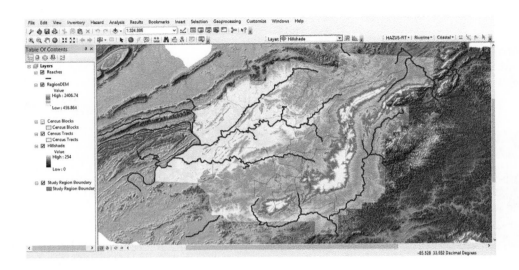

■ **FIGURE 11.15** Stream network of the study region.

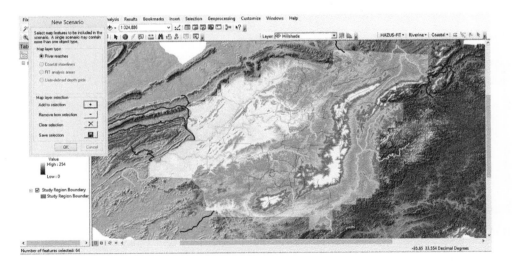

■ **FIGURE 11.16** Selected stream reaches for the flood analysis.

Sselection button to manually select the streams in your study region to incorporate in the analysis. In this case, we select all of the streams located in our study area (Figure 11.16). Once the streams are selected, click the Save Selection button in the scenario window to save the selected streams. Click OK to close the New Scenario window.

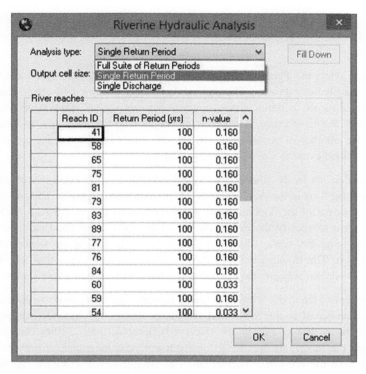

■ **FIGURE 11.17** Hazus-MH Riverine Hydraulic Analysis window.

Now, we will select Hydrology from the Riverine submenu under the Hazard menu. Click Yes to do the raster processing. This calculation will take a few minutes. Then, select the Delineate Floodplain option from the Riverine submenu under Hazard menu. The Riverine Hydraulic Analysis window will open (Figure 11.17). Here, you will see the following three options to choose for the Analysis Type:

■ *Full Suite of Return Periods* will calculate flood depths and floodplains for the 10-year, 25-year, 50-year, 100-year, and 500-year return period floods on each of the stream reaches in your scenario.
■ *Single Return Period* lets you specify a return period between 10 and 500 years for which the flood characteristics will be calculated. For this option, you can choose different return periods for different stream reaches.
■ *Single Discharge* allows you to input anticipated stream discharge levels for each stream reach. Similar to Single Return Period, the user can enter different discharges for each reach (FEMA, n.d.e).

For this example, we select the Single Return Period option. Click OK, and then click Yes again for raster processing. This will also take some time.

Now, select the Parameters option under the Analysis menu. Then click on the Shelter submenu. The Shelter Parameters window will open. This will allow us to define the parameters for our shelter assessment. We would like to estimate the number of people who will evacuate, as well as the number of people that will require short-term shelter for a 100-year flood event in Calhoun County, Alabama.

The first tab in the Shelter Parameters window is Evacuation. Enter the depth (in feet) in the Access box at which people are no longer allowed to go in or out of the flooding zone. For this example, we use 0.5 feet. Also, we have to specify the evacuation buffer (in feet) under the Evacuation Zone (e.g., 500 feet). This value will be added to the current floodplain polygon. The flood model will then estimate the total population within the floodplain polygon and the buffer to estimate the displaced population.

The second tab in this window is Utility Factors. This tab is used to estimate the number of people who need short-term shelter. For instance, we put 10% in the box of Percent of Affected Households under Utility Outage. Users can modify the weightage applied to certain demographic characteristics from the Weighting Factors tab. The Modification Factors tab can be used to modify the weightage or importance of different age and income groups. In this case, the default weighting factors are used. Besides Shelter, users can also set parameters such as Debris, Casualties, Agricultural Products, Direct Social Loss, and Indirect Economic Loss from the Analysis menu. The next step is to run the analysis from the Analysis menu. Click Run, and the Analysis Options window will open (Figure 11.18).

In the Analysis Options window, users can check the boxes that they are interested in and click OK. General building stock, essential facilities, some selected infrastructures, agricultural products, vehicles, debris, and shelter requirements are the items on which Hazus-MH can conduct default analysis runs (FEMA, n.d.e).

Click OK; it will take some time to process the results. Then, once the results are available, select the View Current Scenario Results By option from the Results menu. Choose the available hazard analysis from Available Results and click OK. Results can be viewed in tabular, map, or printed report formats. To view the results in tabular format (Figure 11.19), we will select Shelter from the Results menu.

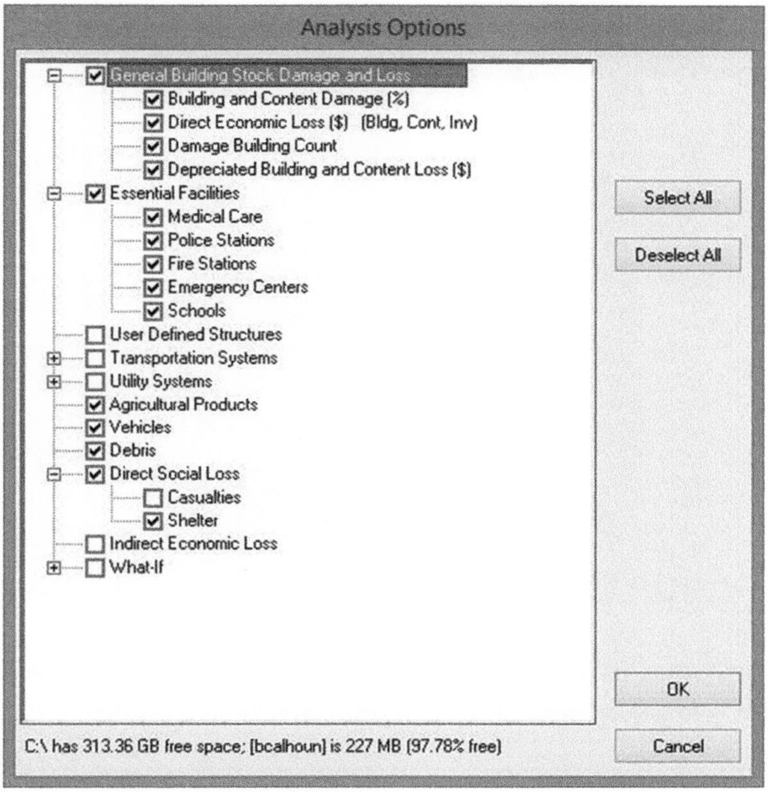

Analysis Options

- ☑ General Building Stock Damage and Loss
  - ☑ Building and Content Damage (%)
  - ☑ Direct Economic Loss ($) (Bldg, Cont, Inv)
  - ☑ Damage Building Count
  - ☑ Depreciated Building and Content Loss ($)
- ☑ Essential Facilities
  - ☑ Medical Care
  - ☑ Police Stations
  - ☑ Fire Stations
  - ☑ Emergency Centers
  - ☑ Schools
- ☐ User Defined Structures
- ☐ Transportation Systems
- ☐ Utility Systems
- ☑ Agricultural Products
- ☑ Vehicles
- ☑ Debris
- ☑ Direct Social Loss
  - ☐ Casualties
  - ☑ Shelter
- ☐ Indirect Economic Loss
- ☐ What-If

Select All

Deselect All

OK

Cancel

C:\ has 313.36 GB free space; [bcalhoun] is 227 MB (97.78% free)

■ **FIGURE 11.18** Hazus-MH Analysis Options window.

CRITICAL THINKING

Suppose that you are using the Hazus-MH flood model to estimate potential losses for your community from a 100-year flood event. Based on the results of displaced population and people requiring short-term shelter, what strategies would you recommend in response to a 100-year flood event?

We can also map the number of displaced people by selecting the column Displaced Population and then clicking on Map. It will show the displaced population by census blocks (Figure 11.20).

Results for
Scenario: calhoun_county

Return period: 100

	CensusBlock	DisplacedPopulation	ShortTermNeeds
1	010150001001003	219.00	219.00
2	010150001001011	4.00	0.00
3	010150001001012	17.00	6.00
4	010150001001013	33.00	33.00
5	010150001001014	51.00	51.00
6	010150001001015	0.00	0.00
7	010150001001016	18.00	6.00
8	010150001002000	0.00	0.00
9	010150001002001	0.00	0.00
10	010150001002002	26.00	26.00
11	010150001002003	15.00	4.00
12	010150001002004	29.00	29.00
13	010150001002005	39.00	39.00
14	010150001002006	70.00	70.00
15	010150001002007	109.00	109.00
16	010150001002008	3.00	0.00
17	010150001002009	0.00	0.00
18	010150001002010	21.00	7.00
19	010150001002011	45.00	45.00
20	010150001002012	0.00	0.00
21	010150001002013	0.00	0.00
22	010150006001013	2.00	0.00
	010150006001014	5.00	1.00

Close   Map   Print

■ FIGURE 11.19 Hazus-MH displaying estimated population for evacuation and short term shelter needs for Calhoun County, Alabama, by census block.

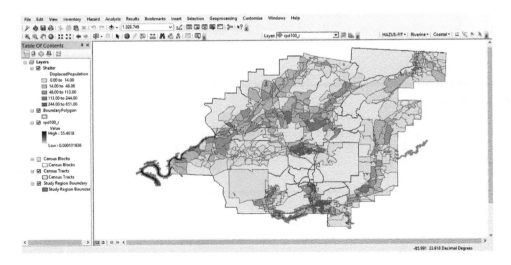

■ FIGURE 11.20 Hazus-MH shelter assessment using the flood model showing displaced population by census blocks.

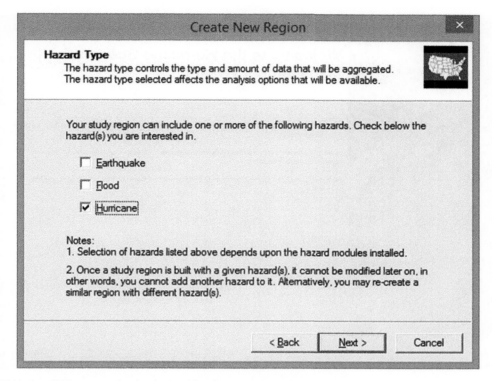

Create New Region

Hazard Type
The hazard type controls the type and amount of data that will be aggregated.
The hazard type selected affects the analysis options that will be available.

Your study region can include one or more of the following hazards. Check below the hazard(s) you are interested in.

☐ Earthquake

☐ Flood

☑ Hurricane

Notes:
1. Selection of hazards listed above depends upon the hazard modules installed.

2. Once a study region is built with a given hazard(s), it cannot be modified later on, in other words, you cannot add another hazard to it. Alternatively, you may re-create a similar region with different hazard(s).

< Back   Next >   Cancel

■ **FIGURE 11.21** Hazus-MH Hurricane is selected as the Hazard Type from the Create New Region window.

Similarly, other results can be viewed from the Results menu. You can also conduct a detailed analysis with user-supplied data. More information regarding the flood model analysis can be found in the *Hazus-MH User Manual for the Flood Model* by FEMA. (Links to these manuals are provided at the end of this chapter.)

Hurricane Model

The next example will show how to run a loss estimation analysis for the Hazus-MH hurricane model using default data. The first step is to define a study region similar to the flood model. For this example, we will use Mobile County, Alabama, as our study region for the hurricane model. Here, we have to select Hurricane as the Hazard Type (Figure 11.21).

Once the study region is created, you can open it using the Open a Region option (similar to the flood model described previously). After opening the study region, we will open the Scenario Wizard from the Scenario option under the Hazard menu (Figure 11.22).

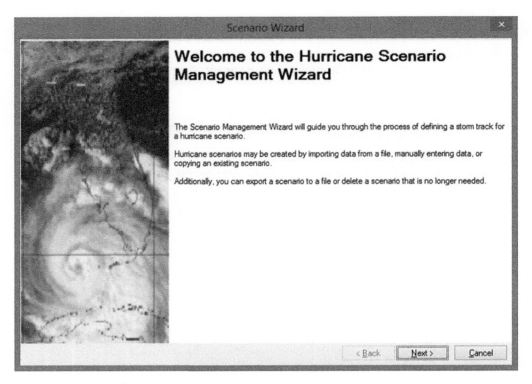

■ **FIGURE 11.22** Hazus-MH Hurricane Scenario Management Wizard.

Next, we will activate the Probabilistic option from the Hurricane Scenario options. The **Probabilistic** scenario option produces seven return period results (for 10, 20, 50, 100, 200, 500, and 1000 years) on total economic loss for the selected study region estimated from a 100,000-years simulated storm database. Sample storms from each return period are randomly selected for the study region (FEMA n.d.f). For the Historic storm option, you can choose a historical storm to run the analysis. Hazus-MH historic storms database is derived from the HURDAT database of the NOAA/National Hurricane Center and only include category 3 and higher hurricanes at landfall (FEMA, n.d.f). You can also use your own storm data or define storm track manually using the Create New Scenario option. For this example, we select the Probabilistic option (Figure 11.23), and then choose "Yes. Make this scenario active" in the next window and click Finish to exit the Scenario Wizard.

Next, we will run the analysis from the Analysis menu. The Analysis Options window will open; here, you can either Select All or select the

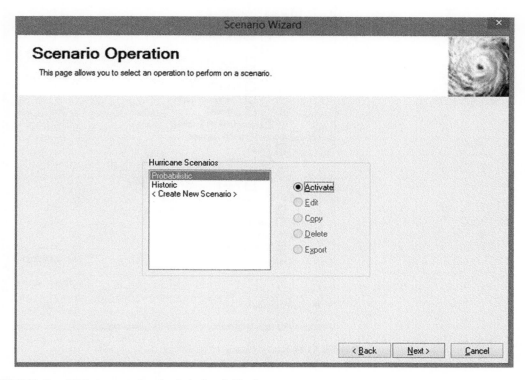

■ **FIGURE 11.23** Hazus-MH Hurricane scenario options in the Scenario Wizard.

specific options that interest you. In this example, we will select the Select All option. Then, click on Run Analysis (Figure 11.24).

The process will take some time. When it is completed, the results can be viewed from the Results menu for different options in either tabular or graphic format.

Figure 11.25 shows the damage probabilities for residential buildings from hurricanes for a 100-year return period in Mobile County, Alabama, by census tract. You can also select the damage probability results for each column and display it on the map. For instance, the At Least Moderate damage probability column is selected here to display the results on the map for the at least moderate damage probabilities for residential buildings in Mobile, Alabama (Figure 11.26). You can also view the damage probabilities for other return periods. Users can also view the summary reports from the Summary Reports option under the Results menu.

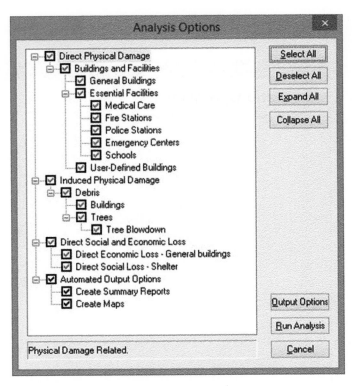

■ **FIGURE 11.24** Hazus-MH Analysis options window.

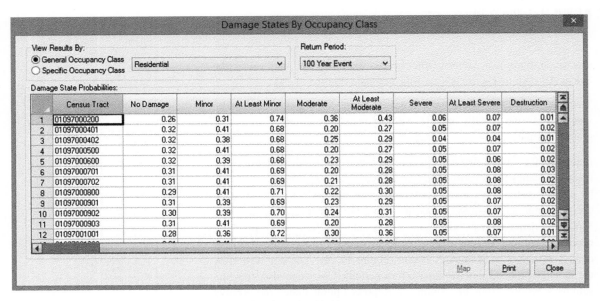

■ **FIGURE 11.25** Results in table format showing damage probabilities for residential buildings.

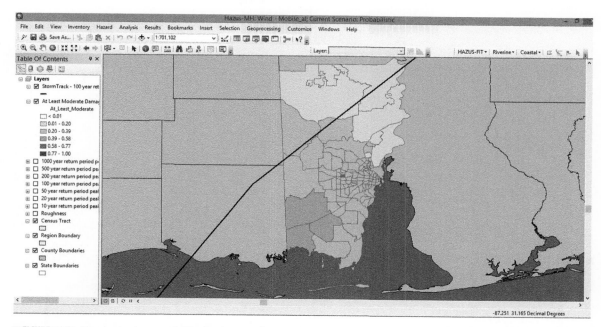

■ **FIGURE 11.26** Map showing damage probability from hurricanes for a 100-year return period of at least moderate damages for residential buildings in Mobile County, Alabama.

Earthquake Model

This example shows the steps of running a loss estimation analysis using only default data in the Hazus-MH earthquake model. Similar to other previous examples, we will first define the study region and then choose the Earthquake option as the Hazard Type for using this model. The study region for this example is San Diego County, California (Figure 11.27).

Next, we have to define a scenario. From the Hazard menu, click the Scenario option. The Scenario Wizard will open. We will select the Define a New Scenario option, and then we will choose Arbitrary Event. Next, we need to select the Attenuation Function (FEMA, n.d.d). Here, we will select West U.S. Extensional 2008 as the Attenuation function and choose the fault type Normal. In the following window, we have to set the Arbitrary Event Parameters and enter the latitude and longitude of the epicenter of an arbitrary event. Click the Map button, and a map window will pop up where you can select any point on the study region as the epicenter (Figure 11.28).

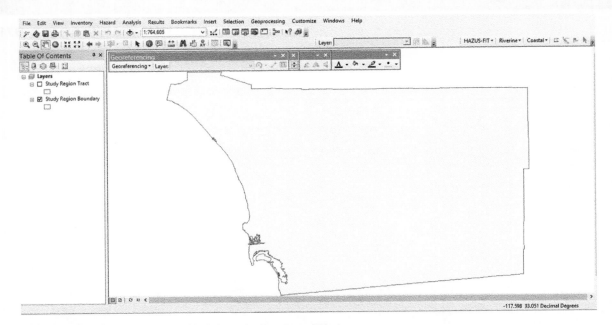

■ FIGURE 11.27 Hazus-MH Earthquake Model Study Region, San Diego County, California.

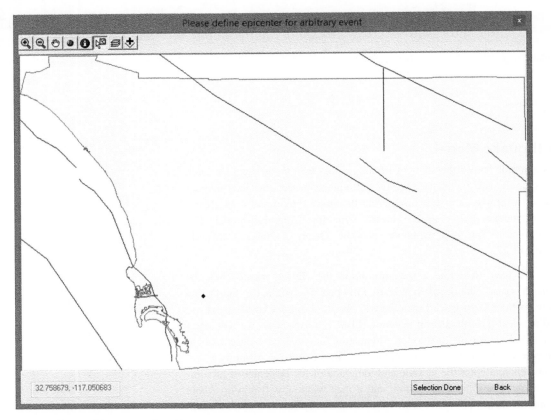

■ FIGURE 11.28 Selection of the epicenter of an arbitrary event.

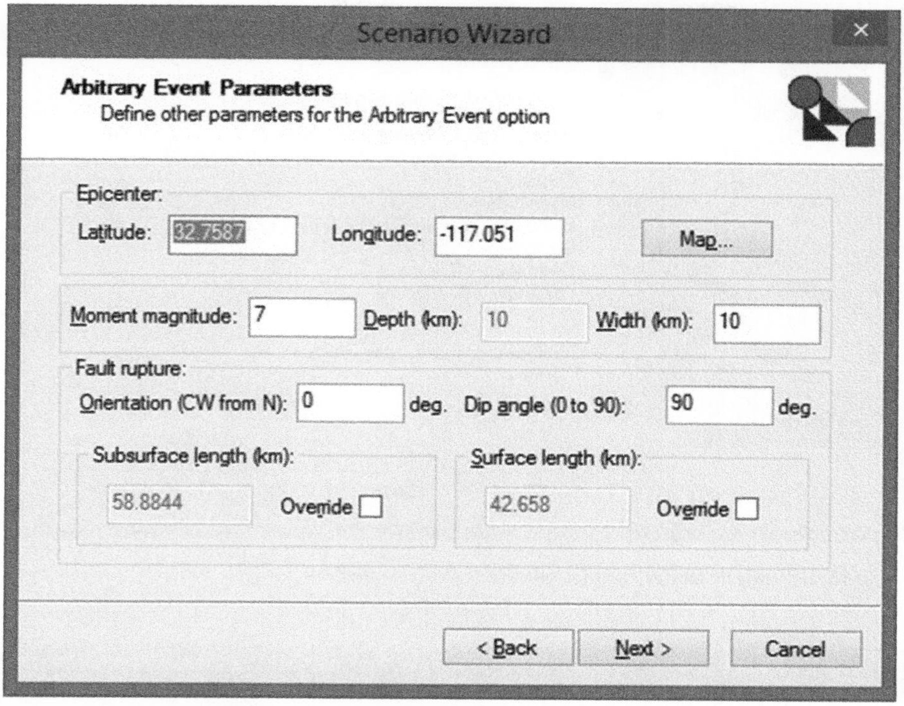

■ **FIGURE 11.29** Hazus-MH Arbitrary Event Parameters window on the Scenario Wizard.

Once you select the epicenter, press the Selection Done button. It will automatically enter the latitude and longitude information on the Scenario Wizard. Here, you also have to define the magnitude of the earthquake. For this example, we entered 7 to represent a 7.0 magnitude earthquake (Figure 11.29) and named the earthquake event as "Arbitrary_M7". Click next to see the summary of the defined scenario (Figure 11.30). Click Finish and close the Scenario Wizard.

Select Run from the Analysis menu to run the analysis. From the Analysis Options window, the user can choose All or select specific options. Once the options are selected, click OK. The process will take some time. The analysis results can be accessed through the Results menu and can be viewed in tabular and graphic format.

For this example, we selected General Building Stock and then Damage by Building Type under the Results menu. The results will appear in tabular format. Figure 11.31 displays the damage state probabilities from a 7.0 magnitude earthquake in San Diego, California, by building type.

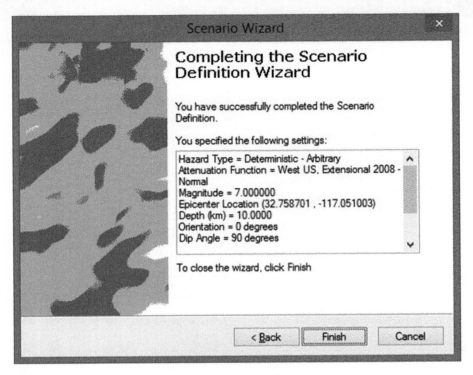

■ **FIGURE 11.30** Hazus-MH summary of the arbitrary events parameters on the Scenario Wizard.

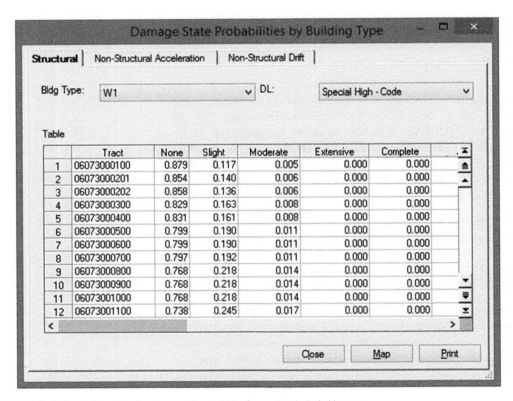

■ **FIGURE 11.31** Result in table format showing damage state probabilities from earthquake by building type.

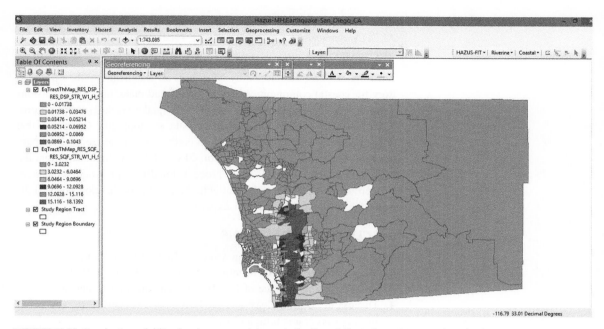

■ **FIGURE 11.32** Map showing probability of moderate structural damage in San Diego, California, from a 7.0 magnitude earthquake.

You can also view the results in map form by selecting a column from the table. Figure 11.32 shows the Moderate structural damage probabilities from a 7.0 magnitude earthquake for San Diego, California. Summary reports can be accessed from the Results menu.

■ CONCLUSION

This chapter described and demonstrated some of the many hazard mitigation tools and map products that communities can use to reduce risks from natural and artificial hazards. FEMA's Map Mod and the Risk MAP programs deliver quality flood mapping products and risk assessment tools that are great resources for communities to conduct flood hazard analysis and risk assessment. HMA grants require the inclusion of a BCA (done in accordance with FEMA-approved methodology) to validate the cost-effectiveness of mitigation projects. The applicants can fulfill the requirement using the BCA tool, which performs BCA for mitigation projects.

The CAMEO software suite assists first responders and emergency planners to obtain key information quickly during chemical emergencies. Using CAMEO and its software applications, they can access, store, and evaluate critical information for developing emergency plans. For instance, the ALOHA application can predict threat zones associated with hazardous chemical release.

The Digital Coast, developed by NOAA, is an excellent web-based repository for coastal communities to assess risks and make informed decisions of using coastal resources. The USGS Earthquake Hazards Program provides real-time and historic earthquake data and tools like OpenSHA that are great resources for communities in earthquake-prone areas. The chapter also discussed the application of GIS and Hazus-MH in mitigation, especially in the risk assessment process. Finally, it provided some step-by-step Hazus-MH tutorials that will help readers develop their skills using the software with Level 1 expertise.

DISCUSSION QUESTIONS

1. Discuss about FEMA's Map Mod and Risk MAP programs.
2. What is the purpose of benefit-cost analysis? What is a BCR?
3. Discuss the importance of CAMEO for chemical emergencies.
4. Discuss the Digital Coast and the Earthquake Hazards Program. How do these programs mitigate risk?
5. Discuss the role of GIS in hazard mitigation. What is Hazus-MH? How can this tool be used to analyze potential loss estimates of a community?

HAZUS-MH EXERCISE

1. Using the flood model, calculate the number of people displaced and requiring short-term shelter in your community from a 100-year flood event.
2. Using the hurricane model and probabilistic scenario option, find the damage probabilities for residential buildings from hurricanes for a 100-year return period in a community near the Atlantic coast of the United States.
3. Using the earthquake model, calculate the damage state probabilities from a 8.0 magnitude earthquake for Orange County, California.

WEBSITES AND RESOURCES

FEMA Mapping Information Platform (MIP)
https://hazards.fema.gov/
CAMEO
http://www2.epa.gov/cameo

Benefit-Cost Analysis Tool
https://www.fema.gov/benefit-cost-analysis
Digital Coast
http://coast.noaa.gov/digitalcoast/
OpenSHA
http://www.opensha.org/
Hazus-MH
https://www.fema.gov/hazus
Hazus-MH User Manuals
Multi-hazard Loss Estimation Methodology—Flood Model Hazus®-MH User Manual:
http://www.fema.gov/media-library-data/20130726-1820-25045-8814/hzmh2_1_fl_um.pdf
Multi-hazard Loss Estimation Methodology—Hurricane Model Hazus®-MH User Manual:
http://www.fema.gov/media-library-data/20130726-1820-25045-8522/hzmh2_1_hr_um.pdf
Multi-hazard Loss Estimation Methodology—Earthquake Model Hazus®-MH User Manual:
http://www.fema.gov/media-library-data/20130726-1820-25045-1179/hzmhs2_1_eq_um.pdf
Using Hazus-MH for Risk Assessment:
http://www.fema.gov/pdf/plan/prevent/hazus/fema433.pdf

REFERENCES

Holderman, E. (2008). CAMEO and ALOHA, *Emergency Management* (October 7, 2008). Retrieved from <http://www.emergencymgmt.com/emergency-blogs/disaster-zone/CAMEO-and-ALOHA.html>. Accessed March 05, 2015.

OpenSHA. (n.d.). About OpenSHA. Retrieved from <http://www.opensha.org/>. Accessed March 02, 2015.

U.S. Environmental Protection Agency (EPA). (n.d.) What is the CAMEO software suite? Retrieved from <http://www2.epa.gov/cameo/what-cameo-software-suite>. Accessed March 02, 2015.

U.S. Federal Emergency Management Agency (FEMA). (n.d.a). Benefit-cost analysis. Retrieved from <https://www.fema.gov/benefit-cost-analysis>. Accessed March 02, 2015.

U.S. Federal Emergency Management Agency (FEMA). (n.d.b). IS-922: Applications of GIS for emergency management.

U.S. Federal Emergency Management Agency (FEMA). (n.d.c). Map modernization. Retrieved from <https://www.fema.gov/national-flood-insurance-program-flood-hazard-mapping/map-modernization>. Accessed March 02, 2015.

U.S. Federal Emergency Management Agency (FEMA). (n.d.d). Multi-hazard loss estimation methodology—earthquake model—user manual. Retrieved from <http://www.fema.gov/media-library-data/20130726-1716-25045-6422/hazus_mr4_earthquake_tech_manual.pdf>. Accessed March 11, 2015.

U.S. Federal Emergency Management Agency (FEMA). (n.d.e). Multi-hazard loss estimation methodology—flood model—user manual. Retrieved from <http://www.fema.gov/media-library-data/20130726-1820-25045-8292/hzmh2_1_fl_tm.pdf>. Accessed March 11, 2015.

U.S. Federal Emergency Management Agency (FEMA). (n.d.f). Multi-hazard loss estimation methodology—hurricane model—user manual. Retrieved from <http://www.fema.gov/media-library-data/20130726-1820-25045-8522/hzmh2_1_hr_um.pdf>. Accessed March 06, 2015.

U.S. Federal Emergency Management Agency (FEMA). (n.d.g). Risk Mapping, Assessment, and Planning (Risk MAP) Program. Retrieved from <https://www.fema.gov/risk-mapping-assessment-and-planning-risk-map>. Accessed March 02, 2015.

U.S. Federal Emergency Management Agency (FEMA). (2004). Using Hazus-MH for risk assessment—FEMA How-to guide #433. Retrieved from <http://www.fema.gov/pdf/plan/prevent/hazus/fema433.pdf>. Accessed March 02, 2015.

U.S. Federal Emergency Management Agency (FEMA). (2011). What is risk MAP? Retrieved from <http://www.fema.gov/media-library-data/20130726-1731-25045-8364/what_is_risk_map_factsheet_07_19_12.pdf>. Accessed March 02, 2015.

U.S. Geological Service. (n.d.). Earthquake hazard program. Retrieved from <http://earthquake.usgs.gov/hazards/>. Accessed March 02, 2015.

U.S. National Oceanic and Atmospheric Administration. (n.d.a). ALOHA. Retrieved from <http://response.restoration.noaa.gov/oil-and-chemical-spills/chemical-spills/response-tools/aloha.html>. Accessed March 02, 2015.

U.S. National Oceanic and Atmospheric Administration. (n.d.b). Digital coast. Retrieved from <http://coast.noaa.gov/digitalcoast/about>. Accessed March 02, 2015.

World Bank. (2014). Understanding risk in an evolving world--Emerging best practices in natural disaster risk assessment. Washington, DC: World Bank. Retrieved from <http://www.worldbank.org/content/dam/Worldbank/Feature%20Story/japan/pdf/101414_event/Understanding_Risk-Web_Version-rev_1.8.0.pdf>. Accessed March 16, 2015.

Mitigation Best Practices and Resources

This may sound trite, but bad things happen to good people, and when you're facing terrorism, natural disaster, you can have every wonderful plan in place, but I am a realist.

Warren Rudman, former U.S. senator

INTRODUCTION

The famous phrase "carpe diem" (which translates to "Seize the day") can be quite applicable to hazard mitigation. The phrase is part of a longer line from a poem by the Roman lyric poet Horace, which refers to the uncertainty of the future, and thus, urging for giving importance to the present day to make our future better. Disasters are unforeseen events; therefore, we cannot prevent a hurricane or a pandemic in the future. But we can certainly reduce the impacts of such hazards by taking appropriate mitigation measures in the present. There are many mitigation best practices in place throughout the United States and around the world that can serve as an example, and even encourage us to adopt mitigation measures for our own communities to withstand hazards. This chapter will provide some examples of mitigation best practices in the United States and in other countries. Toward the end of the chapter, you will find a compendium of links and resources related to mitigation best practices and examples.

MITIGATION BEST PRACTICES IN THE UNITED STATES
Best Practices from Hurricane Ike

Hurricane Ike is the third-costliest hurricane in U.S. history, after Katrina and Sandy, respectively. Ike made landfall at Galveston, Texas, as a category 2 hurricane on September 13, 2008, causing a great deal of havoc and damage. The Federal Emergency Management Agency (FEMA) identified several best practices of mitigation measures after Hurricane Ike, which are discussed in the next sections.

Building Codes
Bolivar Peninsula, Texas

The Bolivar Peninsula is located in Galveston County, Texas. It separates the eastern part of Galveston Bay from the Gulf of Mexico. In 2008, Hurricane Ike devastated this 33-mile-long (53 km) narrow strip of land, which was unprotected by a seawall or any other barrier. During the disaster, 20 people were reported dead and 2087 buildings along the

■ **FIGURE 12.1** A house in the Bolivar Peninsula that survived Hurricane Ike nearly unscathed. In contrast, a neighboring home (right), was built 4 to 5 feet lower to the ground and was significantly damaged. *Courtesy of FEMA; photo by Roy Tyson.*

peninsula suffered varying degrees of damage from the storm. Only 102 buildings were left unscathed, such as the one shown in Figure 12.1. The house shown in this figure was one of the most recently constructed houses in the Sea Breeze subdivision.

Referring to Figure 12.1, note that the house is elevated high above the water. The required elevation was 16 feet (4.88 m), but it was raised an additional 7 feet (2 m), as an extra precaution. This safety feature (the amount of watertight surface between a given level of lake, sea, or river water and the lowest possible entry point during flooding or large waves) is known as *freeboard*, which provides added protection and results in lower flood insurance premiums. In addition to freeboard, the house was built with sturdy materials that were held together with steel connectors and shielded with a storm-resistant roof. Impact-resistant glass on the windows also helps protect the interior from the storm (Figure 12.1). According to one FEMA building sciences expert, houses like this one were built in accordance with Galveston County building codes and used freeboard for additional protection (Patton, 2008a).

Shoreacres, Texas

Another example of using building codes was the house pictured in Figure 12.2 in the City of Shoreacres in Harris County, Texas. The

■ **FIGURE 12.2** An elevated house in the city of Shoreacres, Texas, that survived flood damage during Hurricane Ike in 2008. *Courtesy of FEMA; photo by Bonnie Hanchett.*

12-foot storm surge from Hurricane Ike damaged 575 of the 650 homes in this city as it took on more than 3 feet of floodwater. But this home was not damaged due to following the established codes. The house was built in 2002, and a building inspector enforced the codes very diligently during the process. For instance, the city of Shoreacres requires 1 foot of freeboard above the base flood elevation, i.e., 11 feet, but the inspector required that the home be elevated approximately 9 inches above the city's 12-foot requirement (Figure 12.2). He also ensured that everything was tied down, strapped, and wrapped during the framing to make the house sturdy (Hanchett, 2008). All of these measures paid off six years later when Hurricane Ike blew into town.

FEMA Hazard Mitigation Grant Program and Buyout
Surfside Beach, Texas

In 2006, Mayor Larry Davison of Surfside Beach, Texas, had bought and cleared 9 houses that were along the beachfront on the Gulf of Mexico. The buyout was made possible with funds from the state of Texas and Hazard Mitigation Grant Program (HMGP) funding from FEMA. The program in Surfside Beach also included the planned relocation of 11 other beachfront homes and the construction of a new sea barricade (FEMA, 2008). In 2008, Hurricane Ike wiped out all of the remaining houses on the front row (Figure 12.3). The buyout decision by the mayor

■ **FIGURE 12.3** Aerial photos of Surfside Beach, Texas, before and after Hurricane Ike. Before the storm, nine of the front-row houses were cleared. Ike washed out the remaining first row of houses. *Courtesy of FEMA.*

using the HMGP funds was a good investment for Surfside Beach, as it saved lives and property damages worth of millions of dollars during Hurricane Ike.

Business Continuity Best Practices

Kroger, Galveston, Texas

Located behind the Galveston Seawall, the Kroger grocery store survived Hurricane Ike with minimal damage and reopened in only 3½ days due to its mitigation measures, preparedness, and commitment to serve the community. The initial design of the store included a raised lot, 2 feet higher than the building code and designed to deflect water if it crested the seawall, to either side of the store. Prior to Hurricane Ike, the employees prepared the store for the storm, shuttering the windows, sandbagging the doors, and blocking the large entrances with heavy pallets. They also had a backup generator that ran on natural gas. When the management opened the store after Hurricane Ike, there was only a little bit of damage. It was one of the few places in Galveston where people could find food and essential provisions after the storm (Patton, 2008b).

In order to continue electricity service, backup generators were brought in as the gas supply was disrupted. The company also made arrangements to have the store run by managers brought in from other stores, along with water and emergency supplies. Perishable goods were not able to be kept due to the lack of consistent power. While it was costly for Kroger to open, the commitment from senior management and employees was to be there for the community at its time of greatest need. The mayor and other officials assisted the staff by providing quick access to the store in order to help restore the community.

Galveston County Daily News, **Galveston, Texas**

The *Galveston County Daily News*, the oldest newspaper in Texas, suffered a direct hit from Hurricane Ike, when the eye of the storm passed over the Galveston Island at 2 a.m. on September 13, 2008. As the 110 mph winds, storm surge and rain invaded the newspaper's office building, their backup gas-powered generator failed. Reporters worked out of emergency operation centers using cell phones and air cards to communicate. Located behind the seawall, the newspaper had undertaken preparedness and business continuity planning ahead of time, including significant reinforcement of the building. Preparations also included food, water, and necessities for staff to remain, sending printing and distribution functions to an alternate location (Patton, 2008c). The newspaper did not anticipate losing gas service for their generators or loosing satellite phone service. Their recommendations to other businesses are as follows:

- Know what risks you face and be ready for them.
- Have a strong, elevated building and protecting roofs, doors, and windows.
- Have a written emergency plan and practice it.
- Review technology needs and have redundant systems for data, communication, and other vital needs.
- Determine what you cannot afford to have and what you must have to stay in the business, even if you have to relocate.

Cedar Rapids River Corridor Redevelopment Plan, Iowa

In June 2008, the City of Cedar Rapids, Iowa, was affected by an unprecedented flood, as the Cedar River crested 11½ feet higher than any previous flood and caused more than $6 billion in damages. The flood displaced 310 city facilities and devastated more than 7000 properties, including more than 5000 homes (City of Cedar Rapids, 2011). However, the city responded quickly; within 4 days, it had organized three open houses, which were attended by 2680 persons. They decided not only to recover the city from the flood, but to move toward building a greater community for the next generation. In conjunction with the Sasaki

Associates, a planning and design firm based in Watertown, Massachusetts, the city developed the River Corridor Redevelopment Plan, which was implemented in two phases. Phase One was a four-month-long public process to develop a flood-management strategy. The collaborative planning process included community members, multiple city departments, the Cedar Rapids City Council, the U.S. Army Corps of Engineers (USACE), FEMA, Linn County officials, the Cedar Rapids Downtown District, and the Cedar Rapids Area Chamber of Commerce (City of Cedar Rapids, 2011).

Phase Two of the project focused on creating plans for reinvestment in the flood-affected neighborhoods called the Neighborhood Planning Process. In this phase, the community was able to create a plan for 10 neighborhoods in just four months. By the end of the process, a Neighborhood Reinvestment Action Plan was adopted to guide reinvestment over the next 10–15 years. The River Corridor Redevelopment Plan also included flood management strategy tactics (see Figure 12.4), a community process to prioritize the replacement of flood-damaged facilities, a parks and recreation master plan to integrate the new 220-acre floodplain greenway, and an energy management plan to reduce municipal energy use and promote efficiency among many others. In 2011, the City of Cedar Rapids River Corridor Redevelopment Plan received the 2011 National Planning Excellence Award for Best Practices in Hazard Mitigation and Disaster Planning by the American Planning Association.

SHELTER ETOWAH PROGRAM, ETOWAH COUNTY, ALABAMA

Etowah County, located in northeast Alabama, is vulnerable to tornadoes and other severe weather events. The area was heavily affected from the tornado outbreak on April 27, 2011, as 62 tornadoes ravaged the state of Alabama. Appointed by Robert Bentley, governor of Alabama, the Tornado Recovery Action Council (TRAC) published a report on tornado damage in 2011, and one of its major findings was that people generally do not know where to go when severe weather approaches. In response to the 2011 tornado event and the governor's report, Etowah County emergency management agency (EMA), in collaboration with local businesses, community centers, public buildings and churches, started the Shelter Etowah program to provide residents with specific information on places of refuge (shelters) within 5 miles of every community in the county.

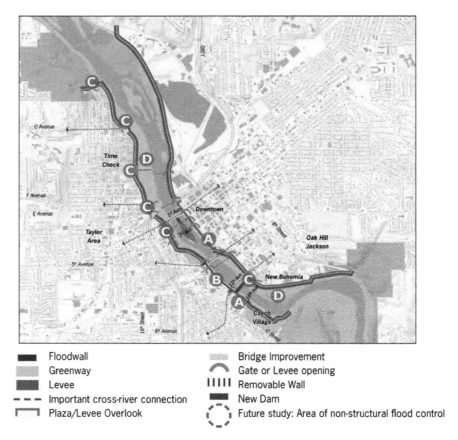

Floodwall
Greenway
Levee
– – – Important cross-river connection
Plaza/Levee Overlook

Bridge Improvement
Gate or Levee opening
IIIII Removable Wall
New Dam
Future study: Area of non-structural flood control

■ **FIGURE 12.4** Flood management strategy tactics in the River Corridor Redevelopment Plan by the city of Cedar Rapids. *Courtesy of the City of Cedar Rapids, Iowa.*

Since the inception of Shelter Etowah, 13 organizations have enrolled. In the event of a direct strike, the EMA has an agreement with the American Red Cross to transition the individuals located in those places of refuge to mass care shelters (Bryant et al., 2014). When shelters are open during severe weather emergencies, citizens are notified through social media, United Way 211, and Nixle, a company that offers notification services. They can also check the status of all county shelters through the Shelter Etowah website (www.shelteretowah.com). The Department of Emergency Management at Jacksonville State University created mobile applications (iOS and Android) for the Shelter Etowah program so that Etowah County citizens can more quickly access shelter information and status using cell or smart phones. The Shelter Etowah

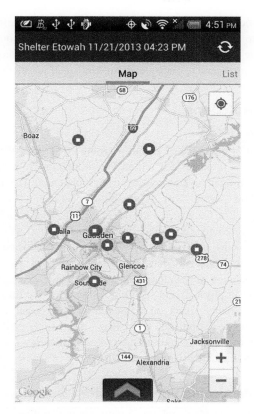

■ **FIGURE 12.5** Shelter Etowah mobile app showing locations of storm shelters in Etowah County, Alabama. *Courtesy of Michael Amberson, Etowah County EMA.*

app helps users quickly navigate to a shelter from their current locations using global positioning satellite (GPS) features. If necessary, users can make calls directly to shelters in one touch using the app (Figure 12.5). The Shelter Etowah program received the Large County Mitigation Award from the Alabama Association of Emergency Managers (AAEM) and the 2014 Technology and Innovation Award from the USA Council of the International Association of Emergency Managers (IAEM) in the Division Two category. The success of the program is leading other jurisdictions to replicate the model. In fact, Madison County, Alabama, recently started a similar program for its residents.

PUTTING MITIGATION BEST PRACTICES INTO A PLAN

In 2010, FEMA published a report called *Hazard Mitigation: Integrating Best Practices into Planning*, in collaboration with the American

Planning Association. The report highlighted a number of efforts around the country to incorporate mitigation best practices into concrete plans. The following sections give summaries of six case studies from the FEMA report representing large, medium, and small jurisdictions.

Large Jurisdictions

Lee County, Florida

Lee County in Florida created a joint planning effort in 2007 with its five municipalities as a model for regional coordination. It is a model for incorporating mitigation into comprehensive planning. The five municipalities are Fort Myers, Fort Myers Beach, Sanibel, Cape Coral, and Bonita Springs. Lee County is a costal, low-lying county facing the Gulf of Mexico. It routinely encounters hurricanes, flooding, wildfires, tornadoes, thunderstorms, and flooding. With planning conducted by the Lee County Disaster Advisory Council, officials developed a prioritized list to address population growth, land use and acquisition, economic growth, and investment in physical and social infrastructure. The mitigation measures of Lee County focus on conservation and costal management, restricting new development, improving evacuations and sheltering, floodproofing of utilities, and repetitive loss structures for compliance with regulatory standards (Godschalk, 2010).

Charlotte-Mecklenburg County, North Carolina

Hazards in Charlotte-Mecklenburg County, South Carolina, include flood, hurricanes, tropical storms, winter storms, thunderstorms, tornadoes, earthquakes, drought, and wildfires. As a result, Charlotte-Mecklenburg officials and stakeholders collaborated to mitigate the impacts of those hazards. Their focus included initiatives to identify both current and future hazard vulnerability, strong collaborative partnerships to solve hazard mitigation problems, and integrate hazard mitigation planning into other objectives, such as water-quality protection, parks and recreation planning, and comprehensive planning policy. Due to Hurricanes Bertha and Fran in 1996, their goal has been to integrate hazard mitigation into day-to-day decision making. They developed watershed-based HM plans, identifying flood-prone properties that were then targeted for acquisition and relocation using grant money.

The county made significant investment in 100-year FEMA floodplain maps and future floodplain maps due to development. They have strong floodplain development ordinances with restrictions on building or renovations in floodplains. Since this would affect development, stakeholders were asked to discuss and put together a solution including developers, environmentalists, representatives of community organizations, planners, engineers, county commissioners, and city officials and their staffs. Charlotte-Mecklenburg Storm Water Services established its Floodplain Buyout Program as part of its hazard-mitigation-planning process, which included its floodplain remapping initiative. Property owners could sell their homes and businesses to the county if their property was a repeat victim of flooding.

Charlotte-Mecklenburg was one of the earliest communities in the United States to quantify and map flood elevations and floodplain boundaries based on "buildout land-use" conditions. It is a vanguard community in the effort to mitigate the impacts of flooding by educating, involving, and assisting constituents in reshaping settlement patterns to avoid high-risk flood zones. Charlotte-Mecklenburg staff secured buy-in for its future floodplain-remapping program among stakeholders and elected officials, realizing that "developers, stakeholders, and elected officials had to recognize the flood hazard problem for themselves if they were to embrace the initiative" (Macdonald, 2010).

Medium Jurisdictions
Roseville, California

Roseville is a rapidly expanding suburb of Sacramento, California. Due to a massive railroad tanker explosion in 1973, Roseville officials rank human-induced events as a top hazard due to a major explosion and chemical-plume release in the rail yards in April 1973. However, their biggest mitigation success was in handling flooding. After a significant flood event in 1986, many steps were taken for flood control improvements, including such things are new construction and land use restrictions, structural emplacements for overland release for floodwaters, elevation of new homes, and buy-out initiatives for vulnerable properties. Roseville also participates fully in the National Flood Insurance Program (NFIP). Their hazard mitigation plan (HMP) is linked to the general safety plan, including planning for vulnerable populations and prioritization of actions. They have established a multistakeholder steering committee, including large business and community organizations. The planning process continues with 5-year comprehensive reviews and updates to the plan focusing on compliance and development for the common good (Topping, 2010).

Roseville represents the best convergence of local capacity to build and sustain disaster resilience through the support of state and federal laws and requirements. California has state mandates aimed at the local level. The community's comprehensive general plan provides a base for leveraging federal Community Rating System (CRS) benefits and FEMA hazard mitigation assistance (HMA) financial incentives to accomplish objectives of hazard mitigation. They have shown strong commitment and collaboration in systematically setting priorities for mitigation actions and implementation to achieve a better future.

Berkeley, California

Berkeley is an older city in the San Francisco Bay Area and home to one of the campuses of the University of California. It has a history of earthquakes and wildfires. Berkeley officials have involved community stakeholders and completed seismic retrofitting of many established public buildings, improved building codes, incentives for residential retrofitting, and disaster preparedness training programs for college student housing off campus. Berkeley's significant achievements include strengthening older, seismically vulnerable public and private structures (Figure 12.6). It has encouraged property owners to retrofit most private buildings through tax incentives. Between 1992 and 1999, approximately $1.1 million in fees were waived for 4100 seismic retrofitting permits (Topping, 2010).

The University of California at Berkeley also has a strong retrofit initiative known as the Seismic Action Plan for Facilities Enhancement and Renewal (SAFER). The program involves an investment of $1 billion over 30 years to strengthen seismically vulnerable buildings on the campus, which has already resulted in significant improvements (Figure 12.7).

Small Jurisdictions
Bourne, Massachusetts

The town of Bourne, Massachusetts, is a waterfront community of fewer than 20,000 people adjacent to Buzzards Bay on the Atlantic Ocean. Hazards include hurricanes, coastal storms, and erosion, flooding, and high tides from storm surge. Massachusetts does not have state-level hazard planning requirements, but the commonwealth does encourage communities to create their own HMPs. It also does not have county governments. Localities use either regional planning groups or consultants to devise plans. In 2004, the Cape Cod Commission (CCC), the area's regional planning and land-use regulatory agency, worked with emergency managers within a 15-town region to produce the *2004 Cape Cod Emergency Preparedness Handbook*. This effort entailed each town creating its own plan. The town of Bourne formed a committee that

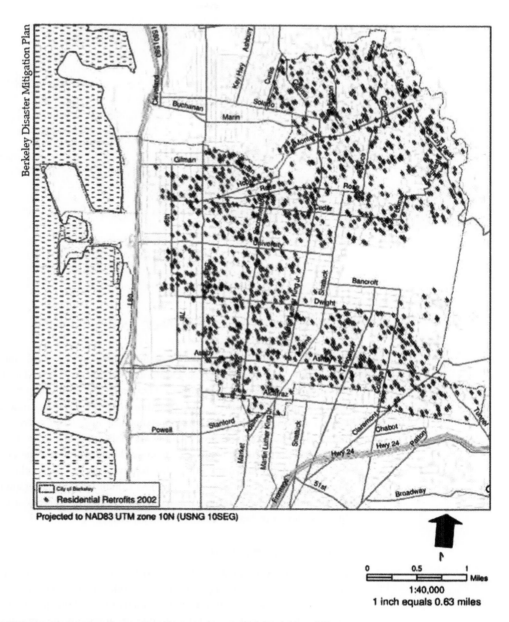

■ **FIGURE 12.6** Map showing seismically strengthened houses in the city of Berkeley. *Courtesy of FEMA.*

Completed buildings

Buildings in process

Still in planning stage

■ **FIGURE 12.7** Accomplishments of the UC-Berkeley SAFER Program. *Courtesy of FEMA.*

included a town planner, an engineer, and a building inspector. Community groups, local businesses, and media were also included in the town's 27-member committee. Their primary focus included future and current development designed to minimize flood hazards, address the effects of severe weather damage, rising sea level, storm erosion, and revision of floodplain zoning. The town of Bourne has been addressing the reinvestment needs of the flood-prone downtown area. The architects used a flood hazard mitigation study to revise their master plan for the project and work creatively with the new floodplain zoning regulations to design innovative solutions that included multilevel, mixed- use buildings, as shown in Figure 12.8 (Dillemuth, 2010).

Morgan County, Utah

Morgan County is located 30 miles to the southwest of Salt Lake City with a population of approximately 10,000 people. Hazards include earthquakes, flooding, wildfire, and landslides. Their planning group includes four people with skills in code enforcement, geographic information systems (GISs), planning, and administration. They invite the public to all their meetings to get citizen buy-in for their initiatives. Their focus has been on quality of life, esthetics through the construction of riparian corridors (plants along a waterway), and implementing

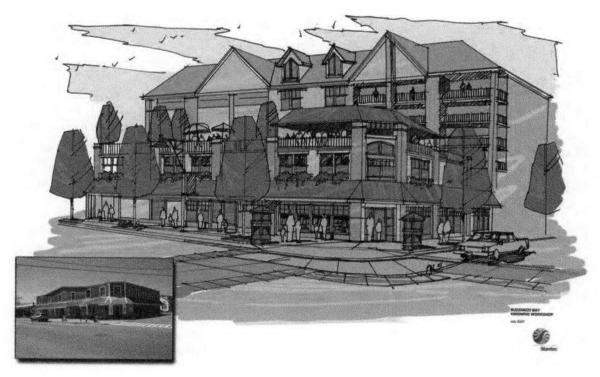

■ **FIGURE 12.8** The Vision Plan produced for downtown Buzzards Bay, Massachusetts, envisions the renovation of existing structures, such as the Christopolus Building shown here, to comply with floodplain regulations. *Courtesy of FEMA.*

their policies into action. They are managing development by encouraging farming and vegetation growth, while restricting development, especially on hillsides. Additionally, collaborative monthly multiple county agency meetings are conducted to coordinate fire and building code requirements, development, and public safety input. They have also identified vulnerable areas that now have rules restricting land use (Leitschuh, 2010).

MITIGATION BEST PRACTICES IN OTHER COUNTRIES
Maldives
Safe Island Programme (SIP)

Maldives, a small island nation located in the central Indian Ocean, is highly vulnerable to climate change and associated impacts such as sea-level rise (SLR). The country consists of more than 1000 small, low-lying coral reef islands encompassing an area of about 35,000 square miles (90,000 sq. kilometers). However, more than 85% of Maldives is estimated to be less than 1.5 meters above mean sea level; thus, Maldives is prone to both short-term changes in sea level (e.g., flooding produced by storms), as well as long-term SLR. In addition, 70% of the nation's critical infrastructure is within 100 meters of the coastline, including 44% of the settlements on all islands (World Bank, 2014). The vulnerability of Maldives was evident during a massive Indian Ocean tsunami that struck in 2004 and caused $470 million worth of damage, which was 62% of the country's total gross domestic product (GDP) for that year. The tsunami destroyed a number of small islands that were highly exposed, with little or no coastal protection.

In response, the government of Maldives initiated the **Safe Island Programme (SIP)** concept to reduce the social, economic, and environmental vulnerability of its widely dispersed population across the islands and to encourage people to move to larger islands. The long-term objective of the SIP concept is to "reduce the number of inhabited islands and consolidate the population in fewer settlements across an identified number of islands" (World Bank, 2014). The goals of the program are to:

- Protect the islands from natural and manmade hazards.
- Rebuild and improve existing infrastructure and economic facilities.
- Develop a capacity to plan and implement risk reduction measures and build community resilience to disasters[1].

The islands selected for the SIP would have improved housing, infrastructure, social services, communication and transportation facilities, and appropriate mitigation measures for coastal hazards, including adequate preparedness for emergencies and disasters. The islands would also have additional stocks of food, essential supplies, and drinking water. Figure 12.9 shows the cross section of an island with enhanced mitigation features where elevated areas can be used for emergency evacuation schools and public buildings.

Initially, 10 islands in the Maldives were short-listed for development as safe islands where detailed risk assessments were undertaken in three phases to recommend specific mitigation options beginning in January 2007. In phase 1, hazard assessments were conducted for tsunamis, high tides, windstorms, heavy rainfall, storm surges, droughts, and earthquakes, with return periods of 25, 50, and 100 years for the safe islands.

[1]Note on Safer Islands Programme (Draft) January 2005, Ministry of Planning and National Development.

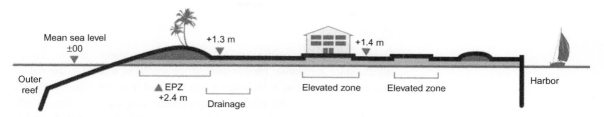

■ **FIGURE 12.9** A cross section of an island with enhanced mitigation features. EPZ refers to the Environment Protection Zone. Schools and public buildings up to two stories in height can be constructed in the elevated areas, which can also be used for emergency evacuation. *Source: Ministry of Planning and National Development Maldives. Image courtesy of the World Bank.*

The assessments also examined the effects of coastal erosion and included the mapping of coastal vegetation. The exposure of buildings and infrastructure to the selected hazards was calculated, and safe buildings were identified. It also determined the capacity of safe buildings to serve as potential shelters during emergencies and identified public structures that required retrofitting.

In phase 2 of the detailed risk assessment, hazard data from phase 1 were used to determine the vulnerability of fishery, tourism, agriculture, small business, and home-based industries. This included a comparative analysis of livelihood opportunities and relocation costs since the SIP program requires relocating people. Also, a social assessment was conducted to incorporate community input into the program. In the third and final phase, all information from phases 1 and 2 was integrated, and recommendations made for adopting island-specific hazard mitigation measures based on a benefit-cost analysis (BCA).

The SIP program, which is still ongoing, has contributed significantly to a number of disaster risk reduction measures in the Maldives. The Strategic National Action Plan (2011), endorsed by the government, was built on the recommendations of the risk information and BCA of the SIP program. The risk information has also helped develop national building codes, a national training program, and a national public awareness campaign for disaster risk reduction, early warnings, and response actions. Started in 2009, an awareness campaign called *Rakkaavethibiyya— Dhivehiraajje* ("Be Aware—Be Prepared") was the nation's first public awareness campaign addressing disaster risk; it was initiated by the National Disaster Management Centre and Maldives Meteorological Service in partnership with the UN Development Programme (UNDP; World Bank, 2014).

Canada

CCAP

Canada is looking at the use of adaptation to address climate change issues. Since mitigation for climate change would be related to the reduction or elimination of greenhouse gases, adaptation is the adjustment necessary to respond to potential or actual climate change events. Since 1998, Canada has experienced some of the warmest years on record (Feltmate & Thistlethwaite, n.d.). Extreme weather events are occurring more frequently, as evidenced by excessive precipitation and long dry spells. The Climate Change Adaptation Project (CCAP) was designed to identify and implement practical, meaningful, and cost-effective adaptation solutions to meet the challenging impacts of climate change in Canada. The goal of the project is for Canadians to be better prepared to face and withstand severe weather conditions that will affect drinking and irrigation water, transportation routes, utility usage, and other human needs.

After reviewing 24 sectors, the project identified five priority areas of focus for climate change adaptation:

- City infrastructure
- Biodiversity
- Freshwater resources
- Aboriginal communities
- Agriculture

In terms of city infrastructure, climate change effects have already raised concerns over the magnitude, seriousness, and implications of their impact on existing infrastructure. Adaptation solutions include evaluating existing infrastructure for its ability to withstand more severe weather while structures are aging, shortening their useful life; and conducting vulnerability/risk assessments to define risks and determine necessary upgrades or replacement needs. Finally, project leaders have identified a need for adaptation protocols to be incorporated into city planning policy. The main challenges for adapting city infrastructure to a changing climate include uncertainty about the rate of climate change, unknown risks of climate change impacts, and developing effective knowledge and training to meet changing needs.

In terms of biodiversity, natural ecosystems may be disrupted, with both plants and animals being unable to migrate or adapt to weather changes. Invasive species may take over where native species thrived. Habitat corridors and increasing habitat density are being considered, along with new ways to manage negative effects and invasive species.

Availaility of fresh water is also another concern; water availability and water pollution may very well be the two most significant challenges that occur as the planet's climate changes. With current water demands by both residents and industry, the Saskatchewan River system is already disrupted, with more water being taken out than replenished. There is less snow and ice available to contribute to water sources. While long drought periods are common, with the current shortage of water, this could be a tremendous problem in the Alberta and Saskatchewan areas. Lower water levels affect the quality of existing water supplies. Restoring wetlands and increasing land and water conservation will help, as well as furthering land development efforts in areas where water is abundant (Feltmate & Thistlethwaite, n.d.).

The aboriginal, or native, communities will be significantly affected as well, due to their dependency on the land. Many lack insurance coverage, which limits their ability to rebound from a disaster event affecting their personal property. New building codes and possible relocation is being considered. This is being done in conjunction with aboriginal community leaders. Renewable energy sources need to take the place of diesel-dependent processes, which further contributes to greenhouse gases, exacerbating the problem.

Agriculture is also very sensitive to climate change. However, many in the agriculture community do not believe in climate change or the potential impacts on farming. Their buy-in is essential. So educational programs that emphasize the effects of climate adaptation and its relevant attributes should promote understanding.

Insurance can play a role with both building codes and the mitigation practices that private homeowners can take to reduce their vulnerability, insurance costs, and damages. By identifying damages, land use planning, building relocation, and retrofits and education, residents' risk can be reduced. Insurance can also incentivize the implementation of necessary adaptations to be taken by lowering or raising homeowner's insurance premiums, purchasing additional coverage, and aligning premiums more accurately with risk.

The Philippines
Seismic Retrofit Program for Public Schools in the Metro Manila Region

It is important that communities ensure the safety of their local schools and public buildings, as many people, including children, gather in those facilities often during earthquake and severe weather events. The Philippines's National Capital Region, Metro Manila, has made an exemplary effort to prepare for and respond to disasters, initiating the Seismic Retrofit Program to strengthen its public school buildings to withstand earthquakes, as well as other natural hazards.

The Philippines, an island nation in the western Pacific Ocean, is disaster-prone and exposed to multiple hazards, such as typhoons and earthquakes. In October 15, 2013, a 7.2-magnitude earthquake struck Bohol province, killing about 222 people and damaging more than 73,000 structures (National Disaster Risk Reduction and Management Council, 2013). About a month later, Super Typhoon Yolanda (also known as Typhoon Haiyan) caused catastrophic destruction in the islands. According to the Metro Manila Earthquake Impact Reduction (MMEIRS) study in 2004, 10% of the public schools in Metro Manila would incur heavy damage or collapse from a magnitude 7.2 earthquake in the West Valley Fault System (Figure 12.10), and 210,000 students would be affected. The study also found that over 50% of the total public school buildings in the region are at high risk from earthquakes (World Bank, 2014).

The government of the Philippines, in partnership with the World Bank, has focused on improving the construction and maintenance of critical infrastructure, especially public facilities that need to withstand the effects of natural hazards. Preliminary results from a pilot analysis in Metro Manila show that systematically strengthening and upgrading the most vulnerable public school buildings would greatly reduce the number of projected fatalities if a magnitude 7.2 scenario earthquake in the West Valley Fault System occurred. A prioritization method was used to determine the public school buildings that were most in need of a seismic upgrade based on the 7.2 scenario earthquake described in the MMEIRS study. The method took "no retrofit" as the baseline and also quantified the benefits derived from and the costs associated with a seismic retrofit program. Based on the prioritization study, the Philippine Department of Public Works and Highways decided to retrofit 200 school buildings in the Metro Manila region (World Bank, 2014).

Japan

Private Sector Initiative for Safe Use and Restoration of Natural Gas in Tokyo

Japan is highly vulnerable to earthquakes and earthquake-associated tsunamis. The 2011 Great Tōhoku Earthquake (9.0 magnitude) was the most powerful earthquake ever recorded in Japan; it also triggered powerful

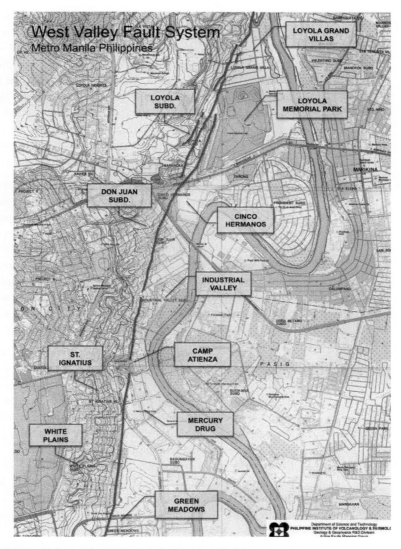

■ FIGURE 12.10 West Valley Fault System in Metro Manila, Philippines. *Courtesy of the Philippine Institute of Volcanology and Seismology, Department of Science and Technology, Government of the Philippines.*

tsunami waves up to 40.5 meters (133 feet). Tokyo Gas is a private company that supplies natural gas to 10 million customers in Tokyo and seven surrounding prefectures in the capital region. The company has adopted extensive earthquake disaster management policies to ensure continuous supply for its 10 million customers, as well as reliable and safe access to gas service.

While natural gas is a clean fuel, disruption of pipelines during an earthquake not only limits fuel for heating and cooking, it poses a major risk of fires and explosions. Tokyo Gas has implemented several structural and nonstructural measures to reduce damages and improve safety. In terms of structural measures, the company ensures that the facilities and equipment used in the manufacture and delivery of natural gas are of solid quality and the structures are able to withstand even a massive earthquake. As for nonstructural measures, the company conducts annual disaster drills for its employees, participates in government disaster drills, and collaborates with partners and other gas companies for large-scale events (UNISDR, 2008).

The company addresses three key phases in its earthquake management policies: prevention, emergency, and restoration. The prevention policies ensure a continued supply of gas to the customers even during a disaster such as an earthquake; the emergency policies are in place to prevent secondary disasters when an earthquake strikes; and the restoration policies exist to restore service quickly if there is an interruption. By creating such an extensive system, along with adopting structural and nonstructural mitigation measures, Tokyo Gas has been very successful in their efforts to reduce the impact of disasters on its 10 million customers.

Australia
Protecting Animals in Disasters

Australia has suffered about 265 disasters in the past 30 years from various types of hazard events that include floods, storms, tropical cyclones, droughts, and fires (National Advisory Committee for Animals in Emergencies, n.d.). After determining that over half of Australians own pets and looking at the history of previous disasters, it was concluded that people will resist evacuating and will return into harm's way to save their animals. Animals enhance human health and well-being and provide economic value. Loss of livestock is not only financial; farming communities also suffer psychologically from the loss of their livestock and their livelihood. These animal-related behaviors reinforce the need to account for animals (companion animals and livestock) in order to ensure the safety of people in times of disaster. In 2012, the World Society for the Protection of Animals and the Department of Agriculture, Fisheries, and Forestry Australian Animal Welfare Strategy cohosted a workshop called "Building Resilience: Animals and Communities Coping in Emergencies," in which over 50 stakeholders participated. The workshop participants reviewed guidelines to address animal needs. Then the

National Advisory Committee for Animals in Emergencies was established to address the animal needs in Australia.

The guidelines developed from this effort suggest several key points to integrate into planning; recognizing that planning for animal welfare will also include human safety and welfare. Several highlights of best practices for an animal welfare plan include:

- Clear roles and responsibilities within command and control for implementing animal welfare measures
- Include animal welfare partners in the planning and response process
- Reference to legal and authority requirements, as well as benefits to the community for animal welfare
- Address the various types of hazards and related animal needs, mitigation, preparedness, and response measures necessary, along with resources required
- Emphasize the animal owners' ultimate responsibility during disasters
- Incorporate animal measures into training, drills, and testing of the plan

Bangladesh
MCSP

Bangladesh, in South Asia, is a disaster-prone country, and tropical cyclones present the most serious hazard in the coastal areas. The world's deadliest cyclone occurred in Bangladesh in 1970, which killed approximately 300,000 to 500,000 people. In 1991, a category 5 storm killed about 140,000 people. After this deadly event, Bangladesh started the Multipurpose Cyclone Shelter Programme (MCSP) in the coastal districts, which received worldwide attention. Cyclone shelters are concrete buildings where the ground floor is kept open for the free flow of tidal surges (Figure 12.11). The structural design is prepared in such a way so that it can withstand the strong wind of storms. When specific warnings for cyclone and tidal surges are announced by the authorities, the shelters are opened for local communities and cattle. During the normal period, the shelters are used as schools/education centers, office, health, or community centers (GOB, 2011).

There are currently 2583 cyclone shelters located in 16 coastal districts of Bangladesh (CEGIS, 2009). Figure 12.12 shows the location of these cyclone shelters. Since 1991, casualties from cyclones have been greatly reduced due to the implementation of cyclone shelters, along with other mitigation and preparedness measures. For instance, Cyclone Sidr

■ **FIGURE 12.11** A multipurpose cyclone shelter in the coastal area of Bangladesh. *Courtesy of the government of Bangladesh.*

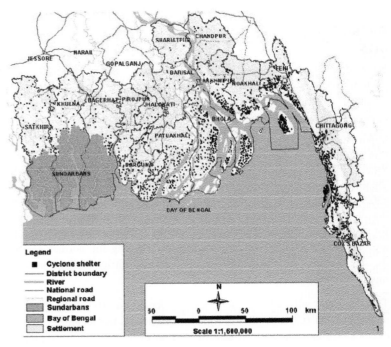

■ **FIGURE 12.12** Location of cyclone shelter in Bangladesh. *Courtesy of CEGIS, the government of Bangladesh.*

(category 5) in 2007 and Cyclone Aila (category 1) in 2009 killed 3406 and 190 people, respectively. Although cyclone shelters are useful, the number of cyclone shelters is insufficient compared to coastal populations. The capacity of the 2583 cyclone shelters is approximately 2.8 million people, which is only about 7.3% of the total coastal population.

■ CONCLUSION

This chapter described a number of mitigation best practices implemented in the United States and in other countries. FEMA identified several best practices during Hurricane Ike, including building codes, buyout, and business continuity. The city of Cedar Rapids adopted the Cedar Rapids River Corridor Redevelopment Plan after being devastated by a massive flood in 2008. The Shelter Etowah program is a collaborative effort that provides a list of refuge to the residents of Etowah County, Alabama, during severe weather emergencies. The chapter also discussed the initiatives of several jurisdictions to integrate mitigation best practices into planning. At the international level, many countries have implemented very successful projects, such as the SIP in Maldives, CCAP in Canada, Seismic Retrofit Program in the Philippines, safe use and restoration of natural gas planning in Japan, animal protection during disasters in Australia, and the MCSP in Bangladesh. Next, a compendium of links and resources will be provided on various hazards, disasters, and HMPs at the state, county, tribal, and regional levels.

Available Resources
Mitigation Best Practices Resources

FEMA Mitigation Best Practices:
https://www.fema.gov/mitigation-best-practices
Mitigation Best Practices: Public and Private Sector Best Practice Stories for All Activity/Project Types in All States and Territories Relating to All Hazards:
https://www.hsdl.org/?view&did=683132
Best Practices in Local Mitigation Planning:
http://mitigationguide.org/
Mitigation Best Practices Portfolio: Hurricane Katrina—Alabama
https://www.fema.gov/mitigation-best-practices-portfolio/mitigation-best-practices-portfolio-hurricane-katrina-alabama
Safe Rooms and Community Shelters Case Studies:
https://www.fema.gov/safe-rooms-and-community-shelters-case-studies
Developing and Promoting Mitigation Best Practices and Case Studies—Communication Strategy Toolkit:
https://www.fema.gov/media-library/assets/documents/3751?id=1774

Telling the Tale of Disaster Resistance: A Guide to Capturing and Communicating the
  Story
https://www.fema.gov/media-library/assets/documents/3747?id=1762
Innovative Floodplain Management, Kinston, North Carolina
https://www.fema.gov/media-library/assets/documents/3807?id=1790
Missouri Buyout Program:
https://www.fema.gov/media-library/assets/documents/3811?id=1791
Performance Analysis of Mitigation Projects in Louisiana (2002):
https://www.fema.gov/media-library/assets/documents/3815?id=1792
Shelby, Ohio—The Economic Upside to Mitigation, Case Study:
https://www.fema.gov/media-library/assets/documents/29964?id=6737
Climate Change Mitigation and Adaptation Best Practices:
http://www.aer.eu/main-issues/environment/best-practicesonclimate-change.html
Best Practices on Flood Prevention, Protection and Mitigation (European Union):
http://ec.europa.eu/environment/water/flood_risk/pdf/flooding_bestpractice.pdf
Malawi—Climate Change Adaptation and Mitigation Best Practices (2012):
https://www.undp-aap.org/resources/projects/aap-malawi-climate-change-adaptation-
  and-mitigation-best-practices-2012

Disaster Databases

The International Disaster Database:
http://www.emdat.be/database
Global Disaster Loss Data:
http://www.desinventar.net/index_www.html
Australia Disaster Database:
https://www.emknowledge.gov.au/disaster-information/
Bangladesh Disaster Management Information Center (DMIC):
http://www.dmic.org.bd/
Canadian Disaster Database:
http://cdd.publicsafety.gc.ca/
Caribbean Disaster Events Database:
http://www.cdema.org/doccentre/disasterevents.php
India Disaster Data and Statistics:
http://www.ndma.gov.in/en/disaster-data-statistics.html
Philippines Disaster Response Situation Map:
http://disaster.dswd.gov.ph/maps.php
Vietnam Disaster Database:
http://www.ccfsc.gov.vn/KW6F2B34/Disaster-Database.aspx
Spatial Hazard Events and Losses Database for the United States (SHELDUS):
http://hvri.geog.sc.edu/SHELDUS/
U.S. Billion Dollar Weather and Climate Disasters:
http://www.ncdc.noaa.gov/billions/overview
Munich RE Disaster Database:
http://www.munichre.com/en/reinsurance/business/non-life/natcatservice/index.html
Swiss RE Disaster Database:
http://www.swissre.com/clients/client_tools/about_catnet.html

Hazard Databases

Tropical Cyclones/Hurricanes

Japan Meteorological Agency Tropical Cyclone Database: http://sharaku.eorc.jaxa.jp/
    TYP_DB/index_e.shtml
Bureau of Meteorology, Australia:
http://www.bom.gov.au/cyclone/history/
NASA Tropical Cyclone Information System:
http://tropicalcyclone.jpl.nasa.gov/
National Hurricane Center Data Archive:
http://www.nhc.noaa.gov/data/
NCAR/UCAR Tropical Cyclone Best Track Data:
https://climatedataguide.ucar.edu/climate-data/ibtracs-tropical-cyclone-best-track-data
UNISYS Hurricane/Tropical Data:
http://weather.unisys.com/hurricane/
Database for Mid-latitude Cyclones:
http://www.atmos.washington.edu/~robwood/data/cyclones.html

Earthquakes

Global Earthquake Model:
http://www.globalquakemodel.org/what/seismic-hazard/historical-catalogue/
Fault System:
http://www.ig.utexas.edu/research/projects/plates/data.htm
U.S. Geological Survey Earthquake Archives:
http://earthquake.usgs.gov/earthquakes/search/
National Oceanic and Atmospheric Administration (NOAA) Earthquake Database:
http://www.ngdc.noaa.gov/nndc/struts/form?t=101650&s=1&d=1
European-Mediterranean Seismological Centre (EMSC):
http://www.emsc-csem.org/Earthquake/?filter=yes
Australian Government:
http://www.ga.gov.au/earthquakes/searchQuake.do
Canada Earthquake Database:
http://www.earthquakescanada.nrcan.gc.ca/stndon/NEDB-BNDS/bull-eng.php
Global Significant Earthquake Database:
https://catalog.data.gov/dataset/global-significant-earthquake-database-2150-bc-to-
    present

Tornadoes and Severe Weather

Tornado History Project:
http://www.tornadohistoryproject.com/
Database of Tornado, Large Hail, and Damaging Wind Reports, 1950—2006:
https://catalog.data.gov/dataset/database-of-tornado-large-hail-and-damaging-wind-
    reports-1950-2006
European Severe Weather Database:
http://www.eswd.eu/

NOAA Storm Prediction Center Severe Weather Database:
http://www.spc.noaa.gov/climo/online/sp3/plot.php
Severe Weather Data Inventory:
https://catalog.data.gov/dataset/severe-weather-data-inventory

Tsunamis

NOAA Tsunami Data and Information:
http://www.ngdc.noaa.gov/hazard/tsu.shtml
NOAA/WDS Global Historical Tsunami Database at NGDC:
http://www.ngdc.noaa.gov/hazard/tsu_db.shtml
Tsunami Observations and Data:
http://www.tsunami.noaa.gov/observations_data.html

Shoreline/Coastal Resources

NOAA Shoreline/Coastline Resources:
http://www.ngdc.noaa.gov/mgg/shorelines/
EPA National Coastal Assessment:
http://www.epa.gov/emap2/nca/html/data/index.html
Global Coastal Program Data:
http://cdiac.ornl.gov/oceans/Coastal/

Other Resources

Wetlands Inventory Data:
http://www.fws.gov/wetlands/data/
Global Lakes and Wetlands Database:
http://www.worldwildlife.org/pages/global-lakes-and-wetlands-database
Federal Wildland Fire Occurrence Data:
http://wildfire.cr.usgs.gov/firehistory/data.html
Wildfire- National Climatic Data Center:
http://www.ncdc.noaa.gov/sotc/fire/
Climate Data Online:
https://www.ncdc.noaa.gov/cdo-web/
Climate Maps and Data:
https://www.climate.gov/maps-data

HMPs

State HMPs

State of Alabama HMP: http://ema.alabama.gov/filelibrary/AL%20Standard%20State%20Mitigation%20Plan.pdf
State of Alaska HMP:
http://ready.alaska.gov/plans/documents/Alaska%20HMP%202013%20reduced%20file%20size.pdf
State of Arizona HMP:
http://www.dem.azdema.gov/preparedness/planning/mitplanning.html

State of Arkansas HMP:

http://www.adem.arkansas.gov/adem/divisions/admin/Mitigation/Documents/State%
20All%20Hazard%20Mitigation%20Plan%202013.pdf

State of California HMP:

http://hazardmitigation.calema.ca.gov/docs/SHMP_Final_2013.pdf

State of Colorado HMP:

http://www.dhsem.state.co.us/sites/default/files/2013%20Colorado%20Natural%
20Hazards%20Mitigation%20Plan%20-%20Final.pdf

State of Connecticut HMP:

http://www.ct.gov/deep/lib/deep/water_inland/hazard_mitigation/ct_nhmp_adopted_
final.pdf

State of Florida HMP:

http://www.floridadisaster.org/mitigation/State/Index.htm

State of Georgia HMP:

http://www.gema.ga.gov/Mitigation/Resource%20Document%20Library/2014%
20GHMS.pdf

State of Idaho HMP:

http://www.bhs.idaho.gov/Resources/PDF/SHMPFinalw-signatures.pdf

State of Indiana HMP:

http://www.in.gov/dhs/files/Chapter_1_Intro_to_Prerequisites.pdf

State of Maine HMP:

http://www.maine.gov/mema/mitigation/mema_mit_plans.shtml

Commonwealth of Massachusetts HMP:

http://www.mass.gov/eopss/docs/mema/mitigation/state-hazard-mitigation-plan/section-
01-introduction-cover-and-executive-summary.pdf

State of Minnesota HMP:

http://www.rrbdin.org/wp-content/uploads/2011/08/MN_state_mitigation_plan.pdf

State of Mississippi HMP:

http://www.msema.org/wp-content/uploads/2012/06/State-Hazard-Mitigation-Plan-2013
.pdf

State of Missouri HMP:

http://sema.dps.mo.gov/docs/programs/Logistics,%20Resources,%20Mitigation%20&%
20Floodplain/mitigation/MO_Hazard_Mitigation_Plan_2013.pdf

State of Montana HMP:

http://montanadma.org/montana-mitigation-plan

State of Nebraska HMP:

http://www.nema.ne.gov/pdf/hazmitplan.pdf

State of New Hampshire HMP:

http://www.nh.gov/safety/divisions/hsem/HazardMitigation/documents/hazard-
mitigation-plan.pdf

State of New York HMP:

http://www.dhses.ny.gov/oem/mitigation/documents/2014-shmp/2014-SHMP-full.pdf

State of North Dakota HMP:

http://www.nd.gov/des/uploads/resources/845/nd_hazard_mitigation_plan_2013_update.pdf

State of Oklahoma HMP:

http://www.ok.gov/OEM/documents/Oklahoma%20State%20HMP%20%20Public.pdf

State of Oregon HMP:
http://www.oregon.gov/LCD/HAZ/docs/OR_NHMP_2012.pdf
State of Rhode Island HMP:
http://www.riema.ri.gov/prevention/mitigation/RI%20SHMP%2011-26-2013.pdf
State of South Carolina HMP:
http://www.scemd.org/files/Mitigation/State_Hazard_Mitigation_Plan/
   1_SHMP_FINAL_2013.pdf
State of South Dakota HMP:
http://dps.sd.gov/emergency_services/emergency_management/documents/
   SD_SHMP_PublicReviewDraft_rd.pdf
State of Texas HMP:
http://txdps.state.tx.us/dem/Mitigation/txHazMitPlan.pdf
State of Utah HMP:
http://publicsafety.utah.gov/emergencymanagement/documents/IntroductionMarch2011.pdf
State of Vermont HMP:
http://vem.vermont.gov/sites/vem/files/VT_SHMP2013%20FINAL%20APPROVED%
   20ADOPTED%202013%20VT%20SHMP_scrubbed_cleanedMCB.pdf
State of Washington Enhanced HMP:
http://mil.wa.gov/other-links/enhanced-hazard-mitigation-plan
State of West Virginia HMP:
http://www.dhsem.wv.gov/SiteCollectionDocuments/2013%20WV%20Statewide%
   20Hazard%20Mitigation%20Plan%20Update.pdf
State of Wyoming HMP:
http://wyohomelandsecurity.state.wy.us/library/2014mitigationplan/
   MITIGATIONDRAFTPLAN.pdf

County HMPs

HMPs of Counties in Alabama:
http://ema.alabama.gov/county.cfm
Maricopa County, Arizona HMP:
http://www.maricopa.gov/emerg_mgt/PDF/Hazard_Mitigation/Maricopa%20County%
   20MJMHMP_2009_Final_10Feb2010.pdf
Dallas County, Texas HMP:
http://www.dallascounty.org/department/osem/documents/
   DallasCounty_HazMAP_June2014_FinalDraft.pdf
Orange County, California HMP:
http://www.hazardmitigation.calema.ca.gov/docs/lhmp/Orange_County_LHMP.pdf

Local/City HMPs

City of Santa Monica, California HMP:
http://www.smgov.net/departments/oem/sems/hazard-mitigation/santa-monica-local-
   hazard-mitigation-plan.pdf
City of Berkeley, California HMP:
http://www.ci.berkeley.ca.us/uploadedFiles/Fire/Level_3_-_General/2014%20LHMP
   .pdf

City of Boston, Massachusetts HMP:

http://www.cityofboston.gov/images_documents/Boston%20Hazard%20Mitigation%
   20Plan%202008_tcm3-31971.pdf

Tribal HMPs

Snoqualmie Tribe HMP:

http://www.snoqualmienation.com/sites/default/files/linkedfiles/snoqualmie_
   tribe_hmp_final_11.1.11.pdf

Tulalip Tribe HMP:

http://www.tulaliptribes-nsn.gov/Portals/0/pdf/departments/emergency_management/
   2010-plan/TulalipHMP2010Sec1.pdf

Ute Mountain Ute Tribe HMP:

http://www.utemountainuteenvironmental.org/umep/assets/File/Home/Blog%20Intro/
   Ute%20Mountain%20Ute%20Tribal%20Hazard%20Mitigation%20Plan%20Public
   %20Review.pdf

Oglala Sioux Tribe HMP:

http://shannon.sdcounties.org/files/2014/06/OST-_-Shannon-County-_-HMP-_-061214
   .pdf

Yurok Tribe HMP:

http://www.yuroktribe.org/departments/planning/documents/Yurok_Tribe_HMP&CWPP
   _2013-01-16.pdf

Regional HMPs

Houston-Galveston Area Council HMP:

http://videos.h-gac.com/CE/hazard/2011-Hazard-Mitigation-Plan.pdf

South Central Region, Connecticut Multi-jurisdiction HMP:

http://www.scrcog.org/documents/hazard_mitigation/plan/
   SCRCOG_HazMit_Plan_2014.pdf

Alamo Area Council of Governments Regional Mitigation Plan:

https://www.aacog.com/index.aspx?NID = 405

Northern Colorado Regional HMP:

http://mitigationguide.org/wp-content/uploads/2013/05/Northern-Colorado-Hazard-
   Mitigation-Plan-Final.pdf

DISCUSSION QUESTIONS

1. Discuss some of the mitigation best practices identified by FEMA from Hurricane Ike in 2008.
2. Describe the Cedar Rapids River Corridor Redevelopment Plan. Why is the project considered by some to be unique?
3. Describe the Shelter Etowah program and its importance in severe weather emergencies.

4. Discuss about integrating mitigation best practices into planning for any two of the following jurisdictions:
   a. Lee County, Florida
   b. Berkeley, California
   c. Morgan County, Utah
   d. Roseville, California
   e. Bourne, Massachusetts
   f. Charlotte-Mecklenburg County, North Carolina
5. Describe the SIP in the Maldives.
6. Discuss climate change adaptation initiatives in Canada. What are the priority areas identified for climate change adaptation?
7. Discuss the Seismic Retrofit Program for public schools in the Metro Manila Region in the Philippines. Would you support such a program in your community?
8. Discuss private-sector initiatives for safe use and restoration of natural gas in Japan.
9. What measures are taken to protect animals during emergencies in Australia?
10. Describe the role of the MCSP in Bangladesh.

REFERENCES

Bryant, M., Amberson, M., Cooey, D., Richardson, C., Islam, T., & Richards, R. (2014). Shelter Etowah: Providing safe refuge in Alabama. *Bulletin of International Association of Emergency Managers,* 31(2), 12–13. February 2014.

Center for Environmental and Geographic Information Services (CEGIS). (2009). Cyclone shelter information for management of tsunami and cyclone preparedness 2009. Government of Bangladesh. Retreived from <http://kmp.dmic.org.bd/handle/123456789/104>. Accessed March 07, 2015.

City of Cedar Rapids. (2011). City receives 2011 National Planning Excellence Award. Retrieved from <http://www.cedar-rapids.org/city-news/media-releases/Lists/Releases%20and%20News/dispform.aspx?Id=501>. Accessed March 06, 2015.

Dillemuth, A. (2010). Bourne, Massachusetts. In J. C. Schwab (Ed.), *Hazard mitigation: Integrating best practices into planning.* American Planning Association/FEMA.

Feltmate, B., & Thistlethwaite, J. (n.d.) Climate change adaptation: A priorities plan for Canada. University of Waterloo. Retrieved from <https://uwaterloo.ca/environment/sites/ca.environment/files/uploads/files/CCAP-Report-30May-Final.pdf>. Accessed March 08, 2015.

Godschalk, D. R. (2010). Lee County, Florida. In J. C. Schwab (Ed.), *Hazard mitigation: Integrating best practices into planning* (pp. 60–74). Chicago, IL: American Planning Association/FEMA.

Government of Bangladesh (GOB). (2011). Cyclone shelter construction, maintenance, and management guideline 2011. Retrieved from <http://kmp.dmic.org.bd/handle/123456789/6>. Accessed March 09, 2015.

Hanchett, B. (2008). Mitigation best practices: House built above building codes stood strong against the storm. FEMA, Region 6 Mitigation Division. Retreived from <http://nhma.info/uploads/bestpractices/2008%20Ike%20-%20DR%201791%20TX%20-%20Best%20Practices%20-%20House%20built%20above%20building%20codes%20stood%20strong%20against%20storm.pdf>. Accessed March 02, 2015.

Leitschuh, R. L. (2010). Morgan County, Utah. In J. C. Schwab (Ed.), *Hazard mitigation: Integrating best practices into planning* (pp. 121–130). Chicago, IL: American Planning Association/FEMA.

Macdonald, J. (2010). In J. C. Schwab (Ed.), *Hazard Mitigation: Integrating Best Practices into Planning*. Charlotte-Mecklenburg County, NC: American Planning Association/FEMA.

National Advisory Committee for Animals in Emergencies. (n.d.). National planning principles for animals in disasters. *World Society for the Protection of Animals*. Retrieved from <http://www.australiananimalwelfare.com.au/app/webroot/files/upload/files/PDF/FINAL%20National%20Planning%20Principles%20for%20Animals%20in%20Disasters.pdf>. Accessed March 09, 2015.

National Disaster Risk Reduction and Management Council. (2013). SitRep No. 35 re: Effects of magnitude 7.2 Sagbayan, Bohol earthquake.

Patton, A. (2008a). Mitigation best practices: Building codes helped Bolivar Peninsula home survive. FEMA Region 6 Mitigation Division. Retrieved from <http://nhma.info/uploads/bestpractices/2008%20Ike%20-%20DR%201791%20TX%20-%20Best%20Practices%20-%20Building%20codes%20helped%20Bolivar%20Peninsula%20homes%20survive.pdf>. Accessed March 06, 2015.

Patton, A. (2008b). Mitigation best practices: Quick reopening of supermarket served Galveston citizens. FEMA Region 6 Mitigation Division. Retreived from <http://nhma.info/uploads/bestpractices/2008%20Ike%20-%20DR%201791%20TX%20-%20Best%20Practices%20-%20Quick%20reopening%20of%20supermarket%20served%20Galveston%20citizens.pdf>. Accessed March 06, 2015.

Patton, A. (2008c). Mitigation best practices: Read all about it—Galveston newspaper never misses a beat. FEMA Region 6 Mitigation Division. Retreived from <http://nhma.info/uploads/bestpractices/2008%20Ike%20-%20DR%201791%20TX%20-%20Best%20Practices%20-%20Read%20all%20about%20it_Galveston%20newspaper%20never%20misses%20a%20beat.pdf>. Accessed March 06, 2015.

Topping, K. (2010). Roseville, California. In J. C. Schwab (Ed.), *Hazard Mitigation: Integrating Best Practices into Planning* (pp. 87–96). Chicago, IL: American Planning Association/FEMA.

U.S. Federal Emergency Management Agency (FEMA). (2008). Mitigation best practices: Storm proves Surfside Beach buyouts a good investment. FEMA Region 6 Mitigation Division. Retrieved from <http://nhma.info/uploads/bestpractices/2008%20Ike%20-%20DR%201791%20TX%20-%20Best%20Practices%20-%20Quick%20reopening%20of%20supermarket%20served%20Galveston%20citizens.pdf>. Accessed March 07, 2015.

UN International Strategy for Disaster Reduction (UNISDR). (2008). Private sector activities in disaster risk reduction: Good practices and lessons learned. Retrieved from <http://www.unisdr.org/files/7519_PPPgoodpractices.pdf>. Accessed March 07, 2015.

World Bank. (2014). Understanding risk in an evolving world—Emerging best practices in natural disaster risk assessment. Washington, DC.

Epilogue

PUTTING IT ALL TOGETHER

The purpose of this textbook is to provide a comprehensive overview of hazard mitigation with regard to natural and manmade hazards. In our discussions with numerous emergency management professionals and former students, we have found that there is significant concern about hazard mitigation principles and planning. Unlike response and preparedness, rarely are there opportunities for emergency managers to be educated and trained in hazard mitigation. Effective mitigation planning and programs take a great deal of understanding, insight, and effort to put together. Like many other complex programs, hazard mitigation projects are funded by multiple sources. There can be long delays in getting a project funded, so it often seems like a waste of time for an emergency manager or business continuity professional to invest so much of his or her time and effort in something that may not come to fruition.

It is our hope that the information presented herein will be useful to you, and that you have learned some things that you may apply to make you more effective in the difficult journey that lies ahead. Before you try this at home, have a discussion with one or more people who have developed a good mitigation plan, received mitigation funds, and employed them in accordance with the mitigation plan.

Glossary of Essential Terminology

100-year floodplain An area that has a 1% chance, on average, of flooding in any given year.

Acquisition/buyout The most permanent form of mitigating hazards. In this case, the government purchases a private property that is located in a hazard area and makes it public property by acquiring the title, which removes the people from harm's way forever.

Agroterrorism Terrorist acts intended to disrupt or damage a country's agriculture, especially the use of a biological agent against crops or livestock.

All-hazards All hazards, natural and man-made, which includes acts of nature (e.g., hurricanes, earthquakes, tornados, etc.) and technological (accidental and intentional).

All-hazards approach A mitigation and preparedness planning process should utilize this type of approach. There are many different threats or hazards to consider: natural and technical or manmade. The probability that a specific hazard will affect your community is hard to determine. That's why it's important to consider a multitude of most-likely threats and hazards in your planning activities and mitigation strategies.

Amortization The process through which communities can require nonconforming structures to be replaced within a certain time, as the former uses become illegal once the structures are replaced or destroyed.

Areal Locations of Hazardous Atmospheres (ALOHA) A modeling application of the CAMEO software suite that predicts threat zones associated with hazardous chemical releases.

Asset A distinguishable network entity that provides a service or capability. Assets can be people, physical entities, or information.

Avalanche A layer or mass of snow that slides or falls down a sloping surface.

Base flood A flood with a 1% chance of occurring in any given year.

Base map A map showing the basic topography, physical elements and infrastructure, and political boundaries such as city limits, streets and roads, rivers, etc.

Benefit-Cost Analysis Tool Software from FEMA that can be used to perform benefit-cost analysis (BCA) for applications submitted under FEMA's HMA grant programs.

Biosafety The prevention of large-scale loss of biological integrity, focusing both on ecology and human health. These prevention mechanisms include conduction of regular reviews of the biosafety in laboratory settings, as well as adherence to strict government guidelines.

Biosecurity A program encompassing policies and measures taken for protecting a nation's food supply and agricultural resources from both accidental contamination and deliberate attacks of bioterrorism.

Bioterrorism The intentional use of microorganisms or toxins derived from living organisms to cause death or disease in either humans or the animals and plants on which we depend. May include such deliberate acts as introducing pests intended to kill U.S. food crops, spreading a virulent disease among animal production facilities, and poisoning water, food, and blood supplies.

Blizzard A weather condition that persists more than 3 h with large amounts of falling or blowing snow, wind speed greater than 35 mph (55 kph), and visibility of less than ¼ of a mile (400 m).

Buffer zone Wetlands that are located at the edge of deep water bodies that can hold floodwaters that overflow rivers, lakes, and other water bodies.

Building code A set of regulations governing the design, construction, and maintenance of structures. They specify the minimum acceptable standard required for structural design, integrity, and construction materials used in buildings and structures, thereby reducing casualties, injuries, and property damage.

Bulkhead A vertical wall similar to a seawall on the shoreline, but designed to retain loose fill and sediment behind it.

Business continuity Refers to maintaining business functions or resuming business operations quickly in the event of a disaster or a major disruption.

Business impact analysis (BIA) A process that involves calculating the consequences of disruption of a business operation and process and collecting the information needed to develop recovery strategies.

Capability target A target that defines success for each core capability and describes what a community wants to achieve by combining detailed impacts with basic and measurable desired outcomes based on the threat and hazard context statements developed in step 2 of the Threat Hazards Identification and Risk Assessment (THIRA) process.

Capital Improvement Program (CIP) A program taken by local governments to implement large-scale projects in the community, such as schools, bridges, police stations, recreation centers, and other public facilities.

Category A agent The most potentially dangerous biological agent that may be employed in an act of bioterrorism. The criteria for this category is that the agent has the potential to cause high morbidity and mortality, may be easily disseminated or spread from person to person, could cause public panic or social disruption, and presents serious challenges to and special preparedness efforts by public health organizations. Examples of agents/diseases fitting into this category are *Bacillus anthracis* (anthrax), *Yersinia pestis* (plague), *Francisella tularensis* (tularemia), smallpox virus, Ebola virus; viral hemorrhagic fever (VHF) viruses, and botulinum toxin.

Chemical, biological, radiological, nuclear, and explosives (CBRNE) A term used in homeland security training and programs to refer to those technological hazards that may make up a weapon of mass destruction (WMD).

Chemical warfare agent (CWA) Highly toxic chemical agents, including nerve agents [Sarin (GB) and VX], pulmonary agents [phosgene and chlorine], and blister agents [mustard (H) and Lewisite (HL)].

Civil Contingencies Act A law in the United Kingdom that introduced a single framework for civil protection and brought several changes, such as replacing and updating former civil defense and emergency power legislation.

Civil Defence Emergency Management Act The key law in New Zealand that provides the legal framework for the Civil Defence Emergency Management (CDEM) agency.

Clean Water Act (CWA) The primary federal law in the United States governing water pollution. It also helps reduce the impacts of hazards in communities throughout the country. The law was passed in 1972 as the Federal Water Pollution Control Act.

Coastal Barrier Resources Act (CBRA) Enacted in 1982, this U.S. law addresses numerous problems associated with coastal barrier development. It made federal expenditure and financial assistance ineligible for relatively undeveloped coastal barriers along the Atlantic and Gulf coasts.

Coastal erosion The wearing away of land surface and loss of beach, shoreline, or dune material as a result of natural or coastal processes or human-induced influences.

Coastal Zone Management Act (CZMA) Passed in 1972, this U.S. law encouraged coastal states to develop and implement coastal zone management plans. It establishes a national policy to "preserve, protect, develop, and, where possible, to restore or enhance the resources of the nation's coastal zone."

Code of Federal Regulations (CFR) The codification of the general and permanent rules and regulations published in the Federal Register by the executive departments and agencies of the U.S. government.

Community outreach project A project that is designed to educate citizens and potential homebuyers about hazard risks in a specific community, possible mitigation strategies, and how to prepare for and respond to a disaster. These include newsletters, workshops, brochures, meetings, and seminars.

Community Resilience This is a core capability within the Mission Area of mitigation indicating that the community can lead an integrated effort to recognize, understand, communicate, plan, and address risks so that it can develop a set of actions to accomplish Mitigation and improve resilience.

Comprehensive emergency management An integrated approach to the management of emergency programs and activities for all four emergency phases (mitigation, preparedness, response, and recovery), for all types of emergencies and disasters, and for all levels of government and the private sector.

Computer-Aided Management of Emergency Operations (CAMEO) A system of software applications developed by the National Oceanic and Atmospheric Administration (NOAA) and Environmental Protection Agency (EPA) to plan for and respond to chemical emergencies.

Context A community-specific description of an incident, including location, timing, and other important circumstances.

Core capability Defined by the National Preparedness Goal, 31 activities that address the greatest risks to the United States. Each of the core capabilities is tied to a capability target. Specific core capabilities that are linked to the Mission Area of mitigation include Community Resilience, Long-Term Vulnerability Reduction, Risk and Disaster Resilience Assessment, and Threats and Hazard Identification.

Coriolis force A force caused by the Earth's rotation on its own axis. Cyclones do not form between $0°$ and $5°$ latitude, as the Coriolis force is weak near the equator.

Critical infrastructure Systems and assets, whether physical or virtual, whose incapacity or destruction would have a debilitating impact on security, national economic security, national public health or safety, or any combination.

Critical infrastructure All community assets, systems and networks that are considered to be vital to security, health and safety of the public.

Dam An artificial barrier designed to hold back water or other liquid-borne materials for any of several reasons, such as human water supply, irrigation, livestock water supply, energy generation, containment of mine tailings, recreation, and pollution or flood control.

Desired outcome The standard to which incidents must be managed, including the time frames for conducting operations or percentage-based standards for performing security activities.

Digital Coast A web-repository developed by the NOAA Office for Coastal Management to provide geospatial data, training, case studies, and a number of tools related to coastal hazards to help make informed decisions.

Dike An earthen or rock structure built partially across a river to maintain the depth and location of a navigation channel.

Dillon's Rule A principle stating that a local government may engage only in activities specifically authorized by the state government.

Dirty bomb A combination of conventional explosives and radioactive materials that yields a more devastating terrorist threat than a traditional bomb. It can potentially cause death, destruction, and contamination, which would greatly complicate response and recovery efforts and present a serious threat to public safety. Such a device is only theoretical (at least as yet).

Disaster A singular event that results in widespread losses to people, infrastructure, or the environment.

Disaster Countermeasures Basic Act A law providing the institutional framework for disaster prevention and management in Japan. The act was passed in 1961 and later revised in 1997.

Disaster legislation A body of laws and regulations that govern and designate responsibility for disaster management concerning the various phases of disaster.

Disaster Management Act 2005 A law that provides a legal and institutional framework for effective disaster management in India and establishes disaster management authorities (DMAs) at the national, state, and district levels.

Disaster Mitigation Act (DMA) A law passed in 2000 that amended the Robert T. Stafford Disaster Relief and Emergency Assistance Act of 1988. DMA 2000 authorizes the creation of a predisaster mitigation program to make grants to state, local, and tribal governments. It further stipulates that state governments have responsibilities to prepare and submit a standard or enhanced state mitigation plan; review and update the state mitigation plan every three years; provide technical assistance and training to local governments to assist them in developing local mitigation plans and applying for Hazard Mitigation Grant Program grants; and review and approve local plans if the state has an approved enhanced plan and is designated a managing state. This legislation is intended to facilitate cooperation between state and local authorities. It encourages and rewards local, tribal, and state predisaster planning and promotes sustainability as a strategy for disaster resistance.

Disaster Relief Act The first law passed by Congress to authorize a coordinated federal response to major disasters; its formal name is the Federal Disaster Relief Act of 1950. In this legislation, funding was authorized for an entire disaster relief program rather than responding to a single incident. The responsibility for determining when federal disaster relief is required was transferred from Congress to the president. The basic philosophy of federal disaster relief was developed establishing that federal assistance is supplemental to state and local resources. The basis for later legislation on cost sharing between federal, state, and local governments was put into place. Provisions were made for emergency repairs to or temporary replacement of essential public facilities. Aid was provided only to state and local governments.

Disaster risk reduction (DRR) The systematic method we employ to effectively reduce disaster risks by focusing on causal factors.

Drought A water shortage for an extended period of time caused by a deficiency of rainfall.

Earthquake Sudden, rapid shaking of the Earth caused by the breaking and shifting of rock beneath the surface.

Earthquake Hazards Program A program by the U.S. Geological Survey (USGS) that provides earthquake data. It includes real-time and historic earthquake catalogs, geographic information system (GIS) data, and seismic hazard analysis tools that create customized hazard maps to assess individual and overall hazards.

Easement An alternative to fee simple acquisition, where the government acquires lesser rights to a property such as a right of access, leaving the remaining rights to the owner. It is also known as the Purchase of Development Rights (PDR).

Emergency Planning and Community Right-to-Know Act (EPCRA) Legislation passed by Congress in response to concerns regarding the environmental and safety hazards posed by the storage and handling of toxic chemicals. To reduce the likelihood of such a disaster in the United States, Congress imposed requirements for federal, state, and local governments, tribes, and industry. The Community Right-to-Know provisions help increase the public's knowledge and access to information on chemicals at individual facilities, their uses, and releases into the environment. States and communities, working with facilities, can use the information to improve chemical safety and protect public health and the environment.

Emergency response services A category including first responders such as firefighters, police, emergency medical services (EMS), and other services that protect people at the scene of a hazard event.

Eminent domain The right of the government to take private property for public use; however, the owner must be given just compensation for the taking.

Enhanced Fujita Scale (EFS) A rating system used to measure tornado intensity.

Erosion A natural process that affects all landforms. It involves the wearing down of the land surface and transporting the eroded material through the actions of wind, fluvial processes, marine processes, and glacial processes.

Extreme heat A condition in which a temperature which is over 10°F or more from the average high temperature for a region and persists for a prolonged period, such as more than a week.

Fee simple acquisition The government can acquire the full bundle of rights to a piece of land in a hazard area.

Financial capital The financial resources that are required if one want to fulfill objectives.

Flooding The accumulation of water within a water body and the overflow of excess onto adjacent floodplain lands.

Floodproofing Flood retrofitting measures that protect property against floodwaters.

Floodwall A structure made of stone or reinforced concrete that acts as a barrier against floodwaters similar to levees.

Geographic information systems (GIS) The use of specialized software with geographical information (precise data points) to determine spatial relationships and produce elaborate and accurate maps.

Groin A shore-perpendicular structure designed to interrupt or slow the movement of sediment along the shore (spelled *groyne* outside the United States).

Hazard A natural or manmade threat that may result in disaster occurring in a populated, commercial, or industrial area.

Hazard analysis The process by which dangers that threaten the community are identified, researched, and ranked according to the risks they pose and the areas and infrastructure that are vulnerable to damage from an event involving hazards. The outcome of this step is a written analysis that quantifies the overall risk to the community from each hazard.

Hazardous materials Hazardous materials (hazmat) come in the form of explosives, flammable and combustible substances, poisons, and radioactive materials. These substances are most often released as a result of transportation accidents or chemical accidents in industrial settings.

Hazard mitigation assistance (HMA) Grant programs by FEMA that are designed to provide funding to protect life and property and mitigate disasters. There are three types of HMA programs: Hazard Mitigation Grant Program (HMGP), Predisaster Mitigation (PDM) Grant Program, and Flood Mitigation Assistance (FMA).

Hazus-MH A multihazard version of Hazards U.S. (HAZUS), a geographic information system (GIS)−based loss estimation software developed by the Federal Emergency Management Agency (FEMA) that contains models for estimating potential losses from earthquakes, floods, and hurricanes.

Home rule A delegation of power from the state to its subunits of governments (including counties, municipalities, towns or townships, and villages).

Human capital The skills, knowledge, labor ability, and good health that collectively allow people to pursue their livelihood.

Hurricane The name for a tropical cyclone in the Atlantic basin.

Hyogo Framework for Action (HFA) Provides a guideline to reduce vulnerabilities adopted by the United Nations member countries that are committed to take action for disaster risk reduction (DRR).

Impact The evaluated consequence of a particular outcome.

Impact analysis A method used to measure the effect of the loss of community resources or increasing losses over a period of time. Impact analysis is used to aid in the decision-making process for hazard mitigation strategies.

Information technology disaster recovery plan (IT DRP) Focuses mainly on restoring information technology (IT) infrastructure and operations after a crisis.

Jetty A wall-like structure built perpendicular to the coast to protect navigation channels and trap sediment by restricting the movement of materials transported by longshore currents.

Landslide The movement of massive rock, debris, or accumulation of earth down the slope of a landmass, which often can cause great damage to a community.

Law of nuisance Pertains to modern property law, which requires that private property owners must refrain from using their property in a way that interferes with the rights of adjoining property owners, causes injury to the general public, or both.

Levee A manmade structure, usually an earthen embankment, built parallel to a waterway or a river in order to protect lives and properties behind it from some level of flooding.

Long-Term Vulnerability Reduction This is a core capability within the Mission Area of mitigation indicating that the community can build and sustain resilient systems, communities, and critical infrastructure and key resource lifelines so as to reduce their vulnerability to natural, technological, and manmade incidents by lessening the likelihood, severity, and duration of the adverse consequences related to these incidents.

Magnitude The size, extent, or importance of an event; with respect to earthquakes, the amplitude of seismic disturbance as measured by the Richter scale.

Major hurricane A tropical cyclone with maximum sustained winds of 111 mph (96 knots) or greater, corresponding to a category 3, 4, or 5 on the Saffir-Simpson Hurricane Wind Scale.

Map Modernization Program (Map Mod Program) A program of the Federal Emergency Management Agency (FEMA). Funded by the Congress from fiscal year 2003 to 2008, it updated the nation's flood maps and provided flood risk data in geographic information system (GIS) format on Digital Flood Insurance Rate Maps (DFIRMs).

Mission Area One of five broad areas specified in the National Preparedness Goal that defines essential capabilities for each community to have in order to be prepared for a multitude of hazards and threats.

Mitigation (1) Mitigation is an ongoing effort to lessen the impact through predisaster and postdisaster activities. It can take place years, months, and even decades before a disaster using long-range policy and decision making. Success is measured by what does *not* occur. Mitigation is most effective when planned in conjunction with community development. (2) A Mission Area found in the Core Capabilities featuring those capabilities needed to reduce the loss of life and property by lessening the impact of disasters.

National Environmental Policy Act (NEPA) An environmental law that establishes a U.S. national policy to promote the enhancement of environmental quality and to consider environmental impacts of major federal projects. It was passed in 1969 in response to public concerns about the degradation of the quality of the human environment.

National Flood Insurance Act Passed in 1968, this law led to the creation of the National Flood Insurance Program (NFIP) to help reduce the growing cost of federal disaster assistance by making flood insurance available.

Natural capital The natural resource stocks from which resource flows and sources are derived, including such elements as nutrient cycling and erosion protection, both which are useful for maintaining people's livelihoods.

Nonstructural mitigation Any measure not involving physical construction that uses knowledge, practice, or agreement to reduce risks and impacts, in particular through making policies and laws, public awareness raising, and training and education. Nonstructural measures seek or serve to reduce the likelihood or consequence of risk through modifications in human action, human behavior, or natural processes.

Open Seismic Hazard Analysis (OpenSHA) A tool jointly developed by the U.S. Geological Survey (USGS) and the Southern California Earthquake Center (SCEC) that can estimate earthquake risks accommodating past and future models.

Overlay zone A designated area that allow communities to isolate and protect regions such as floodplains or historic districts that are not covered by the rest of a zoning ordinance.

Pathogen A specific causative agent of disease. Mostly thought of as being an infectious organism (e.g., bacteria, virus, rickettsia, protozoa, etc.).

Physical capital The resources available to support a viable livelihood. This may include clean water, adequate sanitation, and effective shelter; these items are often encompassed by basic infrastructure.

Preparedness A term within the field of emergency management that can best be defined as a state of readiness to respond to a disaster, crisis, or any other type of emergency. This can be accomplished through the development of functional response and recovery plans, training and exercises, public education, and the creation of alert and warning systems.

Prevention This Mission Area found in DHS Core Capabilities that features those capabilities necessary to avoid, prevent, or stop a naturally occurring disaster, incident or an act of terrorism.

Private sector Usually defined as organizations and entities that are not part of any governmental structure.

Probability The likelihood that an event will occur.

Protection This Mission Area found in the Core Capabilities features those capabilities necessary to secure a nation against acts of terrorism and either manmade or natural disasters.

Public-private partnership A collaborative relationship built on the needs, capabilities, and communication channels of public- and private-sector partners.

Real estate disclosure Notification to potential homebuyers or mortgage applicants if their property is in a hazardous area such as on a floodplain as shown on the Flood Insurance Rate Map (FIRM).

Recover This Mission Area found in the Core Capabilities features those capabilities necessary to assist communities affected by an incident to recover effectively.

Recovery The effort that follows the Response phase to return an affected community to a state of normalcy. Recovery operations can be subdivided into short term- and long term-efforts. Priorities include the provision for basic human needs (food, water, shelter, etc.) and societal needs (counseling, rebuilding infrastructure and businesses).

Relocation A process whereby the housing, infrastructure, and other assets of an entire community or a segment of a community are rebuilt in a new location.

Repetitive Loss Property (RLP) A term referring to a building with two or more National Flood Insurance Program (NFIP) claim payments of over $1000 each within a 10-year period since 1978.

Reservoir A manmade lake formed by the construction of a dam. Reservoirs are located behind dams and reduce flooding by storing water during peak runoff periods.

Resilience Simply put, resilience can be viewed as the ability to rebound from a disaster. Resilience is often characterized as a community or region's capability to prepare for, respond to, and recover from significant multihazard threats with minimum damage to public safety and health, the economy, and national security. This state of preparedness and disaster-ready posture prevents and mitigates cascading failures, often characteristic of critical infrastructure impacts.

Response (1) Immediate and ongoing activities, tasks, programs, and systems to manage the effects of an incident that threatens life, property, operations, or the environment. (2) A Mission Area found in the Core Capabilities includes those capabilities necessary to save lives, protect property and the environment, and meet basic human needs after an incident occurs.

Retrofitting Strengthening or modifying a building in order to prevent or reduce damages from hazards.

Revetment A sloping structure placed on riverbanks or cliffs designed to protect the backshore from high tides and surges.

Richter Scale A logarithmic scale to measure the energy released during an earthquake.

Risk A measure of the probability of damage to life, property, and the environment that could occur if a hazard manifests itself, including the anticipated severity of consequences to people. Risk is generally defined as the combination of the frequency of occurrence, vulnerability, and the consequence of a specified hazardous event.

Risk and Disaster Resilience Assessment This is a core capability within the Mission Area of mitigation indicating that the community can assess risk and disaster resilience so that decision makers, responders, and community members can take informed action to reduce their entity's risk and increase its resilience.

Risk Mapping, Assessment, and Planning Program (Risk MAP Program) A program by the Federal Emergency Management Agency (FEMA). Started in 2009, the Risk MAP Program aims to identify and mitigate flood risk through more precise flood mapping products, risk assessment tools, and planning and outreach support.

Saffir-Simpson Hurricane Wind Scale A scale used to measure hurricane strength used by the National Hurricane Center.

Seawall A hard engineering structure built on the shoreline designed to protect areas from the action of tides and waves and also from shoreline erosion.

Seismic retrofitting Seismic retrofitting involves adding braces, removing overhangs, and providing flexible utility connections and tiedowns to reduce damage.

Setback regulations Regulations that establish a minimum distance between the building or lot and a hazard area.

Select Agents Program A federal program that oversees the possession, use, and transfer of biological select agents and toxins, which have the potential to pose a severe threat to public, animal, or plant health or to animal or plant products.

Severe Repetitive Loss Property (SRLP) A building that has four or more NFIP claim payments of over $5000 each and the cumulative amount exceeds $20,000; or if at least two claims cumulatively exceed the building's value such properties.

Simple Listing The Simple Listing is a comparison of advantages and disadvantages of a mitigation strategy or action when one cannot quantitatively evaluate or measure the costs and benefits of that strategy or action.

Snowstorm Any storm marked by heavy snowfall.

Social capital Social capital consists of the specific social resources that are necessary to pursue one's own unique livelihood. These can be fostered via establishment of networks, trusting relationships, and membership of formalized groups.

Social, Technical, Administrative, Political, Legal, Environmental, and Economic (STAPLEE) An analytical process formulated by the Federal Emergency Management Agency (FEMA) to help community and organizational planners evaluate possible mitigation measures. Criteria used in the evaluation of those possible measures include social, technical, administrative, political, legal, economic and environmental considerations. From this type of analysis, community and organizational mitigation planners may determine a few specific projects that could help mitigate potential hazards, while improving the response and training of staff, as well as helping to protect infrastructure and the environment within that entity.

Special Flood Hazard Area (SFHA) The shaded area on a Flood Insurance Rate Map (FIRM) that identifies an area that has a 1% chance of being flooded in any given year (100-year floodplain).

State Preparedness Report (SPR) A self-assessment of the capabilities required to prevent, protect against, mitigate the effects of, respond to, and recover from all threats and hazards. This annual assessment is mandated for any state or territory receiving preparedness assistance that is administered by the U.S. Department of Homeland Security.

Storm safe room A hardened structure that can be installed in a private residence or business or somewhere in the community to provide shelter during wind events, especially tornadoes.

Structural mitigation Any physical construction to reduce or avoid possible impacts of hazards, or application of engineering techniques to achieve hazard-resistance and resilience in structures or systems. Structural measures are those that involve physical construction to avoid possible impacts of hazards or application of engineering techniques to achieve hazard resistance and resilience in structures or systems.

Subdivision regulation A regulation that governs how land will be divided into small parcels for development and set construction standards for developers.

Subsidence The gradual settling or sudden sinking of the Earth's surface due to the subsurface movement of the Earth's materials

Sustainable development Development that meets the needs of the present without compromising the ability of future generations to meet their own needs.

Sustainable livelihood A situation when it has the ability to cope and recover from unexpected events, while at the same time enhancing current and future capabilities.

Taking law A regulation that results in action comparable to eminent domain.

Technological hazard A wide-ranging, manmade hazard that emanates from manufacturing, transportation, and the use of substances such as radioactive materials, chemicals, explosives, flammables, pesticides, herbicides, and disease agents.

Terrorism The use or violence or the threat of violence to achieve political objectives or draw attention to a cause.

Threat and Hazard Identification and Risk Analysis (THIRA) A tool that allows a jurisdiction to understand its threats and hazards and how the impacts may vary according to time of occurrence, season, location, and other community factors. This knowledge helps a jurisdiction establish informed and defensible capability targets.

Threats and Hazard Identification A core capability within the Mission Area of mitigation indicating that the community can identify the threats and hazards that occur in its geographic area; determine the frequency and magnitude of them; and, incorporate this information into analysis and planning processes so as to clearly understand the community's needs.

Thunderstorm A storm occurring over a local area produced by a cumulonimbus cloud and accompanied by lightning and thunder.

Tornado A violently rotating column of air in contact with the ground that extends from a thunderstorm.

Toxin A poisonous substance that is a specific product of the metabolic activities of a living organism and is usually very unstable, notably toxic when introduced into the tissues, and typically capable of inducing antibody formation.

Transfer of Development Rights (TDR) Programs treat development as commodity separate from land itself. The government awards development rights based on value or acreage of land, and establishes sending and receiving areas for these rights.

Tropical cyclone A rotating, organized system of clouds and thunderstorms that originates over warm waters and has a closed low-level circulation.

Tsunami A series of water waves onto land generated by any disturbance that displaces a large water mass.

Vulnerability A characteristic of individuals and groups of people who inhabit a given natural, social, and economic space, within which they are differentiated according to their varying position in society into more or less vulnerable individuals and groups. It is a complex characteristic produced by a combination of factors derived especially (but not entirely) from class, gender and ethnicity. Differences in these socio-economic factors result in hazards having a different degree of impact.

Vulnerability assessment Involves identifying structures and areas of a community that are vulnerable to hazards using current knowledge or some degree of existing building stock.

Warning An emergency notification issued when a weather hazard is imminent and requires immediate action.

Warning system A system that alerts communities about potential hazards in advance so that residents can get enough lead time to prepare and implement protection measures before a hazard event.

Watch An emergency notification issued when weather conditions are favorable for a hazard to occur. During a severe weather watch, it is important to continuously monitor the weather and discuss emergency/evacuation plans with your family in case of threatening conditions.

Wetlands Under the Clean Water Act (EPA), wetlands are defined as *areas that are inundated or saturated by surface or ground water at a frequency and duration sufficient to support, and that under normal circumstances do support, a prevalence of vegetation typically adapted for life in saturated soil conditions. Wetlands generally include swamps, marshes, bogs and similar areas.*

Whole community An approach to emergency management that reinforces the fact that the Federal Emergency Management Agency (FEMA) is only one part of the U.S. emergency management team. We must leverage all of the resources of our collective team in preparing for, protecting against, responding to, recovering from, and mitigating against all hazards; and that collectively, we must meet the needs of the entire community in each of these areas.

Whole community approach An approach by the Federal Emergency Management Agency (FEMA) that brings together state, local, tribal, and territorial partners with private-sector organizations such as nongovernmental organizations (NGOs), faith-based and nonprofit groups, and industry.

Wildfire An uncontrolled fire that spreads quickly over a large wild area such as a forest.

Wind chill The temperature that the human body feels outdoors due to the combined effect of air temperature and wind speed.

Windproofing Focuses on modifying design and construction of a building to withstand wind damage.

Zoning An instrument that regulates development in a community by dividing areas into different districts (called *zones*) within the jurisdiction.

Index

Note: Page numbers followed by "*f*" and "*t*" refer to figures and tables, respectively.

Printed and bound by CPI Group (UK) Ltd, Croydon, CR0 4YY

08/06/2025

01896873-0015